ZOMBIE NATION AWAKES

Welsh Football's Odyssey to Euro 2016

THE DIARY OF A REPORTER SUPPORTER

'Bryn is a fan like all of us, and this book reflects both sides, the fan and the reporter. Great insight into a great journey that we all thought would never happen. Bryn is genuine, always willing to stop for a chat, and he was in the right place at the right time to tell the selected few in Zenica that we'd finally done it...together...this is a book all Welsh football fans will enjoy!'

Tommie Collins

'I've been doing interviews with Bryn for many years now, since I got into the u21 side in fact. I know he sees it as more than just a job, he's a fan and he's been as desperate as we have to see Wales qualifying. It's been tough at times, to stay upbeat when we've been struggling, but the last year and a bit's been brilliant and there's nobody better placed than Bryn to tell the story of how we finally made the dream come true!'

Chris Gunter

ZOMBIE NATION AWAKES

Welsh Football's Odyssey to Euro 2016

THE DIARY OF A REPORTER SUPPORTER

Bryn Law

ST DAVID'S PRESS

Cardiff

Published in Wales by St. David's Press, an imprint of

Ashley Drake Publishing Ltd
PO Box 733
Cardiff
CF14 7ZY

www.st-davids-press.wales

First Impression – 2015

ISBN
978-1-902719-46-7

British Library Cataloguing-in-Publication Data.
A CIP catalogue for this book is available from the British Library.

Typeset by Replika Press Pvt Ltd, India
Printed by Akcent Media, Czech Republic

Contents

Foreword by Roger Speed   vii

Acknowledgements   ix

Preface by Chris Coleman   xi

1. **"We'll never qualify"**   1
Andorra v Wales

2. **"I don't think we have to win, but I know we must not lose"**   35
Wales v Bosnia

3. **"We'll take a win, no matter how we get it"**   77
Wales v Cyprus

4. **"We've done very well but I still think we can do better"**   90
Belgium v Wales

5. **"We fear no one now"**   128
Israel v Wales

6. **"Too soon Barry, too soon"**   181
Wales v Belgium

7. **"He's Gareth Bale. what can you do to stop him?"**   225
Cyprus v Wales

8. **"We've waited 57 years, a few more weeks won't hurt us"**   249
Wales v Israel

9. **"The best defeat of my career"**   262
Bosnia v Wales

10. **"We're so proud of what we've achieved"**   298
Wales v Andorra

To my fantastic family, Rachel, Megan and Millie;
sorry for all the events I've missed and thanks
for letting me go! X

Foreword

It's over 20 years since I first met Bryn, when he came over from north Wales to cover Leeds United games. He used to commentate with Norman Hunter and the pair of them sat in the middle of the West Stand. Bryn and Gary had already become friendly, I'm sure the Welsh link helped, and I'd always stop for a chat as I headed off for my half-time cuppa. That wasn't the only time our paths crossed though. We'd often see each other at far flung locations across Europe on Wales trips, when we were both travelling to support Gary and the team. Then, of course, when Gary got the Wales manager's job I'd see Bryn down in the tunnel before and after games, as he was waiting to do his interviews with my son. I know he was every bit as thrilled as I was when Gary got that job and even more so with the way things began to turn around in those first few months in the position.

I could never, ever in my darkest nightmares have imagined that the next time we'd meet would be at Goodison Park, a week after I'd lost my beloved son and he'd lost a friend. On the night of the Wales v Costa Rica tribute game, I took Gary's lads Ed and Tommie, and we all sat next to Bryn, down in the reporter position on the touchline next to the home dugout. Many more tears were shed as the Welsh public showed just how great their sense of loss was at Gary's passing. I know the fans continue to sing Gary's name at games and it means a lot; it helps with all the dark days. We have now set up a charitable trust in Gary's name and Bryn comes over from Leeds to help with the annual golf day we now hold in Gary's memory.

I'm delighted that things have turned out so well for Wales in this campaign and I'm absolutely chuffed for Chris Coleman, another person who was a big friend of Gary's and someone who's been such a big support to me and Carol, Gary's mum, since that awful day. I know Chris has done this in Gary's memory, as have all the players, lads that he so enjoyed working with and so admired as fine, honest and talented young men.

When Chris, the players, and our amazing fans were celebrating in Bosnia, I just know that Gary was there, chuffed to see the country he loved finally achieve its dream, and knowing that he'd played his part.

It's been a tremendous effort to qualify for Euro 2016. It's a great story and I know that Bryn's the right man to tell it. He's been right in the thick of it, covering games for Sky Sports for so many years, but he's still a fan at heart, just as he was when we shared a beer or two at bars in Helsinki, Moscow and across Europe, following the men in red .

To the people of Wales, I say thanks for all your support and enjoy France. To Bryn I say, good luck with the book and maybe I'll see you over there!

Roger Speed
October, 2015

Acknowledgements

There are so many people I need to thank for their part in this long-term labour of love. I'll begin at the beginning with my parents, my mum takes the blame for ensuring I supported Wales, even as a little lad in Liverpool; and my dad, for taking me to watch football from a very early age. There's so very much more I have cause to thank them for, of course, but it's too long a list for this book, so I'll stick to the usual stuff, like love, support and new trainers.

Then there's my own wonderful family, my longsuffering wife Rachel who's had to share me with football for so long. I was heading off to far flung internationals and missing our wedding anniversaries long before I started covering the team for Sky. Her support and understanding's been crucial during many extended absences. When Megan was celebrating her fifth birthday, I was in Azerbaijan, working on a Wales game and I've been missing those birthdays regularly ever since, including her 16th this year. It doesn't get any easier. Millie's not suffered so badly on that score but I have just missed her first proper netball match as I was on a plane from Sarajevo to Cardiff. My two girls are fantastic and their births will forever be the greatest days of my life, even if Wales go on to win the World Cup!

Then, it's the Sky guys, 'Tîm Cymru'. I couldn't have done any of this without their support. Alex Gage has been at my side all the way, a fantastic cameraman, and a great friend. Barry Horne's been covering Wales games since day one as well. I first knew him as a great player for my club and country, I now know him as an all round top bloke and pal. The Johnny and Jilly come-latelys, Bill and Sarah, have been terrific signings, helping make this the best experience of my professional career. Then, there are all the other members of the Sky Sports crew, starting with Jim Curthoys, the producer, a cool, calm and focused leader.

On the FAW side, I've made so many friends and received so much help down the years that I've been covering the national team, but special mention has to go to Ian Gwyn Hughes, Peter Barnes and Mark Evans for their day-to-day assistance. It's a sign of something that I found myself hugging each of them in the aftermath of that game in Zenica.

Thanks to Chris Coleman and the players, the finest group of people I've ever dealt with in nearly 25 years in the business; great company and great interviews, an absolute credit to the nation.

To the many fans I've met along the way, such a good natured and passionate bunch, in particular Gary, Gwilym, Rhys and TC.

I've started this book so many times and never seen it through. The fact I got it done this time is largely down to the team, of course, but also Ashley Drake for his invaluable guidance and encouraging words, ditto Robert Endeacott who set the ball rolling with invaluable advice and assistance.

And Gary; we'll never forget you. X

Bryn Law
October, 2015

Preface

As a management team, we've worked hard to establish a successful routine around Wales internationals and part of the itinerary for each game involves dealing with the media. Sky Sports have been covering our games throughout the time I've been in charge and Bryn's been their reporter for the Welsh national team for over a decade, so he's the guy who interviews me before and after each match.

It's fair to say there have been good times and bad, none worse than those dark days when I took on the job, in the aftermath of a terrible tragedy. I'd lost a lifelong friend, Wales and football had lost a highly talented manager. I know Bryn was a mate of Gary's as well and our first few interviews together were amongst the hardest he or I have probably ever had to do.

There have been the footballing low points as well, with Serbia away being the worst. I left Bryn waiting a long time after that one, I was so distraught at the way the night had turned out that I needed to compose myself and try and come up with the right words. He's a fan, so he must have felt every bit as bad. At that time, it must have seemed to him and many other supporters that the long cherished dream of qualification was as far away as ever, further maybe. We stuck at it though and, steadily, things got better, much better. I don't think I've enjoyed any of our interviews more than the one conducted in the rain in front of the away supporters in Zenica and I'm pretty sure Bryn would say the same!

I know he's established a strong bond with many of the players in the years he's been covering the national team, seeing up close the likes of Chris Gunter, Gareth Bale, Aaron Ramsey and Wayne Hennessey progress from the under-21s to becoming highly experienced senior internationals.

This diary tells the greatest story the nation's enjoyed since our one and only previous involvement in a summer tournament way back in 1958. I hope there are more glorious chapters for him to reflect upon in future, starting with France next summer!

Chris Coleman
October, 2015

1

"We'll never qualify"
Andorra v Wales

'Viva Gareth Bale, Viva Gareth Bale'

Sunday 7ᵗʰ September

It starts as it always does, with a bag chucked in the boot, a kiss, some hugs and a wave, and so I pull away. The destinations occasionally change. It's Cardiff, generally. Today though, it's Spain via East Midlands Airport. It's 90 miles away from my home in Leeds, 90 minutes drive under normal circumstances. It's 7.45am, my flight is in four hours. I've already checked in online so leaving this early in the morning might seem overly cautious. But I know my roads, put it down to 25k a year at the wheel and a lifetime working to deadlines. Huge swathes of my southbound route have been reduced to 50mph due to roadworks, the dreaded 'managed motorways', that seem to take longer to complete than Gaudi's Cathedral in Barcelona, the city I'm flying to. On top of that, it's the British Bike Championships at Donington Park, the track adjacent to my departure airport. Huge crowds could cause delays, I've been warned by the airport's website.

So it is that a stress/delay-free 90 minutes later, I'm parking up at East Midlands. Sometimes I'm too organised for my own good. I can hear the high-pitched roar of the bikes as I get out the car but it's obviously still a bit early for the spectators. I pass the long hours with a sausage sandwich, a tea and a copy of the Non-League Paper, purchased because there's a big photo of Wrexham's match-winner from the previous day celebrating his goal on the front. I check

I

my emails. I'm still awaiting the green light to confirm that I'll be interviewing Aaron Ramsey the following day. I've requested his assistance via the FA of Wales as the producer of the live coverage on Tuesday wants to use the interview in the build-up. There is a reply that refers to some difficulties in confirming arrangements as the manager needs to be consulted. I had asked if we could do the interview at the team hotel this evening, but I've already been informed they don't want any cameras at the team base in Barcelona at all today. Tomorrow morning will likely be my last chance, before the team set off for Andorra.

The email alludes to some issues which may interfere. I check online versions of the papers and soon discover what they probably are. The manager, Chris Coleman, is the subject of a Sunday tabloid expose. His ex-wife has been pretty candid about their marriage with a reporter; and I understand now why he may not be feeling best disposed towards the media just at the moment. Fingers crossed he calms down. The flight's called.

Remember the organisation? Pre-booked seat with extra leg room, which is a good job as I need a rest after queuing for 45 minutes to get on board. Ryanair won't be playing that annoying trumpet on arrival today.

There are a few travelling fans on board. It's nice to hear Welsh being spoken. These lads are from the North-West. I can tell by the accents, it's the accent I heard all the time as a lad on holiday with my grandparents near Bangor. They're a long way from home; they must have had at least a three hour drive already. Mind you, it takes them even longer to drive to a 'home' game, so they're used to making a big effort to go and support the national team.

The flight's fine and so is the weather on arrival. In fact, it's really warm and I've packed for the thunder, lightning and heavy rain predicted on all the forecast apps I've consulted. Way too organised!

My cameraman, Alex, is already in, on a flight from Birmingham and he's going to pick me up in the hire car we've got for the next stage of the journey. It turns out Barcelona's a pretty big airport and his terminal is a fair drive from mine so I get 15 minutes sitting in the sun whilst he navigates his way to find me. We use mobile phones like walkie-talkies as I try to help him find me by describing buildings I can see – it's a communication industry we're in after all.

2

We have been working together covering Wales for 10 years now, and working together for Sky for much longer. We started in the same week back in 1998, both part of a new channel called Sky Sports News and both, at that time, based in Yorkshire.

We've always got on well, even after a first day mishap when Alex said he wouldn't film my piece to camera from down low as I'd requested, because then everyone would see my double chin. I suppose he was trying to be helpful, tough love? Anyway, we're still together, so I must have got over it. On trips like these, it really is essential to work with someone you get on with. It's also a massive help to have someone who knows 'the job in hand' and knows the people you're going to be dealing with. Alex ticks both boxes. He's a proper football nut – not all sports cameramen are – and we share a very similar sense of humour.

I took on this role with Sky in August, 2004, as I'd always been a Wales supporter, I'd travelled many times to games across Europe as a fan. When I got wind of the fact that Sky might be in for the broadcast contract, I put my name forward, hoping they might see value in turning me from supporter to reporter, especially given that I could readily prove that – if nothing else – I definitely had a passion for the subject. Happily, they said yes. I can still remember where I was when I took the call confirming it, no more paying to go and watch Wales, now I was going to get paid for doing it! There was further good news to come when my request to get Alex on board as my cameraman was granted as well. He isn't Welsh but he loves the game and by now he'd moved back to the Midlands, so was closer to Cardiff. He's a really good operator so I requested his assistance and we've been an international partnership ever since, 'Tîm Cymru'!

On top of his talents as a cameraman, he likes to drive. So, the hire car was, is, and always will be, his baby. He even brings his own satnav with him. The car's already got one but it won't be as good as Alex's. He loves his gadgets, this guy, so it's a new wide screen number, it also makes a nice cup of tea and our first stop is already plumbed in. We're heading for the Princess Sofia hotel. Alex knows it already from previous trips he's made to film Champions League games in the city. Apparently it's right by *Camp Nou*, the famous stadium. I used my spare time in the airport to check whether there might be a game we could go to somewhere tonight and it turns there's one right on our front doorstep – Barca's B team vs Real Zaragoza. So, we've got our evening sorted, especially as there's a nice tapas bar he knows close by.

We check in and unload all our bags. I've got a carry-on bag only, saving the company money. Alex, on the other hand, has got six. He's brought two cameras as well as all the other kit, his usual one and a brand new state-of-the-art one that does lots of clever things with lots of different lenses. Then there are the lights he'll need to put up for indoor interviews, cables, batteries, chargers, play out machines and editing kit. Basically, we are a two-man band. We do the lot - set it up, light it, film it, do the interview, edit it and send it back to the UK. That means we also lump all the gear around so I have to muck in when it comes to getting all this stuff from the car, to the lobby, to his room. I'm like Sherpa Tenzing to his Sir Edmund Hillary.

Once it's all been delivered, I can delve into my small piece of luggage for a pair of shorts and head out for a walk. Barcelona's famous stadium is a couple of hundred yards away. The museum looks busy, even on a Sunday afternoon. I've been once to watch a game here many years ago, Leeds' first ever Champions League fixture, they got hammered. Tonight's fixture's actually going to be played across the road at the small stadium, the Mini Estadi as the Catalans call it. It looks like a pretty drab concrete bowl. Mind you, the *Camp Nou* is beginning to look its age now, dilapidated despite the club's status as one of the biggest in the world. After a wander round to suss out the lie of the land and see where we might get tickets for the game, I head back to the hotel. There's an email request from Sky Sports News HQ on my phone. Could we film the team arriving?

I'll admit, this sets a few alarm bells ringing in my head. We don't usually get a request to film the team coming into the airport or getting to the hotel. Now we've been asked to do it on a day when the manager's the subject of an unflattering piece in a national newspaper. Tomorrow, I'm hoping to be allowed to film an interview with both him and a player at the team hotel. Those factors make me nervous about complying. I understand the guys at Sports News want some new shots to put on the channel but I have to weigh up whether a few second's footage of players walking into a hotel is worth the potential problems it could cause. We've built-up a good relationship with the Welsh FA people over the years and they help whenever they can.

Today, they've asked me to stay away. I err on the side of caution and long-term harmony and suggest to HQ that it might not be a good time to go after the arrivals shots. Commendably, the man on the news desk concurs. He's an experienced operator, he knows there's often a bigger picture.

It wasn't my motivation, but this does now mean the evening's clear and we can go and watch our game. I collect Alex, we have a drink at the hotel bar and then head back to the Mini Camp. It's an appropriate name as we find the ticket office and the windows are set at about waist height. There's a queue of people bent double for a conversation with an invisible person behind the bars and dark glass. I take this as further evidence of the club's unimpressive infrastructure. Maybe people were much smaller when they developed this part of stadium, or perhaps they only employ Oompa-Loompas in the ticket office. The queue is long and kick-off is close so, when a somewhat shady looking character shuffles over, clearly a tout, and offers two tickets for €20, we agree the deal. He disappears to get them, another tout approaches but before he can make his pitch, our guy returns and we get our tickets and both slither away again. I see why he hasn't hung around to receive our thanks when closer examination shows they usually cost €3, ouch! I suspect this won't be a sell-out.

This theory's confirmed as we enter a near-empty stadium just before the teams emerge from the tunnel. Just like its big brother, the ground is desperately in need of an upgrade. There are non-league stadia in England with better facilities. It's a second division fixture, against a well-known former top division club, but there's hardly anyone here. I can't help but reflect on the English FA's recent 'B-team' suggestion, letting Premier League clubs put a reserve side in the lower divisions. The scene that greets us here doesn't advance a strong case in favour. Zaragoza have brought fewer fans than Wrexham would take to Torquay on a Tuesday night! I've actually seen the away side play before, against Wrexham, in a pulsating Cup Winners' Cup tie in the 1980s. We should have won, their 'keeper was amazing, we ended up drawing 2-2 and going out on the away goals rule. There must have been three times as many people in the ground that night.

So, there are plenty of seats to choose from and we end up sitting alongside an ex-pat. He explains that the €3 tickets are sold to the season ticket holders at the *Camp Nou*. It's usually about €8 to come and watch a game here, which makes me feel a little better. Given how cheap it is and the fact that some of the home players have already been named in the senior side's Champions League squad, a crowd of around 4,000 seems pretty unimpressive.

Still, I can now say I've been a to a Spanish second division game and I've seen Adema, a young player I'm sure Arsenal, Chelsea or Man City will be trying to sign soon. Or maybe Wrexham, on a season-long loan?

It's been a long day, so, at half-time, Alex queues at the one concession stand for hot dogs and alcohol-free beer. We eat and drink as Barca's babies run away with the game and record a 4-1 win. How that must have hurt the small group of travelling fans. They're here supporting a proper club with a proud tradition, and they've been stuffed by Barcelona's youth team.

Zaragoza aren't the only ones with problems at the back. The hotdog has not gone down well with Alex and our tapas trip is cancelled as he performs a fast, short-stride walk back to the hotel. Left alone, I retire to the bar to watch Germany v Scotland over a salad. There's the obligatory email check as well. The confirmation of our interview has come in now, hopefully vindicating the earlier decision to stay away. I communicate this good news when Alex reappears, looking a little wan. He has a sorbet, then retires for the evening, again, quickly. The game over, Scotland got an impressive draw, I go for another walk and soon find the Hilton hotel where I thought the Wales team was staying, and whose proximity was the reason why we are staying where we are. It turns out they aren't staying here but at another Hilton, on the same road, but 25 minutes drive away across the other side of the city. This is not such good news, and means another early start in the morning. This is my first planning failure.

Monday 8th September

It's 8.15am and we reconvene over breakfast. Alex is a little tentative still, and nibbles at a small croissant. I indulge myself on the basis that it's going to be a long day and the next chance to eat may be some way off. All that gear has to be loaded back into the car before we can get going, then we follow instructions that take us across town, through rush hour traffic to our first job. Again, there's an unloading job to be done, to get from the car to the hotel and then we're directed by one of the FAW media team up to a room that's been set aside for our use on the second floor. This is the floor the FAW are using to store all their kit, they have rooms for team meetings and for physio and massage for the players. If you think we travel heavy, all this stuff, boxes and boxes of it, has been transported across on their charter plane.

The fact that we're able to make our way up unhindered, highlights how easy-going it is around the Wales squad. I can't imagine it's like this with Team England. No checking passes, no holding areas or instructions not to look any of the players in the eye. After all these years, Alex and I know pretty much all the travelling party, the travel organiser, the medical guys, the video analyst and the rest. There are over 40 people in the group, just about half and half, players and support staff. There are also two security guards, one is new but the other's been doing it a long time and we exchange greetings. Since Gareth Bale became the world's most expensive footballer, the presence of guards around the group has become necessary but the familiarity helps to ensure relatively free movement for us in the midst of the area they're being paid to patrol.

The next big challenge is to get everything set up in time. The meeting room we've been given offers nothing in the way of an interesting backdrop and is full of furniture. It's one of those drab meeting rooms that look every bit as boring in every hotel around the world. Chris Coleman is due to meet other members of the travelling media in the hotel lobby at 10.30, at which time Aaron will come in to do his interview. We have 20 minutes to get tables and chairs moved, two cameras rigged and lights set up and in the right position. I always get a bit anxious at this stage because it needs to be done right, the interview has to look as good as we (well, Alex really) can make it despite the drab surroundings, and the clock is ticking. We have to stay calm and focused, but it's a tense time. Tension levels rise even higher when Aaron arrives 10 minutes early. It's an unwritten rule that footballers are always late, just when I want that to apply, Aaron's here, ahead of schedule. Another unwritten rule says they tend not to like hanging around.

This is where we're lucky, though. When Aaron was made captain by the previous manager, Gary Speed, our broadcast contract included an interview with him prior to every game. It has to be said he always fulfilled his duties, but he always seemed a pretty reluctant interviewee. He was a young guy still trying to find his feet at Arsenal, a massive football club. He was nervous about saying the wrong thing, so he tried to avoid that by pretty much saying nothing at all. I see it a lot in young players who've supposedly had media training but this generally seems only to consist of someone advising them about what they shouldn't say, rather than what they should. They interpret caution as being defensive no matter how innocuous the question.

However, that was then. He appears in front of us now, older, wiser and a thousand times more confident in his ability to deal with whatever may be coming his way. He's blossomed into the role, coped with serious injury and a loss of form under the scrutiny of one of the biggest fanbases in Europe. He's even been slagged-off by rent-a-quote Arsenal supporter, Piers Morgan! He's learnt the hard way, but he's learnt. I hope that he feels relatively relaxed in our company, he's known me and Alex for a few years now so I hope he feels we're okay. I've always looked on the role of covering Wales as a long-term commitment, building levels of trust with all the people we deal with on a regular basis. In these instances, hopefully, that effort pays off.

Aaron's happy to sit and make small talk whilst Alex beavers away in the background to get everything ready. We chat a bit about 3G pitches. I recount my own experiences, gained in a long and inglorious career of Sunday league and Wednesday night kickabouts. He's good enough to feign interest and recounts his own concerns about the risk of injury. 3G is supposed to be an unforgiving surface if you're at risk of muscle injuries. Indeed, the pitch is the potentially controversial issue in this interview but he handles it well, and swerves past it as easily as if it were a third division defender.

His interview's a good one, he's improved dramatically from those early, nervy days. He's learnt to embrace the media. I always say to players, if you want to get better at something, do more, practise, don't hide away. Aaron's a great example of somebody who found it wasn't so bad after all and it can have a very positive impact on your career. Like so many of this Wales squad, he's a really nice lad, with a very supportive and sensible family. We're very lucky on that basis.

We've been told we've only got 20 minutes all in to do our two interviews and then de-rig as there's a team meeting supposedly taking place in our tiny room at 11am. So, we let Aaron go after a good five minutes or so. It's enough, we're not making a documentary. I know we've got enough good material to work with, so Aaron says his goodbyes and we await the arrival of Chris Coleman.

I wander out of our cubby hole to let the head of media know we're good to go for our second interview. He's still overseeing the manager's appearance in the lobby. Half a dozen reporters are clustered around Chris, dictaphones and microphones held under his nose as he holds forth. There's another 'official' media conference scheduled for this evening in Andorra. It's a UEFA regulation that each association has to adhere to before a game, but this 'unofficial' access in the morning is helpful because it means we've all got something to send back to our offices much earlier in the day.

I'm pretty confident no one will have mentioned that tabloid tale from yesterday. These reporters are all here to cover the football, they're the Wales regulars, and the manager's private life is not really of much concern, unless it's going to intrude upon the forthcoming game in some way.

It's a pretty bizarre scene downstairs. The general business of the hotel's busy reception area goes on around the Welsh gathering. Phones ring, people chat and there's the obligatory muzak in the background. That would have driven me to distraction if I was trying to record an interview there, in fact I wouldn't do it there unless the muzak was turned off. It sounds terrible underneath a TV interview, even worse on the radio. We often have to go and find the man who knows how to turn it off when we're filming in public spaces like this. The BBC Radio Wales reporter is recording his interview in these circumstances, I'm not sure that's going to sound very good!

None of this, of course, is of any concern to Chris Coleman. He just wants to fulfil his media obligations as quickly and painlessly as possible. For him, it's a necessary chore. Still, he seems in good spirits as he follows me to our quieter location. Whatever went on yesterday, this mood shines through in his interview. He's had a tendency in the past to be a little unfocused in these situations. He's not been great at delivering the punchy soundbite, that 25 second quote that we're likely to use over and over on our 24/7 sports news channel. Not today though. Maybe, like Alex, there's some fire in his belly still and he delivers a strong, upbeat appraisal of the team's chances in this qualification campaign. The thorny issue is this brand new 3G pitch and the serious doubts raised about its readiness for this game. In fact, it wasn't clear whether the game was even going to be able to go ahead in Andorra until a few days ago. He acknowledges the concerns but refuses to be drawn into any great discussion about them, it's simple, he says, no matter if they play on 3G, grass or a car park, Wales should win.

Interview done, we chat briefly then Chris goes off to worry about that awful pitch and we begin the big pack-up/put-back exercise before transferring all the equipment back to the car. We're in and out in under an hour. If I ever make a hash of this career, there could be a future as a removal man.

The day is far from over. In fact it is just beginning, and we've a long drive ahead.

The satnav suggests about two and a half hours to the tiny principality. We head out of Barcelona and up into the Pyrenees, in the direction of the French border. It's a scenic drive, mostly on dual carriageway but as we get closer, there are numerous tunnels blasted through rock, the road narrows and we look out over green lakes and rugged mountains. We enjoy a road trip, Alex and I. It adds a bit more adventure to the usual routine of arrive at airport, transfer to hotel. You see more. There's a border to cross and this adds to the journey time, although not much. Alex has to carry a detailed kit list, called a carnet, on trips out of the European Union. Andorra isn't in the EU so he has to present the list to customs on leaving Spain and then again on entering Andorra. Only once it's been stamped can we proceed. This can be a time-consuming exercise, waiting for customs officers to work through it all, they're meant to cross check every serial number on the list with every piece of kit in the bags. Mercifully, this occasion is straightforward and he gets the necessary clearance pretty swiftly.

Ten minutes on from the border post, we're at our destination, the Hotel President, Andorra. Here we encounter the toughest part of the journey – getting into the car park. It's got a crazy, narrow, twisty uphill slope which Alex, never the most confident of parkers, negotiates tentatively. Sometime later, he comes to a stop without having damaged car or hotel. Then, guess what? Yes! We have to unload all the gear again, check-in and lug it all up to his room. It's a security measure, there's tens of thousands of pounds worth of equipment here and he wouldn't want to leave it in the car all night, even if no Andorran scallywag in his right mind would try and make a swift getaway down that toboggan run.

The Hotel President is, apparently, four-star. That pre-planning meant I'd picked it out due to its proximity to the stadium. It's a lot closer than my Barcelona attempt but a short walk takes us to the Holiday Inn, where the rest of the Sky team are staying and that's even closer to the ground. And the rooms have air-conditioning. Next time, maybe, I'll leave it to our highly efficient travel team to make the arrangements.

We have an hour or so to chat with our colleagues and grab a sandwich. Bill Leslie, the commentator, is already in place and we catch up on everything that's happened since the last Wales game we did, back in October. Having had a brief look around, Bill and I agree that this next fixture will be played against one of the most spectacular backdrops either of us have ever seen for a football stadium. A tiny ground, dwarfed by the mountains that climb above it on all four sides.

We stare up at the distant, craggy peaks as we head to the ground to check out the broadcast facilities. We will be using a satellite truck. It's been hired-in so it has a Spanish crew but they all speak decent English and clearly know what they're doing. Our production manager, Lee, is also on site. It's his job to oversee all the technical aspects of transmitting coverage of the game back to viewers in the UK. Sometimes Sky send the entire crew over, cameramen, sound engineers, the lot. On this occasion, we'll have ten people in all out here, which is about twice as many as we've been used to over all the years of covering Wales' away games. Extra resources have been allocated, because the games have taken on a higher profile since the new international fixture arrangements came into place for this tournament. Games are now spread out across a week, not all on the same night, so tomorrow, Wales will be the only home nation in action. Other qualifiers will be shown on our new Sky Sports 5 channel, but we are the Main Event!

There's a lot of work in progress as we arrive, cables are already in and checks are being made. We still have all the material we shot in Barcelona to send back, but we won't be in a position to do this until the satellite truck's established proper contact with HQ. We have a quick look to see where everything is, the geography, the compound for the TV vehicles, the entrance to the stadium etc, etc, then we climb the steep hill back to our hotel to collect everything for some more filming.

Our next task will be to interview the current captain, Aaron's replacement, Ashley Williams and then cover Wales' 'open' training session on the pitch. We'll be allowed to film the first 15 minutes only. Again it's a UEFA mandate that every country should have access to the venue to train the night before the game, and that the media should be allowed to attend at least some of that session. Given the controversy surrounding the playing surface and the fact that it's the first game at a brand new stadium, there's bound to be extra interest in this one.

We're up and down the hill, like Sky's version of Jack and Jill. At the appointed time, whilst everyone else – including local reporters and news crews – is at the manager's press conference in a basketball court at the back of the main stand, Alex and I are heading pitchside, awaiting the arrival of the players.

Things have already been a little tetchy. The groundsman's not at all happy about us standing in the tunnel, so he pushes Alex to move him away. Alex is not best pleased, to put it mildly. I see the danger signs, a flash of anger, but he manages to keep his protestations just the right side of reasonable. These are the little flashpoints that tend to be part and parcel of the build-up to these international games, a culture clash perhaps, lack of communication issues, or maybe just the hosts being deliberately unhelpful? We try and stay calm no matter what the provocation. We've both long since learnt that when it comes to people in high-viz bibs holding walkie-talkies, ranting rarely works. They have the power.

Blazers also bestow authority and there are a few of those to be seen around the stadium as well. These are the dark blue blazers of the numerous UEFA officials who all seem to be holding another essential accessory to power, the clipboard. The tournament organisers appear to be taking a much more hands-on role with these games now, and UEFA has taken control of the whole process of staging the tournament, even selling the TV rights for all member nations. I believe it's a bid to boost the popularity of international football in Europe, which has been increasingly squeezed out of the picture by the growth in the strength of the clubs. The new format is meant to help counter this, although I'm puzzled as to whether it's going to work.

When we started covering Wales, matches were on Saturdays and Wednesdays. A Saturday home fixture was the ideal but even an away game meant travelling fans could make a weekend of a trip. Then they changed it all to accommodate the big clubs' demands to get their players back sooner, so it all shifted to a Friday/Tuesday format. That meant fans could only watch their national teams on evenings in the working week. The impact has been a big European-wide drop in attendances. Perhaps more importantly, TV interest and income has also been falling. So now they've devised another way, they've spread the fixtures out across the week. This means more weekend dates, more games to televise but also shorter gaps between games, so players can get back to their clubs with more time to recover for their next game. Three days is the minimum recovery time according to many experts but next month Wales will play Bosnia on Friday, then Cyprus on Monday. Still, the players should be well rested for their next domestic league game and that appears to be the most important thing. The threat is that the big clubs will withdraw co-operation in releasing their players, so the compromise has been essential for keeping access to the star names.

Anyway, a UEFA man, with his regulation blazer and clipboard, moves us from the edge of the pitch and tells us we have to film from behind the advertising hoardings. Sky has invested millions in the rights to show these games, so it's a little galling that we don't get a bit more freedom. But it's not worth a battle, so we smile, comply and whisper oaths under our breath.

While Alex sets up for the arrival of Ashley Williams behind the barricades, I risk another trip up the tunnel to watch the press conference underneath the basketball net. It involves the captain and the manager. It's a stipulation that all associations have to provide media access 24 hours prior to the fixture, and as the Welsh guys all got the chance to speak to Chris Coleman earlier in the day, it's the local press asking him the questions now. It all has to be done through an interpreter as well, questions and answers, so it's a bit of a drawn-out process. Still, the message remains upbeat. Wales have a real chance of qualifying, now is the time.

Once Ashley's done, he departs the top table and comes out to fulfil his duties with Sky. He's the most easy-going Wales captain I've dealt with over the last decade, and there have been quite a few. Unfailingly affable and helpful, it's a pleasure to deal with him. Ashley came out of non-league and worked in various jobs, such as on a fairground and as a waiter, whilst playing semi-pro football, before finally getting his big break. This means he knows what real life's all about.

In my experience, lads like Ashley, the late starters, are always the easiest to deal with. They know how lucky they are and they appreciate it still. He's a model pro as well, as his stellar rise at Swansea shows. He's grown into the captaincy and, despite his Brummie accent, it's obvious he really feels it, really wants Wales to succeed.

Whilst we've been inside, Alex has got some striking footage of the effect a bouncing ball has on the 3G surface. He's used his fab new camera and when he plays it back in super slo-mo, we can see a foot-high cone of rubber bits flying up, after the ball has sprung off the artificial turf. I've played on this stuff myself plenty of times before, but I've never seen so much of the black rubber they lay on top to try and naturalise the bounce. It looks like they've spread tons of the stuff to try and slow the ball down. The staging of the game was in doubt after UEFA sent their people to check the pitch. They calculated that the ball was travelling too quickly for them to allow the game to go ahead, unless the Andorran FA took action. It seems the action has involved two tons of rubber being shovelled off the back of a trailer.

At the point we speak to him, Ashley hasn't had the chance to get out on the pitch and take a proper look at it. He plays down any concerns, and reiterates the fact that no matter what, Wales should win.

Interview done, he goes off to join his teammates and a collective inspection begins. They stand around rolling balls to each other. These training sessions are pretty low-key affairs at the best of times. The visiting nation know that the home nation will have people watching and making notes, so nobody really does anything, just a bit of stretching, a jog and perhaps a few small-sided games. Tonight, however, Wales don't plan to get much beyond the stretching stage. The worries over picking up injuries on this strange pitch predominate. The whole farcical situation is neatly encapsulated in one instance by the manager, now out on it, looking concerned. With our camera pointing at him, he bounces the ball on the pitch, having already indicated by pointing where it's going to go. As predicted, it spins up and over his shoulder, landing a couple of feet behind him.

He stretches out his arms in an exasperated gesture that highlights his concerns. I have a feeling this shot will be used quite a lot on Sky Sports News in the run-up to the game.

We have our 15 minutes access to film, but are done in a little less than that. Alex has used his two cameras, normal stuff on one for Sky Sports News purposes, super slo-mo stuff for the live show. I also get him to record a 'piece to camera', or PTC as well call them in TV land. It's something of a tradition to finish off an edited piece with one of these on international trips, it kind of highlights the fact that you're on the spot, out there, with the team. Much like a war correspondent, but thankfully, incoming footballs are the only missiles I have to keep an eye out for.

All done, we head back around the ground to our satellite truck. It's early evening now, getting on for 7pm and we've been at it a long time since setting off from the hotel in Barcelona, but the key jobs are still to be done. For a start, we've got to send all the material we've filmed, back to the UK. With people on hand to help out, Alex can hand over the memory card that contains all our footage and I start writing a script for the edited piece that Sky Sports News want to run the following morning. Actually, they asked for two pieces, including one for today as well but I've had to point out that it might be difficult to edit two pieces. Under the new rules of the TV contract, we aren't allowed to show any footage from previous Wales games, even though we've filmed pretty much all of them for the last 10 years. That archive now belongs to the FAW and if we want to use it, we have to pay for it, which means we won't be using it, so the only footage I can call on is what we've filmed today at training. Even though each piece on SSN is only likely to last 1'30", if we do two pieces, we're going to struggle to find enough shots from that brief access we've been given. It's remarkable how many shots are needed just to fill a 15 second gap, so it makes sense to avoid repetition and keep the good stuff for one piece, to be edited for broadcast tomorrow.

Alex is a jack of all trades, so he can edit as well as film, using an Apple Mac to bolt the shots together. My job is to come up with a script, select which bits of the interviews to include and oversee the choice of footage. I've cut thousands of these things down the years so I've already got a good idea in my head what we'll be using before we sit down to put it all together. I know the best lines in the interviews,

Alex knows the most striking shots, so we work together and get stuck into it pretty quickly.

Sometimes, less is more and with so little to choose from, the shot selection can be made swiftly. Sometimes wading through the interviews for a decent soundbite is more time consuming but Chris Coleman's punchy performance makes that an easier task today as well. We finish the piece with the little bit I did on the edge of the pitch, the pay off is, as always, "Bryn Law, Sky Sports". After 16 years, this is a phrase I must have uttered ten thousand times and it still puzzles me a bit, as the pieces actually go out on Sky Sports News.

The timing's good, we lay the final shots as the last frames of our footage are on their way back to the UK. So, we can send our item to them straight away and with that in and the all-clear from the other end, the day's done. We arrange a rendezvous with the rest of the crew and head off back to our hotel on the top of the hill. The calves are already beginning to tighten with all this climbing! There's time only to make a quick call home, have a quick change of clothes and we're already late.

The chaps are already in the bar finishing an aperitif when we arrive. So they set off as an advanced party, a scouting mission, to check out a restaurant. It's not going to be easy finding somewhere to eat. It's been a bank holiday in Andorra. Most places are shut, and a phone call from the advanced group a few minutes later confirms this includes our intended destination. New directions are relayed, and we get to see a little more of the town/country as we hunt for our colleagues. Guided in by mobile, we find them in the back room of a busy bar/restaurant called *Mama Maria*. Little do we know we're in for one of the more bizarre eating experiences of the last decade when travelling to the far-flung corners of Europe following Wales.

We peruse the menu, not extensive, pretty straightforward, but just about something for everyone, as long as you're not vegetarian. Starters are ordered, then mains. The staff have a harassed look about them and ordering doesn't prove easy, even with us doing our best with a bit of Spanish, and a touch of French. When all else fails, we resort to pointing and finally, we get there. Or so it seems. After a bit of a wait, a wild-eyed waiter returns with some steaks. More main courses arrive. But there's no sign of the starters. Despite our protestations, the plates are put down in front of us. The serving staff have now adopted a policy of pretending not to be able to hear us. We look at each other bemused, but there's more to come, literally, because now our starters are served. So, I've got a big plate of bits of lamb and a single potato and another plate of risotto rice and a scallop. We've all got two plates, so there's not actually enough room on the table to accommodate them all. One waiter suggests 'this is how we're doing it I think..', before he goes off to hide. It's clear nobody's going to help us out, so we stoically pile our plates one on top of the other and dig in.

Lee, our production manager, sends his steak back as it's cold already, even before he's tucked into his top layer. It gets whipped away, and only returns when we've all finished both courses. We have suspicions about what happened to his piece of meat before it was possibly reheated and sent back out. Remarkably, the surly staff suddenly become much more friendly around about the time the bill's being produced. They point out that some of the drinks have been taken off, they even whip out a bottle of Grappa and offer everyone a shot. Too little too late? It's been a long day for everyone, we're too tired to argue. We drink up, pay up and head off.

As we're leaving, I see two supporters of my club, Wrexham, standing by the bar. I stop for a chat and lose the rest of my party. Their presence reminds me to make contact with Barry Horne, our co-commentator, who set out from Manchester late afternoon and has driven himself from Barcelona airport. I get through to him. He's arrived in Andorra but sounds pretty stressed so I walk the streets, phone to ear, trying to give him directions in a place I've never been to before! We use the old church as a prominent central landmark and somehow contrive to find each other.

A former Wales captain, Barry has also been covering the games since the start of the Sky contract. I'd watched him, as a supporter, when he played for Wrexham and then interviewed him when I became a reporter, but we've become firm friends since we started working together. More recently we've been brought closer together by the fact that Barry's become a Board member at Wrexham as well. He's a great guy and I'm always pleased to see him, even when he is, as now, somewhat stressed out. He's had a very bad journey. His flight was full of well-oiled Welsh fans, he sat next to a bloke who was violently sick just after take-off, then he got stuck in a late night traffic jam just before crossing the border from Spain, all on top of a day's teaching at his school near Chester. The poor guy needs a drink, so I take him back to *Mama Maria*. Surely they can't mess up a beer?

We talk, have a drink and have pictures taken with some Wales fans. Even after his experiences today, Barry is approachable and chatty. The guys coming over to talk or have a photo seem to have been on the ale all evening, but it's good natured and everybody goes away happy. This includes the barman, who looks like Rio Ferdinand but who wants a pic with Barry Horne, once he realises he's in the presence of a former Premier League footballer.

We wander back through town, the sky illuminated by flashes of distant lightning, the big hands of the church clock having just crossed into matchday. So, to bed, to sleep, perchance to dream. Of actually seeing Wales qualify for a tournament. To be honest, winning the first game in the group would be a start. It hasn't happened for a very long time.

Tuesday 9th September

Well, here we go, Match Day 1 (MD1). Omens? The dog's banshee howls that woke me in the early hours? The street sweeper that drove noisily up the road even before the sun came up? Whatever, this was not the best night's sleep. It's going to be a long day as well. The game doesn't kick-off until 8.45pm local time. Alex has a plan to go and get an overview of Andorra, so he's going to drive up a mountain. He'll be able to offer the shot to the live producer. If he doesn't want it, we'll keep it for our own little plan. If, big If, Wales actually make a genuine fist of qualifying for this, we're keeping aside some footage. We both know there's a good story here if Wales can finally qualify for a summer tournament, as it's actually never happened at any level. In 1958, Wales got to the World Cup in Sweden only as a result of a special play-off game against Israel, staged because nobody else in their group would play them for political reasons, so they were given top spot without playing a game. FIFA wanted to ensure they didn't go through in that manner, so arranged a play-off. Wales had finished as runners-up in their qualifying group but were drawn out of a hat to provide Israel with competitive opposition, Wales won that and went on to claim a quarter-final slot in the tournament. They lost

1-0 to Brazil, the goal scored by a young lad called Pelé who didn't amount to much thereafter.

In 1976, Wales actually won their qualification group for the only time, and got into the last eight. But in those days European Championship finals only involved the last four, and Wales didn't make it past their quarter-final opponents Yugoslavia.

The 1980s was the time when I started actively following the national team. I was born in Liverpool in 1969, to a Welsh-speaking mother and an English father. When it came to allegiances, it was the maternal side that won. We spent many holidays at the home of my nain and taid in a little village, high up in the hills of north-west Wales. I loved them and I loved being there. I played with the little boy from the post office across the road who barely spoke a word of English. I picked up lots of Welsh words. It was all very exciting, a different language in a land that looked very different to the busy streets of Liverpool.

My first memories of making a conscious decision to be 'Welsh' come from this time. In the playground at primary school we used to play football almost every break. Different teams were announced and each individual decided who he wanted to play for. Most days, it was Liverpool v Everton, I was a Red, but we played internationals as well. One day, someone suggested England v Wales and, once again, I chose Red. I don't know how many came with me but I suspect my team's formation might have been 1-1-1. England's was 14-12-16. I think we got a draw.

There's another standout day in this process. 1977 was the year of the Queen's Silver Jubilee. Sometime around my eighth birthday, she was coming to visit Liverpool and we were all given a day off school to go and see her. I'd identified the striking new Wales national team kit, manufactured by Admiral, as the present I most wanted. Politically, my mum was a left-leaning Welsh nationalist so cheering the Queen of England on her triumphal passage was not high on her list of priorities for this extra holiday. So, whilst my classmates went and waved the red, white and blue on the city centre streets, I headed off to a sports shop, Jack Sharp's probably, to get my glorious new red, yellow and green football strip.

I must confess that around about the same time, I also got the Admiral England away shirt, in red, but I didn't feel any emotional attachment to it, probably just liked the design. Those Admiral strips were the start of my generation's collective obsession with kits I'm sure. Lots of logos, matching tracksuits and slick marketing; Admiral has so much to answer for.

I had another year and a half in exile in Liverpool before I moved 'home'. It didn't begin well though. The day my dad came home and announced he'd got a new job and we were moving to Wales, I sobbed my little heart out. Liverpool had just won a second European Cup, this place we were moving to, Wrexham, only had a second division football team! Then there was all the other stuff about going to a new school, leaving friends behind and the rest.

A week or so after the big move, we all went as a family to The Racecourse to watch this second division club. They beat Blackburn Rovers 2-1. There were 'just' 10,000 people there, but grudgingly perhaps, I actually quite enjoyed it. I'd been to Goodison and Anfield before, this felt different but not in a bad way. And so I came to relinquish the chance to support Liverpool and England and went for Wrexham and Wales instead. There hasn't been a lot to celebrate since.

Through the 1980s – apart from a 4-1 win against England at The Racecourse, which I missed because we'd gone to Pwllheli for the weekend in our new caravan – it was an endless tale of near misses for the national team. We always seemed to be in with a chance going into the last couple of games, then we'd blow it. We had a good side, nearly 30,000 people packed into The Racecourse to see the game against the USSR (the Soviet Union), in the qualification campaign for the 1982 World Cup in Spain. I was there. It was my first international match. A few games later in the same group, with Wales in with a great chance of getting through, the floodlights failed at Swansea and a game we should have won against Iceland ended in a 2-2 draw. Hopes dashed.

So it happened, again and again. There were great days. I was present when Wales again beat England on their next visit to Wrexham, the winner scored by a lad who'd been to the school I was now at, Mark Hughes. I was on the Kop when the same player scored probably the best goal I've ever seen live, against Spain. I was there when we thrashed Romania 5-0. But we couldn't win the games we really needed to. I still remember the crushing failures, from the

Iceland game, to Yugoslavia in 1983, to Scotland in 1985, Romania in 1993 and finally Russia in 2003.

All of which means there's a real sense of a dark cloud over Welsh football, a black mark even, something that says this nation won't ever qualify. Ten years ago, when I'd converted from being a supporter to reporter, the first Wales game broadcast on Sky was Latvia away. We had a very good team, we'd just failed to qualify from the previous campaign after losing by one goal to Russia in the play-offs. There was real reason to hope this squad, with Giggs, Bellamy, Hartson, Savage, Speed et al could crack it.

Before the Latvia match, a friendly in Riga, I lined up a group of Wales fans to record a 'vox pop', the first of many over the years. I knew some of them from my own travels as a fan, including Tommie Collins from Porthmadog, who was last in line. As I moved along the group, the chaps all spoke optimistically about the country's chances in the next set of qualifiers. Then I got to Tommie. "What do you think Tommie? Can they do it?", I asked in my bright-as-a-button reporter's voice. No pause, no expression, Tommie came straight back, deadpan, with the immortal phrase; "We'll never qualify." We all chuckled awkwardly, me and his mates. I made light of this lone, dissenting voice after all the optimistic noises. A decade later, a decade older, I'm with TC.

The upshot of all this gloom and doom is that, if by some miracle, Wales do qualify, there will be the biggest outpouring of joy ever witnessed in international football. A loyal hardcore have stuck by the nation throughout, TC included, but their away trips are as much, no, more about the beers and the nights out than the matches. There is no expectation of anything anymore, it doesn't hurt as much that way. That doesn't mean these fans aren't incredibly passionate. They are, this is their life in many instances, but it never leads anywhere and, by now, nobody dares torture themselves with thinking what it would be like if Wales ever did line-up for a first game at a World Cup or European Championship finals. But, if it did happen? Perchance to dream?

Anyway, if it should happen, we'll have a load of great, unseen archive material we can use to make a decent documentary. Listen, I know it won't happen. I've started these diaries on numerous previous occasions, thinking 'this could be the one'. Two games in, two defeats later and the writing already on the wall, I've given up. It's become a standing joke in the family. They laugh at me when I say I'm starting another diary. I'm no Samuel Pepys, that's for sure.

Still, hope springs eternal, and the prospect of anything other than a winning start to this campaign is not even on my mind as I pass a couple of hours looking around the shops that pack the centre of this tiny place.

Omens? How about nearly getting arrested for shoplifting? I have bought two apples, two bananas and a sports drink from a supermarket. They didn't give me a bag, and I didn't ask. Mistake. When I attempt to exit another shop that happens to sell food a little later, I get shouted at by a security guard. He comes over, points at my fruit and the drink, and points at the tills I've just walked past. I respond in English first, then in French, to explain that I bought the items in another shop. He doesn't get either attempt and takes the bottle off and starts to walk in a different direction, angrily gesturing me to follow. I'm going to the tills, or the cells, it would appear.

I have one last chance to avoid Richard Madeley-style headlines. I shove the fruit under my arm, and search frantically through my pockets. I find it! Incredibly, for once, I've actually kept the receipt. I wave it at him in triumph. He looks, shakes his head and says something in Catalan that may refer to deportation or a two-year stretch? I wave it and point again, it's itemised. He ponders the words, then concedes defeat with a cursory wave of the hand. The game's not over though. I'm now up on the moral high ground, overlooking all of Andorra. I get indignant, proper Brit-abroad indignant. "Are you going to apologize? You've just accused me of theft!!" He, of course, hasn't got a clue what I'm saying but he gets the anger and barks back something featuring the word 'police'. 'Fetch them', I think, as I hold the receipt up, still triumphant. But we're not really getting anywhere here, so I stride out of the store, seething but still a free man.

I calm myself by splashing out on four cotton work shirts in a liquidation sale for the princely sum of €20, for all four, result! I remember to get a bag.

Shortly after finding my bargain, I bump into Barry and Bill, the commentators. They're having a coffee in a café and have their own tale of Andorran woe. They've been back to *Mama Maria*, apparently working on the basis that it couldn't be that bad twice. It was, it seems, even worse.

I phone Alex to come and join us. He's back down from the mountains and we tuck into chicken and chips, our last chance to eat before the day begins to get busy.

I've been requested to be in position at the stadium four hours before kick-off, as there'll be a live update to do for Sky Sports News from the pitchside, a conversation with the producer back at HQ confirms the details. So, I head back to the hotel to get changed. It is shirt and tie all the way with Sky Sports. The sun's shining and the temperature actually appears to be rising even as the afternoon draws on but I've even added a cotton blazer that's been a staple on so many of these September trips overseas.

I pick up my match pass from Lee, the production manager, then wander into the ground. This is where my match day really begins. The crew are already set up and waiting for me. It's the pitch that's going to be the major pre-match topic for discussion. Our footage of the clouds of black rubber rising up underneath the ball has whetted the appetite for a chat about just how bad the surface seems to be. I walk across the pitch to get to the live camera position, so that I can make a swift assessment based on experience. It's almost moving under the sole of my shoes, it's a strange sensation but I get a sense of just how difficult it might be running at top speed wearing a pair of football boots.

The plan is to start the live report by rubbing the artificial surface with my hand, so the viewers can see the bits of black rubber moving about, so I bend my knees in anticipation. However, the 'cross' from London is delayed by other events, so I'm stuck in this crouching position, waiting for the presenter to speak to me, for several minutes. In fact, I'm in danger of seizing up, which won't be good as I'm meant to stand up to finish the report with those incredible mountains as the backdrop. Just before any upward movement becomes impossible, possibly for the rest of the evening, I hear, "Wales now" in my little earpiece and I know I'm next in the running order.

A couple of questions later, it's one down, four to go. It was three, but now Sky News have made a late request. There's actually quite a bit of horse-trading around these live 'crosses'. One that Sky Sports News have requested for later, is close to the time the Wales manager might be arriving and I have to interview him for the live show, the producer of which is not too keen as the live show is always the priority

23

and he wouldn't want anything to potentially get in the way. His view is final, so a negotiation starts.

I take part in this dialogue, and suggest a compromise where we do something a bit earlier which can be recorded and that seems to keep everyone happy. I'm a servant of two masters on these assignments and successfully serving both is the biggest challenge.

Subsequently, we talk more about the pitch, but I'm also keen to talk about the incredible backdrop as well. I've never been to a more spectacular international venue than this tiny ground surrounded by these Pyrenean peaks. It's the sort of ground that seems made to feature on HD widescreen TVs, so I ask the Sports News people if we can mention it as well as the pitch again. They agree, and the wide shot must work because at the end of our chat, the presenter closes by saying, "what a fantastic place to play a football match."

There's always an interview to do with Barry before the game as well as one for Sky News; more pitch talk and a frank assessment of the opposition. Andorra are ranked 199th in the world, they've lost all 40 of the Euro Qualifiers they've played and they've lost their last 44 competitive games going into this one. Or, to put it more succinctly, they are rubbish. It's not surprising really, given that the population's only 80,000. They're one of those nearly-nations UEFA has begun to recognise as the map of Europe has been redrawn in the last 20 years. Gibraltar, with an even smaller population, is the latest example. They will lose pretty much every game they ever play, often heavily. It all seems a bit pointless. But, it's the world game I guess, so there's a place at the table for everyone.

Once these two chats are 'in the can', I'm clear to concentrate on the stuff I need to do for tonight's show. Alex and I both have different jobs to do at this point, he's waiting to film the team bus pulling up and the players getting off, 'arrivals' as they're known in TV language, whilst I'm now looking to do the managerial 'pre-match'. This is an established part of the routine, but I've made sure I mentioned it to the FAW. Not all managers are so accommodating, John Toshack always refused to do anything for us before the game so we had to pre-record all his interviews, which is a problem if there's an issue with an injury in the meantime. Most managers are co-operative but they might have different routines. Chris Coleman likes to do his interview pretty much as soon he gets off the bus so I have to be in position with the camera at the agreed interview location, usually in the tunnel, before he gets there. To be elsewhere, to miss this, is a major *faux-pas* in terms of the rules of match coverage.

I hang around in the press room for a bit, chat with another former Wales player – now BBC Radio Wales pundit – Kevin Ratcliffe, have a sandwich, pick up a match programme and then make sure I'm already heading in the right direction as the team coach pulls up outside. I get warning of its imminent arrival in the earpiece that allows Sarah, the director in our truck in the compound, to communicate with me and the rest of the crew around the stadium.

Sarah arrived late last night, one of Sky's top directors and one of the very few females employed in the role in the industry. She's worked her way up through the ranks at Sky, no mean achievement in a world of blokes.

The confirmation of the teams is another aspect of tunnel diplomacy that has to be strictly observed. Nobody can be sure which players are starting the game until the official team sheets have been filled in and submitted to the referee, an hour before kick-off. In this instance, Chris has verbally confirmed his team to our commentator. This helps him prepare his notes but must be keep secret to ensure the other team don't get to know about it until those sheets are handed in. I've been a commentator, so I know how handy it is to have this information to hand when you're preparing for a game, and how important it is too keep it confidential. On the basis that I know the protocol, Bill has passed on the information, so I now know the team prior to interviewing the manager. This is very useful info for me as the pre-match interview needs to reflect on any surprises in selection. Again, some managers are incredibly cagey about this stuff, refusing to discuss specifics until the team sheet has been submitted, Chris is more easy-going. Hopefully, that bond of trust has been established here as well, he trusts us to look after this information in the appropriate manner. As an example, I'm put to the test as I walk towards the interview position. One of the regular Wales reporters stops me, a good guy and we get on well. He wants a steer on the team, but I daren't divulge it. If I do it might stay under wraps, or it might swiftly appear in a Tweet on his well-followed Twitter account, and that would inevitably get back to the manager within minutes. So, 'mum's the word'. He understands, I think. If I break the cycle of trust once, I may never get back in.

There's a sponsors backboard in place at our allocated interview position, all designated by UEFA. This is an improvement on the past, when some host FAs have kept us out of the tunnel area or even forced us to work at the edge of the pitch.

Chris, however, walks straight past me, and the interview point to the dressing rooms, but it's a brief delay before he returns, we shake hands and get ready to start. The interview will be recorded, but nobody wants to prolong the process unnecessarily; he has a team to prepare. So, I want to get it right first time. Chris knows the interview won't be broadcast until after the teamsheets have been handed in, so he's relaxed about talking about the side he's selected. Bale's in and Ramsey's in, but he's starting with three at the back for the first time since he took charge. That's the most interesting aspect of the line-up and this interview allows him to explain his thinking. We do talk about the pitch but only to discount its significance, Wales should win. The same message repeated again and again. I wish him luck, he turns and heads off to the dressing room.

My next job's a little more mundane but possibly no less important. Barry Horne has an interview to do, with the studio, about this blooming 3G surface. They want him to bounce a ball on it as they talk to him. This is fine but there are logistical issues. For a start, we need a ball. I've got to know all the backroom staff well down the years, they're friendly and helpful and they're the guys to turn to in this sort of situation. Sure enough, they come up with a spare ball and I'm straight off around the pitch to deliver it. The next challenge is for Barry to talk knowledgably with a microphone in one hand, whilst bouncing the ball with the other. This proves a problem in rehearsal until I suggest a solution, he's right handed but trying to bounce the ball with his left. Try swapping? It works. He successfully multi-tasks, all under the watching eyes of the viewers at home and the people who've climbed up a wall behind the ground a few feet away from where he's standing. Barry manfully ignores their catcalls to interact with Dean Saunders, Ian Rush and Simon Davies, all former internationals, a top notch line-up of pundits assembled back in the studio. The talk is pretty much all about the pitch but also about how many Wales should win by.

Kick-off is fast approaching, the ground's filling up and the travelling supporters have been busy putting up their flags, which highlight just how many communities will be represented in the away end this evening. Rhuddlan, Denbigh, Merthyr, Cardiff, Wrexham, Bala – the unification of a nation in a way that nothing else in Wales manages – certainly not rugby, which is viewed by most north Walians, as a game for the south. The football supporters come from Welsh-speaking areas, English-speaking areas, north, south, east and west, in a country with an internal transport network that makes it a tortuous trek to get from top to bottom.

I head back around the ground, to return the ball and to collect my own bag from our interview position near the dressing rooms. I have my pass visible as I walk up the tunnel and turn right. There's a fresh-faced police officer standing there, on guard. Normally this area would be entirely under the charge of stewards and stadium officials, but the Andorran FA have been struggling to find enough people to work on a game that's going to attract their country's biggest crowd for many years.

Already, I've seen young kids wearing bibs and working as stewards as I've walked around the ground but there are also lots of cops in riot gear, including my guy. He looks at my pass as I walk past, and shouts after me to stop. I already suspect he has an issue, but I fall back on a communication breakdown as he shouts again and waves me back towards the tunnel. I make various noises about working for television, 'televisio' tends to work in the Latin countries, that I need to collect my 'equipment' (manbag), he's clearly not happy and barks "Rapido!", presumably to suggest I do it more quickly. I walk on but he follows me and shouts "Rapido!" again, as if I should be running. After the supermarket episode, it's about all I can take but I restrict myself to swearing under my breath just as Ian Gwyn Hughes passes, obviously with all the right accreditation. He chuckles at my plight, all part of the fun of international football at a foreign ground.

I'm back in double-quick time, knees up like a squaddie on parade, the scowl of the young cop following me all the way, and head for my seat on the far side of stadium, where I've got a plastic chair to the left of the Welsh dugout. As I arrive, the teams emerge. There's a big roar from the still-filling away end, a more dignified round of applause from the Andorrans. The crowd's split about 50/50. About half the Welsh fans have travelled in on a fleet of coaches from Barcelona but wherever they've come from today, they'll have had a drink. It's part of it. A very big part of it in some cases. It's an excuse for a trip abroad, a bit of fun and a good singsong. The national anthem's a big part of that. I've done a few foreign trips as a fan when hanging on for that last beer has meant running to the turnstiles, trying to get into the ground in time for the opening notes of 'Hen Wlad Fy Nhadau'.

It's a fantastic anthem, gets me every time. The Wales fans belt it out brilliantly and by the end, I've got tears running down both cheeks. Now, it all begins. I settle back in my plastic chair to watch this Wales win.

The first five minutes of the campaign are fine. Chris Gunter gets into a good position in the box, ball at his feet, and the 'keeper has to stop his shot. Then it all goes awry. Andorra mount their first attack with a throw-in taken from about five yards in front of me, about level with the edge of the area. The ball is hurled into the box, towards a red-shirted attacker with his back to goal. Neil Taylor's up close, very close, with a hand on his back maybe and the Andorran topples forward, as if propelled by contact. He immediately looks towards the ref, arms outstretched in appeal. I take a breath but the game goes on another couple of seconds at least and the ref is running away, following the ball. Suddenly there's a blast on his whistle and now he's stopped and he's pointing to the penalty spot. He has assistants behind each goal, introduced for the first time in this competition, and one of these assistants must have seen the 'foul'. The message is communicated between the officials via their headsets, the whistle sounds, penalty given. Calamity! It's all down to Wayne Hennessey, but the Andorran captain, and his country's leading scorer, Ilderon Lima, steps up and strokes the ball confidently to the right as Hennessey dives left. Andorra, who've lost 44 qualifiers in a row, who haven't even scored a goal for four years, are 1-0 up! Even in my worst nightmares, I couldn't have come up with this scenario. I genuinely feel physically sick. We've had all the hype, all the hope before but it's never unravelled quite as spectacularly as this. I think back to the dog howling in the street. Omens!

It's only 360 seconds into the qualifiers and I'm already considering the tricky questions I'm going to have to ask Chris Coleman in around another 5,000 seconds time. He's currently standing, looking somewhat shell-shocked, a few yards to my right.

The next 15 minutes pass in a blur of misplaced passes and abject misery. Bale is doing his best, he flashes a header over the bar then spirits lift briefly as Ben Davies floats in a pinpoint cross and the same number 11 shirt rises brilliantly to guide a header down and into the corner of the net, beyond the stretched arms of the tiny Andorran 'keeper, 1-1. Wales are back at square one but it doesn't feel like it. Nobody anticipated Andorra getting anything, so now there's a nervousness every time they actually manage to cross the halfway line. Play becomes ever more disjointed as Wales labour their way towards the interval.

Small clouds of small black rubber shards fly up at every bounce, big clouds at every tackle and the players must be covered in the stuff. The surface is almost unplayable and I begin to wonder whether all the talk of it not being a problem has actually been a cover for it being a really big problem. Heads have dropped. Wales have the look of a team that feels it's all going against them. It's a sight and sense I'm used to after so many years following the national side, a mentality bred of decades of failure. The whistle blows for half-time and I follow the players off, all of us in a state of despondency. The FAW people I encounter look glum. Sure, we're used to despair. we're used to hope being extinguished prematurely in these campaigns but we usually get a bit more than six minutes!

It all feels bad already. The pitch is awful so Wales have asked for it to be watered in the break. Mark Evans, the big, bearded match delegate is angry that nothing's happened so far, apart from one brief spurt from the sprinklers apart. Clearly the Andorrans are not of a mind to do anything that will help Wales at all. Given their atrocious run of results, I guess you can't blame them. Mark goes off to find a UEFA official to complain to. Then the sprinklers do come on again, but only in the half Wales will be defending after the break, presumably to help the home nation? They must sense that, in their new stadium, in front of this bumper crowd, they're all set up to record probably their best result ever. The mood remains sullen as I head back to my seat for the second half. I send the office a message to confirm Wales will line-up for the second half as they did for the first. This is a talking point in itself. The new formation hasn't worked. We were anticipating a re-jig at half-time. It didn't happen. Still five at the back, or is it three? If things don't improve, this will be a question, one of many, Chris Coleman will have to answer, did he get his tactics wrong?

The one thought that consoles me as the game restarts is that, surely, Wales can't be as bad as they were in the first half? But, like *Mama Maria*, they're actually worse. The home side line-up behind the ball, close down Gareth Bale and Aaron Ramsey in groups of three and commit as many fouls as it takes to stop Wales players progressing. The away fans keep supporting the team but there are murmurs, more than murmurs, a few chants actually, directed at the manager. He's still to win over many supporters. Coming from Swansea probably doesn't help him in terms of the large numbers of Cardiff fans who follow the national side, but neither do performances like this. Wales were thrashed 6-1 in Serbia in the previous campaign. He arrived late in Macedonia for another match after losing his passport, and again Wales were poor and well beaten. Now the prosecution's warming up for another series of accusations of incompetence.

It's torture sitting at the side of the pitch. In the olden days, at least my senses would have been dulled by beer, now I'm suffering every overhit cross, every misplaced pass and there are lots of them. Every now and again I dare to glance at the stadium clock, which is moving forward far more quickly than Wales. They should at least be peppering the home goal with shots from every angle, but it's not happening. The whole game's being played in the Andorra half, a Bale free kick's beaten away by the 'keeper and Andy King misses a good chance with a header but those moments apart, they're not even creating chances. Andorra foul incessantly to stop Wales getting into any sort of stride. The performance becomes ever more ragged.

It's awful. I'd rather be anywhere else than right here, right now. I've spent so many days away from my family over the years covering Wales, missed so many birthdays and anniversaries, parents' evenings and school events, and for what? I'm not alone in my anguish. To my right, the whole of the coaching staff look equally downcast, even Dai the kitman looks resigned to it. He's no more than six feet away from me. Our eyes meet as Wales launch another attack that breaks down. We raise eyebrows, puff out cheeks, shake heads, then he offers me a piece of chewing gum. I accept. Maybe it'll bring a change of fortune. I flick another glance at that ruddy big, shiny clock. It's almost up to 80 minutes now, the scoreline still glows out 'Andorra 1 Wales 1'.

I'm chewing furiously, the end is nigh. Soon, I have to head round

30

to the interview position, to conduct what can only be described as 'the post mortem'. I always leave my reporter position on 85 minutes, I need to be ready and waiting when the final whistle blows and it's a final whistle that will all but bring an end to the campaign as well as the game. But first, a flicker of hope with another foul and Wales get yet another free kick just outside the box. Dai looks over, "now we'll do it!", he tells me. I smile weakly. Anticipation levels rise, in the commentary in my headphones, Bill Leslie's voice goes up a notch. Up steps Gareth Bale. Has the 'Great Man' found his range, after that precursor a few minutes earlier? Gareth awaits the whistle, hands on hips, standing square on to the ball, legs wide apart. The whistle blows, he runs up, strikes the ball over the wall but the tiny 'keeper positions himself well again, flaps at the ball, makes contact and as it bounces back up, with white shirts converging on him, he punches it away. AAAHHHHH!! Last chance gone!? Hold on though, the whistle's been blown. The ref's talking to Andorra's number nine, Riera, now he's booking him, the sixth yellow card for Andorra. I look down to the small monitor at my feet that shows me the TV coverage of the game and I see that he's raced free of the wall and was almost upon Bale when he hit the ball. It's a clear infringement and it means a retake. One more chance perhaps?

The same precise routine precedes the second strike. This time though, he gets the ball up and just over the defensive wall, before it dips sharply beyond the dive of the diminutive goalkeeper! It's perfectly placed and the ball nestles inside the corner of the net, 2-1!! AAAAAHHHHH!!! I scream and do a frenzied little punching movement, the coaching staff race off the bench, so do the subs, as fans pour on the pitch, players dive on Gareth Bale and the relief rolls down from those Andorran mountain slopes; an emotional avalanche in the Pyrenees.

Gareth's disappeared below a pile of teammates and fans cavort around them. They've spent a lot of money getting here, taken days off work, scrimped and saved. They've done a windy three-hour coach trip from Barcelona, they've been drinking and singing all day and at the end of it all they thought their team was going to fail in the most embarrassing of circumstances. It's no wonder they've run on to the pitch. No sign of Mr Rapido or his pals at this point either, by the way. The stewards, many of them brought over by the FAW, are left to herd everyone back into the stands. Even Gareth Bale assists with big 'calm-down' gestures in their direction. Good order is eventually restored.

The delay's taken the clock round to my designated departure time. Mentally, I've torn up the first interview and scattered it to the warm night sky. As long as we hang on, 'Cookie' Coleman's off the hookie and, surely, we must hang on?

To get to the tunnel, I walk round the pitch in front of the away fans. They're singing raucously again and as I walk behind the goal in front of them, I can't help but clap. I get quite emotional to see them so happy. They didn't give up on the team, their faith has been rewarded. I've met many of them down the years as supporter and reporter, they're good people. Let's face it, I'm one of them, just a fan who got lucky. A few shout my name, I wave and then I see him, TC, Tommie Collins, all smiles. We've become mates having met on most trips. He loves football and music, like me, grew up watching the matches when we all started obsessing about which trainers to wear, like me. I reach over the low barrier and we shake hands. Maybe we'll never qualify, but these moments are what keep us all coming back for more and, despite everything, he's always kept travelling with Wales. He's a Chelsea fan, goes everywhere with them, which isn't easy when you live in Porthmadog. He's flinty, straight-talking, not easily impressed, but he's smiling. There's a collective broad grin stretched across the entire away end.

I disappear up the tunnel to the interview position. There's no monitor to allow me to watch the game so I don't see anything of the closing stages, including the six added minutes. As it ticks down, I pace nervously up and down in the company of IG (Ian Gwyn Hughes), the FAW's head of media. I don't throw Dai's lucky chewing gum away until I finally hear the shrill blast on the whistle that brings the game to an end. We've done it! Just.

There's no time to dwell on it. Now I have to get my own game head on and I pass on the request for interviews with Gareth Bale, obviously, and Ashley Williams to Ian. We have something called a 'super-flash', an interview as soon as the players leave the pitch. But Gareth arrives with no shirt on, having already swapped it with an eager Andorran international chasing a decent souvenir. He goes off to find something to wear and Ashley Williams sneaks past at the same time. Ian heads off to get them out the dressing room. I need them back, and in front of the camera, quick!

Then a UEFA official arrives and asks who we want to interview. I tell him who we've already requested, plus the manager and another player. I select Neil Taylor. He's a great talker and he gave the penalty away, so there's a bit to discuss. Gareth reappears in a training top. We don't get a lot of chance to talk to him when he's on Wales duty. He's got a contract as an ambassador for BT Sport, our big rivals, so it's a bit tricky but in fairness, he's always come when we've requested him at the end of games and given that he's almost always Man of the Match, that's quite a lot. Like Aaron, he was another nervous talker who's grown in confidence the more interviews he's done. He comes across well, he's bright, articulate and one of the world's best footballers. I'd settle for just one of those three. Amidst the elation, the relief, Gareth also describes the pitch as the worst he's ever played on.

ITV now have rights to the highlights for these games, under the terms of a new contract. They've had a low-key presence up to this point, but for this game they have a reporter and camera next to ours in the flash interview position, so Gareth moves on to them. Then Ashley Williams arrives, we interview him. Before that's finished, Chris Coleman is at my shoulder so we put him in front of the camera next. All these interviews are being recorded at HQ, they'll fit as many as they can in but Bale and Coleman's will definitely be broadcast. Chris is clearly relieved and praises his players for not giving up. He mentions the pitch, says he couldn't say how bad it was beforehand but now he feels it's okay to be critical. He stresses there won't be any official complaint about it because he wants all the other nations in the group to have to play here as well. He predicts others may also find it tricky.

The manager's night suddenly gets better, as news filters through that the top seeds for the group, Bosnia, have lost at home to Cyprus. Our games next month against both of those teams now have an even greater importance.

Once Chris has moved on, Neil Taylor comes to the position, another hugely articulate player from this squad. Commendably, he acknowledges his error with the penalty and praises the talents of his teammate, Gareth, for the way he saved the day. We've whistled through the four interviews and HQ are happy with what they've got. In TV terms, we get a 'clear'. Job done.

Alex has been elsewhere throughout the game, filming Wales. He was right in the heart of the post-goal pitch invasion. He sends me a text to say he's safe and all done and dusted and that we're meeting up for a debrief in the bar of the Holiday Inn. Too often in the last 10 years, these have been more of a post-mortem. It may only be Andorra but I can only remember three previous away wins in qualifiers we've covered, and not one of those in a game that really meant anything in terms of possible qualification, so we deserve a small celebration. There is a genuine sense of elation and, by turns, desolation, depending upon the result, when we spend so long building-up to a game. If it goes right, all the effort seems worthwhile, if it doesn't, it's a long trip home. There have been far too many long trips home.

The Sky crew gathers briefly. Barry and Sarah are heading straight off for 6am flights back to Britain. Barry's got a full day's teaching ahead of him. It's an incredible effort on his part, I don't know how he does it. So, they make the three hour drive back through the night whilst we sip on a couple of beers, chat with Wales fans who've clearly also had a long day, and then head back to our hotel. We've got our own early start and sleeping after these games is never easy, with the adrenaline still pumping. Despite the dog howling again and the return of the street sweeper, I manage a few hours before the alarm goes.

Wednesday 10th September

We're both up and ready for the off at 8am. The drive back's trouble-free and I'm at the airport well in advance of my flight. Tantalisingly, there's the Leeds flight still on the board. If we'd left a few minutes earlier, I'd have made it. The fact that my car's parked at East Midlands airport obviously means I couldn't actually catch it but the thought of being home a few hours earlier is appealing. I go shopping instead.

I see FAW blazers as I'm wandering around the shops in departures. Then tracksuits. The Wales charter flight's leaving from this terminal, as it turns out. So I catch up with Mark Evans, Ian Gwyn Hughes and a couple of the travelling councillors before I bump into Chris Coleman. We have a chat, and I tell him I was preparing to ask some tough questions before Gareth's free kick. "Don't worry!" he responds cheerily, "I wouldn't have been there. I'd have got a taxi straight back to Barcelona at the final whistle!"

34

2

"I don't think we have to win, but I know we must not lose"
Wales v Bosnia

'Ashley, Ashley Ashley, Ashley Ashley, Ashley Ashley Williams
Jonny, Jonny Jonny, Jonny Jonny, Jonny Jonny Williams'

Friday 3rd October

I've kissed the kids and the wife, patted the dog and the car's packed ready for departure. This time the boot's really packed, though. This is no flying visit, this is proper long-haul. I won't be pulling back onto the drive for another 11 days so I've had to pack accordingly. That means suits, shirts and ties for match coverage, running gear, going out gear, hanging round the hotel gear – clothes and shoes for work and play. That's not all I've got crammed into the back for this one though, I'm lacking a kitchen sink but I can claim a mini deep-fat fryer and a mini surf board that's lying across the rear shelf. Shoved behind one of the seats, there's a wetsuit, behind another there's a big bag of food.

Why the provisions? I'd better explain the plan. First destination is Swansea. As the name implies, it's a coastal city and as I discovered on my last visit, it boasts some excellent surfing beaches. I'm not a proper surfer, I'm an old bloke with a body board but I love it. I love getting

35

out in the sea, being battered by some big waves and occasionally being swept back into shore by one of them. So, as I'm working on Swansea v Newcastle tomorrow, I need to make the 300 mile drive the day before, which should give me the chance to grab an hour or so in the sea. It's October, hence the wetsuit.

The onward destination after the game explains the food. I'm not heading for a hotel, I'm heading for an apartment in Cardiff. It's self-catering so I travel with provisions. In fact, I make an immediate deviation from my route to add to them, calling in at a shop called Foodies in Harrogate that sells lots of locally produced stuff. Saturday night tea and Sunday's lunch are purchased before the journey can start in earnest.

As for the itinerary, well, Wales have a game a week today and then again the following Monday, both at home. First though, there's this, pre-international break, weekend of fixtures for the players to get through unscathed. I'd be happy if they all got sent off in the first minute of their respective games. The manager must spend the next couple of days with everything crossed, hoping for the best and fearing the worst. He's lost out already. After the Andorran pitch debacle, Joe Allen's had to have a double hernia operation and hasn't played since. Aaron Ramsey limped off for Arsenal a couple of weeks ago and some suggestions are that he might be missing until December. So, two key players already out and still one more round of matches to get through before the survivors gather at the team hotel on Sunday. Chris Coleman will dread the sound of his mobile phone ringing for the next 48 hours.

Swansea's a long way from Leeds, further when you divert to Harrogate first and then factor in the dreaded 50 mph stretches on the M1. It's a dispiriting thought that I'll be enduring this motorway roadwork madness for the duration of the qualification campaign. I can't help thinking it might speed things up a bit if the contractors deployed more than what appears to be, just half a dozen chaps in hi-viz jackets, standing round, chatting and checking for texts. Still, like them, I'm not in a hurry even though the waves are calling. The drive's a familiar one, and four hours later I pull into the car park of the Swansea Marriott, check into a room with a seaview and then head straight out in a pair of swimming shorts, a hoodie and a pair of Converse pumps.

I drive the few miles from the hotel to Langland Bay, just as I'd done the last time I did a game in Swansea. It was a dark, stormy September day then, so the waves were big. There were quite a few surfers out as well, real ones. I had a great hour or so, messing about in the shallows under the watchful gaze of windswept lifeguards. No lifeguards today, the season's over so we're all alone. Well, not quite. Dogs are allowed back on the beach from the end of September onwards, so there are a good few of them bounding around. There are a few hardy souls in the sea but they're just young lads, the sky is blue and the waves are small so the real surfers have stayed away.

I've driven a long way for this and, besides, I've already put a pound in the parking meter, so I'm not going to give it a miss. The sea's that bit colder, invigorating, and every few minutes a half decent wave squares its shoulders and manages to carry me back in. It's enough. I think it's also great exercise. Wade out, grip the board, then roll over and push back up to do it all again. I had two weeks of this on holiday this summer and I've never felt fitter.

I stick it out for the hour, then drive back to the hotel for room service, a glass of wine, a swot up on the two teams for tomorrow and bed.

Saturday 4th October

My job done in 'ugly lovely' Swansea, a 2-2 draw with Newcastle, I'm back in the car and heading east to the capital, 45 miles away. My satnav leads me to my destination, Century Wharf. It's a massive complex of apartments built in the redeveloped Bay area of the city. As I approach I have to phone to arrange key collection, and my courier then directs me into the midst of this enclosed community. He takes me up in the lift to the eighth floor. The moment of truth is that one when the front door swings open, first impressions count and mine are favourable. It's really quite smart actually and I'm pretty relieved as I've had to work hard to persuade Alex that this is a better option than a hotel, I think he'll like his surroundings at least.

I have had to agree during the persuasion process to give up the ensuite bedroom. So even though he's not even arriving until tomorrow, I dutifully head for the smaller room, bathroom facilities located across the corridor. We've done this apartment thing a few times before. I've always much preferred it to being in a hotel – more space, more freedom and no need to go out and eat in restaurants every evening. That might sound like a treat not to be missed but to me it's a bit of a ball-ache, you have to agree what it is you want to eat, find somewhere, then order; there's the waiting and then the food that you might not really want but it's the closest thing you can find on the menu is served, sometimes quickly but invariably late. That palaver is okay now and again, but not every night.

The first time we did this apartment thing, two blokes with limited culinary experience, Alex's wife came up with a few idiot-proof 30 minute recipes. They were a big success, and we've repeated the experiment since. I actually enjoy doing a bit of cooking now and Mrs Gage definitely takes some credit for that. I'd never eaten sweet potatoes until that first apartment stay, now I love them and include them with lots of dishes I prepare for the family.

Needless to say, you have to get on well to forego the safety of the hotel room for the wide open spaces of the apartment. People often accuse Alex and me of being like a married couple (not least by our actual spouses!), an accusation I'd be quick to dispel for any number of reasons but I think we know enough about each other's 'buttons' to make it work. Oh, and it saves the company a small fortune as well by the way. The apartment is almost half the cost of the two of us staying in a hotel, without even factoring in the reduced spending on meals and parking.

Once I'm settled in, bags unpacked, mini deep fat fryer unloaded, there's another important task to perform, part of the ritual, the Skype call home so that the family can see my new surroundings. My wife's very much into interior design so I have to do a full tour, waving my iPhone around at all the nooks and crannies and ending up on the spacious balcony overlooking the River Taff. In fact, I can also see the Cardiff City Stadium, Friday's match venue, from up here, but I think Rachel's more interested in the fact that I can also see a big Ikea which appears to be even closer.

Sunday 5th October

A decent night's sleep and I treat myself to a bit of a lie-in. There's nothing scheduled for today in terms of Wales coverage, but I've got to make sure everything's organised for tomorrow, when there's a big Sky shoot taking place at the team hotel. Emails are exchanged, times and locations confirmed and Alex decides he can afford to come down on the day, so the apartment's all mine for the next 24 hours.

The chance to just potter around for a bit is a rare one, so I seize it with two hands. I go for a run, always a good way to explore new surroundings. Even though I know this part of Cardiff reasonably well, I like to get my jogging routes worked out early on. There's actually a gym and pool as part of the complex but I prefer a bit of adventure and fresh air.

It gives me a chance to work out my best route into the city centre as well, important as I'm heading out this evening to meet up with my brother and an old pal, both of whom have moved back to Cardiff recently.

There is the somewhat exotic option of a river taxi from the Bay to Bute Park but ultimately I decide to keep it 'old school' and I walk it, working off some more calories before I put them all on again. Our rendezvous is at the far side of the city centre but there's actually a direct route there from close to the apartment, a path following the river and it's a nice evening so I enjoy the stroll. We've agreed to meet at a pub called Y Mochyn Du, The Black Pig for those who don't speak the lingo. I know it as it's close to where my brother lives, and near to where Alex and I first shared an apartment together in Cardiff. I'm the first to arrive but I'm not waiting long. We all went to the same school, Ysgol Rhiwabon, and we come from neighbouring villages near Wrexham, so there's lot to catch up on. A bit of tea turns into a bit of a session, involving another former haunt, the nearby Cameo Club, and sometime past midnight I make the return journey in the back of a cab. There used to be a lot of these sorts of nights out when I first started coming down to Cardiff to cover the games but now they're rarer than Wales away wins. We're all grown up, and we know there'll be a price to pay tomorrow...

Monday 6th October

...and so there is. Head banging, stomach churning, the morning passes slowly. At times like this I regret being generous enough to let the absent Alex claim the ensuite. Ultimately, I have to make the effort to drag myself up to welcome my compadre – *mi casa es su casa*. He seems pleased with what he finds, particularly the fact that I've given up the best room, and he produces the all-important recipes from Mrs Gage that should help ensure our survival over the next seven days.

I have to get back on the ball now anyway, as we're due at the team hotel shortly. Alex has a lot of gear to set up for a shoot involving all the squad. It's for the fancy stuff we broadcast in the build-up to kick-off these days, there's a graphic of the team line-up accompanied by head shots of all the players. It's a little thing but it takes a lot of effort. The team base is really close to our apartment, but there's a load of equipment to carry from the car to the hotel, so it's a two minute drive but a 15 minute baggage transfer.

A Sky Sports assistant producer, an AP, arrives to oversee things and make sure Alex is filming it all in the right way. He's a good guy and it's going to take a while so he sets about ordering sandwiches for lunch as his first major task. I don't really have a role other than knowing most of the players and team staff if there are any issues; a liaison officer if you will.

This kind of shoot is common practice for the Premier League clubs but this is the first time we've done it with Wales. The players start arriving almost as soon as we're all set up and ready to roll. Chris Gunter's the first. He's a nice lad and one of those we've both known for a long time because he's become a mainstay of the squad in the decade we've been covering Wales with Sky. It doesn't seem to put him at ease, he finds it difficult to keep a straight face and pose in the way required. He keeps cracking up. His session alone takes 15 minutes. We've got about 20 more to get through and only a two hour slot in the players' agenda in which to do it. Fortunately, most of the rest find it a little easier. All the Premier League players know the score; look down, look up, then finish with a smouldering stare into camera. Generally, players are more camera-aware and comfortable than ever before, even the young ones, and there are quite a few of them in this injury-depleted squad. So much so in fact, that even I don't recognise one or two of the faces, but as we need to tick them off the list when they appear, I consult Google to find images that will confirm my hunch in a couple of instances.

Generally, it's a good, fun session. It merely reinforces my high opinion of this group of players. I've watched a lot of them mature, from timid teenagers joining the senior ranks, to the confident men who laugh, joke and take the mickey out of each other now. And there's no way Joe Ledley could have grown that Desperate Dan beard when we first encountered him a decade ago. Our sandwiches cause a bit of a commotion as well. One lot is ordered and doesn't arrive, so another lot is ordered and then both arrive, so now we've got loads of sandwiches. A couple of the players dip in to help out. The rest we manage to tuck away ourselves. Once it's all done, we've got to de-rig and then carry everything back to the car to be transported back to the apartment.

For Alex at least, it's a tight turnaround. He's got to get dolled up for a swift return to the team hotel, venue for tonight's annual Player Awards dinner. This has become another fixture in the calendar for us over those last 10 years. In fact, I've hosted the event every year, until now. This year, they've got someone else doing it, wanted a bit of a change apparently. I won't lie and say I wasn't annoyed. I've put a lot into making a good job of it down the years, hopefully helping to professionalise what was, I believe, a bit of a shambolic do previously. I've MC'd a lot of events down the years, including some pretty big deals. It's something I really enjoy. I got into acting at school and joined the county youth theatre. I even appeared on stage alongside Rhys Ifans, later destined to head off to Hollywood and stardom. After that I did an English and Drama degree at Uni, more acting, so I enjoy working in front of an audience. This year they want a change though. Last year, the First Minister, Carwyn Jones suggested, on stage, that I'd introduced him as Carwyn James, a revered former rugby player, coach and commentator. I don't think I did, as I know as little about James as I do Jones, but he seemed convinced. In my paranoia, I wonder if he's put the boot in, highly unlikely but, hey, I'm a highly strung actor.

On the basis of my annoyance, I have decided not to attend at all, despite an invitation. Actually, that's not the only reason. The FAW invite a lot of the journalists who cover Wales to the event and some who don't. I would find myself sitting at one of these 'media' tables, and then I'd spend the evening being asked by various people why I wasn't presenting it this year. I don't really have an answer to this, so I decide the best course of action is just to stay away. I do fear popping up as an item in a Welsh newspaper, 'the Sky reporter, 45, sat stony faced as his replacement chatted with Gareth Bale on stage.' Again, it probably wouldn't happen, but I don't want to be the subject of anyone's story so better not take the chance.

So I'm staying away. But then Alex manages to rub salt into the wound. "Any chance you could run me back to the hotel?" he asks, the little monkey, now dressed as a penguin. It's a five minute walk but he's taking an expensive camera so he can get some shots for Sky Sports News to use, so I run him across town, dropping him off at the top of the red carpet. He disappears up it, barely turning to wave. In the past, we've always done an interview with the three winners, if they are actually there. But I know who's won this time and I know that we're already lined up to speak to them over the next couple of days. In particular, we've already made a request to speak to Gareth Bale, which we understand will happen on Wednesday, so I don't want to compromise this by shoving a microphone in his face this evening.

It's tricky with Gareth, you see. He's a lovely lad, from a good, stable background but he's become a brand since his mega money transfer to Real Madrid. He has a management team working for him, and they negotiated an 'ambassador' role with Sky's arch-rivals BT Sport whilst he was still at Spurs. The irony of this is, now that he's in Spain, Sky currently holds all the contracts to show him play, both for club and country but we haven't had the chance to interview him prior to a Wales game for a number of years now. When our latest request got a pretty positive response from the FAW, it was a surprise but a pleasant one. After all, he's box office. The FAW want a good crowd for Friday and he's the guy to put bums on seats, so they're keen for him to do something we can use in the build-up to the game as well. That's why I don't want to compromise anything by grabbing a quick chat with him tonight.

Anyway, I've got other plans. I bash together a quick tea, grab a shower and head off into Cardiff.

There's a gig for me to go to, The Tea Street Band are playing at Clwb Ifor Bach (Little Ivor's Club) and they've stuck me on the guest list.

I love my music, sometimes I think I love it more than football. It doesn't let you down as much and a gig's another place to go to let inhibitions drop, to just get into the music. I keep my eye and ear on what's going on still, as I have since I first started listening to John Peel even before I was in my teens.

It's a pretty small venue. The support act wander on shortly after I arrive. There are probably 20 people in the room at this point. They play in the corner, no stage. They're called Houdini Dax, from Cardiff, and they're decent. I make a note to check them out again later and leave a complimentary message on their Twitter account.

By the time my guys walk on, there are about 50 people in the room. These Tea Street lads are older, probably been in bands since they were little, but this is their first ever tour and they're determined to enjoy it. It turns into the sort of night that makes me think music is my first love, particularly when they invite me backstage afterwards to share a beer and have a chat, but only after they've packed their equipment away into the van though, I know that feeling.

We talk football and music over a couple of beers then they have to get on the road, it's a long drive back to Merseyside. As we're saying our goodbyes and they're piling into their tour bus, actually tour minibus, they offer me a lift home. I thank them but decline the offer and set off, just as a monsoon sweeps over south Wales. Bad decision. No coat. On my way back, I wipe the rain off out of my eyes and off my phone screen sufficiently to read a text from Alex at the dinner that says the Bale interview is off, his management people have turned down the request. Plan B it is then. Not sure what plan B is though?

Tuesday 7th October

There's work to be done but not until this afternoon. Alex has more info from the dinner. The FAW will be offering up four players for interviews. We get an itinerary ahead of the international get-together but these names aren't generally confirmed until the day before and even then they can be subject to change. In general, we have three criteria, we want to interview someone who'll be playing, we want to interview someone most of our viewers will recognise and we want to interview someone with something interesting to say. In terms of recognition, it's sadly predictable that lads with Premier League clubs are deemed to be more familiar to the audience. In terms of their ability to talk interestingly, well, we're lucky with Wales, very lucky. The team's full of good guys. That doesn't mean they're likely to come out with anything startling or controversial, it just means they'll talk confidently and cleverly for three or four minutes. Again, I've seen a lot of the players develop these abilities over the decade we've been doing this.

Today, we're getting Ben Davies, Joe Ledley, James Chester and Chris Gunter. On the tick box list that's three Premier League players and four good talkers. Seeing Chester's name on the list raises my interest. I've interviewed him at Hull before, in my other Sky role, but we haven't had chance to do anything with him since he first appeared in a Wales squad last summer. That appearance came as a bit of a surprise to me and others, as he'd never featured in any representative team for Wales at any level previously. It turned out that half of his family come from north Wales, Rhyl to be precise. Luckily, someone at the FAW must have got wind of the fact that he was eligible, and a call was made to see if he'd be interested. It's a good story and I contact the live producer, Jim, to see if it might become Plan B.

Jim knows about the Bale decision by now, others are involved in the discussion back at HQ as well. As the FAW's broadcast partner, we have certain contractual rights, and access to players before and after games is amongst them. So, we should really get the chance to interview Gareth occasionally, when he's on international duty. Technically, he's under the jurisdiction of the FAW at these times, just as he's under the jurisdiction of Real Madrid when he goes back to Spain. In this instance, I don't think anyone's naïve enough to think he isn't a slightly different case. It's not a discussion I need to get involved in though, that's for bigger fish. I just have to come up with an alternative. Jim agrees to have a look at the Chester interview when we've done it, although he's keen on using an Ashley Williams interview that we're scheduled to do on Thursday.

All this probably seems pretty minor in the grand scheme of things but much of my time on these international weeks is taken up dealing with this fairly low-level type of hiatus. Sky Sports News might have different requirements to Sky Sports. In this instance, Sky Sports News want some interviews they can put out ASAP to preview the game. Jim wants an interview he can use on the night of the game, an interview with punchy quotes that can be decorated with nice shots. That means the production team needs time to look at it, and work on it. Ideally, Jim also wants something on his show that hasn't been seen before, so I need to make sure that Sports News are aware what material they can and can't access. To achieve this, I'm constantly having to update everyone on what we're doing and for whom. It's easier now that emails can inform everyone at one go, rather than having to make three or four phone calls but emails occasionally get overlooked, so I might find myself going through the communication process, and relaying the same message, more than once.

In terms of routine, it's usually only on the Tuesday morning of an international week that I finally have a clear idea of what we are doing and for whom, even after weeks of planning. There are planning teams at Sky but, the way I see it, I'm the Wales reporter so I'm the guy responsible for organising and co-ordinating who gets what and when and how, in the build-up to the game. That means, I'll also work with the travel department to arrange accommodation and travel, for me and Alex. I'll only be able to have that conversation after communicating with the FAW to work out times and locations for our various interviews. The next job involves liaising with Sky Sports and Sky Sports News to let everyone know where we'll need to be and what we'll be doing at any given time. It's actually quite a big job and previously, fitting it around my daily Sports News duties was sometimes difficult. Since August, my role has changed, I work primarily for Sky Sports now and there's a bit more slack in the schedule for planning.

Even so, things change, often. I can't be sure, for instance, that we'll definitely be interviewing the players the FAW have suggested. The Bale situation is far from the worst setback I've had to deal with down the years, in fact, in relative terms, it's a tiny blip. I've encountered every sort of crisis and every trip seems to throw up new ones, so I always arrive in Cardiff with the mindset of 'what's going to go wrong this week?'

As I look forward to this afternoon, I piece together the relevant information like a jigsaw. I now know we'll be doing the interviews at the Cardiff City Stadium, I know what time we'll be doing them and I know who we'll be doing them with, probably. There's still one job to do however and it's an important one, where exactly are we going to be doing them? Stadium? Yes, but whereabouts in the stadium?

As a broadcast partner, we get individual access to each player. So, the logistics are that the players will arrive at the stadium and be taken into the media conference room to speak to the journalists from other TV companies, radio stations, newspapers, websites and the like. Then they get brought to us, so we need to be set up somewhere else. In this instance one of the interviews, James Chester, might be required for the live show on Friday evening so I need to organise a space that we can claim as our own for an hour, that's quiet, and that has plug sockets for the cameras, monitors and lights Alex will want to set up.

All this is in my mind as I begin a text message dialogue with Mark Evans at the FAW about where we might best get set up. Mark is the guy in charge of planning for these international fixtures. He has the best overview so he'll help with guidance as to which room at the stadium we might be able to commandeer. He suggests the home dressing room, with plenty of plugs, no windows and a door to minimise outside noise. My only concern is the acoustics. From past experience, sound can bounce around changing rooms as they're often tiled and there might be the incessant drip of a shower that won't quite turn off or the hum of an aircon unit. Still, as another tickbox exercise, we're definitely doing okay. I'm relatively reassured, although I won't be really happy until the job's done.

That leaves me time to go for a run, on a new route down towards Penarth, past that Ikea and then back towards the Bay. I cross the water via the road bridge that has a cycle/footpath alongside it. I like to run by water, and these Wales trips have given me ample opportunity; rivers like the Danube, the Rhine, the Vardar, the Moraca and the Black Sea, the Caspian Sea, the Atlantic and the Mediterranean. The banks of the River Taff are those that I've most often pounded along, half an hour or so, three or four miles, nothing too dramatic. It's time to either unwind after work or to get the adrenaline pumping before I go, occasionally it's time to sweat out last night's beer and work off last night's meal. Whatever, I rarely miss an opportunity to get out when a spare hour appears.

There's a fair bit of exercise involved once the job's begun as well, to be honest. There's all that gear to put in the car, take out of the car and set up. Because of this, we always have to make sure we're at the venue well in advance of the time we'll be seeing our interviewees. It can take 45 minutes to get everything ready, and we need extra wriggle room to cope with anything unexpected. The drive from the apartment to the stadium takes no more than five minutes, but we set off over an hour before the scheduled start time of 2pm.

The first big test is getting into the stadium, not always the easiest task when receptionists and security guards are involved, but the staff at the CCS are helpful and we're straight in. Next test, the room. Is it open? Yes. Is it suitable? That's one for Alex? Yes. Plugs? Yes. Acoustics? Remarkably good. No echo, and the aircon unit turns off at the wall. Lights? Not a problem, for now. As luck would have it, they're testing the emergency lighting, so all the main lights in the tunnel area are off. But what if they come back on? Alex can see the flash from ceiling panel sensors that trigger the lights whenever anyone walks in. If we're not careful, we'll have everything set up just right in darkness, then the first player walks in, all the main lights come on and we're stuffed. Alex has a plan, and puts gaffer tape over the sensors. By way of a backup, I go off and find the stadium electrician and ask him if we can ensure the dressing room lights aren't switched back on when everything else comes back on. He's happy to help. This is why we have to get in early.

My next job is just as important, despite appearances to the contrary. I have to sit on a chair for 10 minutes. The chair I'm sitting on is the one the players will be occupying shortly. I'm a test dummy. Alex lines up the lights to illuminate me. Next he wants to position the backlight, a crucial visual aspect of any decent interview. He's created something clever, three FAW crests printed on a sheet of transparent vinyl. But they need cutting out so they'll fit in the bracket he'll put in front of the light. He hands me a pair of scissors. I'm now multitasking. I'm both sitting and cutting. Do I get a Blue Peter badge? There's so much more to this job than just turning up and asking questions. That's the easy bit!

If we were worried about the clock and not being ready, fears are allayed as Peter from the media team pops his head round the door. The players are delayed, and won't be here now until 2.30pm. Again, this is not entirely unusual. It's actually more of a problem if they turn-up early, like Aaron last month, and you're not ready. Times like this are used for checking and sending emails, sometimes ordering lunch, or often just chatting. We do a lot of chatting.

Interviewing is different from chatting, generally speaking. When the first player, Chris Gunter, arrives, we chat for a bit. There's a bit of banter about the 'green screen' shoot yesterday, a bit about his game last weekend, then we start the interview and the tone changes. He'll be mindful of saying the right thing, he'll want to sound upbeat but not arrogant, respectful of the opposition but not fearful. Chris speaks quite quietly, but there's an impressive quality to the way he delivers the message. As I've said, I think it helps that we've both been around lads like Chris for a long time. Over the period, I think we've developed a good level of trust. Some players still seem to be scared of being 'stitched-up' when they speak to journalists. It's a throwback to the times when tabloids were the place most people got their football news. They were hungry for salacious stories, racy quotes that could feed headline writers and, fill a back page. In all honesty, times have changed, the tabloids' influence has waned and the big 'redtop' exclusive doesn't happen very much anymore. Football news comes online, from social media or the internet or the channel I worked for, for 16 years. On top of that, agents, clubs and associations all have media departments, employed to offer greater protection to their players. The players themselves have become ever more savvy as well, they've grown up with a 24/7 sports news channel, they use Twitter, clubs run their own TV stations. In short, they have a far greater awareness of how the media works than any previous generation.

Still, there are challenges. In these instances, with players on international duty, it can get tricky when I get requests from HQ to ask questions that might not appear to have anything to do with Wales. The most frequent example is when I'm told that I need to ask a player a question about something that's been happening at his club. This is particularly the case with the Premier League players. They are so well protected at their clubs, they'd be kept away from tricky questions about rumours surrounding the manager's future or a controversy involving a teammate. It can be a bit of a minefield, but it's a conflict that takes place within every international camp in the run-up to a game. The national association only wants the players to talk about the game, the guys from the media may turn-up with other ideas.

Generally, my strategy with this has been to try and keep as many questions as possible tied to the context of the upcoming game so, if a player's had a poor game for his club at the weekend, I might consider what state of mind he's going to be in as a result. I'll reflect back but focus on what's coming next Sometimes the questions are too specific for that and I might just make it clear before the interview starts that there are questions I've been asked to ask. A good media officer will already have predicted some of these when he's briefed the player prior to arrival, but it can be useful just to forewarn them anyway. Ideally, they'll have prepared a suitable answer but they have the right to say they don't want to talk about anything but Wales in this interview. A lot of it is down to the individual. Some players steer well clear of anything contentious, others embrace it and that can bring its own problems. When Craig Bellamy was Wales captain, I would always make sure I went to his media conference if I could, even though we would be all set up to interview him elsewhere. He would often come out with something unexpected, something interesting and if he said it in the media conference, I had to try and make sure he said it to me as well, if I didn't, my news editor would want to know why I hadn't got the good stuff that everyone else had?

On one occasion, things were going badly awry for him at Manchester City. Inevitably much of his pre-match captain's press conference was taken up with questions reflecting that situation. The room was packed, even ahead of a meaningless Wales game. All the national newspapers had sent reporters along, seeing this as an open goal opportunity to get a controversial character talking about a high profile club. So every question asked was about Man City. Nobody stepped in to stop it, he kept answering, so the questions kept on coming.

As I sat in the room and observed, I knew then that I had to get the same stuff from him in our one-to-one situation. Craig's a complicated character, nice as pie one day, but he might cut me dead the next, so I never knew quite how these interviews would go. I asked him about Man City, and he answered, at length. He said Roberto Mancini hadn't spoken to him for months; a strong line. I asked him some more, then got round to Wales, knowing full well that only the Man City stuff would go out on Sky Sports News, on that day at least.

Sure enough, they ran all the stuff about his problems at City. Obviously it is 24/7, so it ran many times. Manchester City were, by all accounts, far from happy. They employ lots of people in their press office to ensure they control the message, and keep a lid on things. Now, one player on international duty had undone all their hard work.

I'm sure they were in touch with the FAW soon after to express their unhappiness. I was stuck in the middle. The next day, before the game, Craig collared me in the tunnel, "My agent's not happy with you" he warned, "He says you stitched me up in that interview by only asking me about Manchester City." I was a bit perplexed by this accusation. The truth was, if he'd said 'I don't want to talk about this, only about Wales.' I'd have accepted it and moved on, even though I'd watched him talk about it at length with all the rest of the media only minutes before. But he didn't and he seemed happy to use the interview as an opportunity to have a pop at his club, so now, his agent hated me, his club hated me and the FAW probably weren't keen on me either, all for doing my job!

There's another category of question that's become ever more apparent in recent years, what they call 'the global' at Sky Sports News. This is a question, concerning a major and relevant breaking story that had hit the headlines, that we are meant to ask of everyone, regardless of club, country or circumstance. Some are straightforward, some are potentially contentious, particularly as they could get a player or coach embroiled in a debate that doesn't appear to have anything directly to do with them.

The dynamic's a little bit different with this campaign though, as other factors are at play. Previously, international weeks have not appeared a high priority to some in the media, more like an unwanted distraction between Premier League games, hence the desire to keep club football on the agenda even at international events. But the change in the format means home nations games don't clash anymore, so the games get more attention in isolation. In the past, all the home nations lived under England's long shadow. Now they all get their moment in the light.

From Sky's perspective, this has made a big difference as well. All the games were bunched up on one evening across a range of channels. Now they occupy centre stage on a channel especially created for European football, Sky Sports 5. Sky has rights to the vast majority of games, so the tournament as a whole is getting a lot more coverage.

Then there's the team itself. The first game shown on Sky was that friendly in Latvia in August 2004. Wales won 2-0, Hartson and Bellamy scored, the side was strong and seemed well set to qualify for the next tournament, having narrowly missed out in the play-offs for the previous one. Mark Hughes was a big name, a bright young manager and the Millennium Stadium was a spectacular home that was often full for football internationals.

The first qualifier we broadcast gave a hint that maybe things were about to take a turn for the worse. It was away in Azerbaijan, on the same day as my daughter's fifth birthday and I was actually commentating on it as the regular guy, Alan Parry, wasn't available. Gary Speed gave Wales the lead and a repeat of the victory they'd achieved in the last campaign at the same stadium seemed on the cards. Then Azerbaijan equalised from a speculative long-range free kick that somehow found its way into the net and that's how it ended. In the next game, at home, Wales recovered from 2-0 down to draw 2-2 in a frenzied game with Northern Ireland. Two points from two winnable games and Wales were all but out of the race for qualification straight away. That set the template for what's happened since.

Hopes flickered briefly when Gary Speed took charge but then the cataclysmic tragedy that unfolded seemed only to enhance the sense that this was a doomed nation. I'd actually had enough of covering Wales before that period. The six years that John Toshack was in charge were pretty difficult. The team lost all its stars, results were poor, crowds dwindled and he was a hard man to work with. He fulfilled his obligations but only ever, it seemed, because he had to. Despite all the occasions we sat down together, we never really established any rapport and I got to dread that long drive down to Cardiff. Gary Speed was one of those who'd retired, and was now working as our studio pundit, so we socialised together after games. I'd known Gary since I got my first sports job at the BBC in Leeds many years before. We'd always got on well, so I rang him on the way home from another demoralising away trip and told him I was planning on retiring from international football myself now. Gary laughed and told me to get my head down and get on with it. He was right, John Toshack was sacked a few days later.

That hope's flickering again now and that means more interest in hearing what Wales players have to say about Wales matches. And here I am, interviewing the players in a darkened dressing room at the Cardiff City Stadium and enjoying it. Each of the lads who comes in talks with maturity and confidence about the matches to come over the next few days. They refer to the 'self-belief' in the squad, the great spirit that exists between them, and that there's been a change in the dynamics. Yes, we've heard it all before in these instances. This 'Golden Generation' has been promising new dawns for too long, but this time, there's actually a sense it could happen. Success has been the key element missing from the Wales coverage I've been involved in. Now, Wales have two home games coming up, having won the first game in the group for the first time in six years, oh, and they have a certain Gareth Bale.

James Chester speaks well, but there's a still a mystery as to how he got to the age of 25 without ever being called up to a Wales squad. I ask the question, and I'm still none the wiser, he says he was concentrating on establishing himself as a Premier League player first, now he's ready for the challenge. He also says international football's been a very different experience. He talks about the regular team meetings, then the hanging around the hotel, but also the need to earn the respect of his new teammates. He's stepped into a group, the majority of whom have been playing together for over a decade. He's having to adapt. I think it gives an interesting and different perspective so when the interviews are done and the lights are back on, I communicate that thought to Jim, but ultimately, it's his call.

Once we've got everything packed up, we need to organise getting the material back to HQ. This has been a perennial challenge ever since we've been filming in Cardiff, but it's a straightforward exercise these days. Once upon a time, we had to drive over to Bristol where there was a Sky News office that we could use. With two hours travelling, that was far from ideal. Then, Alex embraced new technology and pioneered a way of sending material back via a broadband connection, a revolutionary development in our little world. Again, it was labour-intensive as all the material had to be digitised and squashed into a format that could be sent via Wi-Fi, so sending three minutes worth of footage would take the best part of an hour. Now, there's a box outside the stadium that we can use to plug-in the camera, press play and it goes straight down the line to London. So, second for second, it takes as long as the amount of footage we've got to feed. Four interviews, all a few minutes in length, plus a second camera angle on the Chester interview that will help the editor make it look nice if it's in the live show. The necessary calls are made to arrange to send the stuff back, to make sure someone presses record at the other end, and then we start the 'feeding'.

It's getting dark by now, rush hour's upon us so the roads around the ground are getting busy. I've skipped lunch so hunger's an issue. I nip over to Asda to purchase food for this evening's tea, as it's my turn to cook. On my return, we're just getting to the end of the last interview, then Alex gets a call to say there's been a technical problem, little glitches throughout. Can we rewind and start all over again? Somebody is meant to be watching all this come in, just in case there are any problems. That person must have left their post, and only discovered the problem when they rewound it at the end. You can get angry or you can shrug, and resign yourself to another half an hour hearing the same interviews all over again, for the fifth time in James Chester's case. I know it off by heart by the time we finally get the 'clear', meaning it's all okay, definitely, and everybody's happy, definitely. Getting the 'clear' is significant in TV land, it's the word that generally signals the end of the working day.

It's not a real job, I know, but it can be pretty stressful. The stakes are high. The company has set high standards in the way it covers sport, and there's a real pressure to maintain those levels each and every day. So, it's that 'under the surface' sort of stress, the nagging worry at the back of the mind, asking is that good enough, did I get it right? There's a new challenge to come tomorrow as well, it looks like the Bale interview isn't happening so what do we do instead? I've made a request to film a few minutes of training as we haven't yet got any current footage of this group of players but I'm not hugely confident IG's going to come back with a positive response.

To take my mind off it all, back at base, I hit the kitchen and whip up a little thing I've made successfully for my family before, potato, chicken, green beans stir-fried with red pesto. I've bought a chocolate pudding as well, and some red wine so we'll dine in style tonight. This is where the apartment comes into its own, in my opinion. Normally, it would be downstairs to meet in the hotel bar, a drink and then off to find somewhere to eat. This I find much more relaxing. The slippers are on, literally. We've only got Freeview on the TV, so boring old Alex disappears to watch a movie on Sky Go on his laptop. I arrange a trip out to meet my friend Alun in the pub.

To be honest, I could easily make do with lounging about and a bit of Sky Go myself but Alun's a really good guy and he's become a good friend. He's a Wrexham fan and we're playing tonight so we'll follow scores from the bar, and talk football and music. He runs a record label based in Cardiff, used to manage perhaps my favourite ever band, Super Furry Animals, and now has a great roster of UK and American acts on his books. We chat over a couple of excellent pints of real ale, muse over Wrexham's late equaliser to earn a 2-2 draw and look ahead to Friday's fixture. Alun's going to the game in the company of the lead singer of the Manic Street Preachers, James Dean Bradfield, and I've helped sort out some tickets. Like many people, I guess James is just rekindling interest in the national side. The Manics once changed the words of their massive hit 'Everything Must Go' to 'Bobby Gould Must Go' at a live gig in Cardiff when the unpopular Englishman was leading Wales into another abyss, so they know about the ups and downs.

Wednesday 8th October

When we get the media schedule sent through, Wednesday's generally the gap day. Traditionally, I've sought to set up something extra to do to ensure we're gainfully employed. It's genuinely not much fun sitting around a long way from home doing nothing. So, I like to find something to fill the void, it helps keep the mind occupied when you're missing your family.

Until Monday night, this was going to be a big day. Now, I don't know. Jim comes back to me having watched the James Chester interview through. He likes it but he wants to use Ashley Williams instead. We have an interview lined up with him tomorrow anyway, but I put a request in to Ian Gwyn Hughes to see if we might not be able to bring it forward 24 hours. The more time the live production team get to work on it before Friday, the better, so it would suit us but it might also suit the player. It means one less job for him to do tomorrow, and might just provide a bit of distraction if this is one of those 'stuck in the team hotel' days. IG's up for asking him, so it might happen. If the call comes, we're so close to the team hotel, we can be set up pretty swiftly.

Then things take another turn. Sky's Head of Football gets in touch for an update on the Bale situation. He's had contact with Bale's agent before on this issue and assurances have been made, so he wants to know how this scenario played out. He goes off to speak to the player's management people to see if he can get things sorted.

In the meantime, Alex and I are poised, just in case the call comes. We can't really go anywhere or do anything until we know what's happening. I keep IG in the loop, just in case there's any movement from Gareth's people. It's all a bit crazy, we're only after five minutes with him and we'll only be talking about the game but I understand the forces at play. Somewhat ironically, as we await news from the Wales camp, I get an email that says the Bosnian FA has agreed to my request to interview their star man, Edin Džeko, once they get into town tomorrow. So, we've got their man sorted.

A call back from HQ suggests it's not likely we're going to get our man, although no specific reasons are given. I suppose a complaint could be lodged with the FAW but what would we gain from that? Their overriding concern is that Gareth's on board. They use him for all their publicity material, he sells kits, tickets and he wins games. They need him. It's frustrating but that's the way it is.

Another hour or so later, mid-afternoon now, the message comes back that Ashley's feeling tired so he wants to stick with doing the interview tomorrow. At that point, I'm all out of ideas. The day's almost over so, yes, hands up, Alex and I go for a pint. It can't be more than one, he's cooking so needs to keep a clear head. Homemade Cajun chicken burgers with paprika potato wedges and salad. Once again, we eat like kings.

Thursday 9th October

If Wednesday can often be a 'down' day in these international weeks, from here on it's all 'up', until full-time tomorrow at least. It begins with the now familiar trip to the Cardiff City Stadium, the gear out the car, then into the tunnel routine. This time we're doing interviews at roughly the same time the team will be training, so the home dressing room's in use. The away dressing room, however, is empty, sort of. No sooner have we started shifting the gear in than one of the stadium staff follows us. He asks if it's alright if they get on with the job of clearing out the guttering in the showers? We can't really stop a bloke doing his job can we? He says he'll be done in 15 minutes and

55

we've got a fair bit of time before the captain and manager are due in. There's a brief delay whilst we greet Bill Leslie, just in off the 'red-eye' from London. He's here to get a look at Wales and later Bosnia as they train and to hear what they're saying in the respective camps.

Showerman and his mate get on with their work, whilst we get on with ours. I perform my crucial 'sitting down and looking in the right direction' role whilst lights, cameras and monitors spring up around me. The presence of the guys in the shower is causing one potential problem – those light sensors. Alex has taped over them in the main section of the room but the shower section is directly adjacent, and the lights have to remain on in there. The worry will be that they don't go off in time once the chaps have finished. We go off in search of someone who might be able to actually switch them off again. As we're doing this, in another room, other members of the media are arriving ahead of the two press conferences. The absence of key players apart, there hasn't been too much by the way of controversy in the build-up to this game. I'm still a little wary of some topic appearing out of the relative blue, which I hadn't foreseen. It's always a potential problem when we are doing our interviews at the same time as the press conference is taking place.

In the past, if anyone in the press conference asked a question which elicited a 'newsworthy' response, I wouldn't know about it. New arrangements mean I am now at least covered. UEFA have requested the host broadcaster provides coverage so there will be a separate Sky camera crew filming the media conference. If anything interesting is said, we'll have it, even if I'm not aware of it.

I always spend time ahead of the interviews scanning the media for anything that might crop up that isn't related to the game. Sports News haven't flagged up anything they'd like me to ask, but better safe than sorry. I've picked up on one story on the BBC Football website that relates to the imminent release from jail of former Wales striker, Ched Evans. It's in relation to interviews they've done with various people about whether he should be allowed to play again having been convicted of rape. Obviously, they're setting an agenda on this but I'm aware that it's a story that's going to gain in prominence once Evans is out and particularly so if he gets re-signed by a club. I make a mental note.

The showers are cleaned and the lights go off just in time as Ashley Williams appears, a little ahead of schedule.

Much as with the players on Tuesday, there's a strong sense of quiet confidence underpinning everything he says. The fact that ticket sales are going so well, we're on course for a crowd of over 30,000, seems to be helping convince the players that there's a widespread belief back in the game in Wales. They didn't win well in Andorra but they did win and Ashley echoes the sentiment expressed earlier in the week that the players took a lot from sticking together and getting through it. The lads are most definitely singing from the same hymn sheet.

The manager's in an upbeat mood as well, as he follows straight on in after Ashley. There's much talk of cutting out the silly goals that have undermined his spell in charge so far. He emphasises that the players have to be better at 'game management', even if that means not playing as much nice football. Being 'street wise' is another lesson the manager hopes the players will learn. I suspect he wants this nice bunch of lads to get a bit nasty!

As the interview draws to an end, I ask the Ched Evans question. Some managers might bristle, Chris isn't one of them. He does a fair bit of media work, I think he gets it. Is he concerned that the former player's release might become a distraction in the midst of the preparations for two big games? He deals with it well, says it's not an issue he's even considered and that it is disappointing that a TV company's decided to broadcast a programme on the matter just before kick-off. Matter dealt with, we move on.

Well, actually, we go and film training. Or more precisely, Alex goes to film training. I head off in the direction of the magic broadband box in the car park armed with a 'play out' device and verbal instructions as to what I need to do to get the material sent back to HQ. Once again, I'm multi-skilling. I love a challenge. It's all pretty involved. First of all there's a coded lock to negotiate, then I have a special device that fits in the catch to turn it. Alex bought me this little key thing on one of our previous trips, ahhh, sweet, I've never actually used it since.

I get the code right, the key fits, and the box opens. Now I'm faced with a bank of input and output sockets but I've been briefed, find the right one, plug the cable from the 'play out' box into it and make the necessary call to base. I'd taken the precaution of pre-booking the line so it should be visible to Sky already. But it isn't. They can't see

57

anything but those test card bars. Neither can the people in the big room where all the feeds coming into Sky are controlled. This means a call to the people who operate the boxes. They can't see anything either. I switch sockets, no change. It starts raining. Last chance, I check the back of the player that Alex has handed me. The cable's coming out of a socket that says 'input', next to it is a socket that says 'output'. I'm no technician, but I think I may have identified the problem.

My cameraman gets both barrels when he arrives with his training shots. He laughs. We head back to the apartment for a couple of hours. We'll be back for our Edin Džeko interview later, same location so I'd like to leave the equipment at the stadium, strangely Alex isn't so keen. That might have something to do with the fact that even one of his lights costs a couple of grand.

Instead of heading back to the apartment, I get Alex to drop me close to the city centre. I've got the tickets to deliver to Alun, and it's always good to drop in at the office for a chat and a cup of tea. The company's called Turnstile Records and they have a great base in one of the old shopping arcades. Alun's there, along with Kev, his partner in the business, and Gareth who works for them but who is also the lead singer of Los Campesinos! They're a Turnstile band, so the office work keeps Gareth in gainful employment and shoes, in-between album releases and tours. He's a big football fan as well, heavily involved in a non-league club in his native West Country and, as he reveals, still a Sunday footballer. Except, he's in trouble with the Somerset FA. Over that cup of tea he outlines an incredible tale involving him and a teammate being homophobically abused by numerous members of the opposition team in a recent game. Not that it matters, but neither Gareth nor his pal are gay. But that didn't seem to deter the other team, nor did the ref, who apparently refused to deal with it during the game despite Gareth's prompting. When Gareth refused to shake hands with an opponent at the end of the game, and swore when he told him why he wouldn't be shaking his hand, he's been reported for using foul and abusive language. He refused to let it lie, reported the matter to the FA, as did others in his team and now all have been summoned to appear before a disciplinary panel in Glastonbury next month. With the FA involved in high profile anti-homophobia campaigns, I sniff a story that could come to national prominence. Then, to happier matters and we discuss the Wales game and an event that Gareth's agreed to help out with. He's going to be a celeb DJ at a charity fundraiser being organised by a Wrexham fan I know. He has sold 300 tickets to football fans from across Wales and he's going to provide a daytime venue and entertainment for people coming to Cardiff for the game. I'm going along to do some filming, whilst Gareth's agreed to do an hour on the decks. I say my goodbyes and leave the office with him sorting out a goodie bag for the raffle. Once again, I get drenched in a downpour on the walk back.

There's a bit more organising of my own to be done once I've dried out. I need to work out where we're going to be able to interview Edin. We have been told he's only got five minutes spare before training, so we need to be ready to go when he arrives, it's for the live show so, again, we need to find somewhere we can put all the gear back up. I text Mark, my go-to-guy. The home dressing room's in use as is the away dressing room, by Bosnia. I enquire about the physio room I spotted earlier? That's needed for a UEFA stadium inspection. Mark comes up with a solution, the referee's room.

The next line of communication involves confirming everything with the press officer with the Bosnian FA, just to reassure myself. On the same basis, I let the Welsh FA's liaison man know what we're doing. Steve's an FA councillor but he also acts as the person who meets the travelling squads on arrival in Wales, and tries to ensure they have everything they require on their visit. Steve and I went to the same school, so we have a connection. He's got direct contact with the travelling party which can be a big help and he also gets me the little badges and pennants given out by the foreign FAs as I'm a bit of a collector. All in all, a very useful person to know!

After a flurry of emails and texts, I think we're sorted, so it's back in the car and back to the stadium. There's more activity around the outside broadcast (OB) trucks now. The production crew have been arriving throughout the day, already editing material for tomorrow's broadcast, preparing graphics, checking cameras and communications. It's at times like these that you get a real sense of being part of a big team. Everybody here has an important job to do. I might do the best interview in the world, but if the camera doesn't work or the sound's dodgy nobody will ever know. These people make it all happen. I've been working on Sky OBs for many years so I know loads of the crew, in many cases I couldn't tell you what they do though. We all work in our own areas, the director and production manager bind it all together and if we all do our bit, it works. Working in this big team is one of the great joys of being involved in OB's for me. The Sky Sports' product is widely recognised for its quality, and these are the people who work so hard to keep the standards so high. You get a real sense of everyone pulling together, I genuinely feel nobody does it better.

We exchange greetings with Rachael, the production manager, as we head into the stadium. She can confirm plans to film the Bosnia press conference and the training session which is good news, as we won't be able to cover the former due to the Džeko interview. Then we head back into the tunnel to complete a hat-trick of dressing rooms. We haven't seen the ref's room before so there's a moment of nervousness as we push the door open. It's not as big as the team rooms, but it's okay, so I soon adopt the 'sitting' pose for Alex. There's one major development that comes our way before the interview starts as well. One of the stadium staff comes in to make sure we've got everything we need. We mention the sensors that keep the lights on. He grabs a chair, stands on it, reaches up to the ceiling panel and pops the sensor out of the hole, there's a little socket on the back which he unplugs. The sensor has been disabled. The lights go off. In our strange little world, this is a life-changer. We all but applaud him back down to floor level.

When the Bosnian team coach arrives, we're all set up and ready. We could do with a team shirt to hang as a backdrop but the involvement of several members of the visiting party fails to produce one so Alex opts to keep the background black. He's draped a big black sheet across one half of the dressing room wall to achieve this effect. Edin's led in. I've not met him before, he's a giant. I've been warned that he can be a bit difficult but he arrives with a big smile and a handshake. He then gives a really good interview, in English obviously, and finishes with a great answer. I ask if Bosnia need to win after losing their opening qualifier, he ponders this question for a moment, which gives his response greater resonance, "I don't think we have to win but I know we must not lose". I know that's a great end, I know that will definitely be used when the interview's broadcast tomorrow evening. I can only offer genuine thanks and another handshake at the end of our allotted five minutes. Actually, I wish him "good luck", he smiles, but I can't help myself and have to add, "but not too much good luck", and I smile. Luckily, he laughs. He's a big bloke.

Alex and I follow him out down the tunnel and onto the edge of the pitch. Our allotted 15 minutes of filming has already started, as confirmed by the UEFA delegate. This role is a new one in this tournament as well. Previously, the respective associations were left to sort everything out, now UEFA has a representative present in the build-up to every game. We had a few issues with the guy in Andorra, this time it's a woman and she's really helpful. She will keep an eye on the clock to ensure that pictures aren't taken after the allotted time, but at the moment, we're the only people present. Then the Bosnian journalists start filing out of the press conference that's been taking place in the media room.

I'm guessing they might have had some tough questions for the coach. He should be an absolute hero for leading this young nation to its first ever World Cup finals in the summer. After the catastrophe of the Balkan war in the '90s, this achievement seems all the more remarkable but it seems to have created the level of expectation Džeko talked about it in our interview. Now, they are expected to win every game. Exiting at the group stage in the World Cup then defeat by Cyprus is not what the fans back home expect. There are suggestions the coach is under pressure. He's not unique, Chris Coleman will be very much under the spotlight again if Wales don't take at least four points from these next two games, and there's no great pressure of expectation in Wales, after all, 1958 apart, the team's never really achieved anything.

The Bosnian squad is missing a number of regular picks, like Wales, but there's still a core group playing at the highest levels across Europe lined up for the session. They exude that sort of easy-going confidence I've seen in other successful international sides. That's the level Wales need to reach. No matter what the surroundings, the self-confidence to think, 'we can cope and we can win'.

Alex uses his second camera, the super slo-mo one, to get some additional shots that might be of use to the people editing the Džeko interview. Then we return to the OB unit in the TV compound, where everything can be passed back to those who need it at HQ. All this material is for the exclusive use of the live programme, so, unless they make a special request, Sky Sports News won't get access to it, although they will have the coverage of the press conference. Begović, the Stoke goalkeeper appeared at that, so there will be a player who speaks English, even though the coach doesn't, and all his answers would have come via an interpreter. Unless he's said something startling, like 'Wales are rubbish and we'll win easily', its unlikely Sports News will go to the lengths of broadcasting his answers and then the interpretation. They'll stick with Begović.

It's dark as we wrap up. Bill rejoins us as the last seconds of the interview are played down the line. We now have to arrange our evening. We agree on a time and a place to meet up for a drink, and Alex offers to cook. England are on the telly tonight but it's on ITV and we get that at the apartment, so the night's itinerary appears sorted.

Bill's hotel is the one we usually stay at in Cardiff, the Radisson. It's about a mile or so away from the apartment, but he's had a long day so I agree to go and pick him up as we're going to have a drink at a pub in the Bay, closer to our base. He gets a quick tour of the apartment before we head out. In theory, we'll be back soon.

Theory and practice. We find a good table, the football's on the telly, the beer's good and it's a Wetherspoon's, so it's cheap. Half an hour later, we're perusing the menu. Alex is off the hook. England struggle briefly, then stroll to the anticipated thrashing of San Marino. Wembley looks a pitiful sight, less than half full. The World Cup and the unattractive nature of the opposition in their group seem to have flattened interest to a level not seen since the late '70s and early '80s. By contrast, we're told Wales will be playing in front of the biggest crowd yet seen for an international at the CCS. England will qualify, then they'll fail and that's not good enough. Wales only want to qualify and that would be the best thing ever.

Friday 10th October

There's work to be done but not for a while, so a lie-in is in order. These are long days. I like to get a run done, so I head out after a late breakfast. Then there's admin. I've been tasked with getting some interviews with fans in the city centre and I'm needed in position to do live inserts for Sky Sports News at 4pm, 5pm and 6pm. I know straight away that the one at 6pm can't happen as it clashes with our pre-match Chris Coleman interview, so I warn the live producer. Then I confirm arrangements with the guy organising the charity event. He's going to be at the venue from noon onwards, and it begins in earnest at 2pm. We need to film something for a slot at 3pm, so we'll pop along at 1.45 to interview him and anyone else who fancies it.

It's quite rare to do this sort of filming in Cardiff. It's actually quite difficult. Generally the crowds are relatively small for internationals here, and those who are coming tend to arrive in time for the game. That means you won't find hordes of expectant fans thronging the city centre during in the afternoon. When Wales played at the Millennium Stadium, right in the city centre, on a Saturday afternoon or evening, it was a different story. Now things are much more low-key.

We've often encountered the same problem in games overseas actually, wandering round a town centre in the middle of the afternoon, hoping to spot a red shirt somewhere. Despite that, I do seem to keep bumping into fans who introduce themselves thus, 'Hi Bryn, remember me? You interviewed me in Bratislava/Podgorica/Vienna/Warsaw', etc, etc.

In this instance though, I know where we will find fans and we can turn-up, film and get away again in time to ensure the footage is back at HQ ahead of that 3pm slot. Also, it's relatively early in the day, so, hopefully, everyone will be sober enough to still be coherent. Watching Wales, as I know from my many trips as a fan, is largely a good excuse for a bit of a booze-up. It's a social as much as a sporting event.

When I was watching as a fan, I looked forward to match days. No matter what the outcome, it was going to be a good laugh. My first ever away trip, Germany in Nuremberg in 1991 actually began 23 years ago pretty much to the day. Fourteen of us from a couple of villages near Wrexham travelled by minibus, it was a crazy week with loads of laughs, a lot of beer and little sleep. The game? We lost 4-1, dashing qualification hopes for another campaign. It didn't seem to matter too much. I slept on a picnic table in a service station that night, until it started raining. Now I get a nice hotel or fancy apartment but these days, it matters much more. Maybe it's the fact that I'm always stone cold sober when I'm watching Wales now, but I do think I've actually got more invested emotionally in these games. There's all the planning, then all the time away from home, all the birthdays and anniversaries I've missed, all the grief I've had and the pressures from the office and at the end of it all, what have I got to show for my efforts? Every single campaign I've covered has been over almost before it's begun. It feels like I'm putting everything in and getting nothing back. Just once, I'd love a bit of hope, a bit of glory and the next two games offer the glimmer of a chance that Wales might actually still be in contention come 10pm next Monday night. Then again, it might all be over bar the shouting once more. It actually makes me feel sick to contemplate, that same feeling I had sitting helplessly on the touchline in Andorra.

Mind you, my nervousness is not unique. Our visit to the Moon Club, venue for the charity bash, proves it. There's a good vibe going even as we arrive, and the sounds of the sort of music I like are drifting out to the street, a bit of New Order there I think? Tim, the organiser comes to meet me. He's an interesting guy, from Bala, massive Wrexham and Wales fan but someone who's taken his interest and used it to make money. He designs and sells a range of t-shirts, hats and badges under the label 'Spirit of '58'. The name obviously alludes to Wales' only World Cup finals appearance, He designs and sells to fans of Wales and the Welsh clubs, nobody else, and he sells a lot. His trick is knowing his market. He's a similar age to me, grew up watching the matches when it was all about the crazy fashions, the sportswear, the trainers, the coats and the little button badges people started wearing in place of scarves or bobble hats. It was an underground scene then, and many of the people who embraced it then are still wearing the same stuff now, as are their sons and, perhaps daughters, a new market.

This is branching out though. He's never organised a pre-match event before and the only marketing he's done has been via social media, the same way he sells all his product. But it's worked. There were 200 tickets on sale, they went, so he claimed another floor of the venue and sold a 100 more. He's got a great list of raffle prizes, a band from Wrexham coming down to play, DJs, and he's done pretty much everything himself. And the proceeds are going to two children's cancer charities in north and south Wales. To me, that's pretty amazing. He's an ordinary guy, who does an ordinary job and yet he's got this incredible knack for 'big thinking'. I've bumped into him on numerous Wales away trips and he's always dodged my request for an interview, but not today. He deserves the recognition and he speaks well about the event and about the game this evening. But even here, in the midst of happy fans, beer, good music and the euphoria of an idea well executed, he's realistic when it comes to the match. "I'd be happy with a draw."

It's the same refrain I get from another group of fans we line-up a little later. One of them even says, "I've been following Wales long enough to be realistic. I'd be happy with a draw." I love this. Usually in these pre-match vox pops I'm amazed at how fans of clubs seem deliriously optimistic about their team's chances. 'yeah, we'll win 4-0'. I don't get it. I don't know where that comes from, I always prepare myself for the worst, then anything else is a bonus. That Tommie Collins quote is always at the back of my mind.

Once we've filmed what we need, I hang around for a while whilst Alex heads off to the stadium to send the footage back for broadcast. It's good to have a chat with the lads gathering outside. Many of them are wearing the same sort of gear I used to wear to go to the match at their age, I'm guessing they're copying their dads. They're a good crowd, there's none of the menace you get with some other national teams, they're here to party not to start a riot. I think they've enjoyed their TV appearance, but now they're kicking back and one of them asks me if I want to join him in a pint of Jagermeister. A pint!? Ever the professional, I politely decline. Then some of the lads produce a big Gary Speed banner they've had made and ask if I'll have my photo taken with it? I agree, but it's hard to know whether to smile or not, it's a timely reminder of something dark that will impact on Welsh football for a long time to come. Gary was hugely popular with the fans, they still sing his name at Wales games; he'll be with us all the way.

After a few more photos and lots of handshakes, I have to head home to get my matchday suit on. My progress is halted a few yards down the road by the sight of the FAW President, Trefor Lloyd Hughes. He's in his FAW suit and tie, a big guy, from Anglesey. He's been following the social media build-up to the event and he promised to come along, it's great to see him fulfil that promise. The FAW has come up with a new marketing slogan, a hashtag, #TogetherStronger, so the Association President making time to come and mix with the fans is commendable.

We stop for a chat, there are big political battles going on behind the scenes between the home associations he tells me, it's the English FA vs The Rest over the attempt to have David Gill appointed to an influential FIFA position. In the break since the last match, the FAW have failed with a bid to bring 2020 Euro Championship games to the country. The English, the Scottish and the Irish associations were all successful. He hints at dark dealings and suggests backroom deals have been done. It's a shame we haven't got more time to chat, but I need to get on. My last diversion takes me to the Turnstile office to make sure Gareth's all set for his DJ slot. He's just leaving as I arrive. The guys can see the club from their office window, there's a large and increasingly noisy group of fans outside now, the atmosphere's warming up!

I wish Gareth all the best, we've had a chat about his choice of tunes, he should be fine as long as he doesn't play World in Motion or Three Lions!

I pass a couple of groups of Bosnian fans gathered outside bars in town. They seem in good spirits, being able to follow their national team abroad must seem like a miracle after what many of them must have witnessed in their childhood. That's the underlying importance of international football, no matter how shallow it might seem, it conveys recognition on those countries who have had to struggle to survive.

Back at base, after another soaking in another deluge, I change into a suit. Sartorially, we're always under the spotlight on these Sky OBs. The wrong colour tie can ensure a whole heap of derision; anything vaguely 'flashy' and you're going to be in for a lifetime of grief. About 15 years ago, I wore a pair of straight leg brown trousers in a sort of velvet effect whilst covering an England youth international. Even though they were Armani, I'm still having the mickey taken out of me to this very day. So, I keep it conservative, blue with a burgundy tie.

Alex has important work of his own to do in terms of his costume. He's a cameraman, he dresses to stay warm and dry but hidden away, beneath the layers, he'll be sporting his 'lucky socks'. They were worn for the last couple of games in the last campaign, then again in Andorra and they'll be on duty tonight, hoping to maintain their unbeaten run. I don't think the level of superstition runs to not having them washed, although Monday night's game could be a problem.

We get to the ground in good time ahead of my first live appearance on Sky Sports News. The format for the exchange has been agreed by email, so I know what questions are going to be asked. Welsh injury problems predominate, then Bale, then the mood of the fans. It's good to be able to speculate on a big crowd, it's been a long time since the national side's pulled in more than 30,000 to a game, tonight could be the night.

After the 'live', I can go and get something to eat on the catering bus. This is the gathering place for all the OB crew and production staff. Many of them will have been on site since this morning, so it's a really long day. On that basis, Sky provide decent food for everyone and everyone's working day has provision for this important break. It's not a provision we ever got with Sky Sports News so, for me, it represents one of the major differences between the two organisations. With Sky Sports, you are part of a big team working on a single project, with Sky Sports News, you're working in very small groups and it's very much a case of fending for yourself and grabbing a bite in-between jobs. You can tell an SSN reporter's car, as the footwell on the passenger side will be filled up with old sandwich packets, coffee cups and empty water bottles.

The catering bus is a frontline of OB work. Everyone eats together, although there is a structure to it. The editorial team, the producer, director, commentator and co-commentator and, yes, the reporter, are usually to be found occupying the back seats on the lower deck. I don't know whether things operate the same way with other broadcasters but it's always been this way since I started working on Sky OBs. The riggers, camera operators, VT editors, sound techs etc are all scattered around in different areas but when I get on board, I know to turn right and keep going.

If you don't know the people you're working with, this can be a bit of a daunting experience. As a much younger reporter, it felt like walking into a 'Wild West' saloon, with all eyes focussed on me and the piano player stopping mid-tune as I made my way tentatively towards the back seats. This is the bit where the wrong tie could prove critical, although it could prove an ice-breaker if you can handle the banter that inevitably follows. That's the crucial bit. Taking it, not biting back.

It's just banter. The word's been misappropriated but it's been a big part of my life since I was a lad. It's the leveller. Growing up, I was the middle class kid in a working class village. I did well at school, acted in drama productions, played musical instruments, wrote poetry and went to university; but I also went to watch Wrexham, drank in the bar of the local and played for the Sunday league side. I had to battle to earn the respect of my peers. Banter was my chosen weapon. Give a bit, take a bit, give a bit back.

It's not bullying, or it shouldn't be. It's not about singling anyone out, it's about including everyone. I believe there may have been an atmosphere at some Sky Sports OBs in the past where some of the perpetrators were prepared to give it but not get it back, I haven't experienced that. I've only seen people getting on together, using humour to break down barriers. It happens at every level on the OBs. We're all at it, all the time, taking the mick out of each other, gently.

Some of the familiar faces are there, some are missing. There's no producer or presenter anymore for a start. These games always used to have a studio on site, now it's all presented from Sky HQ so it's a smaller crew working tonight. The studio guests would always join us on the bus pre-match, a good chance to talk through the programme as well as the latest industry and football gossip. We're also missing the two guys, Bryn Tomos and Waynne Phillips, who've been doing the Welsh language commentary service Sky have provided for the last decade. Sadly, this has fallen victim to budget cutbacks. To me, it's a real shame because Sky did a very good thing by introducing this service at the time the initial broadcast deal was signed with the FAW. The Welsh speaking community had expressed concern at the BBC losing the contract as they'd provided bilingual coverage. Sky were complimented in parliament for recognising this issue and taking steps to address it. I was given the task of putting together the commentary team, using my contacts in the Welsh language media. Bryn and ex-Wrexham player, Waynne have done an excellent job for me and the viewers ever since.

The regular floor manager, John Smart, is also absent. He's one of the big characters on these Sky Sports OBs, I've been working with him in the tunnel for many years. Initially scary, I quickly learned his bark's far worse than his bite, it's all part of the act, and he's actually a great guy to work with. Sadly, Smartie's suffered a family tragedy and he isn't able to fulfil his usual role this evening. In his place is his son, Brett. Again, we've been working together for a long time, he's a great operator and it's reassuring to have him on board. He has responsibility for pretty much everything that happens in the tunnel area and at pitchside throughout the evening, from checking cameras are in the right place to getting the game to kick-off at exactly the right time. He's everyone's point of contact, from the FAW, to UEFA, to overseas broadcasters and referees.

The catering bus gives everyone the chance to talk through the event as well. I've been working with the squad throughout the week, so there might be some information I've picked up that could be of use to the director or commentator. For instance, I've organised tickets for James Dean Bradfield, so I know he's going to be here later and where he's going to be sitting, the director might want to pick him out in the stand. Bill's spoken to the manager, so he's got a very good idea of how the team will line-up. He's keeping the three central defenders, despite the struggles in Andorra so we'll discuss the potential implications. The organisation around these games has changed, as we saw in Andorra, so that's a subject for discussion as well. Most of the people here have worked on the Champions League, so they're used to UEFA officials being involved. For the rest of us, including the FAW, it's a learning curve.

We take about half an hour over our meal before we all head off to our various matchday positions. The countdown begins here. I've got another couple of inserts into Sky Sports News, one live, then one recorded with Barry Horne. I find these a welcome and useful distraction, as I can order my thoughts, talk about the two teams, and begin my own build-up. All day I've had a slightly sick feeling. It gets worse as kick-off approaches. It's all about the stakes. If Wales win, it'll feel amazing and we'll genuinely have a great chance of qualifying, even after two games. If Wales lose, it's not over but it's much harder. A draw sits in-between these two extremes. It's the fear of defeat that dogs me, depresses me before it's even happened. I think ahead to how I'll feel sitting in the apartment after the game. I'm already preparing myself for the worst. That's how it's usually been with Wales. I've been present at victories against Germany, Italy and Spain, I've seen a draw with Brazil but that was always as a fan.

Since Sky started covering Wales, we've not beaten a major nation at home.

Once my SSN duties are done, I'm sole property of the 'live' production team and prowl around the tunnel whilst the matchday crew make their final preparations. There's an army of people at work. As well as the stewards and stadium staff, there are people to organise the way the event looks. Small, nervous looking children have to be drilled for their role of walking out, carrying the big flags. The ball boys and girls are lectured on the 'do's' and 'don'ts' of their role for the evening, the national anthem singer gets a rehearsal, coaching staff lay out cones on the pitch ahead of warm-up sessions for the players. UEFA officials buzz around with clipboards, checking everything's as it's meant to be – and that's a long list. In the midst of all this activity, I see familiar faces, take time for a chat and await the arrival of the manager. It's a different world in here. Outside, fans are doing their thing – parking, drinking, eating, meeting friends, singing, collecting tickets. Alex is out there somewhere, filming them as they arrive. I've been there many times, racing to try and get into the ground in time for the anthems after lingering a little too long in the pub. Running around outside trying to find the right turnstile. What I do now is so different. My world is one of busy people preparing for another night at work. This is our job. But it's still something more for me, I'm still a fan, I've just got to internalise it.

It's different again for Chris Coleman. I've got to keep my producer happy, that's all that really counts. Chris is responsible for keeping everyone happy but, in particular, those fans arriving outside the stadium now. If Wales win, more fans come, more fans means more money for the FAW, maybe more jobs, if Wales lose, well, the opposite. That's the real pressure.

As I'm waiting for Chris and the team to arrive, I chat with Adam Owen, a member of the backroom coaching staff. He's a Wrexham lad, big fan of the club and we've been pals for a few years now. Adam's worried. He laments the loss of so many key players. He's saying what the fans earlier were saying. It's the same fear ultimately. If I were interviewing him, he wouldn't give voice to such negativity publicly, but he has the fear. It comes with being Welsh.

If Chris has 'the fear', he doesn't broadcast it. Broad smile and a big handshake as he comes straight off the team bus and over to the interview point. The producer's given me some pointers on questions he wants asking, related to team selection, even though the team hasn't been confirmed officially yet. I check first and make sure that he's okay to discuss this, as the interview's not due to go out until after the teams will have been confirmed. He's fine with that. He repeats the message about game management and not giving away soft goals, discusses sticking with three at the back, then we talk about the importance of Gareth Bale and finally a word about the big crowd. Then, another big smile, a handshake and I wish him good luck.

There's another hour or so to go until kick-off, hanging around time. I go and get a cup of tea from the media room. There are plenty of people I know sitting around, writing previews, looking through stats or just chatting with colleagues. Kevin Ratcliffe's in the room so I go and have a chat, Barry's doing some prep work so I go and interrupt him, more time killed. Then I drift back towards the tunnel, drink my tea, chat with the camera crew and Brett, check team sheets, shake hands and exchange greetings with some of the players as they go out to warm-up, more time killed. There's one more superstition to pander to as well. I call to Dai, the kitman. I tell him I need him to give me some chewing gum, like he did just before the goal in Andorra. He chucks me the last of his packet. I take one out and start to chew. It won't come out until we go behind.

Eventually, the clock ticks past 7.30pm. The anxiety levels rise as the ref and his huge team of assistants arrive in the tunnel, a team in themselves. They're followed shortly after by Bosnia. I catch the eye of Edin Džeko as he lines up and he nods and smiles. Ashley Williams leads the Wales team out. The two goalkeepers shake hands, a tradition, then all the players search for the little hands of the children who'll be accompanying them onto the pitch. There's so often a UEFA message to espouse, tonight's no different and it's anti-racism that's being promoted. The children's t-shirts bear a suitable slogan. Some would see the irony in this big display of anti-racist sentiment when set against the paltry fines levied on some associations for the racist behaviour of their fans, still, better than nothing I guess.

This is where the tension levels really rise, these few moments in the tunnel before the floor manager gives the ref the nod and he leads the two teams out. I still get a thrill from this bit. I tag along at the back, so the cheering's died down a little by the time I emerge from the

71

tunnel, but I suspect it's the closest I'm going to get to experiencing running out for my country. I still haven't entirely given up on the dream, but time may yet defeat my hope of winning that first cap. It won't stop me packing my boots for the next game though, just in case. I've played alongside Chris Coleman in a couple of charity games, he said I did alright, so, you never know.

The Bosnian players have been greeted by a big roar, their fans have travelled in their thousands and they applaud the anthem with gusto, as do the home fans. I think there's a real empathy with them. They suffered so much but their country emerged from the rubble and here stand their countrymen on the international stage, talented, highly regarded and successful.

'Hen Wlad Fy Nhadau' gets everyone going. The singer does a decent job of going at the same pace as the crowd, always an issue. We all hit 'Gwlad! Gwlad!' at the same moment. I'm still not sure having a person leading the singing works better than a band, but tonight's one of the better renditions. This is helped, of course, by the fact that the stadium's virtually full. It's great to see the seats in the new upper tier filled, there's a big roar at kick-off, a proper football atmosphere!

My viewing position at the Cardiff City Stadium is just to the left of the home dugout. Since this stadium became the team's new home, I've watched every match from this pitch level position. I'm in the midst of the fans, technically, but it's the front row and there are usually a couple of seats gap between me and the nearest supporter at least. Not tonight, I'm right next to someone who's paid to be here. I've got a monitor showing the game between my feet, but I've also got headphones on so I can hear the commentary. This helps separate me, isolates me and that's how I want it. I can't sit here and watch like a fan. I find it very hard to talk to anyone during the game anyway. I concentrate really hard, but try and drift away. It's 'the fear'.

A glance down at the teamsheet doesn't allay a sense of foreboding. Wales have the same five strung across the back, as in Andorra. Whereas that was a game the wingbacks were meant to be pushed forward, tonight they're more likely to have to stay back. It's in front of them that things look pretty thin though. No Ramsey and no Allen means a start for young Jonny Williams, a bright prospect but a player whose potential has already been blunted by injury. Andy King's a Premier League player with Leicester now, but he's not been getting a regular start for them. Up front, on his own, there's Charlton's Simon Church. Again, he's battling to claim a first team place but this time at a Championship club. Bale will probably have licence to roam but he might have to put in a shift at the back tonight, against the top seeds in the group.

Wales actually start well but the first save is made by Wayne Hennessey, at full stretch to keep out Pjanić's shot. Still, they don't panic and Gunter's bombing up and down my side to good effect. He actually gets on the end of a cross, nearly scores and the frailties of Bosnia's makeshift defence suggest there might be something in this for the home side. The crowd sense it too, noise levels remain high. Bosnia's fans are singing and jumping about, but they can't really be heard. This is all good. Wales are edging it without creating too much but just as the clock starts ticking down towards half-time, it strikes – a Bosnian whirlwind! All of a sudden they lift their game to another level and Wales are chasing shadows, white shadows. Last ditch tackles, desperate saves, somehow the home side cling on. I'm not one for prayer, but I'll call on any assistance at this stage. The crowd roar on anxiously, before the ref's whistle brings some relief. The players head off to the dressing rooms, the fans sink back into seats or seek comfort in a pie or a pint and I feel like going for a lie-down. It's therapeutic to get into the tunnel and talk through things with various pale-faced FAW officials. IG's there, so is Mark Evans. It seems cruel that this is only the halfway point. Mark and I share a joke about how we'll both be doing our manic pacing-up-and-down thing before the evening's out. He goes through agonies as well, another former fan who's made his hobby his career, although hobby probably isn't the right word. We've paced up and down tunnels during the last five minutes on many previous occasions. If we are doing it again, as someone else points out, that's a good thing, because it means we're desperate to hear the final whistle.

The players emerge from the dressing rooms again, faces set, no laughing just a look of grim determination. No changes either, despite some fairly heavy Bosnian challenges on both Gareth Bale and Jonny Williams.

I return to my seat. The longer it goes on, the worse it gets, especially as Bosnia pick up exactly where they left off. They fly forward, attack down the flanks, through the middle, just attack, attack, attack. Wales wobble, seemingly on the ropes. Only Wayne Hennessey's long, lean frame stands between Bosnia and the all-important and seemingly imminent first goal. He dives full length to tip one shot away, then saves with his legs from close range. I swear obscenely in my head over and over again through this torture. I start counting the game down in five minute blocks, trying not to look at the scoreboard clock until I think another five minutes is up. Still, the crowd roars its support and this is important because it shows they still have faith. Then Jonny Williams gets hacked twice in quick succession. He stays down injured for a couple of minutes before wearily getting back to his feet, ready to carry on. He gets huge applause for his bravery, and the break in play serves Wales well. Players get a breather, a chance to reorganise and suddenly the game turns again. Now it's Bale leading the charge. Hal Robson-Kanu's come on for Simon Church and his height and physical presence make a big difference in the battle that's now unfolding.

Then, the moment, inside the final 15 minutes and a Wales free kick curls from the feet of Bale and into the box and there's Ashley Williams, all alone in the middle of the goal. He jumps, maybe too early, gets the wrong shape to meet the ball and it goes off the top of his head and over. It's a great chance, and it's been missed. I bash the metal bar in front of me in frustration. But Bosnia aren't out of this yet and Hennessey has to make a flying leap to push away a Pjanić free kick. It's become a tremendous game, and the crowd's absorbed. Still I count the blocks of time down. On 85, I have to make my move to the interview position in the tunnel. The producer's requested interviews with Ashley and Wayne at the final whistle, so I'm mentally running though questions. But I've been in this situation before and everything's unravelled, a late goal and everything changes. As I walk towards the tunnel monitor, away from the game, only the crowd noise gives me any sense of what's happening.

There's Mark, pacing up and down, suffering. Steve, the liaison officer looks pensive, Peter and IG take my request for post-match player interviews, with their professional 'business heads' on. Then we all gather round the small monitor screen to see Gareth Bale set off on another run, tight to the touchline, miles out. He shoots, ridiculous, he's too far away, too wide. But we watch as the ball starts to turn, towards goal, suddenly Begović is stretching desperately, it's going in!

At least it is until the Bosnian gets fingertips to it and pushes it away. Incredible stuff. In the tunnel, we're all 'head in hands', suddenly given a glimpse of a land where Wales win. But it's only a glimpse and a few seconds later, the final whistle sounds in a land where Wales don't lose. It's a good place to be. I can finally chuck out Dai's chewing gum. I'll keep the next one for Monday.

The players stay out on the pitch to acknowledge the crowd's support for quite a while after that final whistle. There's no doubt the fans played a big part. They got behind the players when times were tough. Gareth Bale initiates a huddle out in the centre. This is the togetherness that's been talked about. They put everything into this game, they held one of the world's best sides despite having star names out, and might even have beaten them. That level of commitment is etched into every face as they make their way back into the tunnel. They look spent, their shirts heavy with sweat. Ashley and Wayne are led to the interview position. As he arrives, Ashley bashes the sponsor's board in frustration. I know why, it's the header. He seems almost inconsolable, I offer a swift "don't worry about it", before we get the interview underway. He's been a tremendous servant to the national side, he's put in a huge shift this evening, but he can't get away from the chance when we start talking. Wayne gives a good interview as well, not always the most confident of speakers as I've learnt from previous experience, but he's growing up, getting more articulate, more confident and tonight he gets the man of the match award for the first time. Both players agree, it's an excellent point and one they'd happily have taken if it were offered prior to kick-off.

Chris Coleman appears soon after, speaking about his pride in his players. He reflects on the big miss by suggesting, tongue in cheek, that Ashley got in a good defender's header and he looks forward to another important game in just three days time. The final interview is with Astir Begović for the Bosnian perspective. He suggests it's a good point for Bosnia as well, away from home, and looks forward to their next match, another tough game against the group favourites, Belgium. All in all, everyone's pretty upbeat considering we've just witnessed a 0-0 draw!

The message comes through that we've got enough interviews now, it's job done. Time to go home. Alex is already waiting in the car, and we're back at the apartment in 10 minutes. The suit comes off, the slippers and comfy slacks go on, beers are brought from the fridge and we sit and conduct a post-production debrief. We're two games in and there's still hope. It's the first time Wales have had four points at this stage in all the qualification campaigns we've worked on. This is progress.

It's hard to sleep after these games, with the adrenalin still coursing through your body, but I have a long drive to make in the morning, up to Wrexham, so I need to get to bed. It's been a long day. I check Twitter before I switch off. I like to share my thoughts with others after a Wales game. It seems from some comments that I might have appeared in our coverage, footage that suggests I may not be entirely neutral. Sure enough, I catch the repeat on Sky Go as I lie in bed. After Ashley's miss, the camera cuts to Chris Coleman's reaction, I can be seen in the background, smashing my hands on that bar in frustration.

3

"We'll take a win, no matter how we get it"
Wales v Cyprus

'Hal! Robson! Hal Robson-Kanu!

Saturday 11th October

In theory, today's a day off, no media access to the squad is planned but that doesn't mean a lie-in followed by an afternoon watching Soccer Saturday. Instead, I'm up early and on the road for the long drive north, to Wrexham, where my club are marking the 150th anniversary of the club's first ever game. As a club now owned by the fans, great efforts have gone into making a league game with Grimsby an event to remember. As President of the Supporters Trust, the group that owns the club, I want and need to be present, no matter if that means a six hour round trip.

As it turns out, the bit before the game's great, choirs, fireworks and, most remarkably, a crowd of over 8,500! The game, sadly, does not live up to the billing and I tackle the return journey mulling over a poor performance, a 1-0 defeat and the first effects of what feels like the flu.

The only good news to report, an email confirms the Cypriot FA have sorted out a player to interview, tomorrow evening.

Sunday 12th October

I'm feeling distinctly unwell as I rouse myself from a disturbed night's sleep. I picked up Lemsip tablets on the way back last night and I've been dosing myself with them ever since. There's a lot to do today as well, so I'm going to have to man up and get on with it.

We've got the captain and manager to do as normal at the stadium, but there's also been a request for an interview with Joe Ledley, to be used in the live show. This means we're going to be doing all three interviews, one after another, before the players take part in a training session. We can film the first 15 minutes of that as well, then we'll need to organise sending it all back to HQ.

It all sounds a bit routine by now, I guess, but that's what these weeks are like. Managers tend to like to establish a routine, particularly when things are going well. However, I do shake things up a bit when I suggest to Alex that I'm going to take my car to the stadium. I cite not wanting to share germs in the close confines of his Passat estate, but I'm also hoping I'll be able to get back to base a bit sooner if I've got my own wheels.

I think he sees this as a ruse to try and get out of carrying all the gear back and forth again. He may be right, but cometh the hour I can't watch him loading it all himself, like a little pit pony, so I chip in, as much as my weakened body will allow.

We're back in the away dressing room. There's nobody cleaning the showers today, so we pop-off the light sensors; darkness! Now we're cooking! Alex uses his lights to throw another image of the FAW crest onto the back wall and we're good to go. Joe arrives on time. He's another of the good guys, easy going, no edge despite the fact that he's been playing since he was 17. He turns in a good interview as well. Joe's message is clear, Friday counts for nothing if we don't win tomorrow.

It's repeated by Ashley Williams, but with an added flourish. He makes an impassioned plea for the fans to come along and give the same sort of support the team enjoyed on Friday night. This might be seen as just a bit of pre-match promotional fluff, but he sounds like he really means it and it's a great way to finish the interview. After we've stopped recording, Ashley puts his hands behind his head, sits back and says, "It was great though wasn't it? It was like they could see

when we were struggling and they got behind us to lift us through."
He asks me what it was like back in the days of a full house at the
Millennium Stadium? It's a good question. Often the atmosphere was
very good, but those games used to be as much about people having
an excuse to spend a weekend in Cardiff. That was a rugby tradition
and many of the same people descended from the Valleys. Tickets were
cheap and easier to get hold of for the football. There were a couple
of great nights along the way, beating Italy there was amazing, but
it didn't really work as a football venue and Wales record there was
mediocre at best, particularly in qualifiers. As crowds dwindled,
20,000 even 30,000 looked and sounded like peas in a drum. I tell
him Friday night felt much better, more intimidating for the opposition
as well.

Then it's Cookie. I'm intrigued to know how the players are going
to play another key game so soon after seeming to give everything
against Bosnia. He talks about the support staff and the work they
do in planning a programme that gives the players the best chance of
recovery. This was an area Wales only really started to embrace under
the guidance of Gary Speed. He brought in a Dutch guy, Raymond
Verheijen to be his assistant.

His area of expertise was in planning training sessions to minimise
the risk of injury, a technique he called 'periodisation'. He was a
highly controversial figure, still is. He's an arrogant, authoritarian
Dutchman who pulls no punches when it comes to criticising what he
regards as bad practice. He caused Gary trouble almost from minute
one in the first camp, particularly with comments he used to post on
Twitter. But Gary put up with it because he believed in what Raymond
was doing. The players bought into it as well. They were experiencing
the same level of monitoring and direction they'd got used to at their
clubs. John Toshack held no truck with sports science and the rest of
it, but Gary was a different generation and he embraced new thinking
and technology. Players went back to their clubs fit and ready to
play again the following weekend. This had a double benefit for the
national side. It meant the clubs were happy that the players they'd
invested in so heavily, were being suitably looked after with Wales. It
also convinced the players they were far less likely to suffer injuries
on international duty that might impact on their club careers.

Gary's death led Raymond to burn all his bridges with the FAW in a horribly misguided attempt to get himself appointed as manager. He left with all guns blazing, blasting away at his former employers and the incoming Chris Coleman. Chris probably wasn't that *au fait* with the science when he took the job, but neither did he opt to chuck it all out. He recognised the value even if only as a placebo, something that reassured the players and kept them coming. With the help of the staff he kept on, people like Osian Roberts, he's developed a greater understanding of the role sports science plays in the modern game. Analysis and 'recovery' sessions remain a big part of the training schedule before and after games.

Nevertheless, not everyone's made it from Friday. Not surprisingly, Jonny Williams is ruled out. As the manager points out, he was kicked from pillar to post on Friday night, suffered heavy bruising and there's no recovering from that in just 36 hours.

Chris describes this game as now being the most important for a long time. Seven points from nine would look great. Wales are top of the fledgling group and they'd remain there, no matter what happens elsewhere tomorrow. Cyprus surprised everyone by winning in Bosnia in the first game but they lost 2-1 at home to Israel on Friday night, which means they have just one victory from their last 14 games and have finished bottom of their group in the last two qualification campaigns. Still, Chris isn't going to be tempted into any rash predictions. "We'll take a win, no matter how we get it", he repeats, "just like in Andorra".

With the interviews done, we head out to the edge of the pitch where the players are already gathering. Jonny Williams is there as well, leg heavily bandaged. He's suffered a lot of injuries playing for Wales, including a broken leg, but still he keeps coming back. He's another one of the Anglos, the English-born players who've become such loyal servants of the land of their parents.

A shot of his injured leg will be good to use to illustrate Chris Coleman's description of the treatment he received on Friday night. I contact Sports News to give them a heads-up.

After training, Alex stays on to send all the clips back, and I head back home via the huge Asda that's a goal-kick away from the stadium. I've promised I'll cook Sunday dinner so I'm off to get what I need for a proper roast.

There's still a little bit of work to be done. I need to confirm the location for the next interview, and the identity of the player we'll be talking to. An email answers the ID question quickly, it'll be Vincent Laban. That doesn't sound very 'Cypriot', sure enough, a background check shows he's French. He played in Cyprus for a few years and got naturalised. Then there's a flurry of communication as to the 'where'. Mark Evans is now involved, as is Steve Williams, the liaison officer who's linked up with the next set of visitors. The away dressing room won't be available, neither will the refs room or the medical room. It appears the home dressing room might be. There's also some confusion over the time for the interview. It takes another flurry of emails to ascertain that the original time is the correct time.

Alex and I decide to share a car today. The stadium's all but deserted, except one guy and his small son who follow us towards the main entrance. "What time are Wales training?" he asks the security guard standing outside the reception. "It was this morning", comes the reply. The father looks crestfallen, I don't think his son's going to get many signatures in the autograph book he's clutching.

We're let in and gain entrance to the home dressing room as we'd hoped. It's not been swept since this morning's training session so there are still clumps of grass on the floor. The UEFA delegate laughs when she comes in to check on us, she thinks it looks like we've been adding the grass to make the backdrop to the interview look more authentic. She stays on for a chat as we get set up. Well, Alex sets up, I sit and do my thing. If she's going to be the delegate assigned to all these games, a good relationship could come in handy. I've found it's always better to try and work with people rather than against them.

The Cypriot media conferences are due to take place before we do our interview, and Vincent will be talking to us right before he goes out to train, so we haven't got long with him. In all honesty, we won't need too long. Our viewers won't really know a lot about him so I don't think they'll use too much of the interview in the build-up. We've never actually done interviews with the opposition for the live show before but then, previously, we were generally on air just 15 minutes before kick-off. Now there are 45 minutes to fill before the game begins.

The one overriding concern in these instances is that the interviewee has got a decent command of English. Foreign FAs sometimes offer translators, but that doesn't really work for this type of interview. It's perhaps a little selfish but there isn't really time to translate, unless it's a massive star name. We need Vincent Laban to speak some English, the press officer assures me does, and he's right. Vincent speaks good English and he's a thoroughly nice guy. The interview's okay and everyone's happy.

I head back to the OB trucks where the crew are still running though things for the game tomorrow. I can start to send the interview back whilst Alex gets some extra shots of the player training. By the time he's done, so am I. We load the car for the final time and head back to the apartment. I'm ready for bed, past experience tells me a decent night's sleep will have me back on form for MD3.

Monday 13th October

It certainly helps. I'm feeling more like it as I indulge myself with an extra hour in bed, my own recovery time, ahead of another big game.

The morning's clear at least, which is good as I need to get into the city centre to buy some presents for the family. They've suffered (or enjoyed?!) my long absences for a decade now. It makes me feel a bit better to take a bagful of gifts home with me, even now, with both my daughters at secondary school. It used to be easy when they were little, a cuddly toy, some puzzles maybe, a novelty pen or a doll in national costume. It's a bit more difficult now, they're a bit more discerning.

I pop into Turnstile Records as well, interrupting a meeting in the process. We talk about Friday's game and Gareth's DJ set before it. It went well by all accounts, he ended up playing an hour and he's up for doing the next one which has already been pencilled in for the day of the Belgium home game in June.

Kevin, Alun's business partner is also planning on going this evening. They're both taking their children. This is a clear sign of things beginning to build. The crowd won't be as big tonight, those awful road links north to south will prevent a lot of the fans who came down on Friday making the return journey so soon. It's not possible to get a train back north either. It's the downside to this new calendar, two home games in a three day period is an expensive and time consuming exercise.

I leave the chaps to their meeting and head straight for a shop that's great for gifts. I haven't seen this chain anywhere other than Cardiff, so I know the kids won't be able to get the same thing in Leeds.

I fill a bag with goodies and head home. I've got the same request for live inserts from Sports News so we'll need to be at the stadium for about 3.30. That just about gives me a time for a run and guess what, as I return, the heavens open and I get drenched, again. Then, it's shower, shave and suit on. With the time remaining, I pack, ready for a fairly swift away in the morning. Just this game to get through first.

The old anxieties set in as we leave the apartment together for the final time. We've spent so much time talking about Wales, Alex and I, hours and hours and he's not even Welsh. He's like Jonny Williams though, or Andy King, always turns up when the call comes, never lets the country down when asked. He's really got into it down the years. I think if you asked him, Wales would now be his second team, after Wolves. He went away to the World Cup to cover England in the summer, big time Charlie, but I sense that his heart wasn't really in it. Not many people in our business have been able to get as close as we have to this group of players. We know people at every level, and at times it feels a bit like being part of the squad. He's almost as desperate as I am to see Wales qualify. That would be like the end of the journey for us, a long, hard journey.

We've had some good times, been to some interesting places, but there have been many occasions when it's felt like a chore. It hasn't helped that the team's never really been in contention to qualify. We're in the business of hyping up the game, but the reality is so many of the fixtures we've covered have had no meaning beyond the 90 minutes. When things started to pick up after the long, hard Toshack years, we were given a glimpse of something much better with Gary Speed and then it was snatched away in a manner that was tragic beyond comprehension. There were some dark times then. The filming we did with the players and management ahead of the memorial game was very, very difficult. It was all so far away from football. Real, raw, awful emotion. At that time, I wished I'd never got involved but I'd come too far to turn back. I'd actually helped Gary get the Wales job. I felt then and still feel now a nagging sense of guilt about what happened, and whether the job played any part in it.

We just crave a little sunshine after all the darkness. Tonight could

83

either see a break in the clouds, or bring another clap of thunder. If Wales win, we get to game four in the group with a realistic chance of qualification. That hasn't been the case in any of the qualifying campaigns we've covered together.

Some further assignments have popped up on my schedule for the afternoon and evening, so things promise to be quite busy. Sky News want me to do something and a PR company have been in touch about the possibility of doing an interview with Ryan Giggs, who's going to be at the stadium presenting some awards.

On site and back with the OB team, I get my half hour dinner break but there's stuff to be done either side, both live and recorded. Then I'm back at my post awaiting the arrival of the manager. His conversations with Bill suggest he's reverting to 4-4-2 and that George Williams is going to make his first international start. The Fulham teenager's come on as a sub a couple of times before but now he gets his big chance. Hal Robson-Kanu's also going to start after finishing so well on Friday.

Everything goes well, Chris does his piece and now I've only got Ryan Giggs to tick off my list. Except nobody seems to know when or where it will be. Messages pass to and fro. Tony, tonight's floor manager, is deep in discussions about it all. The PR people want the interview to be done upstairs, UEFA want it to be done on the pitchside and they won't allow a camera to go upstairs. Technically, this is their outside broadcast. It's their competition, so what they say is law. Kick-off comes closer, calls are made and still no resolution. I'm waiting for a decision. Finally, with 30 minutes to go, it's all resolved, I race upstairs to one of the hospitality suites. I'm met by Ryan's 'people'. They're anxious that he doesn't get asked a question about Raheem Sterling and his absence from the England side. I explain that it's an interview for a live Wales game, so there's no way we'd be discussing England. They insist we mention the event he's here to promote, which can be accommodated. All the while though, Ryan's on stage, being interviewed by the same MC who replaced me at the awards dinner. Off stage, more of Ryan's people are trying to catch her attention to end that interview so he can come and do this interview instead. They fail. Eventually, he's done and he's ushered over. He was Wales captain for a while under Tosh, so I interviewed him regularly at that time; always liked him.

October 1992, Cyprus v Wales, with my mates the night before the game. I'm on the left.

September 2015, Cyprus v Wales, with my mates the night before the game.

The lucky socks! This photo was taken in a hotel in Canada where Alex was watching Wales v Belgium. Even from afar, the socks worked their magic.

The stuff we gather along the way. It's the first time I've done every qualifier in a campaign, as a supporter or reporter.

The first game we saw during the campaign was actually Barcelona B v Real Zaragoza at the Mini Estadi, next door to the Camp Nou. I got scalped on the tickets and the hot dog did for Alex.

A 'sit-down' interview, with Chris Coleman in Barcelona prior to the Andorra game, the first of many!

A scenic start in Andorra's new stadium. From a distance, the pitch looks lovely!

Close up, it's a real cause for concern as I tried to explain to the viewers.

The away end starts to fill up in Andorra. Wales enjoyed a fantastic following
wherever they went in this campaign.

Relief as well as delight when Gareth Bale rescues the campaign and gets his
manager 'out of jail' with a late winner in Andorra.

The most important goal of the entire campaign? Gareth scores from a retaken free kick, and Wales take the lead in Andorra with just nine minutes to go.

Music's my other big obsession so when the FAW awards event was taking place in October, I opted to go and watch The Tea Street Band at Clwb Ifor Bach instead.

The Wales squad preparing for the Bosnia and Cyprus double-header. Training sessions are a regular part of our international itinerary, although our access is generally limited to fifteen minutes filming per week. As the campaign went on, so the media interest grew. There have been times in the past where me and Alex have been just about the only people there!

In the tunnel for the first home qualifier against Bosnia, with the two captains preparing to lead their teams out. I interviewed both Ashley Williams and Edin Džeko in the build-up to the game.

Wayne Hennessey got the man of the match award for his performance against Bosnia. It was the first of an incredible seven clean sheets! Not bad for a man who barely got any first team club football throughout the campaign.

Hal Robson-Kanu made a massive contribution to the campaign. He only had one goal to celebrate, against Cyprus, but the fans saw how hard he worked for the team.

It started well, got tricky but the ten men hung on for a big win at home against Cyprus. The captain was delighted to hear the final whistle.

This was a big result for a team missing key players through injury. Three games gone, still unbeaten and top of the group. The first sense that something good was happening.

IG and Pete, the FAW media team. This is the moment they realised neither the captain or manager was wearing the correctly branded tops ahead of our interviews in the team hotel in Brussels.

We didn't have much luck with our crew meals on the nights before the away games, but Bill's suggestion of *Vincent* in Brussels was inspired. It was definitely the best culinary experience of the whole campaign.

Brussels in November, sitting in my pitchside position, a study in nervous concentration.

My pal Tim's Spirit Of 58 label proved a big hit with fans during the campaign. I made sure I had a warm hat for a chilly night in Belgium.

Captain Marvel applauds the fans in Brussels after another clean sheet and a crucial point. Ashley was a strong contender, with Gareth Bale, for Wales's Player of the Campaign award. Both were named in UEFA's all-star XI at the end of the qualifiers.

Zombie Nation blasts out of the PA as the fans celebrate and the qualification campaign has it's anthem.

The players go to celebrate with the fans at full time. Gareth Bale's biggest contribution in Belgium was a clearance off the line in the final seconds, a true team player. 'France is that way' says Aaron to Gareth!

Post-match in Brussels and Team Sky enjoy an editorial debrief in the *Delirium Café*. The consensus seems to be that things have gone well!

He's finally arrived in Haifa! Barry Horne enjoys a beer, still wearing the suit he taught in many hours previously, as he regales us with yet another tale of travel woes.

Alex celebrates his birthday for the first time in the restaurant the night before the game in Haifa. It wasn't to be the last celebration, much to Ben's dismay.

A quick stop to admire the view on the traditional matchday run. The Haifa coastline looks okay, the rest of it was not quite so picturesque.

Mr Ofer spent a lot of money on a very impressive stadium, so it's only fair that he should have his name on it!

The stadium was full but there were lots of Bale fans amongst the home supporters but, after an amazing rendition of their national anthem, his performance quickly silenced the Israeli fans.

My view in the tunnel at the moment the teams were preparing to walk out ahead of the game that changed everything. After this I started to believe it might really happen.

Gareth celebrates the second goal that just about ensured a vital away win in Israel.

The race to get to Wembley to watch Wrexham in the FA Trophy enters the home straight, Barry Horne setting a blistering pace that I can't hope to match. We got in just before half-time but we might as well not have bothered!

He smiles as he sees me which is a good sign! There's no time for a chat sadly, so we get straight into it, and a couple of questions later, we're done. It's so late by now that I can't see the interview making it into the show. Not my problem really, I just ask the questions.

I get back down to the tunnel just before the players line-up alongside their mascots. I pop Dai's lucky chewing gum into my mouth. Here we go!

I'm often impressed by how big so many international footballers are when you see them close up, but Cyprus don't really have quite the same impact. They are bigger than the mascots, whose hands they are holding, but not by much. I take this as a good sign. The goalkeeper, their second choice, very much fits this category. I wouldn't think he's over 6ft if he's even that.

There are fewer in the ground to greet the players' arrival, the FAW anticipated about 20,000 and it looks like they were right. Still, it's not bad considering the quality of opposition and the proximity to the last match. Things don't start well though. Just seconds in and Simon Church gets nudged over by a defender. He sprawls across the turf, then rolls over in agony. It doesn't look good. A few minutes treatment follow, before he's stretchered off. It's a dislocated shoulder. The poor lad is going to be out for a few weeks with that. Another one bites the dust. In his place, David Cotterill comes on. It's a long time since he featured for Wales, even within the squad. His career's been on the slide for a while, until a recent upturn with Birmingham. He's another nice lad, I've known him since he came into the team under Tosh, and our paths have crossed at a number of the clubs he's been at since. If Wales are going to succeed, they're going to have to cope with all this adversity.

'Cometh the hour, cometh the man' and with 13 minutes gone, David Cotterill steps up to the mark. He's already put a couple of good crosses in, then he's whipped another right-footed ball in from the left wing and it's sailed past everybody, goalkeeper included, and into the net. What a way to mark your return! Wales are flying now. Nine minutes later, a fantastic flick from Gareth Bale in the centre circle is really well anticipated by Hal Robson-Kanu. He sweeps forward, well clear of defenders and slides as he places the ball under the 'keeper and in; it's 2-0 and less than 25 minutes gone! This has never happened before. I have a vision of a night when I can actually afford to relax and enjoy the game. One more goal will sort it and there's every sign it won't be long coming. Then, with Wales very much in the groove, the game stops for another injury, to a Cypriot player and, just like Friday, it impacts on Wales' performance, only this time, it's negatively. Cyprus up their game, start to play and get a few good balls into the box. Then David Cotterill goes into a rash tackle just outside the area. A free kick is awarded, to the right of centre. Our French Cypriot pal, Vincent, steps up. He floats the ball into the box left footed, Hennessey flaps and misses and it carries on its way, over a number of heads before coming to stop in the back of the net. *Merde*! Forget relaxing, Cyprus are back in it.

Still, one more goal for Wales and I'll truly regard the game as being won, they won't score three goals when they've only scored that many in about their last nine matches. Wales wake up again and Bale crashes a free kick-off the crossbar, with the aid of a touch from that titchy goalie's fingertips. It loops up and Joe Ledley heads the rebound goalwards until a defender leaps up and diverts it away. Wales go close again in stoppage time in the first half as Cotterill breaks through, the 'keeper saves at his feet, the rebound falls for Bale and his drive's going in before another defender blocks it on the line. So, the lead's still a slender one as the two teams come off at the break. There's no sense of elation in the tunnel. We're all too battle-scarred to be caught getting carried away at this stage.

On that basis, I'm hoping there's a swift Welsh goal to settle things after the resumption, as if?! Instead, Andy King catches the back of the ankle of an opponent who rolls around theatrically. The ref's standing a couple of feet away. He goes to his pocket and to everyone's horror, whips the red card out. This ruddy campaign's taken another twist. The whole dynamic of the game changes dramatically. Instead of seeking that third, killer goal, Wales are now going to have to dig in to ensure the win. Ah, Jesus! There are 40 more minutes to go. I slump back and prepare myself for the inevitable. It's always worse when you take the lead, you've been offered a tantalising glimpse of something. How many times have I heard Wales fans say, 'it's the hope that kills you'?

Friday night was nothing in comparison with this. The tension's unbearable. The crowd go a bit quiet for a while as the Cypriots sense they've got a chance. The possession stats start to rise in their favour, Gareth Bale's reduced to tracking back, the world's most expensive footballer is grafting for the good of the team. Meanwhile, I'm counting down the time in blocks on that scoreboard clock, suffering agonies with each passing second. In truth, they aren't actually looking like scoring but there's always a chance, a deflection, a dodgy penalty maybe? The worst moment comes about 20 minutes from the end when the Cypriots launch an attack down the right, for the first time in this tortuous period, the player in possession makes space to get a cross in and it's a good one, in-swinging, onto the head of a teammate, eight yards out. This is it, this feels like the moment, but the header's poor, and the ball sails over the crossbar. Relief all round. It feels like a release.

From this point on, Cyprus seem to lose heart. As I desert my post on 85 minutes, Wales are more than holding on, in fact they're creating chances, although the players look almost out on their feet. I get the call in my earpiece for a Gareth Bale and George Williams interview at the end. Gareth's man of the match, again. I must admit, he wouldn't have been my choice. I think James Chester's been fantastic over the two games and Hal Robson-Kanu's been excellent this evening as well. Still, the MOTM selection should guarantee us a Gareth interview. We're not there yet though and quite a scene greets me back in the tunnel. Clustered around the monitor are the usual FAW frowns, but they've been joined by Andy King, long since banished back to the dressing room. Our monitor is the only place he can watch the game. We stand side by side to endure the last few minutes. He asks me if it was a sending off? I have to tell him it didn't look good, but I think he was unlucky. Then we turn back to the game, into added time now, Wales get a corner. "Right, I want you to take 30 seconds over this", Andy suggests as Gareth picks up the ball to walk towards the corner flag. By the time he gets there, he's almost complied with Andy's instruction. This is the game management Chris Coleman's been talking about. Nothing obvious, just everything slowed down a bit. The first corner's played short, a defender comes in to try and get the ball and Gareth kicks it against him for another corner. The same happens again. Cyprus get a goal kick this time and launch the ball forward, we breathe in, the whistle goes, we breathe out. Three more points. As I wait for the players, I miss more celebrations On the monitor I see Gareth Bale's manic fist pump dramatically conveys the emotion, then he instigates another huddle. That's your #TogetherStronger that is.

Gareth comes across to the interview position, George follows, a young guy we've not interviewed before. The age gap isn't enormous between these two, but Gareth's comfortable with this situation now, George isn't. Gareth speaks really well about togetherness and the spirit, George needs a little more coaxing but we get there. Good, upbeat stuff.

We don't wait long for the manager. We've been asked to get the footage of the sending off on the monitor for Osian and Andy to watch back but we haven't managed to get it on screen by the time Chris is in front of the interview boards. In commentary it was suggested he looked pretty calm on the touchline in the second half, despite everything. I suggest this as an opening gambit, "I might have looked calm, but inside I was having kittens" he laughs. He praises his players again, and acknowledges that whilst they didn't play as well as they can, the win was all-important. After the interview, he stays to watch the incident which is now ready to replay. Osian and Andy have come back as well. First play and there's a moment's silence that says everything. Second play, different angle and they acknowledge the decision as being correct. Andy's gutted that he's going to be missing at least one game. That's sad but it's a good sign, he desperately wants to be involved.

I've requested an interview with Hal Robson-Kanu next. He's a little subdued, I suspect that he's drained, like the rest of us, although, he's probably done a bit more running around. Word comes through that they've got enough now. We're done. Get in!! Top of the group! Job done! As I walk back to the trucks, I bump into Bill. We actually embrace. He must sense how much this means to so many people. I jabber excitedly. It's all a bit daft really, we're only three games in and with two hard away games to come but we're still in the running and, believe me, this is uncharted territory.

It feels good to go back to the apartment, get the slippers on again, crack open a bottle of beer and reflect together on a good night. In fact, it's been a good week and a half. We've fulfilled all the requests made of us, and turned in some decent material, I think. I'm dead keen to get home again tomorrow, but at least I'll drive north in the knowledge that when I do it all again next month, there's still going to be everything to play for. Bosnia have drawn at home with Belgium, so after three games they only have two points, five behind Wales. If they're the team we're looking to pip for second place, a positive result next month will give us a great chance of finishing above them. Elsewhere, Israel have found Andorra a little easier, winning 4-1 on that awful surface so they're second with six points from their two away fixtures, and a game in hand. They might just yet be dark horses in this group.

4

"We've done very well but I still think we can do better"
Belgium v Wales

'Don't take me home, please don't take me home'

Tuesday 11th November

Habit is a great deadener, as Samuel Beckett once wrote. So, today, my car's staying on the drive and I'm heading for Leeds station as a passenger in my wife's car. Belgium away promises to be a little bit different; trains, planes and automobiles. I've already done a drive to Cardiff and back since the last game, so anything that keeps me off the dreaded M1 can only be seen as a good thing. That salvation comes in the form of the 14.15 CrossCountry trains service, with one change at Bristol Temple Meads.

The prospect of a train ride's an attractive one. I've got music, books and films to entertain me, which is great as I normally find them distracting when I'm driving! My wife waves me off at the station's drop-off point and I head south for another week away from home, with Brussels the ultimate destination.

The time since the last set of fixtures has been favourable for Wales. Every weekend there's been a nervy wait for bad news. I reckon pretty much every Wales supporter's been checking team lists for guidance

90

on those Welsh players who are fit and those who aren't. So far it hasn't brought any major disappointments, on the contrary, Aaron Ramsey and Joe Allen have both returned to action for their clubs, although there was a scare when I switched on the Swansea commentary on my car radio, in the aftermath of my own game at Sunderland v Everton on Sunday. The very first words I heard were, "Ashley Williams is still down having treatment and this doesn't look good for Swansea or for Wales." A chill ran through my veins. Thankfully, the commentator might have been a little melodramatic, the news got better and he got up to carry on. Poor old Andy King got a two game ban for his red card against Cyprus and David Edwards and Jonny Williams are both injured, the latter having again been the victim of a ferocious foul challenge. That apart, everybody's expected to turn-up.

There's no access scheduled until tomorrow morning, so this is a clear travel day, I can sit back and relax and let the train take the strain. There's a call from one of my old colleagues at Sky Sports News, with an extra request for assistance with an interview with the boxer Nathan Cleverley tomorrow. He's coming along to watch training apparently, ahead of a title fight on Sky soon. We're getting our usual time-limited access, so I explain we can help but it'll have to fit around the job of filming the training session. We won't get any more access to film the players ahead of the game and Belgian TV have asked to use our footage, so we need to make full use of our 15 minutes.

It takes about the same time to get to Cardiff by train as it takes me in the car, which does make me think I should travel this way more often. Everything's on schedule and I roll into Cardiff Central a little over four hours later. There's no apartment this time, back to convention there at least, so I head for our usual HQ, The Radisson Blu.

Once I've got into my room, there are more work-related requests. We've now popped up in the 'live plan' for the following morning, which means Sports News want to report live from training. This also means they're sending a satellite truck to join us. On top of that, there's more flesh on the bones of the Cleverley shoot. He's going to arrive early to meet the players at 'The Castle' and we can film that. The only problem is, neither Alex nor I know where or what 'The Castle' is? Neither does the person who set it up. These issues are still unresolved as I meet up with Alex a little later in the bar for what might loosely be termed a pre-production planning meeting. Certainly, we're going to have to plan tomorrow at least, as we've got three jobs to do, all at roughly the same time, with just one camera and he, it transpires, has now been asked to go and do another job for Sports News in Somerset in the afternoon. This one we can definitely cross off, as we have an interview with Neil Taylor scheduled for 2pm. It's a problem I flag up to the person now staffing the news desk at SSN. Things are further complicated by the fact we only have a short time span in which to schedule the live report. Reporting live will tie-up me and Alex for a few minutes at least, meaning less time to actually film the session and we've got that limited window of opportunity. The response is realistic and reasonable – the plan to do a live report is abandoned and someone else will be booked for the job in Bath. Another call to IG clarifies the Cleverley arrangements and we now have a slightly better idea where 'The Castle' is. We've seen it, we just didn't know it was called 'The Castle'. We live and learn. Then we eat and chat.

Alex is clearly upbeat about what will happen in Belgium. He talks about getting a win that will, in his estimation, all but guarantee qualification. I can't deal with this unbridled optimism, and warn him against making such ridiculously bold claims in my presence. This isn't the Welsh way.

Wednesday 12th November

The day starts with a call telling me that the boxer's been in touch with someone at Sports News to say that he won't now be turning up at 'The Castle', or indeed the training session after all. That makes life easier for us at least, although Sky doesn't get the chance to use the interview and pictures to preview his upcoming fight.

There have been a couple of tweaks to the schedule already, this training session for one. The original plan was to only allow access to a session on Saturday morning, in Cardiff, and then hold the traditional and required eve-of-match media conferences at 8pm the same day, over in Brussels. These arrangements weren't particularly helpful for us or anyone else. We need some footage of the squad that's assembled as early in the week as possible, newspapers aren't keen on trying to get preview material processed late on Saturday night either. So, now we've got an earlier open session and earlier access to the manager.

The session, when it starts, is noisy and energetic. There seems, quite literally, to be a spring in their step, a spring that's been missing from so many of the sessions we've filmed down the years. Under John Toshack, things were a lot less organised, or at least that's how it looked. Coaching staff would still be laying down cones and markers as the players conducted a 'kick-in' amongst themselves. Now, when they turn-up, everything's ready and waiting. The fitness coaches do their work first – Ryland Morgans takes most of the squad, Adam Owens assists. The one absentee is Ashley Williams. He's there as well, but he's still suffering the after-effects of that tough tackle on Sunday so his session consists of a walk, a jog, a walk and a jog; just a few laps of the pitch under the watchful eye of one of the medical team.

A pole has been erected close to the training pitch, it contains a camera that has an overview of the pitches they're using. The pictures are being fed into a laptop, which they'll use to analyse the session later. It's the first time this piece of kit has appeared, and video analysts are on hand to erect and operate it. Whether the data collected is of any use or not I don't know but, if nothing else, it gives the players a sense that they are being well looked after, that every effort is being made on their behalf. It also means their effort levels can be monitored; no hiding place here for the potential slackers!

Before we leave, I ask about the location for our interview with Neil Taylor. It'll be at the team hotel this time, IG promises to try and sort out a room for us, we promise to be there early so we're set up and ready when Neil appears.

I've already been in touch directly, via text a few days ago, to let him know about it, but players have a tendency sometimes to let these things slip from their mind. Still, IG assures me he has spoken to Neil as well and he's all geared up to do it. As I'm waiting for him to appear from the players' dining room, other members of the squad appear. Sam Ricketts stops for a chat. He's been around as long as we've been covering Wales, and always been friendly. When he had to drop out of the squad for a while due to a bad injury, he actually appeared as a studio pundit for us and he was good at it. He wants to talk about that as it happens, he's looking for more media opportunities and he's had a bit of training from the BBC. I'd be happy to help advise him, he's a good guy, he's always helped me so now I have the chance to give him a bit back.

As we talk, we're interrupted by the arrival of another group of familiar faces, including 'Big Ginge', aka James Collins. He and Danny Gabbidon are the last two survivors of the team that predated even our coverage of Wales. He's back in the squad after a bit of a fall-out with Chris Coleman and it's good to see him again, as we've always got on. As he's heading towards the lifts, he asks me a question, "Have you spoken to Ched yet?" And there it is, the first mention of the one potential cloud hanging over this week's proceedings, Ched Evans. Yesterday, Sheffield United, his former club, confirmed that they'd offer him the chance to train with them, now that he's been released from prison after serving half of a five-year sentence for rape.

Ched earned 13 senior caps for Wales before his conviction. He had been the subject of a big money transfer from Manchester City to Sheffield United in 2009 and had scored 35 goals for them in the 2011-12 season, right up to the point where his trial began. I was there when he scored the last of those goals, the day before he first appeared in court. His conviction was controversial, his pal was cleared, but his appeals have been unsuccessful. Now his release and potential re-employment as a professional footballer has caused a huge furore. Sheffield United have been widely criticised for contemplating giving him another chance, petitions calling on him to be kept out of football have been signed by hundreds of thousands of people. It's a topic that's caused huge debate.

For the Wales players it's awkward, really awkward. Most of them know him and played in the U-21s or the senior side with him. For Chris Coleman, at some point this week, it's going to be made an issue. He will almost certainly have to answer questions as to whether he'll be invited back to play for his country if he gets his career back on track with his club. This is a crucial week for Wales, culminating in a very important football fixture, and yet the fear is that the build-up will be overshadowed by a situation that's currently no more than a hypothetical one.

I know Ched from those previous times at Sheffield United and with Wales. I once tagged along on a night out in Cardiff with him and Craig Bellamy, an interesting experience but one that didn't end up in anything like the same circumstances that led to his rape conviction.

I had him down as a fairly pleasant lad who was almost painfully unintelligent and a bit bonkers certainly – he ended that Cardiff night spinning round and round a sign post. I did subsequently hear more sinister suggestions about his nocturnal habits, but they didn't seem wildly different to rumours I was hearing about the way a lot of other young, rich, footballers were behaving.

Anyway, I haven't spoken to him since I said hello in the tunnel at the end of his final game for Sheffield United. To be honest, it's a subject I'm keen to stay clear of as well. There's been too much awfulness involved in the time I've been covering Wales, Gary Speed's suicide being the desperate nadir. I would love a period of sustained positivity, and I don't really want Ched Evans getting in the way. I suspect that would be Chris Coleman and the FAW's feeling as well.

Sam and I talk briefly about the subject after James moves away. The best I can offer is that I think the way he's been advised to conduct himself in the aftermath of his release has been a bit of a PR disaster. Say sorry to the victim or say nothing at all, would have been my advice; I think he may have made it impossible for himself to resurrect his career. I don't want to get caught up in a big debate about the rights and the wrongs of the situation and the lobby of the team hotel's not really the right location.

I'm saved by Neil Taylor. He's come out of the dining room and is heading upstairs before he comes back down to do his interview, so I tell him where we're hiding. He's a bright lad but I can't help myself, footballers have a habit of going walkabout, so I hang around to make sure he doesn't get lost between the lobby and the lower ground floor.

Neil's another one of the good guys. I've been following his career since he broke into Wrexham's first team as a 17 year-old. He always looked a class above to me, but Dean Saunders, the manager at that time, didn't seem to have the same confidence so it was a big surprise when Swansea stepped in to sign him. They made a shrewd move, paying a couple of hundred thousand for a player now worth a few million. He suffered an horrendous injury a couple of seasons ago, but battled back and got into Swansea's team again, and he's reclaimed his international place as well. He's also a very erudite young guy, one of the best of a very good squad of 'talkers'. We always enjoy a bit of Wrexham chat, he keeps a keen eye on events at his old club and that's how we warm-up for this interview as Alex is fitting the clip mic onto Neil's top. As he's got good things to say, I stretch the interview longer than I normally would. It will all come in handy if we decide to do our campaign documentary. The same messages of unity, spirit, belief and not a little confidence that a positive result can be achieved from the toughest-looking fixture of the lot.

The evening's clear, so we head out to a new restaurant opposite the hotel called The Smoke Haus. It's really busy when we arrive, but that probably has something to do with the fact the comedian John Bishop's on at the Arena around the corner. As we study the menu, Newcastle's Paul Dummett walks in with a group of friends. It must be a night-off for the players, as the manager's gone over to Belgium to watch a friendly against Iceland. We keep a keen eye on him as they order drinks at the bar. He goes for a Coke, good lad! My next concern is that he doesn't order the 'Donut Burger', a whole morning's training on a plate, but we're done and dusted by the time his party are sitting down. I'm sure he'll do the right thing.

Whilst we've been eating, I've been checking scores from Wrexham's game at Woking. A half-time lead is squandered and the side has to settle for a draw, six league games without a win now. It's a result that leaves me needing to be cheered up. We cross the road to a pub called Porter's where it's 'Comedy Night'. It doesn't really do the trick, in fact, it probably makes things worse. So much stand-up comedy now just seems to consist of people saying 'do you remember how when you were a kid you used to...?', then swearing a bit, for no real reason other than to appear 'edgy'. It might be an idea to throw in a few jokes from time to time, I'm not that interested in the fact that you used to ride a Grifter or watch Thundercats. It's all a bit sad. Neither of us laugh and we're off after about 10 minutes, almost hoping to be heckled as we get up and walk out. We aren't. Poor show.

Thursday 13th November

Today should be straightforward. It's the day for access to the players. We turn-up at the hotel, set up somewhere and interview them before or after they appear before the rest of the media. The appearance of the manager's made it a little more complicated. It requires my attention. If we get the chance to sit down with the manager today, there doesn't seem a lot of point in doing the same thing again on Saturday evening, as the schedule previously outlined. So, I suggest to IG that it might suit everyone to get it out the way today. I also point out that I've already had a request from Sky Sports News to ask questions about Real Sociedad and, as anticipated, Ched Evans. The response, by text, suggests Chris is only planning on speaking at the media conference and then only to answer a few questions about the game he went to see last night. IG and I both know, this isn't going to happen. I point out that he's bound to get asked the Ched question and I can't afford to miss out, so we'll have to film him, even if that means foregoing our individual interviews with the players. The issue's unresolved and the players are off to training now, so we'll have to turn-up at the hotel and hope for the best.

I head back to the Radisson via TK Maxx where I purchase a pair of dark blue, wool trousers, despite the incredibly mild November, just in case Brussels is a bit chilly.

From our base, we head off to the team base, a short drive away. The wind's gusting really strongly as we park up, and the satellite truck that's been dispatched to assist in sending material back won't be able to operate. It would be too dangerous to put the big dish up in this weather, even if the engineer could; he'd not be able to maintain the link for long enough to get the interviews sent back. After a brief conversation, he makes a call to base to tell them he won't be able to help us out.

Next up, another problem, there's a slightly worried looking IG in the lobby when we pitch up with all the cameras, lights and cables. The next issue, of course, is where we go, and he hasn't managed to arrange anything. The good news is that it appears we aren't going to have to film the media conferences, as Chris has agreed to do the sit-down interview today. In fact, IG wants us to get the Ashley Williams one done today as well, one less distraction for the skipper over in Belgium it seems, but there'll be no appearance by Joe Allen as had been previously suggested. It's constantly shifting sands, never a dull moment. Now we need somewhere to set up.

IG suggests I check with hotel staff on reception. It soon transpires that we're struggling. All the extra meeting rooms are taken up, even the little box rooms downstairs. The only thing they can come up with is using one of the suites, something we've done on previous visits. That's fine, so I say yes. except that it's going to cost money;

£150, for a stay of less than two hours! Luckily, the FAW agree to pick up the bill so we can get ourselves up to floor four and set up. Just before we ascend, Ashley Williams strides through reception to the lift. IG requests his presence today, but he's not keen as it turns out so, Saturday night it is for the skipper after all.

We've used this suite before so we know it's an ideal location for us. It has two rooms and we use the lounge area. It's quiet, there are plenty of plugs and there's a kettle and espresso machine and nice biscuits! By way of further reassurance, we've got an FAW person liasing with us so she knows which room we're in, and she'll bring the players and the manager up to us. All bases are covered.

Still, we get bored in our room, so we wander along the corridor to the central balcony that looks down on the lobby. We can see all the movement to and fro from up here but it's also a floor occupied by members of the coaching staff. Kit Symons appears from out of the lift behind us. Since the last international, he's been confirmed as the full-time manager of Fulham. Just before the decision was made, I chatted with him at a Fulham game I was covering. He'd made it clear then that he wanted to continue to combine the roles, so he was keeping a lower-profile now, watching the game from the stand not the dugout, in the hope that nobody from Fulham, the fans in particular perhaps, would question his ongoing commitment to his main employer. We have a laugh about this and both assure him we haven't seen him as he heads off to hide in his room.

On the floor below, we spot Paul Dummett. I call down to make sure he didn't have the Donut burger, he assures me he went for chicken, although he did have a few chips – crazy! It's actually good to see him apparently enjoying himself and settling in with the squad. He heads off with the other 'newbie' James Chester and some of the other lads, bit of shopping or a Starbuck's maybe?

Osian Roberts arrives in the lift next and stops for a chat. I ask about Belgium last night. They were, it seems, very good. They rested some regular starters, but still managed a big win against an Iceland side that beat Holland last month. Vincent Kompany was missing through injury, indeed, he's been confirmed as unavailable for Sunday as well and Osh reckons the away side did make quite a few chances, so some hope there perhaps?

The lift door pings open again and Wayne Hennessey appears.

Here's our first interviewee, so we head back to the suite. As we sit down and get the mics clipped on, Wayne's got something other than the game on his mind. He asks if I know what's happening with Ched Evans. I don't, but I need to know if he was asked about the subject in the media conference he's just attended downstairs. He says he was but he just said he didn't have anything to say about it. But now he does want to talk it through. It's becoming clear the players are really confused, they're almost asking to be told what they should think. These aren't easy conversations.

Eventually, we need to start recording and the focus again turns to football, a much easier conversation. As Wayne finishes his last answer, the door opens and Hal Robson-Kanu appears. He's quite a thoughtful guy, well-spoken and very polite. He began his international career with England, playing up to U-20 level but Wales were aware of his potential qualification through a grandparent and when things stalled with England, they offered him the chance to switch. Shortly after, he made his senior debut. He's been another loyal servant and his loyalty's being rewarded now with regular starts rather than a seat on the bench. In fact, as he reveals in the interview, as a kid he was a striker and that's the one big problem position at the moment with Simon Church still out after the injury sustained against Cyprus, and Sam Vokes still a few weeks away from returning to full fitness after a six month lay-off.

By now, Alex has realised that he's in danger of getting a parking ticket in the pay and display car park in front of the hotel, so he nips down to re-feed the meter. As he nips out, Chris Coleman nips in and so we have chance for a quick chat before Alex returns. He remarks on the view from the suite, over the waters of Cardiff Bay and beyond to the Bristol Channel. I ask him why he doesn't get one of these suites as 'the manager'? He says he does have one, but it's round the other side of the hotel, "I'm quite superstitious you see?" I laugh, don't we know it! I think it was in this very same room that he once asked if he could swap sides for the interview we were about to do. Sky Sports News have a preferred 'side', with the interviewee looking to the left of the camera. He'd noticed we always did it the same way and as he hadn't actually won a game up to this point, he asked if he could switch. We agreed. Wales won and straight after the match the first thing he said to me in the tunnel was, "see, I told you it would work!"

Now he's staying in another part of the hotel because that's obviously his 'lucky room'. I sympathise; with my chewing gum ritual and Alex with his lucky socks. we're all as mad as each other.

When the interview finally begins, I start off with the questions about Real Sociedad and their appointment today of David Moyes as their new manager. Chris counts the club as one of the others he's previously managed, so Sports News would like his insight into the task that Moyes has taken on. He's really good on the subject, as it turns out, and he finishes by suggesting that it's quite an intense place to live and work, "so when the team's doing well, you never have to buy a meal when you eat out. When the team's doing badly, you eat in!" Now, that's a soundbite.

It's fair to say that Chris's time at Sociedad wasn't entirely successful. He lasted six months and there were negative tales about his socialising, even as the team was doing pretty well on the pitch. After a decent spell in charge at Fulham, it was a first black mark on his CV and he's been trying to rebuild his reputation ever since.

That's the easy stuff though. Next up, it's the Ched Evans question. Chris has been asked about this by the other media downstairs, I checked as we chatted, so I was right to predict it. Given its predictability, he has prepared a response, which is that there will be a conversation with the people in charge of the FAW, if Ched ever returns to the professional game. He hasn't yet, and the manager is too busy with preparing the team for Belgium to engage in that discussion now. It's all that needs to be said at this stage. There is no point in him entering hypothetical conversations about what might or might not happen, nor is he likely to venture a personal view, knowing that it will likely be seized upon by one side or the other in this polarised debate.

What he has done is answer my question so we can move on to the matter in hand. Again he's bullish, 'We respect Belgium but we're not afraid of them' is the clear message.

That's us done, so our next stop is the Cardiff City Stadium and that little magic box that lets us send our material back to base. There's quite a bit of it as we have the Neil Taylor interview from two different angles to send as well, that alone runs at nearly 15 minutes. As Alex gets everything organised, I make a decision to walk back from the stadium to the hotel as I haven't managed to fit in a run yet. I've put the miles in over the last few days though, so I feel a walk will do me more good. Alex thinks I'm mad, he checks the distance on his iPhone and tells me he'll be back before me. Now, it's a challenge, a race! Man v car.

Man wins. Blame the lights or the rush hour traffic but I completed the two mile journey just ahead of him. The victory comes at some cost though. The running plus the walking has caused an unpleasant and painful case of buttock chafing, and as I strip for a bath back in my room, my pants are a pretty gruesome sight. Too much information?

A bath eases the pain a little and I'm able to stride out to dinner without looking too much like John Wayne after a day in the saddle. Alex gets to choose tonight. He opts for the tapas we missed out on in that other upsetting rear end incident in Barcelona. Our local tapas restaurant, La Tasca, is busy it seems and a waiter tells us he's no idea when we'll be able to eat. Alex is less than impressed and executes a fairly theatrical spin and flounce out, which I follow, minus the flounce. We do Tex-Mex across the road instead.

After we've eaten, I'm heading on. There's another gig for me to attend at at Clwb Ifor Bach. This time, it's a Welsh electro-pop singer called Gwenno Saunders who's performing. I've heard some of her material and enjoyed it, so this looks like a great opportunity to see her sing live for the first time. She used to be part of a fairly successful all-girl group called The Pipettes but she's reverted to being a solo artist and to singing in Welsh. She's signed to another record label based in Cardiff, Peski Records. I go alone. Alex, a little less 'cutting-edge' in his preferences probably foresees a musical version of last night's 'entertainment', so he heads back to the hotel.

Much like last month, we're a select gathering. I hang around by the bar whilst a couple of lads make music with two keyboards or computers or something. They're 'Carcharorion', which means 'prisoners' I seem to remember. After they depart, a young chap with a very long, and therefore very fashionable, beard appears. He's 'Carw' and he plays a guitar and twiddles knobs on some tech gear and sings, and it's a good sound. It's wistful, it's in Welsh and I like it. Unfortunately, he laments some problems with a pedal that forces him to cut short his set.

When he finishes, I'm approached by a guy and a girl. They introduce themselves as Rhys and Gwenno, Rhys from the record label and Gwenno, the act. We have a quick chat before they head off to prepare for the performance, which turns out to be very good. Again, it's just the artist and some equipment, as lo-fi as it gets, but the sound created is 'big'. Gwenno sings in Welsh and Cornish, the audience is small but really gets into it. It's not the daft dancing of the last gig, it's more earnest head nodding but just like last month, it leaves me with a great admiration for these artists who put themselves out there for a handful of people. Given the choice, I'm sure they'd prefer to play to a full stadium rather than a venue the size of my front room, but I get a sense that they still get something from the fact that even a few people turn out to listen and enjoy their work. If they put everything into it and we enjoy it, we tell others and next time there might be twice as many people here. The same approach might serve a few lower and non-league footballers well.

After the gig, I have another chat with Rhys and we agree to adjourn to the pub across the road. As he's helping Gwenno pack the equipment away, the young bearded guy, Carw, walks past. I think it's really important to convey my enjoyment, he won't take any money from tonight's appearance I'm sure, so a bit of encouragement will serve as my contribution to his musical career. I offer some words of praise and ask where I might find more of his music. He offers thanks and apologies for the pedal problems. He'll be gutted about this, not allowing him to perform properly but as I don't know his material, I suggest it didn't make any difference to my enjoyment. We talk a bit more and somehow the topic of Wrexham comes up; turns out he's a fan. He was brought up in north Powys and was taken along to The Racecourse as a lad. We had a 'keeper called Andy Marriott and Carw still has the replica of Andy's goalkeeper's shirt. He's now guaranteed my lifelong backing in everything he does, us Wrexhamites have to stick together!

There are further Wrexham-related revelations to follow. Rhys is from Mold, not far away and so is his label partner, Garmon. They're both fans as well. Now, we have two indie record labels in Cardiff and both run by Wrexham fans, I feel a fundraising festival coming on! Gwenno's keen, so is Owain/Carw, so that's two acts signed up at least.

It turns into a very good night. They're really friendly people, creative but grounded, just the type of people I most admire. Even amidst the usual football and music chat, there is quite a long discussion about Ched Evans, so clearly it's a subject that's caught the national consciousness.

Friday 14th November

I make my way down to breakfast a little gingerly after one of those 'goodness, is that the time!' sessions last night.

The good thing is I don't need to think. Today is a travel day. This is the planes and automobiles bit of my complicated itinerary. We're driving from Cardiff to Heathrow, then it's an afternoon flight to Brussels.

So, with my big bag squeezed into the back of Alex's estate car, it's pretty much at capacity. Wouldn't a transit van have been more appropriate I wonder. He had a van previously, it didn't handle well on snow and ice apparently. Somewhat ironically, he replaced it with a Passat which he then wrote off in a really scary-looking crash early one morning, *en route* to a job. From the pictures he showed me subsequently, he was really lucky to walk out uninjured, and a road sign didn't fare so well. There's a lot of driving in this job, often against deadlines, and often late at night or early in the morning when fatigue can be an issue. It's the bit I like least, which is why the train's been such a pleasant alternative this week. Still, I'm a mere passenger on this leg of the journey, so who am I to complain?

As an international jet-setter, Alex has his systems well worked out and after a straight-forward drive along the M4, he has arranged for a courier to meet us at the drop-off almost by the Terminal 5 doors. It's a great system. They take the car and park it, then return it once you let them know you've landed back in the UK. It's the little things that take away some of the stress of modern travel.

Actually, it's all pretty straight-forward. There's no queue at check-in. I get through the bag check without having to take off my shoes, always a result, and without activating the metal detector. Alex doesn't fare so well. He's put most of the camera gear in the hold but he's still got a rucksack full of wires and electrical bits and bobs that, not surprisingly, tends to invite the attention of the scanners. Sure enough, it's identified as one that needs scrutinising. Once they've established that he's not planning on blowing-up a plane, we head off for lunch.

The rest of the Sky team are travelling out today and tomorrow. Our production manager, Rachael, will be in Brussels before us, as will the sound man, Steve. Bill and Barry are both due out tomorrow, as is Sarah, the director. The match coverage will be provided by a unit based in Belgium so that's the extent of our travelling party, although Sports News have had a reporter and cameraman out in Brussels all week, covering things from the home perspective. Even though it's Wales, it's actually a regular occurrence for SSN to cover things in Belgium. The squad features a number of high-profile Premier League players and their FA offers lots of access to them through the week. They don't seem overly concerned with the fact that players get asked lots of questions about their club, but not very many about their country. The same guy gets sent to cover them ahead of each international, Gary Cotterill. We've been told he's due to fly back to the UK today as we fly in. Our first task on arrival will be to collect a piece of equipment called a Dejero from the hotel he's just left. It's a small box that somehow does the same job as a great big satellite truck. So, it'll mean we can feed our material back, and do live reports as well.

However, after a short flight to Brussels it seems things have changed. As soon as we touch down and phones get switched back on, Alex receives a call from somebody at 'sound' at Sky asking if we can hear everything okay for the 'live'. The fact that he's currently pushing a baggage trolley through arrivals means someone, somewhere, has got the wrong information. It also means that Gary clearly hasn't gone home yet so it appears we won't be collecting the Dejero after all, or not today at least. Alex calls back to base to find out what's happening, there's a degree of confusion but it appears Gary's decided to stay on for the game after all.

This is good news. I've been getting requests from the Belgian broadcasters, via Rachael, about whether we're going to be covering training sessions and media conferences tomorrow. I've now got an email in my inbox that tells me the times and location for these events have both changed. They were going to be in the morning, now they're late afternoon, and we have an interview lined up with Ashley Williams in the early evening. We're meeting him at the team hotel, just as we did last year, so we know already that we need to give ourselves an hour to drive there, as it's a fair way out of the city. Jim had requested an interview for the live show with either Vincent Kompany or Eden Hazard, but the former's injured and the latter's not being made available to the media.

The upshot of all this is that it helps everybody if Gary covers the Belgian stuff, and we'll stick with Wales. As Gary and his cameraman have the magic box, they'll now be doing those interviews with fans on the day of the game as well.

All this is relayed to Rachel after a fairly hairy drive from the airport to our city centre hotel. The satnav in our hire car, the appallingly-named Opel Mokka (a car that sounds like a frothy milk drink?) takes us down narrow, cobbled streets. Darkly-clad pedestrians keep leaping out from behind parked cars as if it's some form of Friday night pastime over here, and the Belgians behind wheels live down to their reputation as Europe's worst drivers. I kiss the tarmac when we finally arrive in one piece at the hotel. At one point Alex had to admonish me for letting out a high-pitched scream as two cars set off to make a left turn across our lane, despite being no more than 20 feet in front of us.

Anyway, we made it and after checking-in, we catch up with our advance party in the rather impressive atrium. It's got a section of the original Roman walls of Brussels as a feature, and fish swimming around in an adjoining pond. Dinner tonight maybe?

Despite the relative ease of the trip over, it's still been eight hours since we left Cardiff so a meal's certainly next on the list. Tomorrow night's venue has already been arranged by Bill Leslie, somewhere he ate whilst he was over here recently, covering Anderlecht v Arsenal; but tonight we're on our own. We're located near the real heart of the city, Le Grand Place, and that's where we head. It's a Friday night, and it's a location that's a magnet for all the visitors to Brussels, so the streets are thronged with people. We were only here a year ago but the first sight of Le Grand Place remains impressive. The Town Hall's a real eye-catcher, its central tower all lit up. A thousand tourists raise a thousand smart phones and take a thousand pictures.

There are loads of places to eat in the vicinity, too much choice really. So, rather than wander round looking in windows at menus, Rachael, our leader, sets two criteria, it has to be off the main square and it can't be somewhere that displays photos of their dishes in the window. This, apparently, is a bad thing. We discover a quiet looking restaurant somewhat bizarrely called Chutneys. It has a nice wooden interior and advertises moules on a chalkboard outside, no picture. We enter. It's *moules et frites* all round as it turns out, well, 'when in Belgium'.

After a decent meal, we head back towards Le Grand Place for a taste of more of what Brussels has to offer. On another adjoining street, we spy an interesting alley. A group of chaps are already turning into it. There appears to be at least one bar at the end of it, as it turns out, there are two. The one on the left is entered through what looks a bit like a green front door. In fact, the whole place looks a bit like someone's house. There's a guy sitting in the corner playing the guitar and singing as well, the strains of Erasure's 'A Little Respect' are reaching us through the clear glass windows. This proves the clincher. We squeeze in through the door. It's an L-shaped room, tiny really, and the bar is round the corner. There's another chalkboard behind the bar with a drawing of something that looks a bit like a four funnelled ship on it. The sharper members of our party, I don't include myself in this, work out that it's a beer tasting board, clever them. They're absolutely right. It's a wooden board holding four small glasses of different tasting Belgian beers. It's served with small lumps of cheese. Outstanding! As a bit of a beer fan, this looks like a great idea. Steve and I both opt for this option and we all retire to a table by the window facing onto the alley; almost on the knee of the singer. He runs through a fine repertoire of '80s and '90s pop hits, does requests, leads a chorus of Happy Birthday for a customer and stops for a chat in his break. It turns out this bearded crooner's picked up on everything we've been saying, he's from Sutton Coldfield.

His set finishes with him accompanying an old French-speaking guy in a couple of numbers that sound a bit like Charles Aznavour hits of the '60s. The old boy's got a proper crooner's voice as well, so it's a 'yes' from me. French songs, beer-tasting, cubes of cheese, wooden tables and chairs, it all adds up to a fantastic end to the evening. *Magnifique!*

Saturday 15ᵗʰ November

There is work to be done, but not until this evening, so a late breakfast's in order. The good news is that they do offer bananas at this Radisson, although they don't do Weetabix, so what I gain on the roundabout, I lose on the swings. Instead, interestingly, they offer a muesli/yogurt combination that's actually pretty good.

Talking of food, Rachael has designated Alex as provision provider for tomorrow's outside broadcast. The stadium's not well served by places to eat, so she's planning ahead and a picnic seems the best way to keep the workers happy. Before that though, he's offered Rachael and Steve a ride in the Opel Mokka, as they need to go to the ground to start the job of ensuring we'll be able to cover the game tomorrow. It's Rachael's first job of production managing an overseas football match, and she's keen to get everything sorted to her satisfaction. She's also fielding lots of enquiries from the UEFA delegates, some of which I can help with.

There's not a lot more I can do to help, so I go for a wander round the city centre whilst the rest of the team do their stuff. There are quite a few Wales fans around now. Flags are being hung outside bars around the edge of the Le Grand Place.

After a pleasant stroll, I've worked off the yogurt/muesli/banana combination and I'm ready for a bite of lunch. The problem is, I'm not entirely sure how to get back to the hotel. The geography of the centre's confused me this time, despite this being my second trip in a year. I have a solution – invite Alex for lunch. He suggests meeting in the Le Grand Place, which is just grand as I'm there already. He can come to me, I'll feed him, he can lead me back to the hotel – team work!

Again, there's a plethora of places to choose from but this time, with Rachael otherwise engaged, we opt for a venue displaying the menu in photo-form.

In the event, after days of meat-eating, we both crave something a little lighter, a little greener, so it's salads all round as we leave space for an evening meal that promises plenty. We wander back to the hotel with a little time to kill before we need to be on the road to the team hotel. Alex uses the time to get some nice shots of Brussels, and I go for a run in the hotel's little gym. The run coincides with kick-off back home and Wrexham are away at Braintree so I endeavour to check the score on my mobile phone, whilst listening to music and pounding away on the treadmill. This level of multi-tasking pretty much proves beyond me as I wobble dangerously at one point, a fraction away from flying off the machine. Wrexham are wobbling as well, going one down and, reports suggest, playing abysmally.

Things don't improve even after I've put some hard kilometres in. I emerge from the shower to find out they've lost to a side that hasn't won or scored a goal for 10 matches. This is not a good omen for tomorrow. There are quite a few Wrexham fans travelling straight over to Brussels from Braintree as well, theirs will not be a happy journey.

Our journey to the outskirts of Brussels and the team hotel is relatively satisfactory. We did the same thing on our last visit, and getting out of town on a weekday evening proved pretty tricky. It's a little less busy on the roads on a Saturday, but it's still a 40 minute drive that takes us well away from the bright lights and deep into the heart of a forest. The team hotel's almost cut into a clearing and its low, angular, modernist design gives it the look of the Baddie's base in a James Bond movie. It's a really strange place, but Wales came here last year and got a draw, so there's no way Chris Coleman was going to opt for anywhere else. Like last year, they've also given up the chance to go and train at the stadium this evening, they trained this morning in Cardiff instead.

The plan is this, they get in at 7pm, when we'll be set up and ready, they go and eat, we catch Ashley Williams just before the meal, get our interview done and sent back in time to make the restaurant booking at 9pm. The first bit goes okay, with a few glitches. We have a room to work in, sorted by the FAW in advance, but Alex doesn't like it, too bland and he wants to use the corridor outside instead. But there's a conference taking place in an adjoining room and the delegates return just after we've got set up. The quiet corridor's suddenly very noisy. Then the players start arriving and Bale, Ramsey, Collins and Gabbidon all head straight for the table tennis table that's been set up in the dining room. Table tennis has always been a big part of these international get-togethers, the ping-pong sound's something I've heard from behind closed doors so often down the years. The competitive streak in these professional athletes means there's often a lot of shouting, swearing and, from the sound of it, some big shots. It's certainly the smash that's put paid to plans to interview the skipper out here, much to the satisfaction of Pete, the FAW media man, we retreat back into the room they've arranged for us.

Still no sign of Ashley so whilst we're waiting, we're watching England v Slovenia on Alex's i-Phone. Incredibly, Slovenia go ahead! I pop my head round the door of the dining room and relay the news to the table tennis players. For me, as a Wales fan, this is good news. There's a long-standing rivalry, mostly from our side I guess, and England's occasional setbacks used to be the cause for much celebration over the border. I have to confess I was once part of a group of Wales fans standing on chairs in a bar in Cyprus, miming digging actions as we sang, '*I'm from Norway, yes I am, shovel snow all day long as we sing this happy little song. I'm from Norway, yes I am, shovel snow...*' over and over again. Why were we all doing this? Because England were on the TV and guess who they were losing to? It all seems a bit daft now, particularly as many England fans are as likely to mock their own team these days but, the memory lingers on. As a fan it does anyway. The players seem relatively uninterested, certainly no one punches the air when I relay the news, and then England equalise anyway and quickly score again, so I get back in my box.

There's other stuff going on anyway, really important stuff. IG's arrived by now, as has Ashley, but he's gone in to eat first, so plans of getting him done early are very much over. But that's not the only bit of bad news, Ashley's not wearing the right top. He should have a polo shirt with the sponsor's logo on both collars, he's wearing a v-neck top with no logo on at all. To compound matters, Chris Coleman's also supposed to be wearing something similar and he's travelled in an open necked white shirt under a v-neck sweater, it might be smart casual but you try telling that to the man from Vauxhall, who just happens to be in the hotel as well.

The FAW media team are in bits. The commercial guy's not here but they know how he'll react. As if all that wasn't bad enough, I have a chat with the guy I recognise as the former team chef. He's been brought back in for this game, at the instigation of some of the players it seems, but there have been problems. The hotel has, apparently, run out of pasta for an evening meal that's supposed to be all about the players 'carb-loading' so the main ingredient was supposed to be pasta! They've had to try and bring extra supplies in before the players drift away from the dining room. Alex and I speculate about potential skullduggery, probably instigated by a Blofeld-like figure from the Belgian FA, sitting in a swivel chair in a darkened room in this strange and slightly sinister location. 'Let's see how quickly this Bale can run without having had any pasta for tea. Mwwwwhahahahahaha!'

Actually, these are the moments when it does really feel like being part of the whole set-up. They're suffering the same miniscule little setbacks that often affect our days, to anyone outside they seem utterly insignificant, but when it's your job, it seems calamitous. There's not a lot to be done but have a laugh about it, 'blitz spirit' and all that. I suggest that I'll be calling into Sky Sports News with this 'pasta news exclusive', and that it'll shortly be appearing on the yellow ticker that runs across the bottom of the screen when there's big, breaking news. When Ashley then shows up, still in the wrong shirt, we speculate as to whether the sponsors will demand the return of his Nova?

As we both get settled into our swivel chairs in our rather dull-looking room, I do suggest that as we've got a table booked in what's reported to be a very nice restaurant in the middle of Brussels in an hour, this interview might not get much further than 'Hi Ashley, how are you feeling?' I'm joking of course, and we hit the two and a half minute mark before I wrap things up. The truth is that the interview needs to be relatively short, because we're going to be sending it back via broadband from the hotel and the longer it is, the longer it will take. Once the process is started, it'll be about 45 minutes before the people at Sports News actually receive it for broadcast.

Job done, we head for the car and our hotel. On the way out, I bump into Chris Coleman and confirm our hopes of interviewing him pre-match, usual arrangement, straight off the team bus. He's in a good mood, the media conference has been brief, he reckons when there are no injuries and things are going well, he doesn't get as many questions.

We're back at base in time to meet the rest of our team, now including the director Sarah and commentator Bill, who are waiting for us in the lobby. Alex heads off to his room to organise the transfer of material from us to them and I join the group heading out into Brussels. Alex will hopefully catch up with us shortly.

The restaurant's no more than five minutes walk from the hotel, through one of the fabulously ornate 'galleries' that have survived so spectacularly in the city centre. They're full of chocolate shops, naturally, but also a glove shop, a milliner's, a pipe shop, businesses that hark back to a different era, before every city centre came to look the same.

The restaurant has the same look and feel of a place that belongs to a bygone era. The red, neon sign over the wooden panelled frontage says *Vincent*. Through the big glass window we can see it all. Bench tables, waiters, chefs and a lot of customers. We enter and join a queue that actually intersects two areas of the kitchen so we stand in the midst of all the cooking, it's amazing! Chefs pass dishes for serving between us as we wait to be seated. Around us, the walls are decorated with fabulous tile murals that look like they've been there since this place opened in 1905.

The whole atmosphere is enhanced by our *Maitre d'* who is bald but makes up for it with an elegantly trimmed goatee beard, he looks a little like Ming The Merciless but he's all smiles and civility as he shows us to our table, then returns to take our order. A text message from Alex arrives to say he's on his way and what he wants to eat and drink so by the time he arrives, his meal is just about to be served. It's a relatively basic fish and meat menu but the food, as we soon discover, is fantastic. We wash down our steaks with a fine tasting house red and it's all brilliant. It stands as such a contrast to the places we've eaten in Cardiff in the days prior to this. They've been 'chain' restaurants, okay, in their own way but completely lacking what makes this such a good night. There's the quality of the food, the service and the atmosphere and authenticity, created by 109 years of serving food to people on a Saturday night.

We congratulate Bill on his choice and then head off into the evening. The mood's good in the group, everyone's getting on and there's no real desire to call it a day just yet. The same little bar we stumbled upon last night is next on the agenda. It's much busier this evening, there are Wales fans everywhere now and for a while we stand before a table becomes available. There's no beer tasters or cheese tonight, which is a bit of a disappointment but our man from Sutton Coldfield's on again, and he's been joined by a pal who's beating out a backing rhythm on an old wooden box. The fact that he's playing songs people can join in with seems to stir a desire amidst some in our party. The dread word 'karaoke' gets mentioned, then seized upon. Someone spotted a bar just round the corner from this one the previous evening. Steve the soundman has now called it a day so I'm the only non-karaoke fan in the group that remains. It's a democracy and I'm a team-player, so we leave this fine, traditional bar with its excellent range of Belgian beers, my idea of Heaven, for something completely different, my idea of Hell.

There's a neon light flashing on and off in the window shouting 'Karaoke' but inside, it seems to be host to a largely Korean or Vietnamese clientele, a few of whom are dancing on a small stage to Belgian techno. This is not promising and I'm all set for a swift departure and a relatively early night when 'Team Sky' switches into overdrive. These guys have come to do karaoke and, by God, they're going to do karaoke! The bored looking owner's accosted, a dusty old song book's produced from under the bar and the techno dancers retreat as a karaoke tsunami washes over them. Rachael's first up, pushing through the small crowd in front of the stage as she hears the first bars of the Amy Winehouse number, 'They tried to make me go to rehab..'. "This is my choice!" shouts Rachael as she grabs the mic off the bar. And that's the start of it. For the next hour, my colleagues flick though this vast songbook, searching for things they can sing. Others have emerged from the shadows or been drawn in from the streets. It turns out at least one guy's from Wrexham, he recognises me and it turns out I knew his dad. I suspect for the first time in a long time, this karaoke bar is doing what it was meant to be doing when an ambitious young chap first hung the sign in the window. The singing's pretty poor, my colleagues will be dismayed at my saying that, but what they lack in musicality, they more than make up for in enthusiasm. Even quiet Sarah, who deflects early promptings to do a song on her own is swept along and by the end she's throwing her head back, her arms in the air and giving it all she's got. It's almost bizarre what's come over them all, maybe it's a generational thing? I'm the oldest in our party and I'm the one sipping on a bog standard Euro lager at a table in the corner whilst they throw themselves into another MOR pop hit. At one point, Alex brings the mic over to where I'm sitting, it's ruddy Bohemian Rhapsody that they're murdering now. He points the mic towards me, "Go on, join in!" he commands, my answer, broadcast through the sound system for all to hear, is short and to the point and definitely not what it says on the overhead TV screen.

Thankfully, Bohemian Rhapsody seems to involve pretty much everyone in the room, bar me, and it's the sort of big group number a showstopper should finish with. At last, my elated but somewhat hoarse companions agree it's time to face the final curtain.

Sunday November 16th

They're a little gruff still as we meet for breakfast on the day of the match, MD4. Over yogurt/muesli, croissants and coffee we arrange departure times, finalise plans and flag up any issues we might encounter later. It feels like a pre-production meeting, the type we'd normally have in the catering bus on a domestic OB. My biggest concern currently is my mobile phone which has run flat and I've left the charger lead in Cardiff. Rachael comes to the rescue. She carries a spare, now that's what I call crisis management!

This game kicks off at 6pm local time, so we work our timings out by counting back from that. The programme goes on air 30 minutes earlier, so I'll be aiming to be at the stadium around three hours prior to that. It's reassuring to be on site well in advance, for me and the producer. There is no worse feeling than getting delayed on the way to a game when you're up against the clock. I've had it a couple of times in the past, I once ended up running the final mile to Brunton Park in Carlisle as the car ground to a halt in traffic on the approach to the ground, with the referee about to conduct a pitch inspection. Many years ago, I actually missed the kick-off in a Leeds United game at Anfield that I was meant to be commentating on for the radio. I still break into a cold sweat at the recollection of those and other similar incidents.

Rachael confirms a request from Sky Sports News for a live chat between me and Barry from the pitchside at 4pm local time, so Alex agrees to bring me, Barry and Bill in for 3.30. That sorted, we've all got a couple of hours to ourselves so, for me, it's a chance for another stroll into the centre. Normally, Alex and I would be looking to nip out and find some fans to interview but Gary's on the case with that, still, old habits die hard, so I go out to 'gauge the mood'.

I see the first couple of Wales fans a few yards from the front door of the hotel, as I turn right then left. I pass Vincent and the Emperor Ming's there, back at work already. The weather's been really mild for the last couple of days and many of the brunch seekers are sitting outside the bars and cafés, as are many of the Wales fans, already cradling the first beer of the day, probably no more than a handful of hours after the last one.

After a few metres, I spy a familiar face, a Wrexham and Wales fan I bump into on pretty much every one of these trips; Kevin, an ex-army lad. I stop for a chat with him and his mates. In their midst, on the table, is a handwritten cardboard sign that says 'Wales fans in need of tickets'. They aren't the only ones. The FAW received 2,400 tickets but there were twice as many applications. There's been a clamour for tickets for the first time in many years. It's the first time I've had people asking if I can get them tickets since I started covering Wales. I know the players have experienced it as well, and they've actually submitted a request for a bigger allocation of comps such was the level of demand. Things probably haven't been helped by the fact that the lucky ticket applicants were only informed a week or so ago, so many people had already booked travel and accommodation in the hope they'd be successful. Many of them will have travelled anyway, up to two thousand by some estimates. The reality is, the game's a sell-out, so many of these guys will be watching the game on a TV in a bar somewhere close to the Le Grand Place tonight. Still, there are worse places to spend a weekend watching football.

As we're chatting, some of the karaoke crowd from last night roll up. It's a very small world, 'Wales Away'. There's the guy who's dad I knew and spoke to last night. He's with another guy who wasn't there last night but who is from Llangollen, where my mum and dad live. Last time I met him was on a trip back home to see them. He greets me as the 'karaoke king' so obviously word's got about, and that's really why I wasn't keen on getting involved last night. The fact is, I get up and sing, a few people film it on their phones, within minutes it's been put up on Facebook or YouTube and some people will laugh at my pathetic attempts and others will say 'what's that idiot up to the night before a game?' I'm a mere nobody in the great celeb scheme of things, so what it must be like for someone like Gareth Bale, I dread to think. He will have that sensation of being filmed almost every time he steps out in public. I've seen it develop as trend over the years. I was once standing next to Ryan Giggs at the luggage carousel on the way back from a game and from a few feet away a father with his family just started filming Ryan, standing, waiting for his bag to appear. What do they do with that footage? 'Here we all are by the swimming pool, oh and here's Ryan Giggs at the airport waiting for his bag.'

Don't get me wrong, if you want to earn a living from a job that puts you in the public eye, you have to be prepared to accept that there's going to be greater scrutiny and adapt accordingly. I'm actually really lucky, I occasionally enjoy a little bit of the limelight, but I actually live a supremely ordinary life: supermarket, pub, Sunday league and gigs. Ordinary is what I like. It's easy for me because not many people know who I am. I've been in that situation of a guy saying to his girlfriend, "Can you take a pic of me and Bryn?", and her saying to me, "I'm not being funny, but who are you?" That makes me chuckle but it's a fair question.

I'm amongst friends here. Lads from my patch, following Wales with a beer in their hand, something I used to do, and will do again when I'm not working on covering the games. These trips are usually all about the beer. Wales fans tend to travel with no or very low expectations for the game, determined to have a good time despite that. Occasionally, optimism burns brightly but briefly, although I have to report that more than a few flames of optimism are being spotted on this trip. Just over a year ago, I stood talking to fans on match day in this same city and they were almost universal in predicting a heavy defeat for a Wales team missing countless key players, and up against a side who'd be well-backed to actually win the World Cup.

In the event, a late Ramsey equaliser secured an unexpected point to give an upbeat end to another disappointing qualifying campaign and, maybe, to give a hint of better times to come. Certainly, talking to the fans this morning, they seem to be setting expectation levels at a point at least! This despite the fact that Belgium are ranked the fourth best side in the world, that they've never lost a qualifier with Marc Wilmots in charge, and that even if they didn't win it, they got to the last eight of the summer's World Cup finals. In the face of all this exuberance, I maintain pessimism as my default setting, I'll leave such crazy talk to the young fellers who haven't experienced quite as many crushing disappointments when watching Wales. Besides, they've had a drink and I haven't.

These trips are generally more about the tales that can be told on future long winter evenings, like my pal from Llangollen who'd had his pocket picked just after I'd waved to him from our alleyway bar the night before, losing all his cards and over €100 in cash. I'd be utterly distraught, he seems philosophical. His experience prompts other tales of pick-pocketing from previous Wales trips, everybody laughing along at the recollection of incidents that would ruin many a family holiday.

I leave the lads to their stories and head back to the hotel. It's good to experience a relaxed, friendly atmosphere. There have been problems with Wales trips here in the past but that was a long time ago, in the 1990s. Wrexham and Cardiff fans had a big set-to just off the ferry in '91, with lots of fans immediately sent straight back to the UK. Less than a year later, Wales were back in Belgium and I travelled over with friends and saw Cardiff lads hunting for Wrexham supporters to fight. The day after the game, I bumped into some Cardiff lads I'd met on a previous Wales trip, one of them was pretty smashed up, apparently he'd been punched by another Cardiff fan! The atmosphere on the ferry back was pretty edgy as fans from north and south Wales mixed uneasily. The relationship's much better now, I think even Swansea fans are beginning to travel to support the national side again after years of being threatened and even ambushed by fans of their arch-rivals from the capital. The Football Supporters Federation have put a lot of effort into asking fans to forego club colours on these trips and to 'Wear Red For Wales'. I certainly see plenty of red and lots of Welsh dragons on my way back to the hotel.

There's about an hour left before our scheduled departure time, so I get in touch with Barry. This might be our last chance to get some food until after the game. There's no guarantee that there'll be much on offer at the stadium so it might be now or never! I've spotted a fantastic looking café very close to the hotel, *La Morte Subite*. It's Sunday lunchtime busy, but we find a table and peruse the menu. There's not an awful lot on it, and, disappointingly, they don't do *frites*, so we go to work on a *Croque Monsieur*, or a ham and cheese toastie if you prefer?

Before we can set off, I have to nip upstairs to get my game gear on and to collect my manbag. This is an important part of the kit, it's the same bag I took to Andorra although not the same bag I used for the two home games. However, this is now the designated 'away' bag. In the bag, there is a small pack of chewing gum. It's the pack Dai the Kitman gave me before the Bosnia game. I also have to pin a small UEFA Euro 2016 badge on my lapel. It was given to me before the Bosnia game so it's now on the list of designated charms and trinkets. Alex is wearing his lucky socks as well. Yes, it's all getting very silly, but, as we've seen, Chris Coleman started it.

It's a 20 minute drive to the stadium and we have a parking space in the OB compound, so I'm in position at the edge of the pitch with plenty of time to spare before we're due on live. Which is a good job as it turns out because word filters through from the Belgian broadcasters that the Wales team bus is almost at the ground. That's a problem because the camera that's been designated to film me and Barry chatting is the same one that's meant to be in position for the players arriving. All this means a swift change of plan and the interview has to be recorded as quickly as possible. We talk about the likely formation, the possibility that the manager will again start with three central defenders as against Bosnia and we discuss the strength of the opposition. Luckily, we get it right first time and as soon as it's done, I follow the guys round to our interview position next to the away dressing room. This is a distinct improvement on last year's arrangements when all interviews were done outside by the side of the pitch. This became particularly problematic after the game as the Belgians were celebrating qualification with a firework display and very loud techno music, far from ideal! It's the UEFA involvement that ensures we have somewhere inside to use as a broadcast position so, for all the extra bureaucracy, there is a benefit.

As it turns out, the predictions of Wales' imminent arrival prove a little hasty, it's 10 minutes or so before the coach glides in through the gates and Chris Coleman emerges, almost smacking his head on the wing mirror. The fact that he ducks in time may be taken as a good sign, given that a few minutes before, DtK (Dai The Kitman) has shown me photos of the van he's brought over to Brussels with all the kit in it. It suffered a blow-out on the way to the stadium earlier, a hair-raising experience by all accounts. Still, he's safe and so is the kit, that new yellow and red number. Prior to the team arrival, I've also been given a glimpse of the team, even though it's not officially been confirmed yet. It turns out Wales will be starting with four across the back, the one surprise perhaps is that David Cotterill keeps his place on the left wing.

This information's vital, because I'm expecting Chris at the interview position any time now and the team selection will be the primary focus of the pre-match interview.

Chris explains the reasoning behind the decision to go with four defenders - he expects Belgium to start with just one striker, he doesn't want to tie up three players watching one man. The back line, Taylor/Williams/Chester and Gunter, is also one I think he feels he can rely on. The two in the middle seem to be forming a good partnership, the two out wide have been amongst his most loyal servants. There are other good defenders on the bench, Dummett and Collins have been playing well for their clubs recently and both in the Premier League, unlike Chris Gunter. Ben Davies has also never let anyone down even though he's not getting regular games for Spurs. What has to be said is that it's a long time since a Wales manager has had so much strength in depth in the defensive positions.

With the interview done, I'm clear until kick-off so now the nerves start to kick in. Or maybe it's hunger? I head up to the media room. I push open the door and it's like entering a speakeasy; a room packed with people, sitting or standing, chatting, looking at laptops, eating and drinking. There's a table at the far end of the room with platters of food laid out on it. It's interesting looking stuff. There are shrimps, mozzarella balls, cold meats, a veritable smorgasbord! Barry Horne's ahead of me, piling his plate up, obviously the *Croque Monsieur* didn't quite hit the mark! There's also a big fridge loaded with bottles of water and cans of beer, ever the professional, I chose the former. Barry remarks that we'll come back for the latter once the night's work is done.

As I look for a seat, I spy a familiar face in the crowd, actually I spot the hairstyle first. It's that blonde bombshell, Robbie Savage. He's obviously working for the BBC this evening, BBC 5 Live I'm guessing. He's from Wrexham, so we always have a chat. When he was playing for Wales and I started covering the national side, he used to rip into me whenever I saw him for apparently being very friendly with John Toshack. Robbie didn't really get on with Tosh and he didn't wait long before calling time on his international career in a row over fried bananas.

Robbie's loved and loathed in equal measures. It was that way through his playing career and nothing much has changed now he's become a regular broadcaster and sometime ballroom dancer. In terms of his punditry, he tends towards a habit of making definitive statements, 'x will definitely go down', only for 'x' to then improve and Robbie to completely change his position. Some people have a perception of him as being a 'big-time Charlie', the hair, the Armani tattoo and the controversial playing career haven't helped, but, in his defence, I once hosted a Q&A session with him in the backroom of the Lager Club in Wrexham, in aid of the Supporters Trust. Robbie was down-to-earth, self-deprecating and entertaining. It was a great afternoon. People from Wrexham don't have a high 'idiot' threshold, Robbie didn't try and be anything other than one of them and everyone in that room appreciated his efforts.

Robbie can't lob too many verbal grenades my way anymore given that he's a media lackey like me these days. In fact, as I point out, he seems never to be off my TV or radio. For once in our jousting, I'm on the front foot, so Robbie changes tack. Have I heard the team news yet? He's standing next to another sparring partner of his from the old days, Ian Gwyn Hughes, but IG claims not to know the starting XI. I do know but I'll go no further than hint at a start for Cotterill, rumours are already circulating along those lines anyway.

The food's great as it turns out and I have to battle the temptation to go back for more. Instead, an hour before kick-off, I'm going back down to my pitchside position to watch the stadium filling up and to begin the mental countdown. Along the edge of the pitch, facing the stands, huge speakers are pumping out techno 'tunes'. The stands themselves are still relatively empty, but there's one guy in the Belgian section by the tunnel smoking a cigarette! It wouldn't be allowed in the UK, I'm surprised it's allowed here. Was there not some EU directive formulated just down the road? The sight's in keeping with the surroundings to be honest. The stadium will look okay when it's full but when it's empty you can see just how dilapidated it is. The scene of a dreadful stadium disaster in 1985, the name's been changed, seats have been added but it still looks like a ground Belgium should have left behind a long time since.

To reinforce that view, I spot Wayne, the stadium manager from the Cardiff City Stadium, looking towards the visitors section. He's over here as part of the FAW delegation. I learn from others that he's not happy with the seating. The fans will inevitably stand up, the rows are very close together and he fears that if Wales score, people could tumble forward dangerously. I suspect it's a risk most of the travellers would be willing to take, especially at 0-0 in the 89th minute.

The flags are going up now, many familiar ones from previous trips: Merthyr; Corwen; Rhos-on-Sea; Rhosneigr and Bagillt. The early birds get to drape them over barriers, claiming the best places, the late arrivals have them laid out on the running track. Many years ago, my group of mates used to travel with a huge Welsh dragon flag, that one of our number 'acquired' from a flagpole outside the old Air Products plant in Acrefair. It was to be used on my first away trip to Nuremberg so my pal, Ceri, something of a design whizz, was given the task of spraying the name of our local pub on it. He created a fabulous stencil, laid it out over the flag on the patio at the back of his parents' house and did an excellent job of spray painting the letters on. We were thrilled with his work, his parents though, weren't quite so impressed. When he lifted the flag up, a lot of the spray paint had soaked through the flag material and onto their paving slabs. I wonder if it still says 'Duke Ruabon on Tour' at the back of their house?

We're getting to the time now where I start having to keep my mind occupied and my jaws as well. I'm back by the dressing room when Dai comes over, "have you got any chewing gum?" he asks. I tell him I have but it's his and I'm supposed to be using it for good luck. He started all this off by chucking me the piece of gum just before Gareth's winner in Andorra, so he reckons it'll be fine if I give it to him and he then gives me a piece. So, he now takes control of the gum. There is a bigger issue for Israel, there's only one piece left, but we'll cross that bridge after we've chewed our way through this evening.

As the start draws ever nearer, I watch the players line-up in the tunnel, then they disappear from view as they turn the corner to climb the steps that lead to the pitch. My match position's a belter, just to the right of the overspill seats being used by Dai and the rest of the matchday staff. Just before I sit down, the masseur, Chris comes over and asks if they can use our monitor to assess any injuries suffered by Wales players? I say I've no problem with it, but UEFA might not approve. They don't like people sitting in the dug-outs being able to see what the viewers at home can see. I guess in case it puts pressure on the officials when they get a decision wrong? Given how many officials there now are, you'd hope getting things wrong shouldn't be a big issue anymore.

The Welsh staff on the touchline and the team on the pitch link arms for the anthem, the travelling fans struggle to keep up with the version being played over the PA but they hit the '*Gwlad! Gwlad!*' in typically rousing fashion. Obviously, the home crowd roar out their own number, then we all settle back into our seats for 90 more tortuous minutes on the road to France.

Now the torment really begins. I'm straight into clockwatching mode, counting down each five minute period again, trying to only glance when I think at least another 300 seconds have elapsed. I know I've started earlier than ever but I'd take this score now so, frankly, the ref can blow that final whistle as soon as he wants.

In fact, Wales start relatively well, Gareth Bale hits a free kick pretty sweetly but Courtois reacts well and beats it away. The Wales bench are up and out of their seats. Then Belgium begin to take control and I begin to chew ever more furiously. Hennessey makes a great save with his legs from Chadli, but then can only watch helplessly as a fantastic shot from Lombaerts whizzes past his fingers before crashing off the inside of the post. It rebounds out into the path of the sliding Origi but he can only touch it past the other post. It's 'heart in mouth' time. Around all this, Eden Hazard's dancing round Welsh players for fun. I mutter my admiration from time to time, it's a masterclass in close control football, a joy to watch, for the neutral, but he just can't find the final pass or shot to inflict real damage. Still Wales hold it together. Collectively, they're working really hard at maintaining their shape and Joe Allen's performing heroically in front of the back four. Gradually, the storm is weathered and by half-time, I still haven't chucked my chewing gum away. This is, as we know, a very good sign.

Back by the dressing room. I bump into Mark Evans. He looks ahead to our 'pacing up and down until the final whistle session', I suggest that if we're still in the mood for pacing five minutes from time, I'll be more than happy. As I head back to my seat, I miss news of a change, and so it's a surprise to see George Williams being sent on as the two teams line-up for the resumption. He's replacing David Cotterill. There was no obvious sign of an injury, so I check with one of the backroom boys briefly before I sit down, "tactical?" is all I need to say, I get a nod in response. There is an argument for saying Belgium need more to think about defensively, Williams' pace might just provide that.

At times in the first half, Wales were on the rack. The second half begins differently. Sure enough, young George sets off on a run. He takes on and beats a defender, almost creates an opening for Bale. Then he switches wings and does it again. Suddenly, Wales have the hosts looking a little nervous. They probably don't know much about this blonde haired teenager from Milton Keynes, none of us did until his first senior appearance in a friendly in Amsterdam five months ago.

Behind him Joe Allen's still working tirelessly to break up Belgian attacks before they reach the backline, harrying the huge figure of Marouane Fellaini constantly, until Fellaini tries to wipe him out with a straight arm that connects with Joe's head. He crumples, then gets treatment, then lifts himself up, blood visible on his face, and launches himself into another tackle. It's heroic stuff.

There's one 'what if' moment as well. Bale and Williams combine down the left. Bale sets off on a run towards goal. He strikes the ball from the edge of the area, beyond the dive of Courtois and for a millisecond it looks like this might be it, then it whistles a couple of inches wide of the far post. Dai turns to me for confirmation of the proximity, with hands outstretched like an angler, I gesture back with a thumb and forefinger, like 'the one that got away'.

Suddenly, a strange feeling comes over me. It's unrecognisable at first, then I realise what it is; it's confidence! I'm starting to feel confident that Wales can do this. The back four have been brilliant. The midfield's working tirelessly and whilst we still don't have a striker, Williams, Robson-Kanu and Bale are all trying to carry the ball forward whenever they can. Belgium throw on a couple of big guys to try and make a change. But their switch to something more direct is meat and drink to our two central defenders, Williams and Chester, who have barely missed a header all night. The home crowd quietens as the away fans raise the volume. Then another Wales chance as Robson-Kanu's shot from the edge of the box forces another save from Courtois.

Operation Clockwatch tells me it's almost time to head to my interview position. I have to ask the question of the producer, via Sarah, "Assuming it stays like it is, who does Jim want?" Bale and Ashley Williams comes the reply. You'll note I prefaced the question with 'assuming', I'm not about to get caught out by being overly optimistic, even at this late stage, in fact especially not at this late stage. I've been back in the tunnel to see Wales concede too many times to fall into that trap. Anyway, there's a while to go still, even when the clock hits 90. George Williams has clashed heads with Mertens who stays down, pole-axed. It's a bad one. As he gets treatment, I head to the tunnel and Gareth Bale goes round his teammates imploring them to keep concentrating.

The game resumes but now I'm watching on the monitor. The fourth official's board's all-important to my mental state now. It goes up, six added minutes, ahhhhhhh!! The home crowd's roused from its torpor. This will not be considered anything like a good result for Belgium. They suddenly liven up and start probing down the wings. Wales have just about everybody back but one ball finds its way through a gap in the yellow wall, only for James Chester to stab it away before it gets to a Belgian. Still the clock ticks down, I pace ever more furiously, bound like a dog chained to a pole by the headset cables that keep me from straying too far. Another ball comes into the box, another clearance, but this time at the cost of a corner. We are now in that 96th minute. The corner comes over, the ball pings around, Hennessey makes a diving block on the line, the ball comes back again, another block on the line, this time it's Bale on the near post. The world's most expensive footballer stopping a certain goal in the final few seconds! The ball gets whacked up the pitch, the clock ticks past six minutes but still we play on, this is pure torture. God knows what sight I'm presenting to the UEFA officials who rather timidly ask for my post-match interview requests. I add Eden Hazard to my list, they make a note on their clipboard, as I turn back to the match. Finally, the whistle goes to the referee's mouth, and the agony is replaced by ecstasy. I keep it together, bar a little 'Yes!' and a clenched fist. Just about.

I happily toss the chewing gum out, for the fourth time, as I await the arrival of the yellow heroes. Understandably, commendably, the players stay out on the pitch for a while, throwing their shirts into the midst of the delirious Welsh hordes. I can see some of this on the monitor. At moments like this, I wish I was out there amongst them to be honest, the only time I ever got to celebrate a big away result as a fan was in Helsinki in 2002, a 2-0 win in the first game in the campaign and what a trip that was. No leaping around for me, there's work to be done.

Ashley Williams arrives first, shirtless, IG tries to corral Gareth Bale to the interview position but he nips into the dressing room to get a drink, so I stand and chat with Ashley. He blows his cheeks out, shakes his head, "Man, I am knackered!" he exclaims, "That was so hard ... had to stay switched on all night ... couldn't let them go." He then stopped and asked "What are we waiting for?" "Gareth", I reply. "Fair enough. I don't mind waiting for him", Ashley responds, with a smile. But Gareth doesn't come. In fact, IG appears and beckons Ashley over, "The manager wants a word with everyone first", he explains. I wanted two, I had one, now I've got no players to interview. In my headphones, I can hear the guys in the studio already analysing the game. Jim will be wanting something very soon.

Ashley reappears, still shirtless. Still, no Gareth. Just as I'm about to start without him, he appears, with a grin. Then we get on with it. Interviews in these circumstances are a real pleasure. I'm feeling elated, so are the players, everybody's so happy. I remember interviewing Gary Speed after Wales had beaten Norway 4-0 in a friendly when things really seemed to be clicking into place. We both sensed there were good times ahead and a mate of mine rang me the following day to say it sounded like we were both about to burst out laughing at the wonder of it all as we stood there in the tunnel. That was the last post-match interview I ever did with Gary.

After the two boys have done a turn, people appear at my interview position with startling rapidity. Next it's Joe Ledley, then Aaron Ramsey and then Chris Coleman, with a smile as broad as the River Taff. I'm told in my headphones that I can take as long as I need with Chris. This is great, the chance to let the interview breathe a bit. Chris deserves that chance as well, he's taken a lot of stick in the two years he's been doing this job; we waited an hour for him to compose himself before we could do the interview after that 6-1 humiliation in Serbia

18 months ago. That was difficult for both of us. This is much better. He praises the players, but also acknowledges the deficiencies in the performance. It's a mature response, it says 'yes we've done very well but I still think we can do better', and it reflects his confidence in the group he's working with, that he feels they can still improve.

Our UEFA man tells me Hazard's said he doesn't want to do anything in English, so Jan Vertonghen appears instead. That's fine, impeccable English and plays for a Premier League club. I get the Belgian version from him, they're disappointed but don't see it as a disaster. There's a lot of games to go yet in this group. That's six interviews rattled off and the message comes through from base that they've got enough, thanks. We're done. And relax.

Actually, the adrenaline's still very much pumping as I find Alex outside. We follow our 'post-draw in Brussels' tradition (Est'd: 2013) and go for chips with mayonnaise. This almost takes the wind out of our sails as it involves a very complex process of buying tokens from one caravan before swapping them for chips at the next caravan, ultimately even the exorbitant cost of €5.50 a tray doesn't take the smile from our faces. Things get even better when we return to the OB compound to find Bill and Barry and some cans of beer they've 'sourced', as promised, from the media room fridge. We toast the result and each other, and the chips and mayo get passed around.

The early kick-off time means the city centre's still busy by the time we get back to the hotel. It's a quick turnaround, up to the room, get changed, straight out. This time, Barry Horne's in the hotseat when it comes to venue selection. Somewhere called Drug Opera's his choice, causing a few raised eyebrows amongst the rest of the team. As it turns out it's another fine looking old building, with a striking façade, on a the corner of a busy square. Brussels may have no shortage of good places to eat and drink, but finding a cashpoint's more of a problem. I know of one, relatively close, so I lead a splinter party in that direction. It's one of those indoor ones, inside, through the glass door, we can see a dishevelled looking bloke lying, as if dead, across the doorway. As we approach, he revives, reaches up an arm and opens the door for us, before slumping back to the ground again. I watch him perform this same action as others attempt to gain entry. Twenty years as a doorman at the Ritz before the drink took its toll maybe?

With cash in our pockets and a spring in our stride, we join the rest of the party in Drug Opera for the debrief. Point one for discussion is the match, point two is the result from Israel v Bosnia, an injury-stricken Bosnian team has been beaten 3-0 in Haifa. That puts Israel on top of the group, played three, won three. It means Bosnia, top seeds, have just two points from four games and it means Wales' game in Haifa next March is massive.

It's another enjoyable evening, good company and food and after we've eaten, I finally get my choice. There's a famous pub nearby called *Delirium Café*, it's reputed to stock 3,000 beers. I suspect some Welsh fans will have got close to sampling all of them by now but, over two trips, I've not had the chance to get there and sample even their own famous brew, Delirium Tremens, so tonight's very much the night!

It's down another alley but it's easily located as hordes of fans are outside, inside, upstairs and downstairs. Their songs echo off the alley walls as we approach, with a degree of trepidation it has to be said. This is a proper beer drinker's paradise. Running the length of a long bar, there's a brass pipe, coming off it are dozens of beer taps, each a different brew, their names scrawled on the chalk boards above the bar. I scan the lists, there's a Christmas beer, 12%, I've never seen anything nearly so strong before. I'll have one of those please. We're celebrating.

The rest of the party order and we retreat to a table near the door. There's a fair degree of mayhem going on around us, but it's all good-natured. There are Belgian fans mixing with Wales fans and, let's be honest, a lot of these guys and girls will have been drinking since at least lunchtime, so a bit of boisterousness is to be expected. This is how I remember it from my days as a young man following Wales around Europe, great adventures. As my companions decide it's time for bed, I hang on to savour it all a little longer. Actually, the bar closes shortly afterwards, and everyone's forced out onto the street. There begins a plaintive chant that goes on and on and on, nicked from Newcastle apparently, but it fits this scenario brilliantly, '*Don't take me home, please don't take me home, I just don't want to go to work. I wanna stay here, drinking all their beer so please don't, please don't take me home.*' I can't help myself, I join the throng and finally, gloriously, I find my voice and start to sing.

126

Monday November 17th

A journey that started with a train ends with a train. I'm booked onto the Eurostar back to St Pancras, then across the road to King's Cross and home.

I've never done Eurostar before so I'm excited at the prospect, even more so when our tickets allow access to the lounge, with free drinks, nibbles and newspapers. My travelling companion is Steve, the sound recordist. He's a really nice guy who was great company on Friday but has been a bit more subdued since. The reason, he explains in the cab from the hotel to the station, is that his mother became very ill on Saturday, she passed away last night, he actually took the call whilst we were having our meal. It's very sad news and a great measure of the man that he slipped off quietly and left us to our evening out. It's one of the great worries with working away that something like this happens. The only home game I've missed since Sky have been covering Wales was when my father-in-law fell seriously ill a couple of years ago. My producer was brilliant, told me to go home immediately, which I did and luckily he pulled through.

It's a downbeat end to an upbeat trip, as good as I've ever had with Wales. Four games gone and we're still in contention. I've started these diaries so many times before then given up when it's all fallen apart after two games. Four games in, I'm still writing!

5

"We fear no one now"
Israel v Wales

'You're just too good to be true, I can't take my eyes off you'

Tuesday March 24th 2015

A new year brings a new adventure with a trip to Israel, a country well beyond Europe's borders, despite their involvement in the European Championships. The planning for this trip has been more complicated than any other I've been on before. The fact it's Israel, a state almost constantly at war with one or more of its neighbours, means extra input from the production manager assigned to the game. He's got to ensure a safe trip for all those travelling over, so flights, transfers and hotels have been booked well in advance, before even the FAW confirmed its plans, and we're going to be in the same hotel as the players.

Despite the travel department's best efforts, I've managed to create a little extra work just when it seemed they had their plan in place. The return trip is scheduled for Sunday 29th, the same day that Wrexham will be playing North Ferriby in the FA Trophy final at Wembley. I saw the possibility of this looming after the club won a delayed quarter-final replay at Gateshead. Our scheduled return flight of 10am wouldn't get us in to Heathrow until 1.25 and it's a 1.30 kick-off. A check on the BA website showed an earlier flight, so I asked for a switch for me and Barry, just in case.

When others amongst the travelling party heard of the chance of an earlier return, they also asked to be moved. This in turn meant a night in a hotel in Haifa after the game has now changed, to a night in a hotel near the airport in Tel Aviv. I can't imagine I'm overly popular with the travel people presently, but they've done a great job in changing things around and Wrexham won the semi-final so that's worked out well.

Packing's been far from straightforward as well. I'm doing three capitals in three days, it's cold in two of them and warm in the other and I want to be off the plane as quickly as possible on my return so I don't want to check in any baggage. I need to be able to travel light whilst factoring in that my Wembley seat is in the Royal Box, with a strict dress code, so I need to be suited and booted. In truth, I've been wrestling with all this for about a fortnight. I've bought a new bag, mid-size for a bit more carry-on capacity. I've bought a new blazer and shirt for Wembley, along with a Wrexham club tie/cufflinks/top pocket combo, none of which I'm planning on wearing in Israel.

I've gone so far as to measure my bags to make sure I can get them on the plane as cabin luggage. I've packed and repacked, clothes have been selected then discarded but, finally, the night before I leave Leeds for Cardiff, capital no.1, I'm ready. I can take two bags in the cabin and I have a suitbag that I'll leave at Heathrow for collection on my return. Once we touch down, I will go and fetch it then change into my Wembley outfit at arrivals before racing off for the reception prior to the game. It's military in its precision! I can't help wondering whether too much time may have been devoted to this exercise? I'm sure it'll all be worth it to see Wrexham lift the cup!

So there I am, lugging numerous bags out of Rachel's car on Tuesday morning, in the midst of the early morning rush of commuters around Leeds station. There's another factor – no car, as I don't want to have the long drive back after Wembley, so the train's taking the strain once again as I head for south Wales. I've pre-loaded my iPad with lots of stuff to watch on the plane as I'm a bit nervous about the relatively long flight over, but on this leg of the journey I'm actually going to read stuff, 'old school'. Gareth Bale's on the front cover of FourFourTwo magazine, so I pick up a copy by way of a bit of background work. In truth, I've been mentally preparing for this game ever since the last one. Every week, I've been scouring the internet for news of the fortunes and fitness of the players we'll be expecting to see in the squad. When it was finally announced last week, only one key name

129

was missing; James Chester, who'd dislocated his shoulder in a game in January. There's a certain ominous irony to the fact that it was James Collins who fell on him, the man now likely to replace him. Initially it seemed he had no chance of making it but I've bumped into him a couple of times at Hull since and he'd seemed confident of being on the plane. Sadly, as it turns out, the closest he's going to get to the action is a spell in the studio as one of our guests on the night.

Sam Vokes is another player I've seen a couple of times in the run-up to this game. In fact, I interviewed him after he came on as a sub in Burnley's game against Swansea, so he's fit again and ready to return after nearly a year out of international football. His presence up front could be a crucial addition at this stage of the campaign.

Then there's the guy featured in the article I'm reading as the train pulls out of Leeds, Gareth Bale. Fitness isn't the issue, he's been playing regularly for Real Madrid, form is the problem here. Or at least it seems to be if you listen to the club's fans who've been booing him and if you can read the Spanish papers which have been highly critical of his performances in recent games, not least the *El Clasico*, Real Madrid v Barcelona, last Saturday. Real lost, the big-selling sports daily *Marca*, described Bale as the worst player on the pitch and another paper refused to give him a match rating as it said his performance didn't merit one. It's a load of over-the-top bollocks, especially as he'd scored two goals in the previous game, but it seems he's public enemy no.1. Fans even attacked his car as he left the training ground the day after the game. It's football, people, just a game, not a war, take a chill pill, as my kids might have said when it was a phrase that wasn't used by middle-aged people.

At least he's assured of a warm welcome back in Wales. His contribution to this campaign's already been immense, and he's probably had to do as much defending as attacking so far. With the likelihood of Sam Vokes starting up front, Gareth might be able to take up a more familiar role out on the left side of midfield. That's what I'm guessing anyway.

The first leg of this long journey's uneventful, and the train rolls into Cardiff only a little late. I drag all my bags across the road and into the hotel where Alex is already waiting with some lunch. We embrace, a big manly bear hug naturally, then sit down to eat. My sandwich stops halfway to my mouth as Alex has something of a bombshell to drop, he's unavailable for the next qualifier! He's been booked by Sky Sports News to go out to Canada to cover the Women's World Cup. He'll be away when Wales play Belgium. This is not good! A lot of the cameramen have been struggling to get their contract days in recently, so this assignment guarantees he'll hit his target of 20 days a month for June. If he sticks with me, he'll get a week or so but no guarantee of any more. It's a blow. I get why he's doing it, we're all just trying to pay the mortgage and feed the children and it's not the first time he's missed a match, it's just the first time he's missed one for a long time. He did every game in the last campaign, and I didn't manage that. This now means I've got to find a suitable replacement, and the more of these games he's done, the harder that gets. Nobody knows his way round the squad like Alex. More importantly, we're mates as well, we work well together, so it's like Clyde planning a bank job without Bonnie, Batman patrolling the mean streets of Gotham without Robin.

Down to brass-tacks, we discuss who might get called up from the Sky Squad in his absence and only then do we discuss what's coming up, for what will now be his last game until September. Our first job's at the team hotel this evening, a sit-down interview with that man Vokes. Tomorrow, it's training in the morning then standard player interviews in the afternoon, and then we're on the road to Heathrow.

I follow the now familiar route up through the floors of the Radisson, dump all my bags in the room and hang up the Wembley-bound blazer. With a couple of hours to kill, I decide there's time for a run. I've acquired a revolutionary pair of running shoes since the last game, they are called Vibram fivefingers and they fit like a glove, for your foot. They have individual toes and a rubber sole that's just two millimetres thick. Whatever else they are, and daft-looking is definitely one of them, they are the best footwear ever for travelling light. I've been wearing them since they appeared in my Christmas stocking so they've survived well considering the weight that hits the floor when I quite literally pound the streets.

In this instance, I head for the little gym at the hotel, no more than a running machine and an exercise bike, but there's never anybody in there so that's more than enough equipment for me. I've never run on a treadmill in my new shoes and my first couple of steps send shockwaves through the machine and cause cracks in the ceiling of the floor below.

Half an hour and one annoying blister on the sole of my foot later, I've got a sweat on and time's ticking, so I head back upstairs to shower and change. I need to spruce up before we mix with the superstars at Team Wales HQ.

My driver's waiting as I emerge from reception in front of the building and off we go, back in the groove. We're all getting a bit better at this the more we practise. There's a sign up outside one of the conference rooms at the St David's hotel that says, BSkyB. Clearly, this room has actually been sorted out for our use by the FAW. This is good, it's just a shame our designated hotel staff member doesn't seem to know anything about it and he leads us straight past the sign to another empty room that doesn't have a sign by the door saying BSkyB. Ah well, it still feels like progress.

These conference rooms are pretty drab so Alex has asked Dai Griffiths, the kitman, if we can borrow a couple of shirts to hang up behind Sam. We come across Dai as we head back up to reception. He's suffered a big loss since the last time we were together, his assistant, the other Dai, Williams this time, has passed away in the last few weeks. He was a really lovely, friendly chap. He was 72 years old but he looked fit as a fiddle after a lifetime's active involvement in football so it was a big shock to everyone. He fell ill quickly, then had a stroke from which he never woke up. He'd had stomach cancer but nobody knew until almost the end. I know his absence will be keenly felt by everyone because he's been working with Wales squads of all ages for many years, but particularly so by the man they call Dai Griff, they were quite a double act. We mourn his passing as we meet and understandably Dai's a bit subdued. There's always that underlying sense that Welsh football's eternally mired in tragedy and sadness.

Back in our box-room, Alex works manfully with Dai's two football shirts, a red light and a black sheet to create a studio-like backdrop that'll impress the viewers on Saturday afternoon. Actually, it'll be evening for us as Israel is going to be three hours ahead, although only two hours ahead when we arrive tomorrow but then the clocks go forward, but not in the UK until after the game. I think that's right anyway.

Eventually, the shirts get dropped in favour of slashes of red light and we're ready for the return of Big Sam. He's a player I've known for a long time now, since he broke into the under-21 squad as a raw-boned young pro at Bournemouth He's a top young chap, unassuming, always friendly and dedicated to his profession. His career's been a bit of a roller coaster. It started well, then a big move from Bournemouth to Wolves didn't really work out, he drifted off to various clubs on loan before ending up at Burnley where it all suddenly clicked into place.

He scored 20 goals last season, making a vital contribution to the club's promotion to the Premier League and winning Alex a fiver off me in the process. He had faith, he bet me Sam would hit the 20 mark and Sam didn't let him down, achieving the target in early April. We were just going double or quits on 30, when he suffered a really bad injury with Premier League promotion almost in sight. I passed the fiver over to him at the Burnley's 'player of the year' dinner I hosted at the end of the season. Sam's promised to bring it along today for the formal presentation. Only, when he arrives, he's forgotten it, or spent it?

We crack on with our interview, nothing too controversial, all pretty upbeat. Fifteen minutes later, we're packing up and heading back to our hotel. We were originally planning to use the box at Cardiff's ground to feed the material back to base but there's been a call from Sports News to say there's a satellite truck on its way over for the training session tomorrow as they want a live report, so we'll wait until then instead. In the meantime, we take tea across the road in the restaurant that's never that busy, but where we always have to wait for 20 minutes because they're 'fully booked'. All the empty tables are, apparently, reserved. A suspicious type might suggest it was a cynical attempt to get us to spend a bit more at the bar before we sit down to eat, but Alex and I are innocents abroad.

After food, it's bed; an early night with a couple of crazy days ahead. Oh, and Wrexham lost, badly, at the hands of mighty Nuneaton. Not a great aid to restful sleep.

Wednesday March 25th

My banana got battered in my bag *en route*, so I'm banana-less at breakfast. Over Weetabix, we discuss the plan for live coverage of the training session. We've had a few of these requests down the years, but it's been quite a while since the last one. The suggestion from the planning desk at Sports News is that we'll have a guest present, to talk thought the opening few minutes. The big issue is the identity of the guest. There are very few ex-Wales internationals of relatively recent memory living in or around Cardiff. On top of that, you need someone who can afford to give up a couple of hours to head 20 minutes out of town to the Vale hotel. If you get someone to agree, they're probably going to request a payment for their assistance.

The upshot of all this is we arrive at the training pitch to find a satellite truck, but no guest. It's going to be down to me to talk over the shots of the players warming up. We are, as ever, only admitted for 15 minutes, so we have to fit the live report into this window. In previous instances, when England have been training and that's taken preference, we've run out of time before we've actually got on air. Today, there's no clash with England so we're straight on after the headlines, 'top of the shop'! We're standing right at the edge of the pitch, the players are going through stretches and warm-up routines just a few feet behind me. This means I can talk through the team, and Alex can pick them out as I mention them, it'll look great. Except, just as they cue into me, the players all follow the fitness coach and he leads them off to another much more distant part of the training ground, but I'm facing the camera so I have no idea this has happened and continue to chat away merrily. I get a sense all is not well when I see Alex panning further and further left, he appears to be searching for the players, not just the ones I'm talking about, but all of the players, any of the players?

After what seems like an age, I get the wrap-up message from base in my headphones. As they leave our live shots, Alex is all but in tears. It's been a bit of a disaster. As I talked through the expected line-up, the viewers could barely see a player, never mind the ones I was referring to. It was, apparently, akin to watching shots of some small figures just visible on the horizon. Remarkably, no one from base rings to ask what the heck was going on. We speculate that they probably just sighed and said, 'it's those two clowns in Wales again.' In truth, there wasn't an awful lot that could be done once the players jogged off into the distance; we couldn't move, the camera's on a tripod, there are cables, we were live, ah well, TV gold!

Still ashen-faced, Alex can now actually get within sight of a recognisable human being and squeeze in a last few usable shots before our 15 minutes are up. We head back to our hotel to pack and check out, ahead of a rendezvous with the satellite truck at the team hotel, then some interviews, then a drive over to Heathrow.

In what is effectively our lunch hour, I nip up to the Turnstile office for a quick chat with the chaps. The gang's all there and we have a bit of Wales-related football banter before time's up and I've got to head back via the Cornish pasty shop. I collect my bags from the room and shove them into the back of Alex's car for the onward journey.

There were lots of cameras at the training session this morning and there's lots of activity at St David's as we arrive in good time for the 2pm start. Clearly, media interest is building but as it grows, so the size of the room for the player press conference appears to have shrunk. Her Majesty's press are all squeezed into a space that makes the Black Hole of Calcutta look like the Tower Ballroom. Alex and I pick our way between and over reporters, microphones, cameras and notepads to a place on the balcony that lies beyond this hellhole, with wide open spaces and a cooling breeze off the Bay. Perspiring journalists look out through full-length windows in envy, this is what the broadcast contract gets us!

Our player interviewees are brought out to us as well, starting with Joe Allen. His career's been very much on the upward trajectory since the last game. He's got back into the Liverpool starting XI and he's been earning good reviews and MOTM awards for his displays. The Liverpool fans finally seem to be seeing what he's all about. He's a very serious lad, Joe, his interviews are incredibly thoughtful, so much so that there are often pauses as he considers the best thing to say. He doesn't hold eye contact much either. He speaks very well though, I like him a lot, even though he rarely indulges me in my clumsy attempts at pre-interview banter. In fact, I like him even more for that.

In this instance, there are issues relating to his club match last weekend, a defeat for Liverpool at the hands of Manchester United. On top of that, Steven Gerrard marked his final appearance against his big rivals by getting himself sent off almost as soon as he'd come on as a sub. I ask about his mood in the aftermath of the game but the Gerrard incident doesn't really have much relevance to Wales, and I don't want to be seen as an opportunist, securing lines about his club when he's on duty with his country, so I avoid it as an issue. More pertinent is the club form of Gareth Bale, might that have a negative impact on his form with Wales? Joe says no, he'll be fine, as does the next man up, Neil Taylor. He's bang on the money with his answers, as ever. The players have been well drilled in how to approach this, they're not getting carried away but clearly feel they can get something from this game.

Sam Vokes is addressing the seething, sweating media conference as Alex and I coolly depart, our job done. Downstairs, the sat truck's ready and waiting to send our material back to HQ. Whilst that's being done, Alex shoves everything back into the car and I head back into the hotel to try and arrange the manager/captain interviews for Friday. We're staying in the team hotel as it happens, which should make life easier. It might be a job we can get done on Friday morning, after breakfast. Ashley Williams wanders by whilst I'm talking it through with IG, he doesn't appear overly keen as he disappears into the lift but IG and I pencil it in the schedule anyway. Pencil, not pen.

We're staying in the Thistle hotel at Heathrow. It's a 6am check-in for an 8am flight so we're not going to be here long. Even as we arrive, Alex is already lost in reverie. After all these years on the road together, I'm only just finding out that he's a plane spotter. He suddenly reveals that he's got an app on his phone that tracks all the flights in the air, even tells you what sort of plane it is. I'm bemused, he's serious. As I unpack my gear and set off for reception, he's gazing upwards, eyes wide with wonder, phone app telling him it's an A340 flight to Dublin. He's like a small child in a toy shop.

Mind you, I've got my own child-like desires to fulfil. I want to take a ride on the so-called Pod that transports passengers from the hotel to Terminal 5. I've read about it online. It's described as the world's first personal transport system, like a monorail made for one. Even though Alex has the car, I pay my fiver at reception and get me a ticket for this 21st century transport experience. Before all the excitement, we arrange to meet in the hotel bar for food. I arrive for our date fashionably late to find Alex on the rooftop terrace outside the bar, staring up at planes, a pint in one hand, his phone in the other. He's really excited now, apparently there's an A380 about to depart, biggest plane in the world or something. Maybe it'll be good to spend a bit of time apart in June after all..?

Thursday 26th March

Although the room's double glazed, I've used my trusty earplugs and managed a few hour's sleep. At 5.15am however, it feels just what it is, far too early to get up.

Too early for breakfast certainly so I stumble off into the pre-dawn drizzle, following signs for the 'Pod'. I've got a code for the entry gate, across the car park and there it is. It looks like a squashed tube train. One pulls away just as I arrive at the entrance to the pod 'station' or should that be 'dock'? As I wait for the next one, shadowy bodies join me at my post. One of them, a female, speaks, "Do you mind if we share?" As I saw the previous one pull away, it did appear there were four seats inside this so-called 'personal transport system'. So, what can I say? "Okay" I respond, a little grudgingly. The woman doesn't say anything back, she can't, she's been consumed by a hacking coughing fit. I swiftly weigh up withdrawing my offer, but the next pod arrives before I can say anything and I'm consigned to five minutes trapped inside a big egg, facing someone who appears to have a very unpleasant bronchial infection. The edge is taken off the whole 'pod experience'.

I hold my breath for as long as possible as we whizz along the monorail through the dark and then into the light. Heathrow is a nether world, timeless. Even at this ungodly hour, it's really busy. Who are all these people rushing about, pushing trolleys, and where the hell are they all going?

I make contact with Alex and we rendezvous at the check-in desk. We're in economy, cutbacks, so he's already paid £50 extra for a leg-room seat. I can't justify spending my own money on a flight for work, so my best plan has been to go online and get myself an aisle seat in the very back row. They fill the seats from the front so maybe it might be quieter back there?

As we're checking-in Alex's bags, Bill arrives. All the Sky personnel are travelling out on this flight, bar Barry. He's heading out from Manchester with Easyjet a little later. That has all the elements to be a tricky flight, much like his trip out to Andorra. I console myself knowing that however bad it is for me, it'll inevitably be worse for Barry.

At the desk, I ask to take my suitbag on board, but I'm told it's a full flight so there won't be room. At this, I'm too dozy to take on the challenge of finding 'left luggage' on another level in this other-world, so I check a bag on and carry the other two with me. My blazer, shirt and tie are all travelling to Israel despite the fact I don't plan on taking them out of the bag. Mad!

There's more comedy to follow. On the other side, through the security checks, Bill suggests we try and get into the BA lounge, to which he has access, as he's got some silver flying card thing, very much the international jetsetter. He's allowed to take one guest in, there's me and Alex. He suggests we blag it so we trail off to a distant corner of the terminal in search of paradise and free tea and coffee. We find neither; entry denied, to the third member of the party at least. Now, this is where the 'Tîm Cymru' ethic really kicks in! Bill declines to access a facility that is rightfully his, without his comrades-in-arms, and together we head off to find Alex's favourite, the 'giraffe' restaurant, where he promises to buy us breakfast. Heart-warming stuff eh? With that sort of togetherness, how can we fail?

Our enforced fast pleasantly broken, we link up with the other members of our travelling party at the gate. There are a couple of new faces to me, Ray, the production manager and Ben, the sound assistant, everyone else I know. As we're waiting to board, I'm doing the ready reckoner, trying to work out just how busy it's going to be. There aren't many Wales fans on board, that much seems apparent. In fact, the only one I can identify is the guy from the Supporters Federation, who's sitting in the row in front of me. He visits the match venues in advance to plot good places for fans to go, meets with police and the Embassy people, and then relays that info back to those travelling out. We see each other on these trips regularly, so we have a quick chat. He says a lot of fans are already out there, staying in Tel Aviv, and a lot more are coming out from London and Manchester later today; that'll be Barry's flight then.

As departure time approaches, there are still a few spare seats at the back, including one to my immediate left. I'm looking good for room to move into a whole row to myself. Then, there's a late burst of activity, and an Orthodox Jewish guy arrives at the back. He's carrying a hat box for his large black hat, he places the box on the seat next to him, just across the row from me, and I wonder if he's bought a ticket for it?

In the row in front of me, another guy's standing up and praying, he and the guy to my right have prayer shawls, the Tallit, and the man on the right also has the straps on his arms and a small black box on his head, the Tefillin. All this is made possible by the fact that we've missed a slot and the plane's still sitting on the runway, otherwise, I'm not sure if use of electronic devices and a Tefillin is permitted during takeoff?

All this adds to the sense of anticipation at travelling somewhere 'different'. It's my first trip to the Middle East. I do have a slight sense of trepidation. If I didn't know it already, it's clear now that I'm travelling to a country where religion remains very important, like life or death important. I know about the ongoing conflicts in this region, the upheaval since the creation of the Israeli state. I'm not big on religion to be honest, it seems to be at the heart of most of the bad stuff that's going on in the world. I would just like people to be nice to each other, regardless of which book they read.

Forty five minutes later, we're finally up in the air and I'm already stuck into a film (keep calm, focus on the film), Birdman. The one downside on claiming the back row of the plane is my seat's proximity to the toilet. The minute the seatbelt light's gone off, the queue starts to form and it only rarely disappears for the next five hours. After an hour or so, Alex joins it. He's having a tough time even in his extra legroom seat. A guy's fallen heavily asleep snuggled right up against him. My Jewish companion has also fallen heavily asleep but he's been able to sprawl across the three seats to my right without causing discomfort to anyone else. He's now using his prayer shawl as a blanket. A little later, Bill appears. Its two hours ahead in Israel, that makes it sometime close to 1pm there, so something about the sun being over the yard arm, means that as he makes the return trip to his seat, he deposits a small can of Heineken on my tray table. This is, after all, a travel day and a long one at that.

The flight passes agreeably thereafter, more films are watched, and I even win the top prize on the 'Who Wants To Be A Millionaire' game on the in-flight entertainment console! Sadly this doesn't translate into a cash prize, or even a mention over the tannoy from the Captain. I'm a little disappointed.

We land, late, at Tel Aviv. The weather's warm, as forecast, high 70s, but we get only a brief breath of outside air before beginning the task of actually entering the country. We have been warned about this bit. Be patient, be prepared for a wait, especially given the amount of kit we're collectively carrying. The queues for passport control are certainly far longer than those for the bathroom on the plane.

It's half an hour before I arrive at the booth window and present my passport. I'm asked questions about the purpose of my visit, who I'm travelling with, and have I been here before? It's one of those situations where even straightforward answers become difficult, even despite my proven prowess for a quiz. I pass on two, but do well on the pop music round and eventually I'm allowed through. There's no stamp on the passport these days as it has caused people too many problems on subsequent trips in the region, particularly to other countries that aren't very keen on Israel – which is probably most of them. I'm the last of our group to get the 'all clear'. The rest have already collected their bags and they're waiting, with mine, and as I go off to get shekels from an ATM, they head out to find our driver. The transfers have all been carefully arranged in advance and we have a driver for the duration of our stay. Ray's responsible for everyone's well-being and, as safe as it probably is here, he's not going to take any chances. It's reassuring and good for morale, because it means we climb aboard our minibus together, a team, with a job to do.

I've checked the map before we set off, and it's a fair old trek from Tel Aviv to Haifa. It's a long straight road up the coast but we run into traffic a little way from the airport, and it's a slow crawl out of the city and towards our destination. By now, of course, it's 4.30pm, and although we've 'gained' time, it still feels like it's been a long day already. After an hour on the road, we're still 70 kilometres from the hotel. Even when we reach Haifa and see the impressive new stadium just off the main route in, we still have a 20 minute climb up, up, up to the top of Mount Carmel. The roads are narrow and snake their way past higgledy-piggledy houses, and up the side of the mountain. Eventually, we pull up outside the Crowne Plaza. It's dark now, and I'm very much ready for a shower, then something to eat. The Wales team are due to arrive a few hours after us, so we can get settled in before they arrive *en masse*. Except that the concierge, positioned outside the front door of the hotel, has a list of expected arrivals and doesn't seem to know we were coming. More worryingly, neither do the staff on reception. We all activate phones and start scrolling through countless emails to find the travel confirmations we've all been sent. I delve into my bag for the printed copies I've brought, just in case.

We slump into seats in the lobby, surrounded by our luggage and equipment, as phone calls are made, and emails exchanged. A round of drinks is bought as someone tries to sort this out. We all have confirmation codes, but apparently there's no record of any booking at the hotel. Eventually, a member of the reception emerges from behind her desk to reassure everyone that it's okay, it's sorted. "You are not actually booked into this hotel, but our sister hotel The Bay View, a few minutes drive away." For a number of reasons, this is a bit of a blow and there are dark mutterings within the group, are we being fobbed off for their error or is it a mistake by the company Sky uses to book travel? Either way, the Crowne Plaza only has rooms for this evening, not tomorrow, so we have to go. A long day has just got a bit longer.

It's all a bit suspicious, because our confirmations all have the name and address of this hotel on them, and they also agree to pick up the tab for a fleet of taxis to take us to our new base. No room at the inn might be an appropriate comparison, in another location not a million miles away. The hotel's assurance of recompense doesn't seem to carry much weight with our guy when the cab arrives. There's a lot of shouting and gesticulating but eventually he's reassured and we set off. Then we start talking football and everything's okay again. He says the Israel team's not as good as people say it is, and there's been a row between the coach and one of his players. Of course he's heard of Bale, but he knows other players like Ramsey and Allen as well. He predicts a draw, 1-1. I think we'd take that.

We're more successful at the old checking-in routine at this next hotel. They're waiting with our room cards, and take pride in explaining that we've all been upgraded to executive rooms, and that all rooms have a see-through shower. I'm okay with this concept as long as I'm not sharing. Luckily we've all got singles.

The hotel has a position atop the mountain and the executive rooms all face out over the port of Haifa, one of the busiest in this region. By now, it's just lights twinkling in the bay down below and I can gaze out on them even whilst I have a shower, yes they really are see-through, like a big glass cell in the middle of the room.

Washed and refreshed, I head down to meet the rest of the gang. Food's a priority. There's not much sign of any life in the hotel so we head out into the night. A place has been recommended, Charley's Bar, just up the road apparently. We walk away from the hotel, passing a couple of potential eateries, but we're fixed on Charley's Bar. I'm trying to locate it on the phone, it seems to be close as we reach the top of the road and round the corner, but there's no sign of any sign. Already spirits are flagging, the party splits at a crossroads. I remain behind, right outside a decent-looking place with outside tables and a varied menu but Ray's our leader, and he's headed off elsewhere.

The impact of a long, arduous day's travel is kicking in, as a second party goes off to find Ray. This has a touch of the Scott of the Antarctic about it. Then Ray's spotted, waving in the near distance, before disappearing out of sight and below street level.

There is a big clue to his destination, a large, raised sign with a flashing arrow pointing downwards and the word 'PUB' on it at exactly the point where we lost sight of him. We find some steps that lead us down into what appears to be a small park. It's pretty dark down here and some locals are sitting on rocks, apparently taking a break from walking some wild looking dogs. To our immediate right, there's a long picnic table, beyond which almost like a cave, is a bar, actually, it's The After Dark Bar. I'll be honest, it doesn't look promising but there's a seat and the prospect of a beer and, who knows, maybe even some food. We claim the long picnic table as our own. We now outnumber all other customers by five to one, however, the anticipated flurry of excited activity doesn't happen. After a while, a member of staff wanders over then immediately wanders off on request to collect some menus. The kitchen, it appears, is at least still open.

Drinks are ordered, then meals. It's a straightforward grill, burgers, steaks, various cuts of meat, a couple of pasta dishes. Already, I have the sense our waitress is somewhat nonplussed by this sudden invasion of hungry customers. Mentally, perhaps, she was already clearing the tables and on her way home. She checks the drinks order again, then the food we've ordered, then disappears.

Ten minutes later, she still hasn't reappeared. Nobody ordered a Pina Colada or Harvey Wallbanger, it's all beer or soft drinks. But no sign of either. Always eager to help and pretty thirsty by now, Alex gets up and heads off to the bar and he returns carrying glasses of beer. Then he goes back to the bar and returns with more drinks. The actual waitress follows in his wake. a glass in each hand, you wouldn't get away with this performance at the Oktoberfest. Still, it's a start.

Memories of Andorra are already stirring as we wait for the main courses. We've experienced the worst restaurant service in Europe in Andorra, the best in Brussels, now we're back at square one in Israel it seems. The meals arrive sporadically. I've ordered a lamb burger, when it apparently arrives, with two other burgers, I ask the waitress to confirm that this is the lamb one? "How would I know?", she replies. It's a good answer, just not the one I was expecting.

Previous enquiries have been answered with a long and indignant, "whaaaaaaat?" Each time she responds in this manner, people start to giggle. Things are getting a little silly. Ominously, the prairie dogs are now circling the table. It's all beginning to get a bit bizarre. Eventually, all the meals are served, all except one. At the far end of the table, young Ben hasn't been blessed with anything, even when some of the rest of the party are already wondering whether to risk a dessert. Repeated enquiries on his behalf seem to make our waitress even angrier. When his dish eventually arrives, she plonks it down in front him, "Chicken sandwich, sorry for the wait", she snarls, before spinning on her heels and stomping back into the cave. This is now so bad it's funny. I've got tears running down my cheeks as poor Ben nibbles tentatively at the meal he's waited so long for.

My hunger sated, I remember the one missing member of our party. It's time to locate Barry. A text exchange tells me he's *en route* from Tel Aviv, Ray's already sent him the name of the new hotel, but the taxi driver's struggling to find it.

We risk the wrath of our waitress to ask for the name of the road we're on. Our enquiry is greeted with the inevitable "whaaaaaat?", then she goes off to ask someone who might know. It appears she's not local, nor is she a waitress. It's all a bit mysterious really, have we stumbled upon a robbery and would we find the real staff bound and gagged in the kitchen?

Address confirmed, Barry's presence seems imminent but a couple of our party are happy to head back to the hotel to make sure he's then directed onwards to our strange subterranean bar and grill. Barry will very much be in need of a beverage, I suspect.

143

Sure enough, a short time later, he appears, still in the suit, shirt and tie he went to school in this morning. A litre's swiftly ordered, the strong stuff. And, as he unwinds, sip-by-sip, Barry tells his tale. His journey's been every bit as bad as anticipated, if not even worse. The flight was full, a mixture of Wales fans and returning locals. Things didn't begin well when the departures area for this flight turned out to be a small portakabin. Small, noisy children ran around the feet of parents who seemed unaware of the cramped and crowded surroundings. Some of the fans had already clearly had a few drinks and were in boisterous mood, with Barry a recognisable face to many. Things didn't get any better on board as Barry found himself sitting next to a large couple, the male partner so large that he couldn't actually fit in his seat. He spent some time trying to squeeze himself in, the cabin crew tried to assist but they couldn't get him in either, so he decided he didn't really want to travel anyway. A row then started with his wife, again the crew became involved, and eventually, collectively, they managed to force him into some sort of sitting position, and the flight could take off. Barry, needless to say, was somewhat restricted in his ability to stretch out as a result. British Airways offers in-flight entertainment, Easyjet offers nothing, so there was little to distract our man over the course of the next five hours. Then there was all the hassle through arrivals, the long drive and now, finally, a long swig from a very large glass of cold beer.

Needless to say, his tale of woe is met with gales of laughter, and very little by the way of empathy. Barry's travel travails have become an integral part of our Wales tales over the years. It all started with a game in Azerbaijan 10 years ago, only the second game into the new broadcast contract with the FAW. Barry travelled out on his own. Much as today, he made contact with me by text to say he'd landed at Baku airport. We were sitting as a group outside the somewhere bizarrely called Caledonia Bar, in the centre of town. An hour or so later, Barry, appeared, again looking a little dishevelled. He described a nightmare cab journey from his hotel, the Holiday Inn, to the bar. It had taken ages and he'd been driven down countless dark side streets, making him suspect that the cabbie was taking advantage of him as a tourist. Barry's travelled the world though, he knows how it works so he'd got his own back, refusing to give the taxi driver any more than 20 US dollars when the guy suggested he wanted twice as much as the car finally arrived at its destination. The cabbie backed down, a small victory, or so it seemed until we urged him to look just across the road. There it was, the brightly lit sign visible from miles away, 50 yards from where we were sitting, The Holiday Inn!

After another round of beers, the clock ticks past midnight, locally at least, at home it's still reasonably early. Currently, we're two hours off the pace but, in the early hours of the morning, Israeli clocks will go forward an hour. That means an hour less in bed, that means time to go home, there's work to be done tomorrow, today, whatever?!

Friday 27ᵗʰ March

The time switch, added to the time change from GMT, means that to catch breakfast before 11am, we have to be up at what still feels like 7am, even if the clock suggests otherwise. Things aren't helped by the physical effects of drinking what was, as it turned out, quite a strong beer last night. It wasn't Delirium Tremens strong but I did have a litre glass and then a couple, so it's a bit of a struggle.

Despite that, there's an early check call to be made as well. The suggestion that we might need to be ready to do something with the manager and captain this morning can't be discounted. It was on the cards for when we were meant to be staying in the team hotel at least. Fears of a speedy dash to their base are allayed with a message from IG to say that they're keeping to UK time for the duration of the trip, which means they won't be having breakfast until 1pm.

The most likely scenario at this point is that we'll do our interviews at the stadium this evening, around the scheduled media conferences. Before that, the Israelis will be holding their open training session after the coach and captain attend media conferences. This is all relevant as Jim, the producer, is keen to get time with either of them. I've already established contact with the Israeli FA's media officer prior to departure. He's been really helpful and another flurry of emails confirms that we'll get a chance to interview Tal Ben Haim, the captain and Charlton player, at some stage today. So, now I've got three interviews to do today, all of which are currently happening 'sometime'.

Alex has arranged to go over to the stadium early as his camera position needs checking, so he'll be there from 2pm onwards. The Israelis have changed the start time for their media conference to 4pm, so I plan to get there for that.

Bill's going to come over and observe the conferences and training sessions as well, so he and I agree to meet for lunch before travelling together. It's about a 15 minute drive from our hilltop location to the stadium which is down below, close to the coastline.

Breakfast was not really what the doctor ordered, all cold meats and sugary cereals, so I'm still not at my best afterwards. I opt for some sort of low level activity to push the blood though my veins, so I head out for a walk. Directly behind the hotel, there's a promenade and it offers fine views across the port down below us. Instead, I head off to see if there are any good shops. Twenty minutes later, I've ascertained that there aren't; the only thing I've seen of interest is that the next hotel to ours is where the Israel squad are staying. It's a warm day, shorts and t-shirt weather, but there's a really strong wind whipping across the hilltop. Prom apart, there doesn't seem to be an awful lot to this part of Haifa to occupy the attention of the visitor.

I return in time to find Bill, Sarah and Alex sitting by the bar in the lobby of the hotel, looking to grab some lunch before work starts. Attempts have been made to contact Barry but nobody's heard anything back from him. He's an adventurer, he'll be exploring, although we do speculate as to whether he's been kidnapped. We speculate further as to whether the ransom will be set on the basis of his international caps, 59, or international goals, two.

Lunch has its moments. There's not a vast choice anyway, so Sarah and I plump for a slice of pizza. They are actually cooked in some sort of mini grill on the bar but the barkeep keeps disappearing, so, like last night, we basically end up serving ourselves. Afterwards, Sarah and Alex head off to work. Bill goes off to do some prep, and I get changed and decide it's time to risk a run. I use the prom as my route finder. It's straightforward, I set off by turning left which means I run on the flat as the promenade traverses the summit of Mount Carmel, then it descends in the general direction of the sea. I keep running in the knowledge that the further I follow it down, the further I have to return running back up it. I pass a lot of tourists on my descent. There are ornate gardens dug into the side of the mountain and the coaches parked outside suggest this is a popular attraction. As I run in-between the holidaymakers and taxis, I'm keeping my eye on the time, even so, I leave it a bit late before turning round to do the homeward stretch and I have to push myself quite a bit harder to get back up the hill in time to fit in a quick see-through shower, another change and a return to the lobby to catch a cab.

It's a fair drive to the brand new Sammy Ofer Stadium, named after a mogul who donated $20,000,000 to the cost of construction on the condition that his name went up in lights, a Madejski for the Middle East. The drive there affords a better chance to have a look at Haifa. It's an odd place, much of it seemingly built on top of the mountain or at the foot of it, with very little in-between. The architecture's uninspiring as well, the places where people live look like they've been built in haste, thrown up quickly before someone comes to try and take the land back. This is a country that's barely 60 years old. Israel was formed in the chaotic aftermath of World War Two, created as a haven for the Jewish people after the Holocaust, but surrounded ever since by enemies. It's the whole reason we're here for a European qualifier, Israel can't play their neighbours. Croatia and Bosnia will play Serbia, despite the terrible war, but the Middle Eastern nations still refuse to play Israel.

It's a complicated place. I don't pretend to understand the nuances surrounding the occupation of the Golan Heights, the land grab in Palestine territories, the relationship between Arabs and Jews living in Israel or the land that Israelis are occupying. I've watched TV footage of Palestinians with catapults fighting one of the best equipped armies in the world and felt sympathy for the apparently oppressed but if you're a Jewish inhabitant, there must be a sense of constant threat, imminent danger. The people we've met so far haven't seemed very friendly. I wonder if this is why?

There's a simplicity to our role, we're here to cover a football match, 90 minutes, then win, lose or draw we head home.

The political and geographical complexities of the Middle East have intruded on this fixture previously and significantly. In 1958, an even younger nation met Wales in a World Cup play-off after all their potential opponents in the Asia and Africa qualifying section refused to play them. FIFA decreed no team could qualify for a World Cup without actually playing a game, so all the teams who'd finished second in their qualifying groups were put into a hat, the first to be drawn out to provide opposition in a two-legged play-off. Belgium came out first but declined the offer; Wales came out next and accepted. A talented Welsh team featuring arguably the world's best player at the time, John Charles, won both legs 2-0 and Wales found a backdoor route to the World Cup in Sweden in 1958. Having got there, Wales made a decent go of it, reaching the quarter-finals only to be beaten by a Brazil side featuring a 17 year-old called Pelé; he scored the only goal of the game. That remains the only time, to date, that Wales have played in a major international tournament.

The play-off in 1958 took place in Tel Aviv, at a half-finished stadium. As we enter this new venue, it's apparent that Sammy's money has been well-spent. It's an impressive venue. Sky Sports News had made a request for shots of any potential 'heightened sense of security' earlier in the trip. In the event, it's all pretty relaxed. A wave of a Sky ID card gets Bill and me entry to the stadium. We follow signs and stewards' directions to the media room. There's coffee, water and biscuits already on offer, sandwiches arrive shortly after, all very hospitable.

I've been liaising with a guy called Eitan, from the Israeli FA. There are a few people from his media team getting things set up in the media conference room as we arrive and when I hear someone in an official polo shirt call his name, I head over and make my introductions. He's a young guy, speaks good English and he can confirm the interview with the captain's likely to happen but he still can't say if it'll be now or later. If it's later, I have a problem, as Wales are due here at 6pm, training at 6.30.

He suggests I get Alex to set up by the pitchside, and he'll see if there's a small window of opportunity after the conference and before the training session. Alex arrives and I relay this information. We both head down to the pitchside. Now, security of the jobsworth variety suddenly becomes an issue. We are turned away from two potential points of entry and have to retrace our steps around the stadium to finally get access to the playing surface. This is my first view of the actual arena, and it looks good. A 30,000 capacity, with high-banked seating but close to the pitch, it's a proper football ground.

Alex does his thing, tripod up, camera fixed on top but it's obvious there might be issues. The stadium PA's currently belting out music for a start, there are fans hanging about in the stands and staff are milling around everywhere; it's far from the controlled environment we favour for these big 'sit-down' interviews. There's not much we can do now but wait and hope. I don't want to let Jim down, I don't want to leave him with a slot to fill in his running order but I've already been in touch to warn him there might be a clash with what Wales are doing, if we don't get to talk to Tal in the next few minutes.

I go and wait near the tunnel as players start to emerge ahead of the scheduled start of their pre-match training session. They pose for pictures, sign autographs, kid around with the backroom staff, the usual stuff. There aren't really any recognisable faces in their number. It's a team that's proved to be greater than the sum of its parts thus far. Eventually, the one player I do recognise, Tal Ben Haim, emerges. I make my approach as he heads out onto the turf. I introduce myself, make my request, he's polite, apologetic even but he wants to start training. "We'll sort it out later, after training", he suggests.

Alex is watching from a distance, I give him the thumbs down. He's going to hang around anyway to film some of the training session. Eitan appears, he's also apologetic but confirms that Tal's said he's happy to do it and that back at the team hotel might be better. So, yes we've got an interview, but no we still don't know where or when it's going to be. After the 15 minutes are up, Alex and I head back to the outside broadcast compound to discuss what happens next.

It now looks like I'm going to be double-booked, unless I can sort something out sharpish with Wales. I contact IG, ask if we can grab our interviews at the team hotel just before Chris and Ashley set off, but it's a negative, they want to do it at the stadium. In these circumstances, I have to refer up. I let Jim and Sky Sports News know that there's a clash, I can do Wales or Israel, I can't do both. There are alternatives I can suggest. The Wales media conference will be covered by the host broadcaster so we can send the shots of that back, although it will mean we don't take up the opportunity to do the interviews that we're entitled to under the terms of the contract. If we give up the opportunity, I can then go to the Israel team hotel, but it's a prospect that does concern me. I've never not done these pre-match interviews before. If we don't do them this time, will the manager turn round next time and say, 'If I didn't need to do this last time, why am I doing it now?' On top of that, Chris is a very superstitious guy, he may almost demand to do exactly what we've done ahead of all the previous qualifiers in this group. I fear setting a dangerous precedent.

The Wales interviews are for Sky Sports News, the Israel interview's for Sky Sports and Jim has the final call as we're all here predominantly to work on the live match coverage. As it turns out, Jim has a very good compromise. He suggests getting Bill to do one interview whilst I do the other. Alex can film the one at the team hotel, we can use our camera in the stadium to do the other two. This is unusual, commentators wouldn't normally be roped in to doing what might be deemed the reporter's job, but in this instance it does seem the sensible way to sort it out so that everybody gets what they want, and we don't give up the interviews to which we're entitled.

Bill's standing next to me as I come off the phone with Jim, so I make the request for his assistance. For a moment or two, he seems reluctant, with some reason. He wants to attend the Wales media conference and training session, in case anything happens that might be relevant to his commentary. However, doing the interview with Tal Ben Haim means he might get the chance to get a bit of useful info from inside the Israel camp, before a short stroll back to base. I can almost hear his brain working through it, then he gives his agreement. Next up, I need to confirm with Sarah that it's possible we can do the Wales interviews from the camera we have pitchside. She's the director, she gets the final call on all this stuff. After checking with the people from the host broadcast unit, she confirms it'll be possible. Next up, she has to confirm that Dave, the extra Sky cameraman, is happy to get involved. Again, he's really here to work on the OB, but we're a team and everyone's ready to muck in for the greater good. Now and only now do we finally have a clear idea of the way this is all going to fit together. Where normally, it's me who gets all this sorted out and Alex who films it all, this time we need the help of lots of people. Our driver's still waiting at the stadium, so Bill and Alex jump in with him and head back to base. I head back to the tunnel area, where Israel are just wrapping up their training session. Only when they have finished am I allowed back to the pitchside.

Eitan's still around so I explain the change in plan to him, he's happy, and promises to get a room sorted out at the hotel, although he explains that the time might be flexible as the Israeli players have a habit of taking their time over the post-training shower. He's not wrong. The home squad's still getting changed at the stadium as the advanced party from the FAW arrives.

There are the usual cheery greetings, but also an invitation. Dai The Kitman says, "You've got to come and have a look at this dressing room, see how you think it compares to Penydarren Park?" Now, I've actually seen Merthyr's dressing rooms. when I worked there on a live cup game on Sky many years ago, and they're fairly basic. I'm wondering whether Dai means these in Israel are much better or worse? I soon see the reality, they're fantastic! There's a gym area with exercise bikes and running machines, there are individual plunge baths, ice baths, jacuzzis, boot showers, a kitchen area, you name it, they've got it. Mr Cfer's money appears to have been spent on top-of-the-range fixtures and fittings.

Back out on the pitch, more of the Welsh party are arriving, including the assistant manager, Kit Symons. He's adopted a low-key policy in the last few games, since he stepped up to become Fulham's manager. He wants to keep working with Wales, and doesn't want anyone at his club accusing him of not being focused on his day-job, as it were. Last Saturday, I was present as his team recorded a much needed and utterly bizarre 2-0 win at Huddersfield, with the home side missing two penalties. He's a very laid-back, affable chap is Kit, not one to get hysterical by any stretch of the imagination, but I can only imagine what he was thinking during the 90 minutes in West Yorkshire – an early goal, then wave after wave of Huddersfield attacks for the rest of the match. With his side sitting precariously just ahead of the bottom three the win was vital, and a timely boost for Kit, in his first full-time appointment. Football management's a crazy, short-term business, where your first job is often, now, your last and the Championship is the maddest division of all for hiring and firing. So, it's no surprise that Kit looks on this role as offering a brief place of shelter from the storm, and in this instance, his shelter's provided by the roof of the dugout, his comfort from the leather chair he's sitting in, surveying the technical staff going about their business, laying out cones, pushing in poles, arranging footballs.

Then I sit down next to him, rolling in like a squally shower, wanting to talk about the game last weekend. He feigns annoyance that I've ruined his moment of relaxation, but we've known each other a long time, and have always got on, so I'm confident he's kidding.

We chat about that game and the one to come. Born in Basingstoke, with the accent to prove it, he qualified for Wales through his father, and won 36 caps as a central defender. He's still utterly committed to the cause, desperate to keep the assistant's job through to the end of the campaign. Like everyone else, he's devoted a chunk of his footballing life to a project that still hasn't been brought to a successful conclusion, that of getting Wales to a summer finals tournament. He's as desperate as any fan to get there, to get over the line. These are the quiet moments when this job of mine seems the best, the proximity, the intimacy of being able to sit and chat with the people who are trying to make it happen. These are the bits I really enjoy, before the nightmare that is watching the game.

After Kit's strolled off, I chat with Dave Rowe, the squad's soft tissue therapist. He's been doing this job for a while now, one of the few faces that hasn't changed with the managers. He's another steady, easy going guy but with that same burning desire. He's Welsh, so he knows all the history. He's been with the association for over 18 years, so he's seen the side come close to qualification before.

Dave's able to reflect on a quiet week in the treatment room, which is good, it means the players are fit and raring to go. Our chat turns to running, he's done the same prom run as me, although he adds, "I turned round after three miles and heading back was all uphill." I don't think I did three miles in total but I don't mention that. Tomorrow, he plans to go uphill first, although I'm not sure there's much more 'up' to do from our lofty position.

As the goalkeepers begin their session under the watchful eye of Martyn Margetson, the Israelis are still at the stadium. One or two of them have wandered to the top of the tunnel to watch. This is why nothing ever really happens at these sessions the night before the game. Players use them as an exercise in getting to know their surroundings, a gentle run out but there won't be any set-piece work done, nor will they line-up as a starting XI, in the knowledge that there are spies everywhere! I send Alex a message to warn him they're unlikely to make the 6.45pm interview time originally suggested. He's back on to say that Bill's made contact with the media man, and it's rearranged for 7.30. That at least means it's a definite now.

My own mission should be completed a little earlier. I wander over to our camera position a few yards further down the running track. Dave, the cameraman, is all set, Ben the sound man has some headphones for me, and the little box they plug into it hooks onto my belt. Through that and the mic, I have a line of communication with Sarah in our OB vehicle in the compound, and she has contact with base. The two interviews are going to be fed straight down the line to HQ, the first time we've ever done the traditional pre-match interviews like this.

IG arrives at the top of the tunnel, which is always a prelude to activity. Sure enough Chris Coleman strides out onto the pitch after him. He glances in my direction, IG mouths to ask if we're ready, I give him the thumbs up. The manager's not quite ready though, he's out in the centre circle having a good look around, taking pictures on his iPad it appears. I'm guessing this is another aspect of the rigorous preparation, but maybe he's keeping his own diary? Before he heads over to see us, Ashley Williams heads out of the tunnel, accompanied by Peter, the other media guy. We have a bit of banter, as always, before getting down to business. It's a big game for Ash, his 50th cap and captain of course, not bad for a lad who was stacking supermarket shelves not so long ago.

The fact that Israel v Wales is a game between the top two teams in the group is probably a surprise to many, not least I suspect, to the two sets of supporters. But I get the sense that, despite their winning start, Israel hold no fears for this group of players. The interview underlines this, nothing overt or cocky, just that quiet confidence thing again. Israel may be described as 'the surprise package', a team of relative unknowns, but nothing they do should be a surprise to Wales. There are no secrets, all the games in the campaign are covered by TV, and all the footage is available to every competing nation. Clearly the players have been sitting down to study footage. and I'm aware that Osian Roberts has also initiated the introduction of a new technology called Global Coach. I've actually seen it demonstrated on one of the coaching courses I've attended. It looks like a pretty impressive piece of kit, and it's been utilised for the first time for this game. It's an online dossier on the opposition that the players can take away and study on tablets and phones. It's what they get at their clubs, it's what they expect when they join up with the national team.

Kit Symons has already mentioned to me how vital it is that everything's done to ensure there are no gaps in the preparation.

He's told me about a coach he's worked with who always talked about match preparation being an exercise in 'filling in all the rabbit holes', meaning no escape routes, no excuses, in the event of a poor performance. It reminds me a bit of Don Revie's infamous 'dossiers', thick booklets containing information on all aspects of the opposition. I once spoke with Norman Hunter about them, he said they were useful but he had a lingering suspicion that the Leeds players were usually so much better than the other team that Revie could have said, 'just go out and play lads'. But Norman's from a very different generation. Now, all the information we seek is available at the click of a button, so why wouldn't you seek to learn as much as possible? Unless you're Gareth Bale, of course, in which case Norman's advice probably could prevail, 'Gareth, just go out and play son.'

Talking of whom, Gareth's out on the pitch, messing about with some of the other players. There's apparently been a lot of interest in him over here and as we stand and watch, a member of the Israeli TV crew sidles up and asks if we think Gareth will sign something for her. It's not something I can answer, but Peter's on hand to suggest she might be best to wait until after the session's over. He says the Israelis have been delighted to see the world's most expensive footballer in their midst. Maybe because Israel doesn't have the best international image, and big stars rarely seem to come here. I doubt Gareth's much aware of this as he practises booting the ball very high in the air, and then trapping it expertly as it descends. He just sees another hand outstretched with a pen and paper, another mobile phone, another selfie, day after day, hour after hour. Where he is now is his 'rabbit hole'. Even more so perhaps as he's away from the madness of Madrid and fans who will boo a player just because he had a shot when he could have passed to Ronaldo.

As Ashley heads off to the media conference room, Chris appears to be walking over to us, then stops, then waits. Peter's escorted Ashley on to his next destination, now he has to escort the manager the 20 yards across the grass and running track to our interview position. Bit daft but I suspect it's something about everything being done right, everyone having their role.

We chat briefly but he's all about business today, with a packed room of journalists awaiting inside the stadium, so we get on with it. The pitch has been an area of concern for him in the build-up, he was critical of it when he came out a couple of months ago, mindful of the Andorra fiasco perhaps. He's far happier with the outcome this time. He's had a look at the problem area, they've done work on it, and it looks fine. I ask whether it's enough for his team to avoid defeat here. He suggests it might be but again, I get a real sense that he sees a chance to do much more than that. Despite that, he talks Israel up, says how well they've done and mentions how upbeat the crowd will be after the start they've made.

It's a sell-out, with around 800 travelling fans coming, but I know just how many people will be watching this back home. By back home, I mean in Wales. This is an event that will literally have the eyes of the nation upon it. If they could do viewing figures for Wales, I'd love to see the percentage of the population that will be sitting down to watch this game. I can picture them, pint in hand, staring at the screen in anticipation, always fearing the worst if they're as bruised as most fans of my generation. But that's a positive as well. There's interest in the national team again, there are stars to worship but it's a team above everything. Chris refers to this, embraces it as something exciting. Expectation is something few Wales sides have had to deal with in the last decade, especially not this far into a qualifying campaign.

The interviews are done, which means I'm done, but I hang around to watch the 15 minute slot. Then I head back to the OB compound. *En route*, I pass the Israel team bus and parked next to it is its escort vehicle, a police motor scooter, complete with big blue light on the box where they usually keep the pizzas. I take a photo and send it back to the editor at Sky Sports News as an example of the heightened security levels we're encountering out here! Then I join the rest of the crew ahead of a lift back to the hotel in our shuttle bus. This bit of the trip has been a big bonus. It just feels like we're being looked after, just like the players, the rabbit holes are filled in so I can concentrate on doing my job to the best of my ability. Ray has already lined up a place to eat for this evening, enlisting the help of a pal of his who's booked us a table at a restaurant that comes recommended. This time, we've got to get it right!

Alex and Bill are all done and back at the hotel but, for reasons I don't really comprehend, Alex is missing the vital piece of kit required to send the interview back to the UK via the hotel's Wi-Fi connection.

Sarah had it, she gave it to Ray, but there's no sign of him as he left the stadium with his pal. Alex looks a little grumpy to say the least. The equipment arrives just as we're preparing to set off, I suggest he could send it back tomorrow but he's diligent and wants it done tonight. He ushers us off to eat, promising to join us when it's done.

We jump into cabs for the trip out. The restaurant appears to be hanging from a rock overlooking the port, it also appears to be extremely popular, with a queue stretching out of the front door. We join it, half in, half out the building. It's the Sabbath now and clearly it's a family night out as kids run, play, shout and generally do their own thing, regardless of the presence of adults. I've seen the same behaviour in the hotel lobby, if it were me, I'd be shushing my two to order, bringing them to heel. Here, the attitude seems very different. I'll be honest, I'm a bit more 'old school', or perhaps British and I find it just a little bit annoying that these children are continually opening and closing the door and pushing in-between adults unadmonished.

After putting up with this for ten minutes or so, our table becomes available and the banquet begins. Our Israeli guide orders starter after starter, salads, three types of humus, seafood, couscous, breads, olives, all sorts. The lights keep dimming as we eat, and, every time they dim, a birthday cake's served up to a diner, it happens every few minutes. Apparently, there's a free dessert for anyone celebrating a birthday. The absent Alex was 40 a few weeks ago, many of us were invited to his party but as it was held on a Saturday, we couldn't attend. Tonight offers the opportunity to mark the occasion. As we order the starters, Alex rings through to say he's on his way. We order him a beer and a steak, should be safe with that, and tip the wink to the waiter. This guy, by the way, is bang on the money, unlike our friend last night.

Alex arrives as the food's served, perfect timing. Somewhat bizarrely, a big sparkler on a plate appears shortly after, accompanied by a song that isn't Happy Birthday but definitely has those words in it. The sparkler, looking a little bit like a distress flare, goes out, we raise our glasses to Alex and then carry on eating.

In the meantime, quiet Ben, the sound man has revealed that he actually does have a birthday tomorrow, his 29th. I'm not sure how it happens but word is passed to our waiter and once the mains have been cleared, the lights dim once more and a proper chocolate dessert appears, again with large sparkler. Clearly, Alex is unaware of the actual celebration in the crew, as he jumps up as it appears and chases it to its resting position in the centre of the table, like John Terry at a trophy presentation. The fact that he's soon piling into the pudding as well has everyone rolling about, except birthday boy Ben, who looks a little nonplussed as our fortysomething cameraman tears into his treat. Luckily, there's quite a bit to go around and a few others dig in as well, it's a team game isn't it?

Well-fed and in high spirits, we head back to the hotel. It being the Sabbath, the bar's closed so the decision's made to give The After Dark bar another go. If it's got one thing in its favour, it's close to the hotel. There are a few more people around this evening, not packed but we're not alone this time. We sit inside the cave, relieved that there's been a staff change since last night. As it turns out, there's a different kind of attitude in the air tonight. If last night's was surly, tonight it's full-on abrasive, up to the point where I'm asked to pay up front for a round of drinks, unlike on every other occasion we've ordered anything. I hand the cash over as ordered and then we wait ages for the drinks, insult to injury, until we have to point out to our aggressive waitress that as they've taken the cash is there any chance of us getting what we ordered?

Things take a turn for the worse when a bearded old chap comes over and, without introducing himself, starts suggesting that there was an issue with a round of drinks that we'd had the previous night and hadn't properly paid for. He says he's going to go and check how much we owe. This is the final straw. We served ourselves the night before, meals arrived ages after they were ordered, we were the only people in the place most of the night, so we certainly put more money over the bar than anyone else and yet we're now being accused of pulling a fast one. We drink up, rise and leave before he can return, flight not fight, it's time for bed, big day ahead tomorrow!

Saturday 28th March

It's a little easier to get up and out this morning, the body adapting to the time changes perhaps? It's all very confusing still. I've got a dual time setting on my digital watch, plus an analogue display so that's three sources, and I don't think anything's actually set to the right time in either Israel or the UK anymore. Actually, there is a dread feeling in my stomach, but that's nothing to do with any beer or humus overload and all about the fact that I'm desperately nervous ahead of another key qualifier. The further they push, the harder it gets; it's MD5.

On that basis, a light breakfast does me fine. I'm planning another run, this time following Dave Rowe's advice and turning right; uphill first, downhill on the way home. It's really humid, temperature in the high 70s I'd guess, and close. The wind's dropped today, so there's less to battle against as I head off. I quickly pass the team hotel, no sign of any activity or indeed security, never mind 'heightened' there's nothing at all.

I keep going a little way, but then the road drops down to the left and I follow it. Down, down, down and further away from the hotel which I can still see high above. This isn't what I had in mind. My crazy shoes are rubbing on the sole of my foot, it's hot and I've now got to go back the way I came, but unexpectedly uphill, again.

As I plod along, retracing my steps, I sense an alternative. There's a sign, some steps, maybe there's a shortcut of sorts? Whilst the road winds its way back up, this route might cut straight through? As it turns out, I'm right. It is a shortcut, of sorts. It's straight up, about 150 steps, my legs are like lead by the time I stagger over the last one. I arrive almost right outside my hotel, sweat now pouring down my forehead.

I bump into Barry on the steps. He laughs at my footwear, predictably. He then coughs quite a lot. He's not on top of his game so I head upstairs to shower and find him some paracetemol. There are no substitutes in our team.

On my return to the lobby, Bill's appeared and we all head off for lunch. The venue rejected on Thursday night is selected on Saturday afternoon, lucky them. It's clearly a popular place, tables inside and outside, but they find room for us. John Hartson and the BBC 5 Live commentary team are in another corner and we go over to say hello. There are worse ways to pass an hour or two pre-match. Food arrives, cold drinks, we chat amidst the locals. It's a well-heeled crowd. I've read of the economic hardships in Israel and the sky-high prices that were set to cost Netanyahu last week's election by all accounts but he came through, maybe these people are still out celebrating his surprise success? The Prime Minister attended the last international in Haifa, the Bosnia game, and caused chaos by staying until the final whistle, meaning no vehicles were allowed to move in the vicinity of the stadium until his cavalcade had left the area. We could do without a repeat tonight, as I suspect the drive back to Tel Aviv will be long enough as it is.

Once lunch is over, it's 'go' time. We head back to the hotel to shed the shorts and t-shirts, and all three of us re-emerge in reception, suited and booted. However, there's now an issue over checkout, Alex and Sarah have had to pay their own room bills but Ray's been on the phone and he's got something sorted in time for our departure. The van and the driver are waiting, so we pack our bags in the boot, climb in and head off.

In terms of superstitions, where are we at? Well, I'm wearing the same jacket I wore in Andorra, but I don't have the same bag or anything else for that matter I will be relying on the chewing gum exchange with Dai the Kitman again. Alex, I know, is wearing the lucky striped socks.

As we approach the stadium, the driver diverts to a busy-looking diner. He has food to pick up for the crew and for us, although we've only just eaten. Then, the next stop is the TV compound. Dark clouds have rolled in from the sea and there's rain in the air as we alight, leaving all our luggage on board for the next leg of our journey.

The evening's first task is to record an interview with Barry by the side of the pitch. The Sports News duties have been curtailed today because there's a Soccer Saturday show all afternoon, the time difference means we will have kicked-off on another channel while they're still on air. I think the interview's going to go into that show, and I've offered to record a quick update on the team news, that they can use, once the teamsheets are confirmed an hour before kick-off.

Conditions have worsened, and the rain is now falling heavily. So we have to delay the interview, it's not live so we aren't working to a strict deadline and it's better to do it without raindrops falling on the camera lens. A five minute wait brings some respite and we get our little chat started, a couple of questions in, the stadium PA booms out and we opt to start again. 'Good rehearsal everyone', is the usual response in these instances. Take two goes more smoothly. We speculate about the team, anticipating the return of Sam Vokes up front and Bale in a more traditional wide left role.

There's more team talk as I head up to the media room afterwards. I bump into Chris Wathan, the *Western Mail* reporter, on the way. He's heard a suggestion that it might be three at the back again, as it was in Andorra and against Bosnia. I express some surprise, given that it didn't work very well in that first game. Maybe it's just a rumour to put the Israelis off?

Except that the next person I see is Bill who's actually been in touch with the manager and, in a quiet corner, he confirms it's true – Williams and Collins as expected, but also Ben Davies in a 'three'. The other bit of news is that Sam Vokes doesn't get a start, Hal Robson-Kanu keeps his place as part of an attacking three with Bale and Ramsey either side of him. It looks a bold move, a view confirmed as I then happen upon Alex on my way back to the OB compound. He's not sure about the formation either. A message pings up on my phone, from Barry, 'what do you think about three at the back?' 'I'll tell you after', I reply, keeping my concerns to myself.

The opportunity to discuss the matter further arrives only shortly afterwards as the Welsh team bus pulls into the stadium a full two hours before kick-off, about half an hour earlier than usual. As Chris emerges and passes me at the interview point in the tunnel, I ask him, "What are you doing here so early?" "They told us we needed to set off early because the traffic gets bad, could take an hour they said" he replies. "So we do. Not a thing on the roads, took us 15 f*#&in' minutes!" The raised eyebrows suggest he thinks Wales may have been the victim of some skulduggery on the part of our hosts.

Still, as he's here, with time to kill, he's keen to get the interview out of the way and after a quick look at the pitch, he returns to the tunnel to talk. It's not quite the traditional pre-match chat, there's no backdrop for a start. The FAW haven't brought one, apparently they were told by the Israel FA that they couldn't put their own up in the tunnel, so it's been left at the hotel. The Israel FA haven't provided one either so we're left with a choice between a blue wall or a white wall against which to shoot the interview. Neither looks very good. Still, it's the words that are most important, and Chris is happy to confirm the formation of the team and the reasons for adopting it.

He also explains Vokes's absence, based on a chat with his club manager that suggested he wasn't operating at the peak of fitness still and Hal's deserved to keep his place anyway. Everything else is about the hostile nature of the crowd and the significance of the game.

Once we've shaken hands and he's headed off to the dressing room, I talk to Sarah in the truck. My concern is that we've done the interview an hour before the teams will officially be confirmed. Israel may not be expecting Wales to line-up like this, the more notice they have, the better they might be able to readjust. I'm anxious that we keep hold of the information until such time as everybody knows it's true. It's happened in the past, that once an interview or even key information arrives at HQ, it quickly spreads through all the myriad tentacles of the Sky operation. Sarah speaks to Jim, Jim sends reassurance back via Sarah that they'll keep it under wraps until the appointed 60 minute deadline.

We're on air 45 minutes before kick-off, so the interview will run quite high up the order I'd imagine, by which time the host nation will know pretty much how Wales are lining up anyway. Or maybe not, because as official team sheets are handed out in the tunnel and the media room, with boxes showing how the teams line-up as a formation, the Welsh box is empty. Israel, it seems, will be 4-3-3.

My work's done for now. I spend the rest of the time walking about, checking the weather, changing from cotton jacket to waterproof jacket, nervously killing time basically. Staff members wander past, hands are shaken, smiles then anxious glances exchanged. With each passing game now, the stakes are raised. A defeat doesn't end anything tonight, but it makes Israel a strong bet for second place at least. A draw's okay, keeps the group leaders in sight and a win's dreamland; top of the group guaranteed halfway through the campaign, at least until Belgium come to Israel for that rearranged game next week. They and Bosnia play Cyprus and Andorra respectively this evening, both will surely win.

As the minutes tick down, the rain passes and I'm able to finally settle on the cotton jacket that graced the touchline in Andorra. My seat is to the right of the away dugout, not quite under cover, but I'm happy to get wet for the greater good. UEFA have provided a Euro 2016 branded umbrella but I don't plan to shelter under it like some sort of lakeside angler.

My latest weather check takes me down the touchline towards the away section, now beginning to fill. The Wales players are out and warming up at this end, Bale banners appear everywhere, not only in the away seats but in the home end as well, 'Bale, I just want a selfie with you' one proclaims, 'Bale, Can I have your shirt?', another asks. In the visitors section, they're unfurling a much more ambitious effort, 'Haters Gonna Hate', it declares in big letters between an FAW crest and an ambitious caricature of the man himself, this clearly in reference to his problems in Madrid. There's only love from the travelling supporters and a fair few of the home ones as well, I suspect. I can see two young women in Real Madrid shirts, 'Bale 11' on the back a few rows up in the midst of the Israel supporters. He's something like a phenomenon in this global sport.

Just as I'm turning to head back in, my phone rings, the name Gary Pritchard appears on the screen, another pal from previous trips and someone else who's been both supporter and reporter. Tonight, he's here as a fan. I know he's going to be somewhere in the vicinity of the ground by now, having flown out for a few days in Tel Aviv earlier in the week. Facebook updates suggest he and his travelling companions have been having a fine time in party central. He's actually made it in ahead of the anthems, always an achievement on these trips in my experience, 'come on, just time for one quick one..'. He describes his position in the stand and I spot him, an arm waving in the upper tier. It's hard to hear him above the cacophony of Israeli techno but I let him know the team news, relayed immediately to his crew, all of whom are lads I know, a mixed group of north and south Walians. All Welsh speakers. I wish him all the best. He's a regular, all the lads he's come with are veteran travellers and ultra-loyal supporters. The real reward at the end of all this would be for them, the people who've stuck with the side regardless. They deserve that summer trip more than anyone.

Shortly afterwards, the Wales players are lining up in the tunnel. As I stand alongside them, they seem have that air about them I've sensed with other international teams when you see them close up at moments like this. There's not a swagger in the stride as such but there's a calm control that suggests they feel they can handle it, whatever it is they're about to encounter. There are a number of players in this team now who are dealing with the pressures of Premier League football week-in and week-out. Only two of the starters play in the Football League. Big crowds and pressure games are what they encounter every game. This stadium might be noisy, but this is a team packed with lads who've played in Champions League games, big derbies and Wembley finals, so this experience should hold no fears. The players start walking out in the midst of a booming fanfare, to the cheers of a packed stadium.

As I wait to tag on at the end of the line to make my own entry into the Coliseum, I remember I still haven't had my chewing gum from Dai. He appears on cue at my shoulder and as our eyes meet, he realises what he needs to do. But there's a problem, he pats his pockets, checks them all, he hasn't got any! Mild panic sets in, he actually sends another member of staff to get some but we have to walk out ourselves now, in fact the mini-delay means I'm not even in my seat as the players belt out the first couple of lines of the anthem; gum-less and now separated by a dugout and 20 metres from my gum supplier. The Israeli anthem takes my mind off this potential catastrophe. There's no band, no music, one guy on the pitch with a mic just starts singing. He's a sort of ageing rock star type with loads of bangles and bracelets, diamond earrings and a shaved head. I don't know what the words are, of course, it's in Hebrew but it sounds incredibly sad, like a lament, appropriate perhaps for this conflicted nation. The crowd join in, it's all pretty moving but not uplifting, like the Welsh anthem or *La Marseillaise*. Only in the last couple of lines does it suddenly lift and become something more bombastic and aggressive, and our man on the pitch finishes with a clenched fist salute, bangles a-jangling.

Birthday boy Ben asks me what I think the score will be as we settle ourselves into our plastic seats. The poor lad's probably expecting some cheery, upbeat response. "I don't do predictions on Wales games". I answer, perhaps rather too tetchily. Mentally, I'm moving into the 'Zone of Dark Foreboding'.

My position on the touchline doesn't give me an overview, but I'm well-placed to spot one of tonight's tactics. Chris Gunter's constantly being urged forward by the bench, pushing deep into enemy territory and the target for long diagonal balls from the back, provided either by James Collins or, more likely in his case, Ashley Williams. It's the same on the other flank, Neil Taylor staying forward even after attacking possession's been conceded. The effect of this is apparent, our three central defenders and two deeper lying midfielders, Allen and Ledley, have smothered the centre of the pitch and their two attacking wide men are having to hang back to counter the threat from the two advanced wing-backs. Israel are not physically imposing, so need to play round Wales, but they're on the back foot right from the off.

This domination begins to manifest itself in the first chance of the night, a swift break leads to a Bale cross from the left, it sails across the box and lands at the feet of James Collins who remarkably is the furthest man forward. It's a manifestation of Wales' intent that it's the big centre half leading the charge. It's great that he's on the edge of the six-yard box, with only the goalie to beat, but he's a centre half! The ball gets stuck under his feet somehow, as if he's trapped it when any sort of clean contact would surely have propelled the ball into the net. Before he can untangle himself, a defender nips in to save the day. To my left, the lads on the sidelines are all on their feet in anticipation, then hands clutch heads in reaction. I wonder whether Wales can really afford to miss chances like that. This level of control needs to produce a goal.

Still, the signs remain encouraging. Ramsey and Bale are switching wings, coming inside then dropping wide. Joe Allen sits in behind them, doing a great job of getting the ball back, keeping possession and the grip tightens. Israel look flustered and far from the world-beaters we'd feared. They give the ball away, often in dangerous positions, panicked into poor passes as red shirts bear down on them. I become aware of just how quiet the stadium is, all the pre-match noise, and now you can hear the players calling to each other. There's one nervy moment that briefly raises noise levels, when an Israeli cross from the by-line that lands in the danger zone but it's dealt with well by Hennessey and the game heads towards half-time with Wales clearly on top. As the board goes up for added time, the one big concern is that the dominance hasn't been rewarded with goals. In commentary I hear Barry making the same point as I prepare to push the headphones off my head, ready for the walk back up the touchline to the tunnel. Wayne Hennessey launches a long ball forward, it reaches the edge of the box then bounces over the head of Kanu, but Gareth Bale's kept his eye on it and leaps prodigiously to flick it forward. Aaron Ramsey's made an instant assessment, worked out where the ball's heading next and he nips in front of his marker to meet it and loop his header up and over the 'keeper. My immediate reaction is that it's going over, then it drops beautifully, under the bar, the net ripples and Wales have their reward in the very last few seconds of the first half.

The goal's scored right in front of the travelling fans and as players sprint to catch Aaron, he races towards the fans, his two index fingers pointing up to the heavens. The Wales supporters are a glorious sight, a writhing mass of joy and euphoria. They tumble over seats and each other in delirious celebration.

Internally, I'm doing something similar, externally, I have to restrict myself to a surreptitious clench of the fist. From my current position, I could actually run onto the pitch and dive on top of the group of celebrating players. Imagine that? I'd be an overnight YouTube sensation! And I'd never work again. I resist the urge. Within seconds, the half-time whistle blows and I'm heading in the direction of the tunnel instead. It's all happened so swiftly. nobody seems to have had chance to take it in yet. Little smiles are exchanged as I catch sight of various members of the FAW staff but the old heads know not to get carried away, that this might be the prelude only to even greater disappointment. 'It's the hope that kills you', and all that. Having said that, the impression gained from the first half does give me grounds for a modicum of cautious optimism. It takes someone like Alex, less damaged by watching Wales, to put things into their proper context. "We'll win this easily. Israel are rubbish", he opines confidently. I agree, but caution that with the response that they can only be better in the second half.

As I'm hanging around at the interview position, a minor crisis develops. The gist of it, I think is that some of the Wales players want a half-time can of Red Bull and there isn't any in the dressing room. The Israel FA can't or won't supply any, suggesting only that the FAW can buy some from a stall somewhere close. The problem is, the cash they bring for this type of event is in the dressing room and nobody wants to intrude at such a key time. I have 200 shekels in my wallet which I happily offer to help the cause. My donation, actually it's a loan, is accepted and a member of staff departs to try and buy some energy drinks. Mark Evans appears and we talk interest rates, is it the VIG they call it in the Mafia movies?

At this stage, I sense a cameo role in any future blockbuster as the man who supplied the money that bought the energy drinks that ensured Wales won in Israel. Except that the member of staff comes back empty handed, and I get my money back. No drinks, no interest.

The players seem lively enough anyway as they begin to reappear in the tunnel. None of the fist-pumping, loud-swearing hysteria you sometimes experience before teams head out at times like this, just that quiet sense of determination displayed by teams who believe in the superiority of their group and who believe in each other. I follow them out, trying to work out just what it is I'm feeling. It's not easy to identify, it's almost unsettling, I think the feeling is confidence. I seek to suppress it; 'prepare for the worst you idiot'. I retake my seat. The second half starts.

Then Gareth Bale sets off on one of his runs, actually they're surges really, aren't they? He's up to top speed and trailing defenders in his wake. As he drifts inside another challenge, a leg catches him and he tumbles to the ground. From where I sit, I can't see exactly where he is but I'm pretty sure he's very close to the edge of the penalty box if he's not actually in it. A glance at the monitor down to my right confirms it's a free kick right on the edge of the area, just right of centre. Tibi, the culprit and a real weak link in the first half, has been booked as a result.

It's a similar position to the one in Andorra, still the most crucial moment in this campaign so far, as it was the one moment when everything balanced on the tightrope between hope and despair. The dynamic's changed a bit since but it feels like another big moment in terms of the way things go from here, and the crowd seems to recognise that. Something of a hush descends as Bale goes through his familiar free kick routine. Suddenly, it all feels more akin to a key penalty in a Six Nations rugby international and, like his oval ball contemporaries Leigh Halfpenny or Dan Biggar, Gareth takes the required and well-measured number of steps back, never turning away from the ball. The crowd's quietness suggest we're all aware that we're about to watch a master craftsman at his work. Then the run-up begins with the player marking a small arc in his path towards the ball before he meets it with a whip-like flick of the foot. I can visualise it but I could never hope to reproduce it. It's a super slo-mo moment but someone on the Welsh bench steps right into my line of vision just as the ball rises over the wall of defenders, so I don't see it dip or see it hit the target. I do see the ripple in the net that travels from the right of the goal to the left and the arms that shoot up at the same instant. It's another masterpiece!

My response? Another clenched fist, a whispered "yesssss", but I'm in control, there's still a long way to go and I'm a massive pessimist. Then, almost immediately the game restarts and the whole thing plays out again. Gareth sets off on another run, a little further out maybe but Tibi lunges in again and Gareth falls over, and I think I know what follows. The ref, a Serbian, Milorad Mažić, who's been excellent all night puts his hand to his pocket and Tibi's fate is sealed. It has to be a second yellow, followed by the red and the defender's miserable night is brought to a premature end. 2-0 up and Israel down to 10 men. Now and only now am I prepared to accept that the worst that could happen now is that we get a point. Believe me, that represents rampant gung-ho, crack cocaine levels of optimism given my usual state of mind an hour into an away fixture.

On the bench, the professionals, the coaches, the manager must now feel the job's been done. I'm a fan, I can't rationalise the situation completely. I see signs that reinforce a sense that I need to remain cautious. For a start, Wales go off the boil. Barry's pretty hard on them in commentary, a flurry of misplaced passes draws his ire but I know it's because he's desperate for the same outcome as the rest of us. Barry is articulating our nagging fears.

Israel do rally briefly and Wayne Hennessey makes another good block from a cross, whipped in from the left. He's had a quiet night of it so far, but when he's been called upon he's done his bit tonight, like so many others.

It's proves to be a temporary upturn for Israel. Joe Allen calms the nerves by getting a grip of the game in midfield again. He wins the ball, makes sure it ends up with a teammate, gets it back again, and keeps the process going. It's a basic bit of play but he's the cog that keeps the watch ticking. The crowd quietens, only the combined voice of the travelling fans can be heard, away to my right. At times like this I'd love to be up there amongst them, hoarse, tired, a little nervy but sensing the imminent outpouring of unconfined joy that the next 20 minutes might/should bring.

I've very much got my eye on the big clock, doing my five-minute thing again. Sam Vokes is on now and almost marks his international return with a goal, but the 'keeper and a defender block his efforts.

Then after a quick glance to confirm another 300 seconds have elapsed, another player returns to international action after a long break, David Vaughan. Shortly after he wins possession back for Wales, midway inside Israel's half, he steers a great pass into Ramsey, who swerves left but keeps the ball on his right and in the same movement rolls it towards the penalty spot. It's an audacious bit of football in itself, but what's even better is that Gareth Bale's anticipated it and he times his burst into the box to perfection, stretching to push the ball in, between the hands of the diving 'keeper. "Yesssss! That's it!" is the stifled reaction from the reporter seat to the right of the Welsh dugout. On the bench and in the away section, it's joy unconfined. All doubts can now be banished. Wales are going to win in Israel! This means I can now relax and actually enjoy the next 10 minutes. For the first time in the campaign, I can enjoy watching Wales for ten whole, beautiful, minutes. In fact, for the first time in 10 years, I can sit back and really enjoy watching Wales. There have been one or two other games when we've had a good lead, but they've either been friendlies or dead rubber qualifiers. So, for the first time in over a decade, I can exude nothing but positivity as the game plays out in front of me. It's all good, everything. Wow! So, this is what it feels like is it? This is what Real Madrid, Chelsea and Bayern Munich fans expect to experience regularly is it? I like it!

In all the other games in this group, I've headed off to my interview position with the result still in the balance, so I've had to prepare questions for different scenarios. Tonight I've got the luxury of knowing exactly what we're going to be talking about in a few minutes time.

In my opinion, this is the most important away win for Wales since Finland in the first game of the qualifiers for Euro2004. I was there as a fan that day, it was the icing on the cake of a great weekend in Helsinki. We partied hard afterwards, as will the dancing masses in the visitor's section tonight. But I feel different on this occasion. Then I'd spent the afternoon drinking beer and the evening singing and jumping up and down in the away end. Tonight, I'm working, and I've still got the most important job ahead of me. I'm looking to do interviews with the two goalscorers, and the big buzz for me will be sharing some of their elation at a job very well done. As I walk past the figures in the away dugout, my grin matches the faces I see there, I feel like clicking my heels as I turn into the tunnel.

Predictably, I'm planning on asking for the interviews on the final whistle to be with Gareth and Aaron. I convey my plan back to base. Then, Sarah passes on a message from Jim, the producer, back at base. Can I ask Gareth about Real Madrid? This comes as a bit of a surprise and I have to make a quick assessment before I respond. I know what he's getting at, the backstory from a non-Welsh perspective is all about Bale being booed at Madrid before scoring twice for Wales. But I've got concerns about pursuing this line of interrogation. I was asked to do something similar once with Craig Bellamy, playing for Wales after being on the bench for Liverpool in the Champions League final, they lost and he didn't get on. The producer wanted me to reflect that in the first question. I wasn't happy about it but I went along with it, trying to form a question that hinted at one event whilst majoring on the matter in hand. It didn't work. As soon as I asked if a draw with New Zealand represented a poor end to a poor week, he went mad. He laid into me verbally, lambasting me for asking a question about Liverpool when he'd just been playing for Wales? It was excruciating for me and, I'm sure, the viewers, as the interview all went out live.

My ordeal wasn't over as he returned twice more in the next few minutes to shout abuse at me, to accuse me of not showing him any respect. It was a scarring experience and one I'm not keen to repeat. Gareth is a very, very different character to Craig but still, there are dangers. There's enough sensitivity around our interview requests with him already as we've already seen. So if I put him on the spot with a question about Real Madrid immediately after a massive win for Wales, he might not go mad with me, but he might not come back and talk to me next time. On top of all of that, if I'm a fan watching back home and I know there will be loads of them, I'm not bothered about Bale and Madrid. I'm bothered about Bale and Wales.

I don't do it very often but I ask Sarah to tell Jim I don't think it's a good idea, that I'm worried if I do, there might be short-term interest in the answer but long-term damage to the relationship. There's isn't time for a massive discussion of course, we're minutes away from doing it and, if Jim insists, I will follow orders. Still, I've been at this game for a long time, 23 years now, so hopefully I've learnt a bit along the way. I'm relieved and pleased and grateful when Sarah relays Jim's acceptance of my suggestion. Good man, good decision.

In the tunnel, there's a sense of calm. Whatever the outcome, there are people here who have a job to do; press officers, stewards, reporters, UEFA officials. For those out there, the night's almost over. We still have things to do.

There are FAW staff around as well of course. They look really happy but it's all controlled jubilation and I like that. It means it doesn't feel like something so utterly out of the ordinary that Wales have come to Israel and scored three goals and won. People aren't dancing jigs, it's the little clenched fist again, a thumbs up maybe; the bigger the win, the smaller the demonstration. Besides, nobody's actually achieved anything yet. It's just another step on the journey, another obstacle overcome. We're still only halfway to paradise.

An interview board has miraculously appeared by now, so the Israel FA's sponsors will get their exposure behind Gareth Bale's head. IG asks who we're after, knowing already what I'm going to say. The UEFA delegate, a helpful, friendly young chap, asks the same question so he can tick names off on the list attached to his clipboard. The game goes on, but there's none of the usual pacing up and down in the tunnel this time. Mark Evans has a look of zen-like calm about him in comparison to the final seconds of pretty much every previous game in this group, when he's been visibly consumed by some type of terror at the prospect of an awful, unexpected, last second twist.

The whistle goes. It's done. Wales are back on top of the group, until Tuesday at least and I can hear the strains of 'We are top of the league, we are top of the league' as the players stay out to celebrate with the fans. The FAW's clever social media campaign, with the hashtag #TogetherStronger comes to mind. At times like these, it feels that way.

As we wait for our two guests, an Israel FA official comes over, do we want to talk to their manager? He's already faced his inquisitors from the host broadcasters, my priority lies elsewhere though, I need the people back home to hear from their heroes. So, I politely decline. There's another game on live, shortly after ours, so I want to make sure we get as much reaction into our coverage as possible.

A bare-chested Gareth Bale appears, closely followed by Aaron Ramsey. I shuffle them over into the corner and get the all-clear to start from Sarah sitting in the truck in the compound. The two lads exude happy positivity. Gareth goes first, bare-chested but with an Israel player's shirt draped round his shoulders. He starts the interview by dedicating the win to Dai Williams, the kitman we lost along the way. It's a nice touch and a reminder that because of what they've seen, this group will always have an awareness of what constitutes real tragedy, not the sporting kind. They both speak really well, neither getting too carried away, maybe in recognition of the unexpectedly poor standard of the opposition, and already focused on the next one, the next big one, Belgium in Cardiff in June.

Once they're headed off to the dressing room, our UEFA man asks if there's anyone else we want? The manager's the high priority for the programme but I ask for another player as well, James Collins, back in the side and no goals against. Moments later the man they/we still call 'Big Ginge' is ushered out to join me. He's been around for the entire time I've been covering Wales, the last survivor of the most recent, decent side. We've chatted in many tunnels in many countries in the years since and I still recall a doleful conversation in Podgorica, after a dismal away defeat, when he lamented the fact that he always seemed to make a big mistake playing for Wales. Players aren't conditioned to talk negatively about themselves, so it was an admission that remains in my memory. For that reason, I'm delighted for him tonight.

He's self-effacing in the interview as well, "I hope you're not going to tell me I missed a sitter" he says. I have to make an effort from answering "you did!" He speaks with genuine pride about being part of this group of younger players, and how much he'd love to achieve qualification with them.

Now, we need the manager. There's still no sign of him, so I wander up towards the away dressing room. I'll catch anyone's eye that I can to get the message passed through the dividing doors. I wander back to my position. Eventually, the doors swing open and a tall, dark-haired figure pushes through them in the manner of a Western gunslinger. I've got more time to talk to Chris, to reflect on the change in formation, almost by way of an admission of my lack of faith. Chris is good on stuff like this, doesn't ram it back down anyone's throat, admits he and his staff took a risk but made their decision based on all the work they'd put into studying the opposition.

171

He sings Gareth's praises but recognises everybody's contribution, including the supporters. This guy was the subject of fierce criticism in the media, on the message boards and even on the terraces not so long ago but still, he resists the urge to bite back. Nothing's been achieved yet, let's look forward to Belgium.

I've asked for Ashley Williams as my final interviewee, but word comes back that he's just got into the shower so he's going to be a while and our studio time's coming to an end, so the people at base are happy to call it a day. Earpiece out, I shake hands with the crew, then head for the OB compound and our ride out of here. Now is the time to relax in the company of friends. There's a little jig, a hearty handshake with Alex, and a bear hug with Bill. It must look to the outside world like the three of us had won the game. Which, I guess, we have. We've had some great times together already as a small team, and we want more.

It's only now that I realise I haven't actually eaten anything for several hours. It's 10.30pm and we've now got the drive back to Tel Aviv before a really early start for the flight back to Heathrow and then Wembley. I'm hungry and I'd love to toast success with a glass of beer. Sadly, neither option is available as the five of us travelling back tonight climb aboard our transport. As anticipated, we turn out of the broadcast compound and into two lines of solid traffic, brake lights blinking away as far as the eye can see. We obviously aren't the only ones heading in the same direction. For a start, somewhere up ahead there's a convoy of coaches carrying the Wales fans back to a big party in Tel Aviv.

It's a long drive, not without its laughs, but it takes a bit of an edge off the euphoria of the evening. In an attempt to keep the party going, I play tunes on my iPhone and Barry suggests a beer stop. Our driver's very obliging and pulls over at a service station. There's a shop and we collect some cans, a sandwich, some sweets for Sarah and join the queue at the counter. Barry nips off for a call of nature. In his absence, a tragic scene's enacted, Alex gets to the counter with our goodies and the bloke behind it tries to tap the code for the beer into his till but it won't work. He tries again, no good. He tries to explain the problem but can't do it in English, the guy behind us in the queue helps out, "he says he can't sell beer after 11pm, the till won't let him." We're so befuddled by now that we disconsolately abandon everything on the counter and trudge back onto the bus. Barry bounds up moments later like a puppy looking forward to chewing a new bone. When we explain what happened, he thinks we're joking, then he's crestfallen.

We return to the slow road, a little bit quieter. The only positive we took is that the guy behind the counter suggested we try the next place along, as they can serve beer after 11. So, we re-enact the whole scenario a few miles further on. This time, it's Bill who nips off to the 'Gents'. He returns beaming and looking forward to a beer only to be told we've failed again. Incredibly, he also thinks we're joking!

The final act in this tragi-comedy is played out at another service station. This time, the driver has vowed to help out and when we pull up he goes off to negotiate his way round Israeli licensing laws. We're actually almost in Tel Aviv by now but, fittingly for the Holy Land, it's become a grail-like search. Once more, he returns empty-handed.

Our next stop is the hotel. It's half past midnight as we check in, via a tricky lift arrangement that requires some working out. The guy on reception is friendly, unusually for this trip, and offers vital assistance to weary travellers. So, A) we need to be at the airport at least two and a half hours before the flight at 8am, and B) yes he will go and get some beers. As Alex has all his gear to get through security, he's adamant he needs to get to the airport three hours beforehand. There's an airport shuttle from the hotel that takes 15 minutes, so he plans to leave at 4.30. Sarah agrees to go with him. For Bill, Barry and me, there's the luxury of whole half an hour extra in bed before we leave at 5am.

Sarah heads off to grab her three hours sleep as we settle back to await the arrival of that beer. Alex heads to his room to drop his kit off, promising to return to join us. Our hotel man is as good as his word and moments later we're finally toasting another great away trip. Alex comes back, it appears the guy's only brought three beers, there isn't another one on the counter. At this point it all gets too much for the G-man, it's been a long day and we're all on the edge, "Thanks for that, I'll just go to bed then!" he hisses at us, then spins round and goes back the way he's just come. The tabloids would say he 'stormed out'. Bill's a bit taken aback, "Come back Alex", he calls after him plaintively but all that's left is a cloud of princess dust. "Was he serious?", Bill asks. I'm too tired to form any serious thoughts by this stage so I mumble "probably", then Barry orders more beers. I

173

climb into bed at 1.30am, set the alarm for 4 and settle down for a whole two and half hours sleep!

Sunday March 29th

Technically, the diary entry for 29th has already started but let's not confuse matters. Certainly, I'm far from at the top of my game as I stagger around the room trying to find my phone to switch the alarm off a few hours into the new day.

Then, I scrape a razor across my chin and shower, all in an effort to normalise the experience of getting up so early after so little sleep. I'm trying to kid my brain into thinking everything's okay.

Now, I've got to dress for a trip that will see me rush straight off the runway at Heathrow to Wembley way. Normally, I'd travel ultra-casual in some shorts and a t-shirt but today's ensemble starts with Wrexham FC underpants, first time on. Over them, I pull smart wool trousers. On my feet, I've got the work shoes I wore last night so my only nod to casual attire is the FAW polo I'm wearing for just the journey.

Of course, I've got my blazer, along with a new shirt and tie, in the suit bag that I've carried across the globe without actually using yet. There is a plan for this. Bill has agreed to take it on the plane as his second permitted piece of hand luggage. That means I then have two bags I can take on and with no waiting by the carousel at the other end, we should get to Wembley more quickly. Military planning.

This, though, is Tel Aviv airport we're going to be heading from. The reason we've been warned to get there early is because of the notorious security checks, more stringent on the way out than the way in. Yet, here I am, handing over my bag to Bill to take through. Even in my bleary-eyed state I'm conscious enough to describe just what it is I've got in the bag, to the best of my memory, in case he gets asked that question about 'packing the bags yourself sir?'

We set off into the night/morning. It's a 15 minute drive through deserted streets to the airport and yet, once more, when we arrive, it's all hustle and bustle. There was a thought in my mind that maybe things would be a bit more easy-going at this hour, but if they are, I'd hate to see it later. The first passport check takes place before we actually get to the check-in desks. It's not any old passport check though, it's a full-on interrogation conducted by two passport checkers. Barry's first up, he gets asked where St Asaph is as it's mentioned as his place of birth? He explains that it's in Wales. Other questions follow about his travel and his reason for being in the country, then he's waved through. Bill's next. He gets even more about his work, does he travel often, has he been working with others, why aren't they here? He mentions the fact he's with other people from Sky and then things change a little. He's asked who else in the queue works for Sky? He points us all out. Sarah and Alex have arrived from his big security check on the equipment by now, and we're told to gather together, then another official gets involved, a thin-faced young chap. I think back to school days studying Julius Caesar and Cassius with his 'lean and hungry look'.

He stands in the centre and addresses different members of the team in turn. He asks what we all do, to each person individually. At this point we have to stifle laughs as Sarah has previously described how difficult it is for some people to accept that she's a director. Pure, old-fashioned chauvinism of course. She joked that she's sometimes resorted to answering the 'and what do you do in television?' question by saying, 'I do the make-up', accompanied by a girlie giggle. We all think the same thing as the spotlight falls on her, go on Sarah, dare you?! She doesn't, probably wise, imagine what would happen if we all burst out laughing at her answer? We'd be in the cells in seconds I'm sure. Besides, I'm already worried that Bill's going to crack under questioning about the contents of my bag. 'What is your collar size then Mr Leslie?'.

The whole process takes about 10 minutes. I actually come through without having to answer anything other than the question about the job I do, which is a relief given my current befuddled state. Next up, for some, it's check-in but I've already done that online, securing myself another backrow, aisle seat. My satisfaction at this has been tempered somewhat by the fact that everyone else seems to have been upgraded. As we march through the airport I complain about the injustice, the only one of our party who anyone occasionally recognises as being on the telly, and I'm the one who doesn't get the upgrade?! I'm joking, honest.

There's still more fun to be had at the airport, as the 'proper' passport check awaits and we queue patiently for our turn. I step forward to the counter and hand over my dishevelled passport. The bearded bloke behind the Perspex looks at it quizzically. "What happened?" he asks, holding it up gingerly. "The dog chewed it", I reply. "Urrrggghhh!" he yelps and immediately tosses it away, face contorted in mock disgust. It appears that as I'm one short step away from leaving the country, I've encountered my first display of Israeli humour.

The fun and games don't end there though. Next up, let's play try and bluff your way into the BA lounge again, this time with five! Alex has been off somewhere doing something important involving his kit. He comes back triumphant, they've given him a lounge pass for everyone! This sounds too good to be true and I follow the group loungewards with the same resigned expectation of imminent defeat I have previously adopted on my way to Wales away games. Now, as then, it's the hope that kills you so better not to hope. So, the predictable knockback comes as no surprise. Alex has got the wrong end of the stick somehow. I'm not sure how, too tired.

Did I mention how hungry I was? I grabbed a biscuit in reception at the hotel but that's it since 2pm yesterday. A table is claimed close to bar/café in the centre of the big circle of duty free shops that form the major throughfare in this airport. A coffee and a *pain au chocolat* appear in front of me and I eat and drink greedily.

Then we move on through to the gate; the flight is apparently on time. Mark Evans had mentioned that some of the players had opted to travel back on this flight, rather than the charter to Cardiff later this afternoon. I'm reminded of this as a large bloke lumbers over towards us, looking a little the worse for wear. It's 'Big Ginge'! He crashes down into a seat next to me and opposite Barry. It's clear he's had more success in celebrating the win than we did, a fact he quickly confirms. "Alright boys? I've had a few beers!" He's in fine form anyway and we have a good chat about the match. He's at pains to emphasise just how well Joe Allen played, in his estimation. "My man of the match", he says, describing how Allen makes life so easy for the central defenders, protecting them, taking the ball off them when the pressure's on.

Then there's Wayne Hennessey, "Why is no one mentioning his ball for the first goal?" he asks. "They think that's just a clearance. It isn't! He's pinged that right onto Gareth's head. There's no 'keeper in the world can strike a ball like Wayne, he does it in training. That's a worked-on move that."

Inevitably, the chat turns to the superstar, "I was talking to Ashley about him in the second half", he says, a good indication of how little they had to do in that period, "I said, how do you play against him Ash? How do you stop him? It's impossible, he's got everything!"

We look ahead to the next game. "We fear no one now" he states, "We think we can beat anyone in the world on our day." Delivered differently, it might sound arrogant, boastful, but he says it like he really means it. All this ends up with laughter about all the long journeys home we've shared after disappointing defeats in far flung corners of Europe, not much cause for celebration that's for sure.

Ginge sways off to join the other players, 'old school'. He joked that he was having a few beers after the game whilst the young lads were all playing on their computers. Barry appreciated that, he was part of a different generation that Ginge just about belongs to. He tells tales of international trips that always began with the golf bag being the first thing lifted out of the boot of the car. As our flights called, I collect the suitbag that Bill's managed to leave draped over the back of his chair and return it to him as he strides off towards the gate.

I pass more players as we board, Chris Gunter's with Aaron Ramsey in the posh seats, small cubicles actually. He calls me back for a quick chat before I block up the aisle and have to keep moving on towards my seat far, far away. I'm not the only one though, the man who started the move that led to the third goal, David Vaughan, the quietest footballer ever, is sitting a couple of rows in front of me, alongside Owain Fôn Williams, the second choice 'keeper. Evidently, they didn't make the cut when it came to allocating the business class seats. Owain's at Tranmere, currently teetering on the brink of relegation out of the Football League and David's barely played a game for Forest in months, maybe that's a factor?

This plane is bigger than the one that brought us out but it's also busier and guess what, I've got the guy eating the smelly cheese biscuits with the hacking cough and sinus issues sitting next to me! My joy becomes unconfined when the pilot comes on the PA to explain that the bags have been packed on incorrectly, and they're having to be repacked and we've missed our slot, so he doesn't know when we'll be taking off.

177

It's an hour as it turns out. A miserable hour spent dodging flying crumbs and bacteria. I start to watch a Benedict Cumberbatch thing about Bletchley Park but a story about posh, clever blokes doesn't really grip me and I drift off to sleep. I awake to the end credits and the plane finally in the air.

My power nap keeps me going for the next four and a half hours. By now, UK time has changed as well, it's 12.25pm by the time we can finally get out of our seats to get bags out of overhead lockers. That leaves just over an hour to get off the plane, onto a train, then a tube, then a walk to Wembley. We won't be seeing kick-off.

I'm last off because of my seat at the back, Barry's racing ahead. He's got a wheelie bag, I've got two to carry plus the suit bag that Bill surreptitiously hands me once we reach the main building. Passport control should be easy, I'm biometric. Barry's never done it before, so I explain the ease of the procedure. He sails through. I, Mr International Traveller, don't. It tells me to take my passport to be checked. Barry, with David Vaughan and Owain Fôn Williams as sidekicks, looks on, and laughs at me from the other side of the barriers.

At the desk, the woman asks the inevitable question, "what happened to your passport?" Again, I explain about my dog's antics. "Oh, have you ever tried to get into America with it?" she asks, somewhat mysteriously. "No", I reply, "might it be a problem?" "I don't know" she answers, helpfully.

Finally through, Barry sets a fast pace in pursuit of the Heathrow Express to Paddington. We arrive at the platform just as a train pulls out. We are prevented from getting on the one on the other platform whilst they carry out a security check. Time's ticking fast towards the 1.30 kick-off and Barry's son is waiting for him at Wembley, ticketless until his dad arrives. He was expecting to sit down for a slap-up meal pre-match, but our delayed flight means we've missed all that. Poor lad's now sitting in a pub somewhere near the stadium nursing a packet of crisps and a pint.

Once we're finally allowed on the train, I head off to do my Clark Kent routine in the toilet. I emerge in blazer, pink shirt, red Wrexham FC tie and matching cufflinks and a top pocket hankie. There's a red and black bar scarf to complete the Royal Box outfit.

I get team news from Twitter, on the train, and by the time we've switched to the tube at Baker Street, Wrexham are a goal up. The last bit of the journey is a long slog from the top of the steps at Wembley Park station, up the red carpet and to the doors of the stadium. Barry's son appears, looking hungry, and we finally burst into the reception room behind the Royal Box five minutes before half-time, eight hours after setting off from the hotel this morning; barely 12 hours since we left the stadium last night.

The sight that greets us is an odd one. To the right, seats well filled with Wrexham fans, probably about 12,000 in all. To the left, almost nobody. North Ferriby's a village with a population of only 3,500 and most of them have turned up but it doesn't make much of an impression at Wembley.

No sooner have we sat down than the whistle goes for half-time and we race back inside for a drink and a sandwich. Apparently, the game's been dull, Wrexham have been poor but Ferriby are worse.

The game seems unimportant. The league season for Wrexham's been disappointing, and we've won this trophy before, two years ago, but when we score another goal on the hour, I do allow myself to think that for once in my sorry football-watching existence, I might actually get to see my two teams win two big games, back-to-back. I always get one or the other, sometimes neither, but now it looks like I'm finally going to get both! The clock ticks down and the game's uneventful. I'm in the front row of the Royal Box and I'll be shaking the Wrexham players' hands in less than 15 minutes.

But this chapter couldn't end like that, could it? That wouldn't be me. Inside the last quarter of an hour, the part-time team pull a goal back from the penalty spot. Now, their left-sided winger, the number 11, is performing like a non-league version of the world's most expensive player. With seconds to go, he tortures our right back again, cuts the ball back and a sub sticks it in for 2-2, Wrexham become the only team to be booed off by its own supporters with the scores level at the end of full-time in a Cup Final.

In extra time, things get worse, North Ferriby score again and then cling on grimly until the 119th minute, when Wrexham contrive an equaliser that sends it to penalties.

I know by now, that there's no way we can win this. The Football Gods are playing with me, they've had their fun, shown me a tantalising glimpse of a world where my teams win, now they need to restore the rightful order. We miss three spot kicks, they miss a couple as well, but not as many as us, so they win. And I stay and applaud them up the steps to lift the trophy.

People have asked me a number of times which was the more important game to me this weekend, Wales or Wrexham? I've answered Wales every time, in the grand scheme of things, qualification is the goal I've longed for almost my entire life. Still, slumped back in my seat in the Royal Box, ahead of a tube trip to King's Cross and a train ride back to Leeds, this afternoon's events have definitely taken the edge off that fantastic win in Israel. That's why I won't be getting carried away any time soon. Give me three points needed from the last game against Andorra and then, maybe I'll have a quick check on ferry times to France.

The Spirit of '58 event prior to the Belgium game in Cardiff, and I have my first ever crack at DJ-ing. The SO58 bucket hats were everywhere!

The SO58 events help raise thousands of pounds for charities and unite fans from all over Wales, a big success!

All smiles as I prepare to interview Ian Rush, a hero of mine, before the game.
He was confident, 'We always beat Belgium' he suggested.

My favourite ever band, Super Furry Animals, played a live set before the
Belgium game. I made sure I was there to see them getting the atmosphere
going.

Eden Hazard and Ashley Williams shake hands in the tunnel before locking horns on the pitch. Two Premier League stars preparing to meet on the international stage.

Belgium manager Marc Wilmots prowls the technical area in the 90th minute, his team on the verge of defeat. I should have been in the tunnel by now but I wasn't going to miss this!

On the streets of Cardiff in the early hours of the following day and I bump into Tim Williams, Mr Spirit of '58 himself. Needless to say I'm wearing one of his hats.

Dale Johnson
@dalejohnsonESPN

New FIFA Ranking top 10:
1 Argentina
2 Germany
3 Belgium
4 Colombia
5 Netherlands
6 Brazil
7 Portugal
8 Romania
9 England
10 Wales

05/07/2015 15:43

The win against Belgium propels the national side up the FIFA rankings, into the top 10 for the first time ever! The side had been 117th only a couple of years before.

New skills learnt along the way included finding out how to disable the light sensors in the dressing rooms at the Cardiff City Stadium. We needed to make the rooms dark before our interviews.

It's not all glamour! Here I am, organising the 'feed' of material we've just shot at the stadium, in a damp and cold Cardiff, before heading for sunny Cyprus.

Pre-match preparations were pretty pleasant in Cyprus. Bill and I stay cool at poolside, with some soft drinks, honest!

Interviews with the opposition were a regular feature of our pre-match build-up. The best interview of the lot was in Nicosia with Jason Demetriou, who was set to play a defining role in Wales's qualification for Euro 2016.

The thousands of Wales fans in Cyprus, many of whom had turned the trip into a late summer holiday, were superb. Belgium played in Nicosia a few days later, with a fraction of the support.

The great thing about the Welsh football team is that it draws support from all parts of Wales, and some of the most loyal fans come from the furthest flung corners of the country.

Almost there! Another win to celebrate in Cyprus but Barry's smiles would fade as he embarked on another nightmare trip home.

Bill Leslie recorded for posterity the moment when I finally let slip that I thought Wales would qualify. 'We'll never qualify' had been my mantra up until this point.

My daughters Megan and Millie. I've missed them, and regretted not being there for some important family landmarks whilst I've been away covering Wales games, including Megan's 16th birthday on the day we flew back from Cyprus.

Andy King, Ashley Williams, Chris Gunter and Gareth Bale. I've been lucky to work with a squad featuring so many bright, articulate young men. Some of the interviews I've done during this campaign with the Welsh squad have been amongst the best in my career.

We arrive in Bosnia having travelled with the team for the first time, still seeking the one point that ensures qualification. As we arrive in Sarajevo, I get news of another Barry Horne travel saga.

We had our own travel nightmare trying to get to our hotel in Vitez. The country's troubled past still in evidence. Luckily we had brought neither Scotty dogs nor handguns.

Four large men pack into a small hire car for the terrifying trip over the mountain from Vitez to Zenica. Don't be fooled by the smiles, our driver's face tells the real story.

It's pouring with rain, he's had hardly any sleep after travelling all night, but Barry's still going to turn in a fine performance as he prepares to talk to the guys in the studio pre-match.

Gary, Alun and Rhys in the away end, belting out the anthem. They're amongst the loyal hardcore that have stuck with the side, home and away, no matter how bad it's been.

The moment the dream became reality. I've just heard Bill announce full-time in Israel, so despite the defeat, Wales have qualified! When these photos are taken I'm the only person in the ground aware of the Israel result. No words are needed as the fans see my celebrations.

Within seconds, word's spread and a party starts in front of the away end. In the midst of it, I have to stay professional and keep the interviews coming...after hugging the FAW's Mark Evans.

The lads who made it happen. The best bunch of people I've dealt with in nearly 25 years covering football.

Chris came in at a difficult time, had a difficult start, and can now celebrate.

Me and Roger Speed at The Cardiff City Stadium before the final game with Andorra. I've known Roger from Gary's days at Leeds United. He's a lovely man and I know how proud he was at seeing the players finish the job his son started. Welsh fans will never forget.

Inside the ground, the party's already started. The Merthyr boys are in the mood. Down at the front is my old mate Fuzzy, Wrexham and Wales, home and away.

We've been through a lot together in the 11 years we've been covering Wales. Alex now talks about Wales as 'we' and I couldn't have had a better guy at my side. Top cameraman, top person.

The players waiting to be called onto the pitch for the post-game celebrations.

Wales has never seen a night like this, for my money the greatest Welsh sporting achievement ever. Diolch!

Team Sky, complete with Tîm Cymru t-shirts, attempt the Joe Ledley dance as we bring an end to a successful campaign. Barry, sadly, is already on his way back home but he, Bill, Sarah and Alex, were just brilliant to work with, thanks guys!

Team Law! Back home and a nice glass of bubbly in the company of my fantastic family. I have to be extra nice to them between now and June when I might be popping away for a bit.

What can I say? This has been an amazing odyssey. I've waited my whole life to see this...and I'm going to enjoy it. Iechyd da!

6

"Too soon Barry, too soon"
Wales v Belgium

'We are top of the league, said we are top of the league'

Wednesday 3rd June

If there's any 250 mile car journey in the world I could attempt blindfold, it has to be the one from Leeds to Cardiff. I'm making it again today and as I cruise control through the endless 50 mph speed limits on the M1, my mind begins to wander and I begin to wonder just how many times I've actually made this journey. It has to be in the hundreds by now. I drove down as a fan many times and as I've been covering Wales for Sky for over 10 years, with about 10 Wales games a year, at 500 miles per trip, I reckon I've done about 200,000 miles at least just on this journey. In more recent years, I've added to the tally as I've been helping the FAW Coach Education program by hosting 'Football And The Media' sessions for coaches studying for their UEFA A and Pro licences.

On that basis, it's the second trip I've made to south Wales in a week. On Sunday, I was one of the guest speakers at the National Coaches' Conference, held at the Celtic Manor in Newport. I got the train down for that one to break things up a bit, knowing that I'd probably be heading in the same direction at some point in the next few days to help with another 'green screen' shoot for Sky Sports, possibly even to do that elusive 'sit down' interview with Gareth Bale.

Requests for both had been submitted weeks ago, but it was still 'probably' and 'possibly' on Sunday evening as I made the trek back north after my presentation to a room full of football coaches. The players were due to assemble the following day, but we still hadn't heard what access we might be getting to fulfil one or the other of the two tasks.

Finally, after a long delay to my connection at Cheltenham Spa, enlivened only by the happy discovery that they sold bottles of Wrexham Lager in the Co-op across the road, an email dropped into my inbox from Ian Gwyn Hughes asking if we could do the squad shoot on Wednesday.

The lack of confirmation up to this point had prompted me to predict a clear week as far as reporting on Wales was concerned, now I knew I'd be back down again to help out on Wednesday and I still had the question mark against the request for the 'sit down' with Gareth.

I'd tried a different approach on this occasion, first submitting a request to his management company rather than to the FAW. Their reply came as a pleasant surprise, as it suggested they'd be happy to let the FAW decide what media activities he'd be undertaking whilst he was on international duty. Suitably encouraged, I mentioned this in my subsequent request to Ian, but that all took place a few weeks ago and I'd not heard anything since.

On Monday, the squad shoot was organised, with rooms and cameras all arranged but the feedback on Bale was not so positive. Our interview request was going to be on a list submitted to his people after all. By Tuesday, their answer came back with another 'no'. This was not entirely surprising, but my hopes had been raised by the initial response. If I was disappointed it was only because this was shaping-up to be the biggest game of the past decade for Wales and I wanted the build-up to reflect that, which meant getting Gareth to sit down for a chat about it. I'm not naïve though, there are often other factors at play these days, and in this instance it's Gareth's contractual obligations to another broadcaster that complicate this process. It's nothing personal, it's business.

Still, it did mean we now needed a plan B, in terms of the big interview for the live show ahead of kick-off on the night of the game.

In discussing the options with Jim, the producer, I'd suggested the other big name, Aaron Ramsey, and he was keen for me to pursue that avenue of enquiry, so another request had been submitted. As I drove down on Wednesday, there was no news on that one either.

For the first squad shoot at the start of the campaign, Alex had been the cameraman but this time, of course, he's over in Canada covering the Women's World Cup so I've been assigned a guy called Matt Cahill, who I've worked with quite a few times before. He's both a good operator and a really nice guy, so I'm happy to have him on board. He's based in Bristol, so he'll be commuting rather than basing himself with me in Cardiff.

I arrive at the Cardiff City Stadium in good time, ahead of the 4pm filming session, to find Matt and another local guy, John, with backdrops and cameras already set up and ready to go. Also there already is Wilko, an assistant producer who's come over from HQ to oversee everything, direct the session and then courier the footage back to base. I'm here to liaise, primarily, but Jim also wants me to chuck in a question or two that we might be able to use in an opening titles sequence.

We've been given a room we haven't been allocated before, the warm-up room, that adjoins the home dressing room via short corridor. It's literally a space the players use pre-match, with exercise bikes and various items scattered around, for a last-minute stretch of their highly-tuned bodies. It's ideal for what we want as well. It has plugs, controllable lighting and good acoustics and there's a 3G artificial grass covering on the floor, Andorra style, that helps deaden any echo. We devise a plan to accommodate this, with players coming into the room in small groups. They're actually coming to the stadium for a 'signing session', putting their signatures on dozens of football shirts and balls that have all been laid out on trestle tables in the tunnel and which, presumably, go to sponsors or charities who've asked for them. They are also scheduled to have both individual and team pictures taken wearing the new kit. They'll call in on us in-between these duties.

The players arrive on time, which bodes well, and the signing begins before they head out for team picture.

FIFA's politics have also threatened repercussions for Wales' qualification hopes in the last few days, with the Palestinian FA having proposed a vote to expel Israel, a move only avoided at the 11th hour, probably due to some backroom lobbying from Blatter. Had it happened it might have wiped out the Welsh win in Haifa, but our anxieties have been allayed. I think many Welsh fans are just waiting for the unforeseen circumstances that will derail another bid for qualification. In 1981, the team needed a home win against minnows Iceland to ensure their place at the World Cup finals in Spain. Wales were winning when the floodlights failed. In the lengthy delay that followed, the team lost momentum and ended up drawing the game 2-2, ultimately missing out on qualification on goal difference.

We're hard-wired for failure, those of us who are at an age to be able to remember all these near misses but not old enough to remember '58. My first harsh lesson came early. I remember watching Wales v Scotland in a World Cup qualifier. It was 1977, I was seven and growing up in Liverpool a year or so before the move across the border. Despite that, because of my mum and those frequent trips to see my grandparents, I was already supporting the team in red. This was meant to be a home game for Wales but they were actually playing just down the road from where we sat around the telly, watching the game in our living room. Due to crowd disturbances at a previous game at Ninian Park, followed by the subsequent UEFA punishment and restrictions, the FAW, in their wisdom, decided to take the home game against Scotland over the border to Anfield in the hope of big crowd and increased gate receipts. They got their bumper gate for sure, the ground was absolutely jam-packed with Scots! They created such a hostile atmosphere that the few Wales fans who were there feared to raise their voice. So, home advantage had been abjectly surrendered when a win for either side would just about send them to the finals in Argentina. With 12 minutes to go, it was still 0-0, then, a long throw into the Welsh box, Joe Jordan leapt to meet it with his long blue-sleeved arm raised high above his head. Alongside him, Welsh defender Dave Jones, also jumped, his two bare arms down by his side. The ball struck Jordan's fist, the referee blew his whistle; penalty to Scotland. Jordan turned away, the same fist clenched in celebration. Scotland scored, you know the rest. We were burgled that night as well, they took the TV on which we'd just watched another robbery. I blame Joe Jordan.

But, that was then. As I look at the current generation, now gathering *en masse* in the warm-up room, 1977 is distant history, so is 1982 and pretty much every other failure since. Unlike me, these lads aren't burdened with this stuff, they weren't even born. Even so, many of them have suffered the most terrible blow ever to strike Welsh football, a tragedy in the true sense, the sudden and shocking loss of their leader.

Still, they aren't thinking about that as they pile into the room, no chance of those little groups of four or five we were hoping for. They're enjoying what they're doing, being noisy and boisterous, as mates, and rightly so. There are 28 names on the list, and they've all come to see us at once. This is great, we've got the squad and the stand-by players who've been drafted in for the experience of training with the seniors, even Jonny Williams and he's actually injured so not included. However, 28 players hanging about, taking the mickey out of each other, suddenly makes this a trickier proposition, not least in terms of the 'audio'. A quiet, controlled environment is now a noisy and somewhat chaotic one. That's the first issue, the second is more serious. A few seconds after the first players stepped in front of the 'green screen', the assistant producer, Wilko, sidles over to where Matt's ready to film them in front of a black screen. He cups his hand over his mouth, a bit like a Premier League manager talking to his assistant on the touchline, and whispers, "You haven't got a blue screen have you? Have you seen the colour of the kit?!" Then it dawns on me, of course, the new kit is not just red, or red and white, but red and ... green! What happens when you put green in front of a 'green screen'? It disappears. So, when the players perform the move from standing facing the camera to turning side-on to the camera, the three broad, green stripes down the shirt sleeves mean their shoulders suddenly disappear!

Matt hasn't got a blue screen, so there's nothing to do but plough on and hope someone back at base can do something clever with it. As it turns out, even the blue screen, had it existed, would have caused an issue, as the new goalie's kit is all blue, so Wayne Hennessey would have just appeared as a head and hands!

I throw in a question about the game to a few of the players as they stand in front of Matt's camera. Some find it a bit awkward to speak in front of their peers; David Cotterill pleads to be spared the ordeal, whilst others like Aaron Ramsey and Joe Allen, perform admirably.

185

The problem is, there's so much stuff going on in the background that even my pleas for 'quiet on set everybody!', don't produce the necessary silence.

As they go through, I tick the names off the squad list, until we're left with the last few, the big beasts. There's some pretty fierce mickey-taking flying about by now, and poor Jonny Williams blushes bright red as he cops for some Bale banter. All in all though, as ever, the lads are an absolute credit. Despite the presence of the world's most expensive footballer in the room, there are no 'Big Time Charlies' in this group, just mates taking the mickey. It's the one common denominator between teams at all levels. Egos get parked at the dressing room door, whether it's Wakefield Vets or Wales. When the players are asked to line-up in front of the cameras, they do so without complaint, do what they're told when they're told and we get through the whole group in no more than 45 minutes.

Between the two cameramen, there's an awful lot of gear, so I hang around to help them pack it away. In fact, I do better than that, as I spot a shopping trolley in the corridor outside the dressing rooms. It seems to have been 'borrowed' from the Asda on the other side of the retail park opposite the stadium. It's swiftly commandeered for the use of Sky Sports and I roll it out into the car park, packed with light stands, kit bags and cameras.

Wilko, still looking a little crestfallen, heads back to London to try and rectify our 'green-on-green' issues whilst I head over to the Radisson. Initially, there was some talk of a media call tomorrow but that was a while ago and I've asked for confirmation since and none's been forthcoming. On top of that, I've seen Peter from the media team today and he's not mentioned anything either, so I'm assuming it's gone away. It's been a long day with the drive and all, so I'm going to stay tonight anyway. I'm also lined-up for a media training session with this year's new group of A license candidates on Friday afternoon in Chepstow, which is about 45 minutes drive away, so I'll prepare for that in the morning then head over in the afternoon.

All this 'normality' takes place against a swirling fog of allegations and accusations surrounding corruption at FIFA. Arrests have been made, Sepp Blatter's resigned and many in the media who've pursued him and his organisation are now scenting blood.

So, when I bump in to the FAW's top administrator, Jonathan Ford, in the tunnel, it's the first subject he turns to after an exchange of greetings. The FAW seems to have enjoyed reasonable relationships with the governing body and Jonathan's keen to stress that he thinks the man at the top's only guilty of being unaware of what may have been going on below. He makes the point that under his leadership, football's truly established itself as 'the global game'. There is a culture that people are suspicious of though, he accepts and he shows me the watch he's wearing, nothing too flashy, bearing the FIFA logo, a gift for attendees at a conference.

Maybe this is a part of the problem, giving gifts has become a part of the organisation's culture leading to a blurring of the lines between the gift-giving and bribes? For some people, it seems, perhaps, the 'gifts' have just got bigger and bigger.

Thursday & Friday 4th/5th June

I spend Thursday morning tidying up the presentation I'll be making to the candidates. I use a lot of video clips of football managers and coaches to illustrate points, and try to keep every session as up to date and interesting as possible. This is particularly important as it's an ever-changing world. When I started doing the sessions, Twitter was barely on the radar, now it plays a major role in the way the game is reported, supported and discussed. Broadcast deals change, media demands change, and all the time, coaches at every level are finding themselves less and less able to hide themselves away from the spotlight. On that basis, the discussion I'll have with the people on this course and others gets ever more significant.

There always tends to be a few familiar faces in the room at these sessions. This Friday's is no different. The FAW courses are run by an offshoot body called the FAW Trust, which is led by Osian Roberts, now coach to the national team senior squad. It was Osian who asked me if I'd help out a couple of years back, and I've got to know him and his team pretty well since. To be honest, I really enjoy the experience of working with them. They're a dedicated bunch, focused on the desire to produce more and better coaches for the good of the game in general, but in Wales in particular. At this level, the courses last two years and cover an awful lot of ground. It requires real commitment, and no little financial input, from the candidates, but they recognise the importance of the qualification. Increasingly, it's becoming like a driving licence; if you want to drive a car you have to have one. If you want to coach at the highest level, you need at least the A, if not the Pro licence, qualification and you can only go for the highest award if you've got the one below.

The reputation of the FAW courses is such that they're attracting an increasingly stellar line-up of candidates from way beyond the nearby border, but there's always a good mix of people from all levels of the game in Wales, England and the world. In this group of 19, I should have a Frenchman, Thierry Henry, although he's away on Sky Sports duty, a Swede, Freddie Ljungberg and an Aussie, John Hutchinson. Then there's a cross-section of people either already working as coaches, or players looking towards a career in coaching. One of the familiar faces is the former Wrexham manager Kevin Wilkin, who didn't have any qualifications when he was appointed and who was accepted on this course when he was still in charge at Wrexham. It's a fast-changing world though and already he'll be wondering and worrying as to whether he'll ever get another full-time appointment. Completing the course will give him a much better chance.

I really enjoy the challenge of trying to come up with something that's as relevant to as many people in the room as possible, despite the wide disparity in terms of the experiences they've had. I come from a line of teachers on both sides of the family so the classroom's probably in my blood, add to that the drama aspect that made up half of my Uni degree and it may go some way to explain why I get such a buzz from these sessions. Being on TV doesn't always give me quite the same buzz as being in front of a live audience, I like the interaction. After 23 years covering football, it feels a bit like putting something back in as well. Everybody in the room's here because they want to learn how they might do their bit to make football better. That might be by fine-tuning the skills of multi-million pound Premier League players, or it might be by encouraging more young people to enjoy the game, no matter what their level or ability. There's a lot in football that disappoints me, these sessions leave me with a much more positive impression of the game in this modern era.

The A licence is a big step up from the B, and the candidates have a familiar faraway look in their eyes by the time they sit down in front of me on the final day of their first week. They work from first thing in the morning until late into the evening. The staff who run the courses push them hard and the FAW incorporate twice as many contact hours as UEFA, who oversee all the courses, stipulate as the minimum for this level.

The session takes place in Newport, at the FAW Trust facility, Dragon Park. It's only been open a couple of years but it's already become a vital component in the improvement of the way players and coaches are educated in Wales. Given the quality of the playing surface, it's a surprise perhaps that the senior squad don't train here, but it's a long drive from Cardiff so their visits are rare. They've actually spent their first week in the capital at the Marriott hotel, right in the city centre, but next week they're returning to the Vale of Glamorgan hotel, west of Cardiff, so even further away from Newport. But before that, I've got a weekend at home but only once I've navigated my way through roadworks, traffic jams, speed limits and the rest of the stuff that a Friday afternoon journey on Britain's motorway network inevitably throws up.

Monday 8th June

The return to south Wales is considerably smoother but my mood is no better than it was as I battled my way home on Friday's five hour slog.

The 'plan B' of interviewing Aaron Ramsey isn't going to happen, because he already spoken to reporters at a sponsor's event the previous week.

I'm all set for the biggest Wales game of the decade and I've never had so many negative responses to my requests for interviews. This pains me because, as a company, we've stuck by Wales even when the football's been awful, the crowds pitiful and the results rotten. Whilst the guys in the written press have often had harsh things to say, we've tried to remain as upbeat as possible. On at least half a dozen occasions, with Wales out of contention two or three games into qualification campaigns, we've fallen back on the line that an emerging 'Golden Generation' of young players promises better times to come. Truth is, it's taken an awful long time and a lot of miserable, meaningless matches for that to happen. In the meantime, until very recently, almost everyone's given up on the national side, except the diehard supporters, and us. Just four years ago, I covered a game at

Dublin's Aviva Stadium between Wales and Northern Ireland in the shortlived 'Carling Nations Cup', when I swear there were more Sky Sports people working on the broadcast, HD and 3D, than there were spectators. The official attendance was recorded at 529 but even that seemed like an exaggeration from where I sat, completely alone save for one steward amidst an ocean of empty seats.

In that same period, Wales dropped to 117th in the world rankings, a joke nation, below superpowers like Togo and Uzbekistan. About the only thing that gave me any hope for the future was Gary Speed's appointment as national team manager, but even he was soon copping criticism from journalists and supporters as, initially, the team continued to struggle.

Throughout it all, I had to try and stay positive, or else what was the point in spending so much time on the road, in hotels and away from my family? Gary gave me hope that things might get better, even if only because we got on so well it was like having a mate as manager. There were, at the very least, a few laughs. In John Toshack's spell, it was all pretty heavy going. Then things did, briefly, take an upward turn, performances improved and hope began to return before it all came crashing down in the most awful and unexpected way imaginable. I guess I could have called it a day at this point, just too much sadness to bear, but I didn't. I came back. And now I'm on the long drive down again and finally, finally, I can see something better just ahead but the route to the Promised Land still seems strewn with obstacles.

I've known IG for many years. I knew of him through his long stint as BBC Wales' football commentator, the voice of the national team really. He went everywhere Wales went, and it was a role he only relinquished when Sky snatched the rights away from the corporation in a daring raid that was very much the company's style at the time. The BBC in Wales clearly didn't think anyone was going to compete with their bid and they calculated their offer accordingly, but Sky were waiting and came in and blew their bid out of the water. IG must have been devastated, as it meant he lost his job as the man commentating on the national team after 15 years in the role. He hid his devastation well, always affable and philosophical even in the immediate aftermath when others at BBC Wales were not quite so friendly. Then he left the BBC and took up a job with the FAW as Head of Media, so now our relationship's changed a little and he's become my go-to guy, but we've remained on good terms throughout. It was IG I called first when Gary Speed invited me into the canteen at the Sheffield United training ground, purportedly for a cup of tea and a chat, but actually keen to make it clear that – despite newspaper reports to the contrary – he was interested in making the switch from club to international management.

I then made the call that set in motion, the process that ultimately led to Gary's appointment. There were a few wobbles along the way, Sheffield United released a statement rubbishing suggestions that they were about to let their manager go, even as I knew they were negotiating his release. IG and I became the conduit for messages from both sides through the negotiations. We both liked Gary a lot, IG knew him from those days on the road covering Wales and we both knew he was a reporter's dream; affable, helpful and eloquent. We both got closer to Gary in the short time he was in charge of the national team. From a personal and professional perspective, it proved to be a dream appointment for us. Then it all ended.

We've both stuck with it and we're both absolutely desperate for Wales to succeed now but IG's under pressure to keep this week 'normal' and 'low-key', so he's not committing anyone to anything that might upset the manager. Tomorrow, he's informed me there will only be two players coming along to speak to the media about the game, rather than the four or five we usually get. I wanted a quick word with Osian Roberts ahead of the training session we're about to film, just a brief word about the France v Belgium game he and Chris went to watch last night. That request's been denied as well. When I finally pull up at the Vale complex, I'm greeted by the sight of a locked gate and a steward who demands ID before I'm admitted. This has never happened before. The final straw? As I slide my window down, he approaches and says, "Press? Oh, it's you! In you go", a cheery recognition that encourages me down off my high horse. Matt's already in and set up on the edge of the training pitch.

Still, I'm not happy and I'm on a mission to let certain people know. The plan is that I'm going to be grumpy. I've always enjoyed this bit, it always feels like returning to the fold when everyone starts arriving for this traditional precursor to the international week. I'm usually ready for handshakes and greetings and a bit of banter, but today I'm employing a different approach. I greet Peter with a cursory nod and I don't catch IG's eye at all. I seek to reinforce the impression by talking happily with other members of the coaching staff, including Osian, who comes over to discuss the timing of the next media session for the second year candidates on the A licence course. It's going to be scheduled for this week, so I need to keep it away from any potential clash with work. A time's provisionally agreed, Wednesday evening and we both go back to the day job as the players start to appear, walking towards the pitch from the hotel.

As Matt films their arrival, IG approaches. He's brought match tickets I was asked if I could arrange, on behalf of James Dean Bradfield, lead singer of the Manic Street Preachers. I'll give them to Alun from the record label, he's a good pal of James so he'll pass them on. I take the tickets, remember my manners and say thanks but I'm business-like, almost brusque. Truth is, it doesn't really suit me, it's not who I am but I'm trying to make a point. I'm just not sure what it is.

My attention turns back to the approaching players and manager. Chris appears at the top of the steps down to the pitch and TV cameras swing in his direction, motor drives whirring as photographers fire off shots. There are a lot more members of the media gathered here than has usually been the case, a fact Chris acknowledges as he sees me in the crowd, "Don't remember there being this many here ahead of Macedonia at home, eh Bryn?", he shouts. It makes me laugh. He's right. It was probably me, Alex and the FAW photographer ahead of the penultimate game in the last campaign, yet another dead rubber when the only real pre-match interest was engendered by the Chief Exec's suggestion that Chris probably had one more game to save his job. Wales won. He's still here.

There's no live update to do today, so when the players move, we can move with them. I point out the players we'll be interviewing tomorrow, Chester and Ledley, and Matt gets shots of them, plus Gareth, of course, and Aaron on the off chance IG changes his mind. The plan C for the big interview is Ashley Williams, who we know we're definitely going to get on Thursday. It seems about the only thing we can currently rely on.

We get the order to stop filming from Pete and, as Matt heads off to feed the footage back from the Sky News bureau in Bristol, I hang around for a chat with one of the fans invited to attend the session by Vauxhall. His name's Rob, he's brought his young son down from Wrexham, after winning a competition. They missed out on tickets for the game, as did many others, so they've come down for this instead. Rob's son has done well with autographs and pictures, hopefully that's made the long drive down from the north worthwhile.

The clamour for tickets has been crazy for pretty much the first time since the decision was taken to start playing games at the CCS. They swiftly sold out after Israel and subsequently there were some suggestions that maybe the FAW should consider moving matches back to the Millennium Stadium. I spoke with at least a couple of the players about the rumoured switch, but they were adamant that they and all the rest of the lads wanted to stick with the current home. There's a financial consideration of course, twice as much gate money for a start, but there's a bigger picture. Long-term, the overriding need is for Wales to qualify, that's the outcome that'll bring the biggest benefit. So, in the short-term, whatever helps the players achieve that aim surely has to be the best way?

All done, I head back to the hotel for a run in the evening sun, some room service, a film and an early night. Such is the life 'on the road'.

Tuesday 9th June

It's interview day today so I'm meeting Matt at Hensol Castle, the mystery castle of a few months ago, now clearly identified as the location for this afternoon's player appearances.

Before I head off, there's work to be done this morning. I need to create a presentation for my appearance in front of the A licence candidates tomorrow. Each one is bespoke, designed, where possible, to utilise issues thrown up by the work of the candidates themselves. So I spend time scouring YouTube for anything I might be able to use. There are some well-known names amongst the group, but none better known than David Ginola. The fact that he's currently putting himself forward as a candidate for the FIFA presidency should at least give us something to talk about! I've been dealing with Sol Campbell on the Pro Licence course recently and he's now putting himself up for London Mayor, so you can see it's all gone way beyond, 'I'm sick as a parrot, Jeff.'

Once the presentation's done, I turn my attention to the interviews. I want to check some stats on the strength of the opposition. It's funny, I've been so wrapped up in other stuff, trying to sort out interviews, booking cameras, travelling up and down to south Wales that I've not had much time to contemplate the game itself. A glance down Belgium's run of results doesn't provide much cause for comfort. One loss in their last 17 games, and that was to Argentina in the World Cup quarter-finals. In fact, they haven't lost a qualifier since Marc Wilmots took charge. He's been the subject of speculation in the build-up, there are rumours this could be his last game before a move to manage Schalke. Mind you, the Welsh stats are beginning to sparkle a little, even in comparison with the side now ranked second best in the world. It's one defeat in ten now, and that was an away friendly, fielding a much-weakened team in The Netherlands.

I travelled to that game on my own as a supporter, I'm now travelling to today's media event on my own as a reporter. Not having Alex to chauffeur me around is one of the big downsides of his absence! Still, I've made the journey from the city centre out to the Vale resort enough times to also have it down on my list of potential blindfold drives. It takes about 20 minutes, then another five before I can find anyone to open the metal gates to the castle. I've seen this building loads of times without ever really noticing it, and that's despite the fact it's got turrets and towers.

The satellite truck that's been sent from London is parked out front, as is Matt. We have a quick conflab about what's required, no live reports just the interviews, and Matt goes off to get set up in what is just about the perfect room for interviews. It looks and sounds great. It's like a big sitting room with leather sofas and armchairs. There's wood panelling on the walls, lilies in a vase, and an ornate fireplace, all good for backdrops. It's also got heavy wooden doors that should keep out any external noise.

I'm feeling more mellow today. Our interviewees list has actually been extended as it turns out, Wayne Hennessey's coming as well as the two players previously mentioned. Osian Roberts will also be on hand, so we'll have enough to keep everyone going between now and the next round of interviews on Thursday. Wayne's first, then James, who gives a good interview about how quickly he's settled into international football and how he'll have loads of the Welsh side of his family down for the game. We then nip outside to interview Osian. By the time that's done, Joe Ledley's already sprawled across a sofa waiting for us. The room proves to be great only until a sit-down lawnmower starts going up and down on the lawn right outside one of the big, shuttered windows. Why does someone always start cutting the grass just when you're doing an interview?! It's as predictable as rain on a British bank holiday.

Tuesday evening sees me leave my cocoon and head into town, first for a run round the usual park, then to meet up with Alun for a couple of pints and a chat about a project he's undertaking for Wrexham. My plan is to eat in the pub, they do food, I've checked. On arrival, I ask for a menu, only to be told the kitchen's closed. So tea ends up being taken in two stages; first, a large Scotch egg and two slices of pizza from jars behind the bar, then a chicken kebab from a takeaway on Caroline Street, the infamous place known as 'Chip Alley', as I walk back to the hotel.

Wednesday 10th June

The FAW haven't scheduled any access today, and there's no sign of a change of heart on letting us have a chat with Aaron Ramsey, so the big interview will be taking place tomorrow. That leaves me clear for my session with the A licence chaps in Chepstow. The base for their week's work is the St Pierre hotel, set in rolling countryside and with direct access to what was once a Championship golf course. There's no point in the candidates packing their clubs though, their schedule's packed with sessions covering all aspects of the business of coaching and, to an extent, management. I have worked with this group already, a year ago, so we're continuing and expanding on the conversations we had then.

Before things get under way, there's news to put a spring in the step, Fellaini's out! He's injured his groin in training. So, that's Kompany suspended and now Fellaini, who scored two goals against France on Sunday, is missing as well. They've got loads more good players, but it still feels like a boost. The French game was apparently played at a high intensity, you've got to wonder whether that was the best idea at the end of a long season. Anyway, their loss could be our gain.

The session is, as ever, good fun. I just hope the candidates enjoyed it as much as I did. I stay to eat with the course tutors. Carl Darlington's running this one in the absence of Osian. Carl's another lad from Wrexham, and he actually ended up caretaker-managing the club for the last few games of the season. When the club then appointed a new manager, Gary Mills, he decided he didn't want Carl around and the manner of his departure clearly still hurts. It wasn't handled at all well by the club, which I found very disappointing. Carl described to me that he'd found out he was sacked through a report on the radio, made all the harder to bear because he's a lifelong fan of the club.

I'm planning a quiet night in on my return but just as I'm about to stick the cocoa on, Gary Pritchard sends me a text, the pal who rang me just before the game in Haifa. He's in town, do I fancy popping out for a pint? Oh, go on then!

These midweek meet-ups in Cardiff were, for a time, a regular occurrence. Gary works for Rondo, the independent production company who provide the football coverage for S4C. At one stage, a few years ago, Rondo held the highlights rights so they used to produce a programme that went out an hour or so after Sky's live coverage ended. It's a rights package that has changed hands a number of times in the decade we've been the main guys. Currently, ITV have access but now, as of this week, S4C have also been granted access, as minority language rights holders. Are you following all this? So, they'll be showing an hour's worth of highlights at 10.30 on Friday night. Gary's down to provide some material for another show they're doing, that's previewing the game tomorrow night, and he's got Nicky, the presenter, with him. She's a familiar face to viewers of their Welsh Premier League coverage.

Gary's another Wrexham fan, despite living at the far end of Ynys Môn, or Anglesey if you prefer. That means he's got a two hour plus drive across north Wales for home games. That makes him a proper fan. We've really become friends since I started reporting on Wales. Alex is a pal too and we've both been to stay with him and his family.

Gary, his wife and two children are all first language Welsh speakers. Welsh is what they speak at home, at work and at school, as is the case for many people on the west side of Wales. Alex has an excuse, he's English born and bred, but it's to my shame that Gary and I will chat in my first language, not his. I absorbed a lot of Welsh on those earliest trips to visit my grandparents, their village was totally Welsh-speaking, before I started studying the language at primary school once I'd moved over the border. I stuck with it all the way and went on to get an A grade at A level, as a second language. But then I went to college in London and I've lived in England ever since so opportunities to speak Welsh and listen to it have been much more limited. Still, I haven't let it slide completely. I can get S4C on the TV, I've always listened to a lot of Welsh-language rock and pop music and I've been asked to do a few things in Welsh over the years, interviews on radio and TV mainly, and it remains my intention, one day, to go back and get fluent. It's still important to me. My mum taught Welsh, all the generations of her family going way back spoke Welsh. I've got two daughters who were born in Leeds, they know 'nos da, cariad' is 'good night, love'. They know 'diolch' is 'thank you' and they can both pronounce 'Llangollen' beautifully but still I suspect the language line ends with me.

Gary, Nicky and I have much to discuss. I'm particularly keen to know what Gary's heard about two subjects, the friendly that Wales were due to play with Northern Ireland last Friday that was then cancelled, and the switch from the usual team hotel, St David's, in Cardiff Bay? It's actually going to be playing host to the Belgians from tomorrow onwards. Gary's always well up with the gossip so I want to hear what he's heard, and whether it tallies with tales I've been told. I've heard two suggestions as to the cancellation of the friendly. One is that it clashed with two events in Cardiff, the Manic Street Preachers and One Direction gigs, that would impact heavily on the crowd and the logistics. The other is that the FAW feared staging a friendly would negatively impact on the nation's coefficient in terms of ranking status, even if they won. There's a World Cup draw in July, and it appears that Wales could get themselves into the top seeds pot with a win over Belgium.

Gary's heard both stories as well. Whatever's right, either or neither, the Northern Irish FA aren't happy and I've heard suggestions of an official complaint to UEFA. The hotel issue's even more confused. Apparently, Wales didn't manage to book their favoured base for either week. Nor did they manage to book their second or third choices for the first week so, instead, they ended up in the Marriott. It's a nice enough hotel but it's literally right in the middle of the city centre, directly opposite where we're sitting now, on Mill Lane, one of the liveliest areas the city has to offer after dark.

This week, they're in the Vale hotel, a base they turned their back on a few years ago. My recollection is there was a sense the Welsh Rugby Union got better treatment there, they also used it as a training camp. It was also a long way from the city centre for bored footballers in-between training sessions and you couldn't get a mobile phone signal from anywhere but the car park. The biggest puzzle to me is that I know how superstitious Chris Coleman is, so I'm surprised he's been ready to break with routine and give up his lucky room at the hotel? Gary's been told that Chris is quite keen to try different bases, but also that the Belgian FA wanted to use the Vale and claim exclusive use of the training pitch that Wales generally use, so the FAW stepped in to prevent that by booking it instead. It's a real mystery. My concern? Things were bad enough with Alex and his lucky socks being absent, now Chris has lost his lucky room. We're doomed, I tell you!

That's enough intrigue for one night. The towels are over the taps, so we head back to our respective hotels with an agreement to reconvene in the morning for the short drive to the Cardiff City Stadium.

Thursday 11th June

I'm getting more excited now. This is always the day when things start to feel more 'real'. We're billing this as the most important game for a decade, which it is. In fact it's longer than that. The last competitive game Wales played before the Sky contract kicked in was Russia at the Millennium Stadium, the second leg of a Euro2004 play-off. I was there as a fan, I'd been in Moscow for the first leg a few days earlier. We sang long into the night at the end of a 0-0 draw, then kept quiet as hordes of Russian hooligans awaited our collective return to the city centre, surrounding the massive Hotel Rossiya as our convoy of coaches pulled up. I was with another Leeds-based Wales fan, Evo, and my brother. We pulled up our hoods and slipped through their cordon, the walk back towards our hotel was edgy to say the least.

Needless to say, having done all the hard work, Wales played poorly, lost the home leg 1-0 and in the manner of the usual, extra twist, the guy who put the cross in for the winning goal then tested positive for a banned substance post-match, but UEFA did nothing other than ban him.

I wasn't as beaten up by that result as you might imagine. I'd only missed one qualifier, home or away. I'd been to Helsinki, Milan, Belgrade and Moscow but throughout it all, I kept expectation under control. Romania taught me that. At full-time in that play-off game at the Millennium, as 73,000 people drifted quietly off into the night, I was sad but not distraught. It was a shake of the head, not days and months of depression.

Then, my focus changed as my role changed. Now, much of my planning revolves around setting up interviews and interview rooms rather than trying to find flights for under £100 and a hotel room with three beds. From this point on though, it's all about the game.

The OB trucks are already at the stadium when we get there. The riggers are running cables into the ground. It's a busy scene. Our team's rolling into town, I bumped into Sarah in the hotel prior to departure, she's on match directing duties again, then Bill appears as I walk towards the entrance to the stadium and we renew acquaintances in time honoured fashion. Then we head on in. I know where I'm heading as I've already arranged the location, the away dressing room. It's nearly an hour before the scheduled interviews with Chris Coleman and Ashley Williams but as I push open the door, the room's in darkness. This is good. It means Matt's already set up. And it means he's worked out how to knock off the light sensors without being told. This guy's good.

The room's illuminated by the three lights set up around the interviewee's chair. As we wait, Bill and I catch up on events since Haifa. He's just back from a crazy charity bike ride that took him up lots of very steep French mountains. Apparently, he keeps nodding off as his body continues to recover. This could be interesting, will there be little snores in the background as Chris and I discuss the merits of playing five at the back? Actually, Bill and I talk through the possible team as well. I suspect he'll go back to four defensively, as he's not got James Collins or Ben Davies, maybe stick Andy King in as another defensive midfielder? We both agree he'll surely have to revert to the four, if only because of the personnel he's got available.

Then, the man himself appears. As Matt's clipping on mics and readjusting lights, we chat. I ask about the hotel situation? He explains it as being a change designed to bring benefits for the fitness levels of the players. He didn't want them to be spending up to an hour a day travelling by coach from the hotel to the training pitch. The Vale facilities have been upgraded to allow them to 'preactivate' ahead of training, then walk to the pitch they use, then walk back to the hotel afterwards. This, he suggests, might just give them that extra one per cent. This is something I've heard Sir Dave Brailsford talk about, the attention to seemingly minute details, that's been cited as being crucial to the success of the cycling teams he's led.

He says The Vale as a venue has been welcoming, the facilities and rooms have been improved and you can even get a mobile phone signal now! I ask about last week, the Marriott. Nice hotel, he agrees, but probably not quite the location they'd have chosen if their other picks hadn't already been booked up. If they've gained one per cent this week, I hope they didn't lose two per cent last week. It's interesting that there's no talk of having to maintain 'the routine', rather he says they might explore other options once the contract with St David's hotel runs out in November. I just wonder whether the science is beginning to supersede the superstition in the manager's mind? He's surrounded himself with people who use the latest technology and sports science to improve all aspects of the preparation, and he's enjoyed success as a result. Has this helped convince him that winning is nothing to do with 'the lucky room', a pair of stripey socks, or swapping chewing gum with the kit man? I'm not sure I'm entirely ready for such advanced thinking, yet.

The interview's good, relaxed but high energy and particularly stirring when he talks about the crowd and the role they have already played in getting the side to this point. Talking of points, he'd be happy with one, especially against such strong opposition. He saw them in Paris on Sunday; awesome going forward but, then a moment's hesitation that suggests they may just feel there's a weakness at the back. He's at pains to stress that this game isn't make or break. If Wales lose, it isn't over. He also makes brief reference to that history of failure. He's a couple of weeks short of being a year younger than me, so he has the same generational hang-ups but he says the players don't, they don't know anything about all that stuff. We talk about the fitness levels of the players, some haven't played a game for nearly six weeks, but he says they all followed their fitness programs. The staff have produced tailored training schedules to match all needs, so they're good to go!

Bill's stayed awake until the end and as we conclude he asks Chris if he can contact him in the morning to check on the line-up, as ever, Chris says no problem, he'll send him a text.

As one departs, another appears, and as Ashley gets wired up, we talk about his holidays. He's managed a few days away between the end of the season and the start of the training camp. Swansea report back for pre-season in early July, so he'll get less than a month off as a result of this game, then another 10 months back in action, maybe even more depending on the next couple of internationals. On that basis, it's a good job there's still something to play for, because you have to wonder how many top level players would show up for this one if there was nothing riding on it?

I explain that this interview's for the live show, so it'll be 'tonight' not 'tomorrow night' if he makes reference to time. He subsequently remembers this midway through an answer, stops himself and starts the answer again, true pro!

As Ash then heads off to train, Bill and I help Matt to start packing his gear, and we head out to pitchside as well. I pass Paul Dummett at the top of the tunnel, flipflops on. This is not a good sign. Chris didn't mention it in the interview but it looks like he's injured, another Premier League defender ruled out. Surely it has to be four now?

All along the touchline stretches a line of cameras and photographers pointing their lenses towards the players who are, unhelpfully, over on the far side of the pitch. It's another indication of the level of interest in this game. The one advantage of this mid-June fixture is that it's a fix for any fans already craving more action, a whole week after the Champions League final brought the curtain down on club football for another season.

The training session continues as we get the 15 minute warning, and we all head towards the exits. Bill's got a rental car to collect, so I drive myself back to the hotel. I have jobs to do before I return to do something similar with the Belgians later on. As I get back, I get an enquiry from Sports News about Dummett being out. Apparently my hunch at training was right, and Chris mentioned it in the media conference, although not in the interview. Luckily, the UEFA camera was filming that so the footage just needs to be sent back to HQ, something I organise with Sarah.

As I'm sitting doing all this in the lobby, a familiar face appears. It's Gruff Rhys, chatting to a family who appear to be checking out, as they're surrounded by cases. I've met him before, he's another Turnstile act and he catches my eye and waves, then comes over for a chat. I've loved this guy and his music for so long! I went to see the Super Furry Animals, probably my all-time favourite band, on their reunion tour last month. I've got pretty much every record he's ever made. Today, he only wants to talk football. He's a keen fan, Wales in particular, and SFA are playing the warm-up slot before the match tomorrow evening. He's told me previously that he's already got a song written for when/if Wales qualify but he wrote it years ago and still hasn't had reason to record it. He introduces the chap he's been talking to, tells me that the last time he was in Cardiff he went to the Romania game, my response to this is to order his friend to leave the country, immediately. This, he reassures me, they are about to do.

The Queen's been in Cardiff this morning apparently, but she appears to have cleared off as well. There's not much sign of it as I walk through town in the direction of a barber's I've used before, just a few people holding those little flags on a stick that get waved at Royal visits. I walk straight into a chair in the salon, which is a result. I've got the scary looking bloke who's cut my hair before. He looks lived in. You'd be worried if you met him in a dark alley at the end of a night out, but he does a decent enough job with the clippers and scissors and he doesn't ask me where I'm going on my holidays, so he's alright by me.

From the barber's, I nip round the corner to Turnstile. I've brought my iPad with me as I have important matters to discuss with Gareth. As well as working for the label and being lead singer of Los Campesinos, he also occasionally turns his hand to a bit of DJ-ing, including his stint at the Spirit of '58 gig last October. There's another event taking place at the same venue tomorrow and this time, I've foolishly offered to do a DJ slot, despite never having done it before. The plan is to nip there once the event's underway, it's virtually *en route* to the stadium, do half an hour, then head straight off to work.

Needless to say, it's all requiring some careful planning, not least the issue of how do I actually go about the playing music bit?

Well, there are no records involved for a start, only proper DJs use them. Gareth has recommended an iPad app called Pacemaker, appropriately enough for one of my advanced years. It's actually called that because the clever trick is that it examines all the music in your iTunes library and then suggests those with the best match in terms of BPM (beats per minute). By doing this, it should ensure a smooth transition between one track and the next. I've been practising on it for a few weeks. I've actually drawn up my playlist, now I just need to know that it'll work with the sound system in the club.

Gareth's already reassured me by email, but I'm anxious not to look a chump so I pop into the office and ask him to talk through the process and to examine my equipment to make sure everything's going to be fine. He's doing another stint this time around, having enjoyed the experience last time. The event's success then has led to even greater interest now. Tim, the organiser, has sold all 350 tickets and there's been a clamour from people wanting to come anyway but he's restricted by the venue capacity. That's created something of a black market and the potential for gatecrashers, so it looks like being the second hottest ticket in town, after the game itself! As well as the DJ slot, I've also arranged for Carw to make an appearance on the bill, the young guy with the beard who I saw play live last year.

We've just started talking though things when Alun and Kev burst in through the door, fresh off a train from London and an appearance at the Festival Hall by one of their acts, Perfume Genius. They're chuffed because that went well, now they're both looking forward to the game tomorrow evening, in the company of James Dean Bradfield. I wonder if one day we'll all have to grow up and get proper jobs?

DJ tutorial done, I head back for the hotel where Bill's waiting for a lift back to the stadium. He wants to see if there's anything more that can be learned from sitting in on the interview I've got lined up with Thibault Courtois, and from the training session Belgium will hold afterwards.

The Belgian FA media man with the senior squad is called Pierre. He and I have been exchanging numerous emails arranging this interview, but we meet for the first time as he's shown into the room where we are, as I'd promised all set up. He's run through the brief

203

with me already but he reiterates that we only have five minutes with the player. That should be ample time for what we need. We requested Hazard, we got Courtois but he's a more than adequate replacement and it's a decent interview for our pre-match build-up. When it's over, Bill has his own mission. Courtois is his son's favourite player and he has a picture for him to sign. As soon as the player leaves the room, Bill's on the phone to his lad to tell him, so he definitely wins 'Dad Of The Day'.

Things are not quite so straightforward for Thibault in the media conference he attends immediately afterwards. The English media reporters seem only to want to ask him about his relationship with Petr Cech, chasing club lines rather than anything about the game, something that clearly annoys the Chelsea 'keeper. Wilmots, the coach, gets similar treatment, with most of the questions relating to his anticipated departure to Schalke. There's a media lesson in itself. I'm doing an interview to preview a game, my questions follow that line, then there's a media conference attended by people who may be under pressure to produce a newsline for today, another one for tomorrow – same event, two very different agendas.

I see my man, Steve Williams, in the tunnel as the visiting players start making their way out onto the pitch for the session. As the liaison man, he'll be with them until they head home after the game tomorrow night. The players are actually starting to train ahead of the scheduled time and the UEFA delegate sets the clock going accordingly, even though camera crews and photographers are still arriving. On top of that, the Belgians have given her instructions to strictly enforce the 15 minute limit, and then to ensure that everybody clears the stadium that isn't part of their party, including Steve. They must fear espionage!

So it is that a few minutes after 6pm, she calls time and everybody's ushered towards the exits, regardless of how much footage or pictures they've actually been able to gather. In some cases, I can only think this was not an awful lot.

I go back to the compound with Bill and climb the steps into the gallery where Sarah will be based. We're actually presenting on site for the first time in this campaign, so there's another director for the studio presentation as well. Ray Ryan's the production manager, the man who got us to and from Haifa safely. There's nothing more for me and Bill to do at the stadium, but I have one more task to perform, I'm leaving my suit here so I can change into it post-gig tomorrow afternoon, I might look a bit odd behind the decks in a suit and tie.

The evening begins with a meal in the hotel for Bill, Sarah and myself. Then I get another of those pesky text messages, this time from David Hughes who's out in town and heading for a bar close by. I arrange to meet up. Except that I get my bearings completely wrong and I end up doing a big loop around the city centre, before finally working out that he's going to be at a venue about 200 yards away from where I started. It's a Barry Horne moment. It's a warm evening and Dave's in the midst of a group of people sitting outside. My big walk's shown just how many Belgian fans there appear to be, crowds of them walking the streets, drinking, enjoying all that the Welsh capital has to offer. The atmosphere's lively but good natured, much as it was in Brussels a few months back.

Dave's with his wife, Eleri, and some of her pals from the BBC. He's actually been observing the senior squad's preparations this week after an invite from Chris Coleman. He tells me he's confident that no group of players in the world can have been prepared better for a game. Dave's not easily impressed, so this is high praise indeed. Even from him, I sense that sort of quiet confidence that comes from knowing you've given yourself the edge. After a couple of drinks, the young people are up for something a little louder and livelier, I leave them to it. It's time I went to bed.

Friday 12th June

Like Andorra, a bad night's sleep. My mind seemed to be working constantly, and it felt like I was lying almost awake for long periods. I think the nerves are kicking in. It must be MD6.

The afternoon promises to be a bit busy so I sneak in the traditional matchday run after breakfast. Then it's a shower, and out to meet Matt who's already been filming on the city centre streets. There are loads of fans pouring into Cardiff now, the red, yellow and black of the Belgians, the red, white and green of the Welsh so it's a colourful scene. The weather's fine so there are large numbers already enjoying a beer outside a bar, as more groups drift in from the station or car parks. Sometimes over the last few years when we've been tasked with finding 'colour' for Sky Sports News, you'd be hard pressed to know there was even a match on, not today. Once Matt and I have managed to rendezvous, we head off in search of fans to talk to. A group of Belgians stagger past, I ask if they speak English? A fairly curt 'non' is the reply but I do better with the next group a few yards further on. In their midst is a man mountain, who speaks passable English and pretty much everyone in the world knows how to predict a scoreline when prompted so we get quite a nice little piece out of them. They all say narrow win for their team.

Next on my hitlist is the Spirit of '58 venue. I want to reprise the chat we did with Tim ahead of the Bosnia game. It's partly through superstition, and partly because it was good and we can discuss what's happened since.

If you want to see the slightly crazy nature of the modern TV world, we aren't the first camera crew on site at the location. S4C have beaten us to it. Tim's also got newspapers coming down later, and he's done interviews on Radio Cymru and Radio Wales. He'll be getting an agent soon. His event's given everyone something to do on matchday, including the media!

Actually, Tim's not there when I arrive so I chat with some of the early birds, many of whom I recognise from last year. They know I'm doing a bit of DJ-ing later, it's on the poster, so I'm asked what I'll be playing. I've plumped for a strictly Madchester half hour, Stone Roses, Happy Mondays, Paris Angels, Charlatans, Inspirals and James. I hope this will find favour with the crew who'll be attending. Adidas trainers and bucket hats are very much in evidence and both were mainstays of any young football fan's wardrobe back in those days, well, they were in mine anyway.

These boys are already hard at it. Whilst we're chatting, one of them emerges from the bar with a look of mock horror on his face, "Christ, Willo's just ordered 20 Jagermeisters...for himself!!" he shrieks. Bear in mind, it's 1pm, nearly seven hours to go until kick-off. Things are going to get a bit messy for some of these lads I suspect.

Tim appears, we film our interview and the lads outside get to join in with score predictions. The difference between us and Belgium is that their fans expect to win, our fans hope to win and it shows in this instance as pretty much everybody says they'd be happy with a draw, just as they did pre-Bosnia. You see, realism still rules optimism, even amongst the younger generation.

Matt needs to head off to the stadium now to send all this TV magic back to HQ for broadcast. I head in the direction of the hotel to get changed ahead of my return to the Moon Club.

I begin to realise I need a dresser today. There was one outfit for breakfast, another for my run, then chinos and shirt for the filming with fans, now a DJ outfit before I pull on the suit I've left at the stadium. That's a whole bag of clothes in a day. I'm like Mr Benn going into and coming out of my hotel room.

For the DJ slot, I dress like the lads. My favourite ever trainers, Adidas Gazelles, jeans and a Spirit of '58 polo shirt, my red, yellow and green SO58 bucket hat's in my bag, along with my iPad and the playlist and timings I've scribbled down on a notepad, lest I forget.

I opt to drive as close as I can to the venue, so I can then drive on to the stadium immediately afterwards. I'm scheduled to do 2.30 until 3, then I have to get off as I'm doing 'lives' inside the ground from just after 4pm onwards.

The drive takes longer than anticipated due to bad traffic, but I'm there 15 minutes ahead of my start time. Tim's busy selling raffle tickets upstairs, he's acquired some great prizes, and I chat with a man they call Pasti, who's currently playing the tunes downstairs. He's using CDs so I can plug my tablet straight into the desk and I'm all set. It's really simple. Any proper DJ must hate the advent of this type of technology. All those years spent learning how to mix and crossfade and some goon turns up with an iPad and starts shouting 'make some noise!' Doesn't seem fair does it?

I'll be honest, I'm a bit nervous about this. First off, what if it doesn't work, then what if I choose the wrong tracks, then what if I choose the right ones and nobody likes them? My start's somewhat delayed as Pasti rounds off his first stint by playing Sunshine On Leith by The Proclaimers. I know this song. I like this song but I know it's quite long. He sticks it on at half past, so I've got one eye on the clock already. I've actually timed my set, it should run a little over 30 minutes so I'm eating into my spare time already.

The House DJ's got me plugged-in and as The Proclaimers fade away, I hit play on my first track. I've gone for the big chords at the start of Sproston Green by The Charlatans, except I can't really hear them, my tech advisor suggests increasing the volume on my iPad, I do and, boom! Now you can hear it! And we're off. It's a bit of strange experience actually. I may be the bloke off the telly, but I'm no superstar DJ and this isn't Ibiza. The lads and a few lasses in the room are here to drink and chat, not to dance, although Perfume by Paris Angels almost prompts some movement in front of me. I scan the crowd for nodding heads, tapping feet, any sign of connection. In fairness, I'm playing stuff that's nearly 25 years old, so a fair few of the people here weren't born when it came out. If they have heard it before, that may well be because they've been rootling through their dad's music collection!

I carry on regardless. At one point I put the headphones on, even though I can't actually hear anything through them, a ridiculous affectation, but I'm living the dream! I'm not working in complete isolation, either. People come over for a chat, to have a picture taken, it's nice. They're good people. One of the lads I was talking to on arrival made the point that he and his pals are a mixed group of Swansea and Cardiff fans. He said they got some grief for fraternising with the enemy from some of the older guys on both sides, but they enjoy these events because they bring together fans from north and south Wales, Jacks and Bluebirds, and Tim's label, Spirit of '58, has played a part in that. It reflects a culture that's about clothes, music and football and you'll see those distinctive bucket and bobble hats at all games involving Welsh clubs. He also made it clear before the event that club flags couldn't be hung up on the walls of the venue, only Wales flags. There will be some very drunk people here by closing time, but I'll make a confident prediction that there won't be any trouble.

WFL by the Happy Mondays is my swansong and as it comes to an end, I shout my thanks, wave and depart. As I walk out into the daylight, my name's being chanted by the guys inside and that feels just fantastic. What a way to really start the day!

Outside, I bump into Bala Town's secretary, Ruth, who I met when I arranged some coverage of the club a couple of years ago. Bala were about to play in Europe for the first time, and they're back again this season, so she's going to be busy but her commitment keeps clubs like Bala going. In its own way, Bala is as big a hotbed for football as a city like Glasgow or Liverpool. They love football in Bala. It's a very small town, but I bet nearly everyone there tonight who isn't at the ground, and plenty will be, will watch the game. It's a shame the players probably can't appreciate the impact their potential success could have on a place like Bala. It's about putting Wales on the map, reinforcing the country's identity, making it clear it isn't the western-most county of England. I talked with Alun earlier in the week about the Romania game and the negative impact that it had on me, he said he thought that defeat had a similar impact on the country. Wales needs to be confident, sporting success can help breed that confidence. When people say 'I'm from Wales', the response may well be, 'ahhh... Gareth Bale!' They now have a global reference point, a marker, something that isn't coalmines, choirs or rugby.

My next clothes change of the day is performed in the home dressing room, where the team equipment's being sorted out and the kit's already hanging up. Dai Griff's blasting out his new favourite album, Brandon Flowers, balls are being pumped up and training tops sorted into piles. This is all so that everything will be just perfect by the time the players arrive. Dai's fastidious and I get grief for having moved one of David Cotterill's flip-flops a little out of line as I make the transition from club DJ to Wales reporter. I've timed things just about perfectly and I stride out of the dressing room, suited and booted, ten minutes before my first 'live' of the afternoon.

I've missed a couple of calls from base while changing, but there's an email explaining the format and it confirms a conversation I've already had with the live producer, so I'm clear in my mind what I'm going to say.

I've been busy all afternoon, the DJ challenge has got me pumped up, and my performance benefits from the extra adrenaline. I'm my own biggest critic but I thought this one was decent. Remember, in over ten years, I've never had a Wales game to report on when there's been so much at stake. Usually at this stage, we're talking about Wales already planning for the next set of qualifiers!

As I'm talking, spots of rain are falling. and I make reference to a storm that's predicted for just about kick-off time. They're talking about the possibility of thunder and lightning. so I round off by predicting something dramatic on and off the pitch tonight. It's a tad corny, I know, but it's all about tempting the neutral to watch. Tonight, for once, we can be confident we've got the Wales fans watching.

After tea on the catering bus, I'm back again at my position pitchside, ready for another hit. Gruff Rhys is close by and I get a thumbs up, the SFA lads are on in a couple of hour's time and they're heading over to the far corner to inspect their stage and to soundcheck. For my own appearance, I've got a guest with me, a proper legend, Ian Rush. He's going to be in the studio tonight, as one of our pundits, alongside the injured Ben Davies. Ian's arrived at the ground in good time so I've grabbed him to talk to me about the match. We've known each other a long time now, since he signed for Leeds in 1996. I was thrilled to see one of my favourite players crossing the Pennines, and he didn't let me down when I got to know him. He was just a really nice guy, and always helpful when I made requests of his time. It didn't go well for him in Yorkshire, but I will always regard him as the best striker I've ever seen play.

As we chat before the interview, Ian can't see a problem, "We always beat Belgium", he says, with a shrug. It's not strictly true but I know what he means. Twice in the early '90s, Wales did just that, in Cardiff, and Rushie scored in both of them. The stats show we haven't beaten them since, in five attempts, but I like the simplicity of his bold statement. Just before we go on 'live', Adam Owen comes across for a chat. He knows Ian as well, as he recalls, he used to clean Rushie's boots as a young pro at Wrexham. He says the camp's gone really well, they feel the programme they set out for the players has worked and everyone's at the required level. More positivity.

Then it's showtime and Ian and I talk Wales for a couple of minutes. As we come to the end of our live discussion, Ben Davies appears on the touchline. I go over to say 'hello', giving him a bit of a pat on the back after a handshake. Only then do I recall that the reason he's sitting in the studio is that he dislocated his shoulder a few weeks ago, probably roughly where I've just playfully patted him. "Oh God, sorry mate", is the best I can offer. He laughs, and doesn't appear to require any medical attention.

I retreat to the safety of the tunnel. Bill's there, still waiting to hear from the manager about the team. I was there when Chris said he'd let him have it in the morning. The fact that there's still no news has Bill concerned that maybe there's a problem, perhaps an injury we don't know about. I tell him I've just spoken to Adam, and it didn't sound like anything's amiss on that front. So, the other theory would be that Chris is doing something unexpected, switching things round again maybe, and he doesn't want to give the opposition any early chance of finding out about it. It's another hour at least before the team bus rolls in, so more time to do some digging.

I've got one more interview to record for Sky Sports News, with Barry, who's currently sitting in the away dugout, reading through his stat pack. We need to get that done before any possible clash with the arrival of Chris Coleman, so I give him the heads up and we get it done.

In the meantime, Bill's been busy and he appears to have devised a starting XI that reads as something of a surprise. He's been told that Wales will start with the same formation employed in Israel, with Chris Gunter moving into the central three and Jazz Richards replacing him at right back. Crikey! Just like in Israel, I'm surprised. I've seen Jazz play a few times this season, for Fulham on loan and for Swansea, he's got potential but he's still working to establish himself as a regular pick. To me, it looks like a gamble but then so did the line-up in Haifa and we all know what happened there. In Chris we must trust.

My next job is to wait for the man himself. Needless to say, I'm going to need to ask him about his selection when we do the pre-match interview. As usual, it's about 6.15pm when he appears at the interview position in the tunnel. Before we start, I need to confirm that the info we've got is accurate so I drop my voice to a whisper and ask. He whispers his confirmation and we start the interview, normal volume, with a suggestion on my part that he hasn't maybe gone with the side that people were expecting? He says the overriding desire was to play the same formation as in Israel, so he's fitted the available personnel into that shape. He also mentions how well Jazz did in his only other start, also against Belgium, when Wales got a 1-1 draw in the last game of the previous World Cup campaign.

Then he sets out to downplay the importance of the game a little, making it clear that whatever happens, qualification isn't decided tonight. It might help soften the blow a little if the game goes the way of the second best side in the world. He asks the crowd to play their part, as they have done throughout the campaign to date. A firm handshake, a hearty 'good luck' from me and he heads back towards the dressing room as the players are going in the opposite direction, out for a look at the pitch. There are already people in the ground and there's applause as they appear for the first time.

In fact, the atmosphere's beginning to build already and I would imagine it's at fever pitch level at the Moon Club by now. They're closing the doors at 7pm and it's a 15 minute walk up to the stadium, assuming you can walk in a straight line still, obviously, or even still walk?

My head is clear. I don't expect Wales to win, I do think they've got a chance to draw but, if you gave me a free bet, I'd put it on a Belgian win because they're very good but more because that's the way it is when you support Wales.

What I am determined to do is enjoy the occasion as much as possible, and the best time to do that is before a ball's been kicked. Normally, I hang around in the tunnel, tonight I spend time on the touchline, observing as seats begin to fill up. I have a wander up to the media room where I bump into Chris from the *Western Mail* again, much as I did in Haifa, only this time I have the surprising team news. He furrows his brow a little before coming to the same conclusion I just have. Then, at 7pm, I walk all around to the other corner of the stadium where the Super Furry Animals will be playing. As I arrive, they're already up on stage and singing, I walk behind them and round to the far side of the stage for a better view. Fans voted for them to start the set with 'God! Show Me Magic', with a fair few suggesting that 'God!' should be replaced with 'Bale!' The seats behind the band are still some way short of full, but the guys get a great reception as they rattle through three tracks in the rain before heading back round the ground to take up their seats in the stand. I follow directly behind, catching-up with Gruff like a besuited, white-haired groupie, and I brief him with the team news before our paths separate.

The players are already out on the pitch for their final warm-up now and the ground's filling rapidly. The away end's an impressive sight, a sea of red. I've been hearing Belgian fans singing all afternoon in the city centre, now though, their voices are being drowned out, both by a top notch playlist of Welsh tunes over the PA and by the noise from the home supporters. You can feel the sense of anticipation.

It's time for me to get back in the tunnel. John Smart's on floor managing duty again, so we're in safe hands. The mascots start lining up down either wall. I've got the mascots in Wales kits on my side, at the front of the line is a little blonde-haired lad with glasses. He's a real character, as are the two little guys standing behind him and they chatter away to me and each other. It's raining outside and my little pal in glasses remarks that this is bad because he hasn't got a coat. Behind him, another suggests that the crowd are all jumping up with their arms in the air because they want the rain to stop. Then Thibault Courtois appears and he becomes the object of their curiosity instead. They ask him better questions than I managed to come up with yesterday, like "Why are you so tall?" and "What's your name?"

Next, it's the ref's turn, "Are you the ref?" one asks. The ref nods. "Can you give Wales lots of penalties then?" "No, he can't" Thibault interjects, perhaps fearful the ref might actually say, 'yes, little guy, no problem'. It's funny, there are 33,500 people out there, working themselves into a frenzy, but in the tunnel we're in a different world.

The Wales players file out of the dressing room, shortly after the visitors. Then there's a moment of confusion and mild chaos as it appears the two teams are actually on the wrong side of the tunnel, and they all have to do a sort of formation shuffle across. The timings for these games are meant to be spot on, but I don't think Smartie will be getting this game off on time tonight. Finally, with everyone where they should be, they set off.

I must admit, tonight feels different, a bit more momentous. I consider it one of the great privileges of this job to actually be allowed to follow the teams out from the tunnel, this is the closest I will ever get to being part of 'it'. This is the bit where I can best try to imagine I'm one of them. We step out into a wall of noise. No chewing gum swap with Dai, Haifa banished the need for that. I am wearing the Euro 2016 badge in my lapel though, apart from that, I'm lucky-item free. If it works for the manager, it works for me! Anyway, I know that somewhere in a small town in Canada, Alex is watching in his lucky socks.

I go and find my seat, accompanied by Andy, the sound man. He's been at my side for pretty much every one of these home games. He knows how it goes next. I stand for the Belgian national anthem, sadly booed by some amongst the home support. Surely we're better than that? The majority shush them down, and there's warm applause at the end. Then there's a collective intake of breath and the home anthem. It's a good rendition tonight, the singer slowing down sufficiently to let the crowd keep up and the 'Gwlad! Gwlad!' is massive. I've belted it out tonight, no holding back. At the end of it, Chris Coleman raises his hands above his head to applaud the crowd, a sign of things to come maybe?

Now, all the good stuff's out the way. There's just the torture to come. And for the first 20 minutes, it's really, really painful. Belgium move the ball around swiftly and incisively. Wales can't get the ball off them, never mind build any possession. On 10 minutes, Wayne Hennessey makes a great full stretch save from Nainggolan, then Hazard wallops a half-volley in from the edge of the area but it's a little too high. These are worrying times but Wales keep their defensive shape admirably and eventually engineer a break out, Bale charges forward and wins a corner. The noise levels surge. Robson-Kanu places a header wide, that's better, but here come the Belgians again. I've been doing my five minute count from the very first minute, such has been the extent of the away team's domination and the first half already feels like it's lasted an age as we approach the 25 minute mark. Now Hal's on the charge down the left, chasing a Bale pass from inside his own half. It relieves the pressure on those overworked defenders. Hal does well. He runs the ball down towards the corner of the Belgian half, pursued by Denayer. All four Belgium defenders are natural centre halves, big guys but not really sprinters. Hal's strong as well as quick and just as he looks to have wriggled away from the grip of his marker, he's wrestled to the ground. It's a free kick in a good position for a cross into the area.

Aaron Ramsey goes over to take it. He delivers the ball towards the near post, but Jan Vertonghen's in there to head away to the edge of the box. To me it looks like the danger's gone as Joe Allen loops a header back towards the edge of the area, Chester jumps and makes connection, but it loops up harmlessly again. There, underneath is it the distinctive blonde Mohican hairstyle of Nainggolan. Somewhat unexpectedly to say the least, he sends another looping header back into his own box. It's a very strange decision. I watch as the ball drops, my heart quickens as it falls perfectly for Gareth Bale. He's got his back to goal but he's all alone, literally, in front of goal, everyone else has pushed out. It all happens in microsecond, he lets the ball drop off his chest, turns to face the goal and I see him sidefoot it calmly under the onrushing Courtois. As the ripple spreads through the back

214

of the net, I let out a noise that comes from somewhere deep within. It's like a muted scream, with all the energy but not so much of the noise, not that anyone could hear me trying to stay neutral, as the stadium's just exploded!

As the game restarts, I take some time to look around the stadium and it's an amazing sight. It looks like everybody bar the Belgian contingent is standing and singing and jumping up and down, and just enjoying this whole experience. After so many years of being rubbish, suffering the sight of another campaign slipping away, this is just brilliant! I love this so much. To me, from here on in, it almost doesn't matter what happens in the game now. All these people have had a moment when their team was 1-0 up against the second best team in the world. Savour it, enjoy it. Pray it lasts.

This is why it's so much better that this game is at this stadium. My guess would be that the tickets have been sold to the real football fans, the ones who showed their faith in the first place by buying campaign tickets, then those who saw the potential and stepped in to snap up half campaign tickets, including my mum and dad, somewhere out there amongst the celebrating masses.

For sure, they could have got more into the Millennium Stadium but I don't think you'd see scenes like this in there. As I remember, it used to attract a fair proportion of people who'd as readily show up for a rugby international or a monster truck event and when Wales weren't good any more, they stopped coming. The rugby's still well supported but it's marketed differently, as an event at the heart of a weekend mini-break in Cardiff. A lot of the football lads remark on the number of pink cowboy hats you see in the crowd, the international symbol for hen parties. That's fine, inclusive and all that, but does the result really matter to anyone? Or are they just there for the fireworks?

There's no way I'm relaxed now, by the way, I'm fretting about the inevitable equaliser. But I keep reminding myself that a point's a great return. Joe Allen's been booked, so I'm already worrying about the fact he'll be suspended for Cyprus. And then Wales nearly score again at the end of the best move of the game so far. Crisp passing and good movement on the edge of the area and Ramsey's in, his cross shot is palmed away by Courtois then sliced clear by a defender straight into the path of Hal Robson-Kanu. The goal is gaping but it

215

comes at him quickly and he sidefoots a few inches wide of the post. Hands are thrown to heads all around.

Still, it's a decent counter jab because it reminds the visitors that they have to be wary of conceding a second. They seem to lose a little heart and time passes relatively comfortably to the temporary relief of the half-time whistle. The players leave the field to a huge ovation but by comparison, the tunnel's very quiet. Time passes too quickly and Belgium emerge first from the dressing room again. Somebody asks Jan Vertonghen if there are any changes? He nods as Lukaku follows. Mertens is being replaced. It looks like 4-4-2, with a pair of big lads up front. I'm actually quite pleased at this development. It means Belgium may start to rely less on Hazard's trickery on the edge of the box, and more on the supply of crosses from the two wings. I think we've got the players to deal with that. Belgium did something similar in the home game and that didn't really work for them. Needless to say, when Wales come out, they remain unchanged, in terms of personnel and attitude. The look on Ashley Williams' face sums up the mood, he's the picture of unblinking determination. The other players have the same look, as if they know there's so much still to do. This, this is team spirit.

I follow them out, Andy a step behind. Poor bloke doesn't get much chat out of me on these occasions. I'm concentrating every bit as hard as the players; daren't relax. As we sit down he says, "you don't look like you're enjoying this much?" He's right and yet, of course I am, because at half-time we're leading the second best side in the world by a goal to nil, Wales are top of the group and could take a huge step towards qualification. Not only that, but they're playing well. So, I'm not not enjoying it, it's not like Serbia away when we were 3-1 down at half-time, I'm not enjoying it because I know there's a possibility I might be enjoying it an awful lot more, if Wales can just hang on. But it's a very big 'if'.

Belgium, unsurprisingly, start off on the front foot. They win an early corner and all the tall players go up. The ball flashes across the area as Benteke arrives at the far post, he makes contact, but Williams is right in there with him and it goes wide. The great thing is that nothing Belgium do in or around the area is uncontested. There's always a red shirt or two bearing down on them, throwing themselves in front of the ball. It's not desperate, just utterly committed. For one second, the wall is holed. De Bruyne's been really quiet but he finds space, works the ball onto his right foot and strokes a shot just wide of the post from the edge of the area. Then Hazard dances through again and tumbles on the by-line as the captain tries to chase him down. The ball rolls out and the ref points for a goal kick. A glance down at my monitor suggests a hint of a touch on his heel but nobody, not even Hazard, appealed. In my headphones, after viewing a replay, a former Wales captain reckons that might be a let-off.

These, though, are isolated moments. Wales aren't doing anything offensively, but defensively it looks like they've got it all locked down. Even the clock seems to speed up. At the hour mark, I genuinely begin to wonder whether we might just get something out of this after all. At this stage, Belgium would probably be happy with a point. They've been playing football for two years almost straight through. They played a hard game last Sunday and they don't look like they've got an awful lot left in the tank.

The crowd sense it. The singing gets louder. The commentators sense it as Barry starts talking about the potential consequences of a Welsh win. Bill's relatively new to this Wales-watching lark, but he gets it and he proves that as he seeks to rein Barry in a little, "Up and down Wales, people are now screaming at their TVs. Too soon, Barry! Too soon!" And I actually laugh out loud. He's absolutely right. Barry's calling it on the basis of what he sees with his professional eye, the rest of us watch as fans and secretly we may think the same but we'd never dare say it. That would be to tempt fate. It's a brilliant bit of commentary.

It might be said that the game's gone into a bit of a lull now but we love this lull, especially as it's so utterly unexpected. In the place of action comes noise and with the clock heading towards 70 minutes, something incredible happens. The strains of the anthem rise up from who knows where but it's quickly picked up and soon it sounds like the whole stadium's singing. Tears roll down my cheeks. I'm sure I'm not alone. It's awe inspiring and, it prompts another memorable moment of commentary as Barry remarks that it looks like the Belgian players were shocked by the intensity because they just rolled the ball round to each other harmlessly during the rendition.

In front of me, though, is the one concern. Gareth Bale is clearly struggling. Every time play stops, he stretches his right calf, to my right there are anxious conversations going on amongst the medical staff. Even in his predicament, Belgium daren't not man-mark him so he's still tying up a defender. Nevertheless, subs start warming up. The psychological impact of taking Gareth off is what worries me, and it must surely worry the coaching staff. It might just be the impetus those tired looking Belgians need for one last push. So, he stays on.

The clock moves on towards that 80 minute mark. Before it gets there, another Belgium corner. It's cleared, Belgium come again and Chris Gunther manages to head a dangerous cross over his own bar. Oh Jeez, here we go again! My stomach lurches once more. My only consolation at this stage is the point, if they score now surely we'll still get a point out of the game. Then Witsel swings at a cross and somewhere in the crowd of players, Jazz Richards falls to the floor and the ref whistles for a Wales free kick, there's a big roar of relief. Jazz stays down a little while. I think back to all that talk of game management earlier in the campaign, this is it in action. Waste a bit of time, let things calm down, take control again.

Then a big let-off for Wales as Hazard goes through the gears in the middle of the pitch and in Wales' half. Joe Allen's chasing but he clips him and Hazard tumbles. Already booked, I switch my gaze to the ref, nothing but a free kick, Joe's a very lucky boy!

A couple of minutes more tick away and it's time for me to leave my seat. It's incredible to me that I'm heading to the tunnel with Wales still winning. The news comes in through my headphones, Gareth is man of the match, so I suggest the Bale/Ramsey combination that served us well in Haifa. Jim's on board. As I reach the tunnel mouth, there are a crowd of officials and staff, all straining for the best view possible of the game. In their midst, John Smart, veteran of a thousand big games, unruffled and intent only on getting everything sorted at full-time. IG's there as well, he looks pale. I pass on the request and he asks where we want to do it? There had been a suggestion that the super flash interview would be conducted on the pitch, I think UEFA are quite keen for this to happen.

In preparation, I ask Andy for a set of over-the-ear headphones, as it'll be too noisy out there for me to get a cue on my little in-ear speaker. There's a problem with connections or something, a screwdriver's required. To be honest, it's an unwanted distraction. I just want to join that throng at the mouth of the tunnel, I want to actually watch the last few minutes, live, not on a monitor.

Then, Smartie turns and mouths, 'inside', pointing to the interview position. He's referring to where we're going to be talking to the players. I'm actually pleased, it's now pouring with rain, the noise will be cacophonous if it stays as it is and we have better control over everything if we bring the players back in. That means I don't need the headphones either, so I rush back out to a position where I can see what's happening.

Bale's finally brought off with the clock on 88 minutes and he gets a tremendous ovation. What a way to mark your 50th cap for your country! Still, it's not done though and the crowd gets involved again as the anthem rises from 30,000 voices, imploring the players to hang on. It's up to 89 now when Belgium get awarded a free kick just outside the area. This is it. I resign myself to what happens next. I know they'll score. A point is still okay but, we were so close! IG and I exchange a glance, we're both thinking the same. The ball's tapped to Vertonghen, his shot deflects off the wall and behind for a corner, there's a huge roar from the home fans but the awsay supporters sense there's something still in the game for their team. As the board goes up, three added minutes, the corner's sent over and Wayne Hennessey stands alone in the centre of the box to catch the ball. It's like a goal has just been scored, people leap up to celebrate a simple catch.

The whistling reaches a shrill crescendo but Belgium aren't done. Wales concede possession badly and the away side get another corner. Courtois comes all the way forward, this has to be their last attack. The ball sails into the box towards Benteke, he stretches, closest to goal, but he can't make contact and it drifts behind for a goal kick. That must be nearly it? On my wrist I'm running my stopwatch and we're heading rapidly towards 48 minutes for this half. Oh my God! I think we're going to do this! IG stands at my shoulder. The ball's pumped forward, then comes back into the Welsh half, another defensive header's won and as the ball loops forward, the ref stops running and I see him put the whistle to his mouth. AAAAAAAAAAHHHHHHHHHHH!!!!!!!!!!!!!!!! I started the week being grumpy with IG, now we're hugging each other tightly like lovers and jumping up and down like lunatics, football eh? Bloody Hell!

I know it's going to be a little while before the players come off the pitch, so I break the habit of a lifetime and stay out to watch the scenes from the touchline. This needs to be savoured! The coaching staff have stayed out to watch as well. Dai the kitman spots me and after a big slap of a handshake, there are more hugs and embraces, I take one last look around the stadium and it's an incredible scene. The joy is sheer and absolute, relief, happiness, pride and excitement. We daren't talk about it before but now we must, Wales might actually qualify for this ruddy tournament after all!

As I turn and head back to work, Chris Coleman's heading in the same direction. There's a bit of me, at the back of my head, that says I shouldn't, that I'm neutral and a professional and not a fan anymore. If I was a fan, I'd rush to give the manager a hug, by way of congratulations and gratitude; aah, sod it! I let him walk into a big embrace, arms outstretched. We've suffered the bad times together, let's at least enjoy this whilst it lasts.

There's a job to be done now. Our UEFA official's on hand with her clipboard, checking who we've requested and where we're doing the interview. I chuck a couple more names at her, including Jazz Richards, who's had such a fine game. Jazz has been selected for a visit from doping control though, a random selection, which complicates matter as it means he can't go back in the dressing room and has to be escorted at all times when he comes off the pitch. I add Ashley Williams and Neil Taylor to my wish list, truth be told, I'd happily interview all of them tonight. They all deserve their recognition for an incredible team display. Bale's MOTM perhaps because of the goal but, if truth be told, any one of the 11 that started could be getting it tonight.

The Belgians slope past looking doleful, in stark contrast to the home players who start coming in. Then our two guests appear, Aaron first, Gareth next. As I start to ask questions, I realise my voice has gone really husky. I'm not sure how or why, I haven't been shouting or singing, honest, but it sounds a bit like it. There's no problem with energy though, words tumble out, the players are absolutely buzzing, but still not out of control. It's joyous but it's measured, a fantastic night but still a job to be done, not achieved anything yet, take it a game at a time, look forward to Cyprus. They really get it, this is an intelligent response from bright lads. They aren't going to commit to anything that could lead them to be accused of complacency.

It's the same with Neil Taylor who appears next, almost at their shoulder. It's very impressive. As Chris is led over by IG, he asks about the Allen foul first, before we get going, could it have been a second yellow? I tell him, yes, that it would have been surely, if he hadn't already been booked. He agrees and says they felt much the same in the dugout. On that basis, we both agree the ref's had a fine game!

Chris has a lot to say, he commends the commitment of his team to the cause, whilst admitting it wasn't the greatest footballing display. He reiterates the confidence the coaching staff had in 'the system' and how well Jazz Richards adapted to his role in it. Then we look forward and he refuses to dampen hopes the fans will have of what lies ahead, although the players know they have more to do. He says tonight wasn't the biggest game, the biggest game will be when Wales can actually, definitely, qualify, whenever that may be. Amen to that.

Vertonghen is put up as the Belgian offering, as he was in Brussels. Now, as then, he's pretty terse but I appreciate the fact that he's been prepared to 'front up' after his country's first defeat since the World Cup quarter-final with Argentina.

Our last man arrives, Ashley Williams, forehead still lined with beads of perspiration. He describes how he pulled the players together in the now-customary huddle at the end of the game and delivered the 'achieved nothing yet' message. It's been another landmark night in a remarkable career, but he knows there's better to come if he can finally lead a Wales team over the line.

Six interviews done and I'm guessing that's probably enough, but I confirm that with Jim before the earpiece comes out, the comms box is unfastened from my belt and my day's work is done. The banter for the last few minutes has all been about what comes next. The lads in the crew have to help pack everything up before they depart, the only thing I'll be carrying will be my bag, back to the car.

Before I head off into the night, I hang around a little while longer close to the dressing rooms, like the big kid I am, I want to mark this incredible evening and I've kept a couple of team sheets for players to sign. Aaron puts his name on one, Joe Ledley and Gareth Bale on another, as he scrawls his signature and I thank him, Gareth says, "That puts us in pot one!" This is the big spin-off from the result.

The players are clearly of the opinion that beating Belgium means Wales will be amongst the top seeds for the World Cup draw in July, having been in pot six for the last one. That's a rise that nobody's ever achieved before.

One of the men who's made it possible emerges from the dressing rooms, Kit Symons. He's got a big smile on his face but as he stops to talk to the under-21s manager, Geraint Williams, I sense all isn't well. He's saying goodbye. I wonder immediately if Fulham have finally said enough is enough, despite his attempts at remaining low-key. We talk about the game, then I ask the question, "Is this your last game then?" The smile slips and he suddenly looks quite emotional, he confirms it is with a nod. I probably don't help matters by exclaiming that he can't go now, not when we're so close! "I'm gutted mate, absolutely gutted", he sighs, crestfallen. "Does that make tonight sweet and sour then?", I ask, "No mate, it's still very sweet!", he replies, the smile back. He'll be missed.

David Hughes is in close proximity as Kit heads off for the final time, with another big grin. He describes an incredible night that encompassed a fascinating evening in the company of Rafa Benitez, over to watch Gareth Bale, a subsequent invitation to go and watch Real Madrid at work next season and, of course, a fantastic result for anyone connected to Welsh football. I think it's fair to say, Dave's had a night he won't forget in a hurry, and I'm chuffed for him.

Another former pupil of my old school appears, Steve Williams. He's got me a Belgium FA badge to add to my collection. More smiles and he might be able to look forward to a celebratory drink later, as the visitors are heading straight back tonight.

Mission accomplished, I head out into the late evening. There are still crowds of people thronging around the reception doors, waiting for that last glimpse of Gareth perhaps? I move through them and stop at the OB compound. More hugs as first Sarah appears, then Bill. Normally, I think he and I would be looking forward to a little celebration but he's straight off to Heathrow to catch a flight up to Scotland at 6am so he can attend the wedding of a family friend. The 2014-15 season finally ends here. For all of us, for a few short weeks, Saturdays are now for families, not football.

Barry's staying over in Cardiff and he's still at the stadium so we arrange a rendezvous back at the hotel. The traffic into town's still backed up one way, so I spin the car round and find another route. Ten minutes later, I'm back at base and I rush straight up to my room to get changed. I switch the TV on and S4C are showing their highlights of the game still, so I delay my exit to enjoy the last few minutes all over again. Suddenly, the emotion overwhelms me, pretty much pent up since full-time and I stand in my room and start to laugh and then sob arms spread wide, fists clenched.

Only once I've seen the scenes at the final whistle and regained my composure can I head downstairs. No sign of Barry, so I order a drink and await his arrival. There are one or two Belgians sitting quietly in the bar, I know that feeling all too well, but they'll be fine and they'll still qualify. In fact we now need Belgium to beat the Bosnians to keep them out of the race in the run-in. I can start to contemplate what needs to happen next. Twenty points has been identified as the magic number. If Wales can win in Cyprus, we're virtually assured of automatic qualification. If we can win the next two games, we'll be in with a great chance of actually finishing top. Andorra to play at home in the last game must mean three points, so three more from three games needed.

My calculations are interrupted by a fan who wants a chat and a pic, it turns out he might well have played against me in a school game many years ago, and then by the man himself. But, true to form, Barry has a travel tale of woe to recount before we can bask in the afterglow. On his drive through the city centre, someone staggered off the pavement and rolled across his bonnet. The bloke seemed to have had quite a few drinks as he bounced straight back up off the floor and began shouting angrily in Barry's direction. His pals then emerged from a bar and joined in. Barry fled but only to find someone in uniform to whom he could report the incident. Keen to avoid a charge of leaving the scene of an accident, he had to hunt for quite a while before finding a police officer, pretty surprising on a Friday night in Cardiff, but he found one, gave his details and was told to carry on with his evening.

Not for the first time, the poor guy now probably needs a drink to help him calm down so we have one at the bar then go to a nearby pub, The Yard, for a couple more. Whilst we're there, I get chatting to another bloke who almost certainly played against my school team in a game as well, this is getting bizarre! I know it's only a small country and all that but it's beginning to feel like we all live on one long street!

Barry calls it a day a little earlier than me, but it's not the same without my wingman, so one more drink and I head back as well. Before I make it, I bump into Tim, Mr SO58. He's survived the day well. It seems the event was a success with loads more money raised, so here's someone else who'll have a big smile across his face still as he closes his eyes at the end of a long, amazing day.

Saturday 13th June

I've got a long drive ahead of me but before I can get going, I have a duty to perform. My parents were up for the game last night, and they've stayed over. So, before I drive north, I walk up through the city to meet them for a coffee.

They've got their half-season tickets, so they'll be at the two remaining home games as well. It was my dad who took me to my first international back in 1981, when we played the USSR in front of the biggest crowd I've ever seen at The Racecourse. We needed a win to be in with a real chance of qualifying for Spain '82; and drew 0-0. You know the rest.

They're waiting for me in the café of the Holiday Inn. The big TV on the wall is showing the game again, and there's a group of Wales fans already cradling pints looking up at it. It seems the party's still going strong.

Then, my brother arrives. I offered him a ticket for last night's game, Dave Hughes had a spare, but Tom turned it down. He said Wales were good until he started travelling with me to watch them, so he doesn't want to jinx anything by starting to come along to games again. It's not strictly true. He was in Finland for the 2-0 victory, in Moscow for the 0-0 draw and his last trip was San Marino away, where, admittedly, Wales recorded a pretty unimpressive 2-1 win, but it was still a win. In truth, I think he's fallen out of love with football, found other things to do with his time and money. I wonder if he'd contemplate coming back for France? Stop it! Too soon Brynnie, too soon!

7

"He's Gareth Bale, what can you do to stop him?"
Cyprus v Wales

'We like to sing, we like to dance,
We've got our passports, we're going to France.'

Sunday 30th August

There's the usual family tableau on the front doorstep of 'Chez Law' at the start of another international week. This time, though, the keen observer would notice an extra kiss, a little longer on the hugs. There's an added poignancy to this departure. By the time I return, my daughter will have celebrated her 16th birthday and my wife and I will have passed our 17th anniversary. So, Wales may be two wins away from qualification, but my trip will be tempered by the knowledge that I'm missing significant events in the life of my family.

It's been this way many times before. The first big mistake I made was not foreseeing the implications of getting married in early September, my first child then being born a year later was something I had a little less control over.

The warning signs were there from the start. We got married on the day Wales lost a qualifier to Italy, and Megan was born on the day we won 2-1 away in Belarus. I watched the highlights on a small TV above my wife's bed, when I was meant to be comforting her ahead of an emergency caesarean. If it had been a boy, it was Ryan, he got the winner.

I've been missing Megan's birthdays ever since, starting with the first qualifier we covered for Sky, 11 years ago in Azerbaijan. She's relatively philosophical about it but, as we break the hug, she reminds me that I'll need to come back with a pretty special present to make up for this one. It's been tough on them though, combined absences for Wales games alone must run at a year plus by now, the parting certainly doesn't get any easier and I take a long, lingering look in my rear-view mirror as I pull away from the drive, a lump in my throat.

If there are tears over the next few days, they could be of sorrow or joy. Wales are so close, and I can't even be sure when I'll be back. I'm guessing it'll be the day after the Israel game if qualification's not been achieved. I wouldn't like to put a date on it if it has, the party could go on for quite a while!

The build-up's brought the usual trials and tribulations, Joe Allen was suspended for the Cyprus game anyway, but a pre-season injury means he won't make the second game either. The weekend fixtures have also brought doubts over the fitness of James Chester and Hal Robson-Kanu.

On the upside, the forecast suggests Cyprus is going to be pretty hot so I've packed accordingly. Shorts, sunglasses and sun cream are all to be found in my bag. I've also made contact with Alex already, back on board for this one, to make sure he's got one vital item in his luggage, the lucky stripy socks he's been wearing all the way through Wales' long unbeaten run.

That run has lifted the national side to stratospheric heights in terms of the FIFA rankings. It's just a few weeks since it was confirmed that Wales were now ranked inside the top 10 for the first time ever; not only that but Wales were amongst the top seeds in the draw for the qualifying stage of the next World Cup, just four years after being amongst the bottom seeds! These are great days indeed, but the one prize that really matters, that of qualification, still has to be achieved.

Plenty to contemplate on the drive down before a reunion with Alex and his socks. We grab a bite to eat and discuss the itinerary, players tomorrow, then training, then Heathrow before a flight to Larnaca on Tuesday.

Monday 31st August

After a decent night's sleep, I stick the kettle on in my room and then collect the copy of the *Western Mail* from the floor outside my door. As I sip, I read and the big sports story concerns the imminent announcement of the Welsh Rugby Union squad for the forthcoming World Cup. It's taking place at midday in Cardiff. Football, as ever, has to fight for the column inches in this part of the country. Still, Sky Sports News are sending a truck over the border, and it isn't heading for the Millennium Stadium, but joining us at the team hotel.

It's already parked when we finally get to the St. David's, still early but later than planned. Alex got stuck for ages waiting for the lift, one of the drawbacks of being up on the 17th floor. The FAW have played a blinder, IG points us in the direction of a room upstairs which is just for us. Chris Gunter is our big live show interviewee this time and we're told that he's ready when we are, so we need to get a wiggle on. Half a dozen tables have to be stacked, chairs piled on top, lights up, cameras, action! As well as Chris, we're talking to Wayne Hennessey, Ben Davies and Andy King and it's the goalie who appears first. He's got his worries currently and we chat through them before the interview. He's not getting a game at Crystal Palace, despite an injury to Speroni, Alan Pardew's first pick 'keeper. It seems the manager's not keen to let him leave either, even with the transfer window set to close tomorrow. So, Wayne's worried that he's not getting match action ahead of the biggest games of his career.

We get the usual glut of good material out of the guys and I warn Ben Davies that the next interview we do might be in Welsh. S4C will again be showing highlights of the game in Cyprus, and I've offered to help them with their post-match interviews as they aren't sending a reporter. This promises to be something of a challenge, so I warn Ben that if I say something daft, he should just talk about the game anyway.

All done, we're back to the hotel to check out then make our way over to the Vale for the 4pm training session. Interviews are sent back to London and, in the meantime, a decent sized crowd of cameras gathers for the arrival of the management team and players. Over the brow of the hill, we see a golf buggy appear and as it gets closer

227

it becomes apparent that it's a buggy transporting about a hundred and fifty million pounds worth of footballing talent! Gareth Bale's standing on the back, bouncing up and down, Aaron Ramsey's sitting next to the driver, who looks a little stressed. Can you be fully comp on a golf buggy?

Alex is in the right place to film it all and he gives me the thumbs up, he knows he's got the shot of the day. IG also looks a little concerned at such an arrival in front of so many cameras, but no one gets hurt and the lads head off happily to join the rest of the group, now arriving in a more conventional manner. Soon, they're all kidding around and playing games of keepie-up and the banter's flying. It's all suitably upbeat. I've learnt to pick up on the mood around a successful squad, they exude a kind of easy going positivity, it's in the air around these lads for sure. It's the camaraderie you rarely get at clubs anymore, even successful ones, because long service is a thing of the past. Players come and go with much greater frequency, so they don't have chance to form such strong bonds as you can sense on this training ground.

Time up, shots sent, I leave my car at the Vale, and we head off to Heathrow in the Alexmobile. It's a Bank Holiday and the M4 is predictably busy, so it's nearly three hours later before we arrive at our next hotel, the Radisson Edwardian. So, like last night, we eat and then swiftly adjourn to our rooms.

Tuesday 1st September

We're not flying until 11.45am, so no need for an early alarm, unlike my former colleagues at Sky Sports News who are all out and about already for coverage of Transfer Deadline Day. As they chatter away about potential comings and goings, I hit the gym for an hour then grab a bit of breakfast before checking out. Alex has promised me bacon rolls in the business lounge, to which he has access for himself and a guest, so I've limited myself to the Weetabix.

No pod this time, we travel in his car, which gets collected at the departure hall doors, and taken off to be parked somewhere before its returned for the minute he sets foot back in arrivals, a great service!

Bill's waiting for us at check-in. There's a bit of a discussion about whether Alex can take his camera on board when we get to the desk. A supervisor is called and confirms that it's fine, so we move on through security without much further delay. Then, as usual, the promise of a lounge place is snatched away as Bill reveals that his BA status has slipped from Silver back to Bronze, so he can't get in anymore. He stuck with the team last time, so we do the same now and all head off for Giraffe again, where we're joined by Sarah, once more on board as the director. We've put the old team back together, minus Barry, who, as ever, is making some crazy trip over tomorrow that already sounds like it has all the makings of another tale of travel woe.

It's a long flight, nearly five hours, and we're all in cattle class again. But it passes pleasantly enough and we rendezvous, along with other members of the Sky crew, at the baggage reclaim in Larnaca. Our production manager for this one is a guy called Dave Weinstein and he's waiting for us in arrivals, holding a Sky Sports sign, as if we didn't know who he is. He's a big lad, Dave, easily spotted and most of us have worked with him before. He's been out since the weekend, getting a bit of sun before the work begins. He's managed to organise a minibus so we head off to find it in the car park. Just before we get on board, he does a head count. There's a problem. We're one short. A check on the travel list suggests there should be a sound supervisor called Victor with us, but there's no sign of him. Calls are made and it turns out he hasn't flown. Further investigations reveal he's been working on another job in London today, crossed wires somewhere, so he needs to catch the first flight out tomorrow morning. This is bad news for the tech crew and is likely to extend their working day, in temperatures that are still in the 30s at half past six in the evening.

It's a 45 minute drive to Nicosia. We check in at the Hilton, which is really rather nice, swiftly reassemble in the hotel bar, then move to the dining area by the hotel pool. A very pleasant evening ensues, and my adventurous choice of octopus as starter proves a winner. I get talking to one of the sound techs who I haven't met before, not a big football fan but he loves his music and ran the BBC Introducing stage at last weekend's Reading festival. My pal, Andy, was running the equivalent stage at Leeds, and I spent some time watching the bands there in the days leading up to departure for Wales. As we compare notes, it makes a change from the usual 'red hot soccer chat'.

As others drift away, Bill suggests a late evening constitutional and he and I head off into the night, looking for a bit of life. It isn't to be found in the immediate environs of our hotel, that's for sure. We walk further, guided by the occasional local we meet. After a while, we arrive at a pub called Finbar's, promising except the lights are off and only two people remain at a table outside. There's a tall, elderly guy in the doorway, hair in a pony tail. We approach him but even before we've uttered a word, he says, in a North American accent, "Sorry guys, I've got the message you don't want to hear; we're closed." Sensing our dismay, he directs me towards other possible venues, someway distant down the same long road. Bill gathers more intel, the old town's down this way, so we keep walking.

Next stop is a seedy looking joint with the word Pub above the door. Again, two people sit outside and all the lights are off. It's small and faces onto a dried-up river and a wire fence, I'm not sure this is the Old Town. If it is, it's in need of renovation. Bill asks one of the old men at the table, "Can we get a beer?" To which, the old man replies, "You want Fanta? Coke? Girls?" Slightly taken aback, Bill responds politely "Er... no, just a beer." A discussion then ensues and a third old bloke gets brought into the scene, he's wearing an apron and appears to have been at work on a kebab stand next door. He's dispatched to the fridge for beer. We sit at our table on the edge of the building site and reflect that, like Haifa, we've ended up at the worst bar in town. We've also wandered so far from the hotel that the return journey's made in a taxi driven by a heavily bearded man who tells us he's not a football fan, but a fan and practitioner of MMA, mixed martial arts. I tell him to be careful as Bill's an expert in Origami. He doesn't laugh, but says his skills are useful for dealing with 'bad passengers'. He doesn't get a tip. We walk briskly back into the hotel.

Wednesday 2nd September

Getting down to breakfast at 10am might seem a bit self-indulgent, but the body and the watch are still set to UK time, two hours behind. There's not a lot of recognition for this from our Cypriot hosts. The second I step into the dining room a member of staff steps in front of me to warn me that they're shutting in five minutes. They're already whipping croissants off the buffet display.

Outside, the loungers around the pool are already beginning to fill up. I can see the familiar red, white and green stripes of a Spirit of '58 bucket hat on the head of one early sun seeker. Tim's stuff's been flying out in the run-up to this trip. He reckons at least one third of the travelling fans will be wearing his most successful line on their heads. With 3,500 travelling out, that's a lot of hats!

After bolting down a bowl of cereal and a cup of tea, I'm on my way out as well, my own bucket hat in hand. My first job will be to interview a Cyprus player just before their training session at 7pm. After that it's the usual interviews with the manager and captain. Wales aren't training at the stadium, and won't get in until early evening.

So, I've got a bit of time on my hands. Bill's following the same routine, so we'll travel to the ground together later. Alex and the rest of the team have an hour or so to kill before they need to get there to make sure everything works. We all get the chance to catch a few rays together before we go our separate ways.

This is one of the good days. Bill and I hang out by the pool for a few hours, then partake of the excellent buffet lunch at the hotel, then head back to our rooms. He's got prep to do, I have a siesta. After a decent power nap, I get the running gear on and head out into the heat for a half hour, stopping only to peer into the window of an Adidas factory outlet. It's closed. Old habits die hard, I'll be back.

I've got half an hour to go until we set off for the stadium and, after a shower, Bill suggests a coffee before we hail a cab.

As we're sitting in the lobby with our drinks, a familiar face appears. It's Robbie Savage, staying here as he's on assignment for BBC 5 Live. He remarks on my hair apparently being whiter than ever. He says I look "like that film star", then can't remember who that is. I suggest George Clooney? It's not him, though, it seems. We go through a few more, all incorrect, he promises to remember it for later, something for me to look forward to.

We head out to find transportation to the stadium. I've had one plaintive phone call from Alex this afternoon, he sounds a little low, not helped by my description of a pretty pleasant day. I send him a message to say we're on our way, ready for a bit of work!

It's a short drive from the hotel to the stadium, even in pretty heavy traffic, and it's handily located right by the side of the main road into town. It's not a bad looking structure, much better than the first ground I went to when I first came to watch Wales play here, in a World Cup qualifier in Limassol in 1992. In fact, as I look out the cab window, I can reflect on a few more dramatic differences than the architecture of the stadium. I came with my mates, we had booked an apartment for a week. I'd not long started a new job as a reporter at BBC Radio Leeds. I'd booked the trip before I got the job and I was here very much as supporter, not reporter. We drank all week long, rising late to spend a couple of hours by the pool, then heading off into the night again. It was messy.

We did have the game, of course, the first ever meeting between the two countries. Wales were going well in the qualifiers and it was October, with the weather still warm. So then, as now, a lot of fans had combined supporting the team with a late summer holiday. We sang our way through the match, including one 20 minute non-stop rendition of '*Terry Yorath's Red and White Army*', led by Jacko and Chris, two lads I see at matches to this day. Mark Hughes scored early in the second half, Wales hung on grimly and claimed the victory. Outside, the Cypriots took their revenge. As we left the ground, they formed a tight phalanx, arms linked, and charged through the middle, splitting the group of away fans, then they charged into battle. It was a savagely well organised attack. I fled in the direction of the safety of the bus that had brought us to the ground. A few weren't so fleet of foot, and got picked off. Mind you, I wasn't so lucky two days later, my last night, when the Limassol bouncers clearly decided they'd had enough of celebrating Welsh fans. I was sitting next to a guy in a club below our apartment block when he stood up to start another chorus of the Terry Yorath song, his fingers flicked the strip light and it shattered. Angry looking Cypriots appeared from nowhere and used this as the excuse they'd been looking for. I didn't make it back to my room this time, I was chased, caught in the lift, dragged out and battered, my blood spattered all across the marble floor of reception as the bemused night porter watched.

I missed the flight home as I went to hospital for an x-ray, nothing broken but a tooth and a disfigured septum, both of which I bear as souvenirs to this day.

And that was our only previous win in Cyprus. I have been back as a reporter twice since, once to Limassol, once to Nicosia, and we lost both. So don't blame me if I don't get too carried away about Wales' prospects tomorrow.

The taxi takes us right into the TV compound where we find a fairly exasperated looking Sarah, they're still hard at it. Things appear to have been every bit as tricky as feared. Inside the ground, Alex has just got his camera position sorted out, and he's also done well to make contact with the media officer I've organised the interview with. He's got us Jason Demetriou, who pays for Walsall and comes from Newham in East London, so the language won't be an issue. Alex has already set up and is ready to go. The man from the Cypriot FA goes off to find Jason, and a few minutes later we're walking down the tunnel together to where Alex is waiting. He's a really nice lad, as it turns out, and it's a very enjoyable interview. I ask him if there any special plans to deal with Gareth Bale. He laughs, a proper laugh out loud laugh, and says, "He's Gareth Bale, how do you do anything to deal with him?!" It's a strong contender for 'Best Answer of the Campaign' award.

He also makes clear that the home side will go all out to win the game. Cyprus have nine points, only two less than Belgium in second place. Beating Wales could make them realistic contenders for third place. The new format and the expanded tournament means that teams who would normally be out of the running still have plenty to play for.

It promises to be a tough night, a point Chris Coleman's keen to emphasise as he joins us an hour or so later, straight from the airport. Before the interview, he gets his first look at the pitch. It's not the best. "We can't really complain about any surface after Andorra can we?" he remarks as he pokes his shoe into a small hole. IG gets involved and says the pitch is meant to look a bit yellow as it's a characteristic of the seed used here. 'Bermuda Grass' he's been told. I make a joke about trying to avoid telling anyone the manager's been on the 'Bermuda Grass' the night before the game. Like my taxi joke, it doesn't get much of a response. Chris seems a bit distant, wrapped up in the magnitude of what lies ahead. He's at great pains in the interview to stress that nobody's looking any further ahead than the next game. Forget the two games to qualify, let's just get this one out of the way first.

There's a chance for a quick chat with Ashley before they all leave. He was a standout performer for Swansea in their win against Manchester United at the weekend, his performance highlight was a late goal-saving challenge on Wayne Rooney, brushing him aside to win the ball back in the box. He's got to be one of the best defenders in

233

the Premier League, arguably the best bargain buy playing in the top division as well. He's definitely one of my favourite ever Welsh players. Before he leaves, he sets me a challenge. He says, "If we win, I want to see a picture of you dancing on a table in Ayia Napa." I promise to comply, if he fulfils his side of the deal.

The guys head off to the media conference. I follow on in case it covers any ground that we haven't discussed, but they stick to the party line, tough night, focus only on the next game, etc. There's been talk about Cyprus's rough tactics in the first game but the manager doesn't really get drawn into that discussion. Suffice to say he hopes the ref will be strong.

Back at the compound, there's still work being done. We've got our interviews and training shots to feed as well. The Sky people and the Cypriots all look done in. The late arrival of the sound supervisor's had its impact, and even once we've sent our stuff there's a bit of a wait in the back of the minibus before we can hit the road for home.

We've got another Ben with us this time, a cameraman, and he's sorted the restaurant already. The hotel is hosting a wedding so we can't eat there but he's found a place across the road and booked a table. Bill and I cheer when we hear it's a buffet, our second of the day! At only €12 per head, it seems like pretty good value as well.

There's not a lot of turnaround time. Those who've been at the stadium all day haven't eaten and it's 10pm now. So, we sit down, order drinks and everyone sets off to pile their plate high. It's the perfect place for this situation. The service is attentive, the food plentiful and instantly available and the ambience good. Spirits rise as the plates pile up. Thoughts turn to our absent friend, Barry. There's much hilarity as we speculate on the nature of his travel travails, anticipation levels rise as contact is made via text and there is a huge cheer when he finally appears in the restaurant doorway! It's genuinely great to see him, the last member of our team. He doesn't disappoint either, "Order me a beer!" he demands, once the hearty handshakes and hugs are out of the way, "I've just had the worst journey yet!" The fact that he clearly means it provokes gales of laughter, ribs ache, tears roll down cheeks, as he recounts another tale of woe, involving tiny seats, big people, delays and all the rest, the laughter goes on and on. This is one of the great moments of what has been a fantastic experience.

This is our team, and the mood is every bit as upbeat as it was in that Wales training session.

Talking of which, by the time we get back, the players are all tucked up in their beds somewhere in our hotel. There's no sign of the management team either, there's a big day ahead.

Thursday 3rd September

It's MD7 and I'm awake before the alarm, set for 9.30am. Despite this, I still end up walking into the dining room at 9.55, where the same member of staff approaches me and points out that the breakfast will be finishing in five minutes. 'Team Sky' are all a little ahead of me and I join them at the table. The production crew are heading down to the stadium at around 4pm, whilst Bill and I agree to leave at around the same time as yesterday, although the game doesn't kick-off until 9.45pm! It's another very hot day but it should have cooled down a little by the time the players step out onto the pitch. Before all that, Alex and I have a request from Sports News to fulfil, they want some 'colour'. They aren't specific but that generally means some shots of Wales fans and a couple of our famous vox pops. I've explained that the vast majority of travelling fans are staying at the resorts of Limassol, Pathos and Ayia Napa, and coming in much later for the game. So, we might have a bit of a hunt on to find any, still, we'll give it a good shot.

Then Barry appears and I mention maybe going for a run later? He's in training for next year's London Marathon, so he's keen, particularly when I mention the Adidas shop, he says he needs some new gear. So, that gets pencilled in post-lunch, my schedule's now full!

The first task is to find the Old Town, where any locally based fans are bound to be found. Bill and I failed on foot, so we take a taxi this time and the driver drops us a short distance away from where we ended our first evening. This is more like it, narrow streets, shops, bars and there, some red shirts! Once again, we're not the first. ITV Wales have beaten us to them so we leave them to their filming and go off in search of some other fans. We turn into a blind alley, literally, and have to concede defeat and go back for the crumbs from ITV's table. The fans should be getting agents as crews line-up to interview them. As we're talking to our guys, the people who do the FAW TV output show up and queue patiently for their turn. It's all a bit bonkers really but all this practice is making for some very good talkers amongst the Welsh support. One down, we stumble upon another group of lads, still with their suitcases in their hands and clearly looking for their accommodation. Apparently one of them was hoping to bump into me in Cyprus, his mates suggest. Alex tells him he needs to set the bar of his ambitions a little higher. Fair point.

They're just in from 'Napa' and it shows in their eyes, it appears to have been a heavy week. Still, they turn in a bravura performance in the circumstances, one of them even suggesting Wales will not only qualify but will win the European Championships! This is all a bit different, unbridled optimism, I point out to them that this isn't the Welsh way but they're not having it, it's a generational thing. We who are white-haired, bear the campaign scars of past failures.

Then it's back in a cab so Alex can get the footage sent via a ropey broadband connection to the UK. Our taxi driver this time is a big football fan and he talks knowledgeably about the two teams. He reckons Cyprus are either good or not good, nothing in-between. They like to attack so they're susceptible to the counter attack. They've got injury problems, two good wide men missing, and Laban, who we interviewed and who scored in Cardiff, is suspended. He says the target will be to beat Wales and draw with Belgium.

As Alex goes off to deal with the material, I leave to change into something a little cooler for an hour by the pool. Soon it's time for lunch and, yes, it's another buffet! This time we're pre-loading for a long night at the stadium, which is completely isolated from anywhere to actually purchase anything to eat or drink.

As it turns out, we could have found more Wales fans on our doorstep than in town. There's a trip from Cardiff using this as their base and they're enjoying the build-up poolside. What's great is that they're sunbathing, eating, having a drink or a dip or whatever, but just being good, decent and nice. We have fans to be proud of. Good people.

After our lunch, with Bill again leading the way with another five-plate pile, Sarah leads off her team to go and do their thing at the stadium. Barry and I agree to let all the meat and fish settle for 15 minutes before we head off for our combined running/shopping trip. Bill's too full so he heads off for a lie-down.

The run's another killer in the heat, we've both got a real sweat on by the time we reach the top of the hill and the Adidas outlet. We drip as we browse. Barry buys a couple of very nice long sleeve running tops for his winter regime, but my pocket money's already gone on a watch for Megan, ordered online from my hotel room to arrive in time for her birthday.

I squeeze in a quick swim on our return, then doze off for 20 minutes or so. Once I wake, it's shower, summer issue chinos, shirt and the cotton jacket that I wore in Andorra and Israel, with the lucky Euro 2016 badge on the lapel, of course! I've got one interview to do with Barry sometime after 7pm, but as I wait for him in reception, a call comes in to say its going to be live and right at the top of the hour. Thinking of last night's traffic, I have a minor panic but Barry appears moments later, we jump into the cab and, thankfully, the road's much quieter than last night. I get a text from Dylan about the Welsh language interviews and he sends me some suggestions for questions but says I can do them in English if I prefer, as long as they answer in Welsh. No way! I'm going to use the Welsh I studied so hard to learn many moons ago! He also asks about team news and hints at rumours of a Ledley injury. Coleman mentioned nothing about it yesterday, and no mention of it has been made around the hotel that I've heard today either and I've bumped into a few members of the coaching staff.

We get straight out of the cab and walk immediately up the tunnel to the live pitchside position. We've got a few minutes to spare so I get set up with my earpiece, although there's a problem with the connection and a panic ensues as I can't really hear the output from Sports News. Brian races off up the tunnel to find another piece of equipment and he gets back in the nick of time. I'm not keen to go down the route of the Ledley rumours in case they turn out to be incorrect, so we talk about the other changes but mainly about the magnitude of what lies ahead for Wales, starting with this game. Barry remains steadfast in his view that Wales will qualify.

As soon as we're done, I head off to the media room, checking my phone *en route*. Immediately there's a story on the *WalesOnline* Twitter feed that says Ledley's out, hamstring injury. This is a blow if true.

Bill's chasing the confirmed team and when the text drops from the manager, it says same team as Belgium with Davies in defence, King and Edwards in midfield. This means Ledley is out, as well as

Allen. It means Jazz Richards keeps his place at right back and Ben Davies takes on a central defensive role again. It's all about the system, players fitting into positions, rather than changing the formation to fit the players. We've learnt not to question.

There's a bit of time to kill before Chris arrives for our interview. I hang around the away dressing room, chatting with various members of the coaching staff as they go about their work. Chris Senior, the masseur, chats then goes in search of a brush so he can sweep out a big Turkish bath in the dressing room for use in the recovery session after the game. He and the others are going to be hard at it afterwards, trying to get the players in the best shape possible ahead of a long flight back to the UK in the morning. Then Dai the Kitman appears, asking if I've got a plug adapter for a continental plug socket, "It's UK style here" I answer, but apparently the socket for the speakers for the sound system are two pin. He goes off in search of one, then comes back asking if anyone's got a black Sharpie pen. I offer green but apparently it has to be black!

There's no Mark Evans on this trip, he's stayed behind in Cardiff to make sure everything's ready for the arrival of the Israelis on Saturday, a visit that's bringing many extra security complications. Amanda's flying solo for the first time as the Team Administrator, she seems pretty calm and very much under control as the tunnel area starts to get busier ahead of the arrival of the team bus, but she confides in me that she's feeling really nervous about the game.

Sean Connelly, the physio, wanders past, "I've heard you're flapping?", he suggests. "You've been around the game long enough to know we'll be alright" he says reassuringly. It's that contrast again between the clear-thinking professionals and us, the daft fans again.

Then the coach pulls up and I know the interview's imminent. A couple of minutes later, Chris appears. He's in the familiar dark suit. It's the one he's worn for every game in this campaign. He's already revealed that he won't take the jacket off now, like he did in Serbia, because of what happened there. Alex is wearing his lucky socks and it's still in the high 20s so they're both going to get a bit warm for the greater good tonight.

Before the interview, I double-check the team news to make sure I've got it all right. That confirmed, we start. It's the Ledley news first, apparently he pulled up in the last minute of yesterday's training

238

session. I've already heard a suggestion that the grass was quite long on the Cardiff pitch, I hope that wasn't a factor. The fact Joe has barely played a game this season, frozen out at Palace, is probably more significant. The manager reiterates the desire for a strong ref and cautions against expecting an easy evening.

With that job done, I'm clear until kick-off so I go out for a look at the crowds arriving. There are a lot of Welsh fans outside the ground, and more coaches arriving all the time. Back in the compound, Dave's distributing sandwiches and crisps to the crew, this is tonight's meal. With the game kicking off so late, we aren't going to be back at the hotel much before before 1am, the kitchens will surely be shut?

I pick up mine but I don't feel much like eating, as Sean said, I'm flapping! Back to the tunnel area and the players are heading out for their warm-up. I follow and chat with the two injured travellers, Chester and Ledley, as they watch from the away dugout. Joe's obviously gutted, it's been a tough season for him so he must look forward to Wales games even more. James can at least look forward to a potential return on Sunday.

When they head back in, so do I. It's almost time. The UEFA delegate is waiting in the tunnel as the players return, "two minutes to teams out", she shouts. IG and I exchange glances, we both think 'that's a bit ambitious, the players are barely back in the dressing room.' There's no Cypriot version of John Smart, it would appear, no TV floor manager to control things, so the UEFA lady's reliant on the ref and his assistants to persuade the teams out of their lair. Wales are second, well beyond the two minute mark. This game's not kicking-off on time, a big negative in UEFA land. I exchange handshakes with a lot of the staff as we head out, and with James Collins as I pass him at the edge of the dugout *en route* to my position, a box to its left. Because of my proximity to the dugout, I'm not allowed a monitor to follow the game on. UEFA don't want the people in the dugout to be able to see coverage during the game. The theory is that the match officials will come under greater pressure from 'the bench' or the technical area, if people have a sense that a wrong call has been made on a decision. It's pretty arbitrary, though. I've sat just as close to the Wales dugout during other games, and have been allowed a monitor, so I'm guessing it's a decision made by the ref or by a delegate on the day. The upshot is that tonight I have to rely on the commentary and what I see with my eyes, from pitch level, and on the far side from the home and away dugouts.

As ever, the events of the evening begin with the anthems. To my left, the away end belts it out with typical gusto and the players raise their hands above their heads to applaud the fans' efforts. The stadium's about two thirds full, not the sell out some had been suggesting, except behind the goal. I'm still expecting the home fans to create a hostile atmosphere. Jason Demetriou joked about it in his interview, "the nice, friendly atmosphere," he chuckled. I have that first trip still in my mind, and the two defeats I've seen here since. Actually, it's pretty quiet. Still, early indications are that it promises to be every bit as tough as predicted. The first Wales pass across the back hits a divot, and almost doesn't find it's target. Wales have the quality though. Bale goes on a charge, skips past a challenge, plays in Ramsey and he curls a shot in from just outside the box. The net ripples but it's the ball dropping on top, not under. An early goal would settle the nerves, mine at least. Wales are kicking towards that packed away end, and those fans roar them on. Then, another Cyprus lunge on Ramsey. The free kick's in Bale range, down the middle, if a little far out. The Cyprus goalie's not the little feller who played in the game in Cardiff, this one's taller and looks a little like Kermit in a pair of shiny green leggings. As Gareth steps up and strikes the ball, the goalie drops to his knees and the ball hits them before flying away into the path of the oncoming Neil Taylor. I'm half up off the box I'm sitting on in anticipation. To my immediate left, the rest of the coaching staff, are also poised. Time slows as Neil sidefoots the ball. There's precision, but not enough power, and the 'keeper uses those frog legs to good effect again. It should have been a goal, his first for his country.

Cyprus are scrapping for everything but aren't creating anything. It's Wales carry the threat. Bale works another good position on the right, chips into the box where Kanu and Edwards await. Hal moves forward, the ball passes him and onto the head of Dave. He nods it in. Now, I'm up on my feet, so are the others, but something's not quite right. The ref's not pointing back towards the centre circle, hands are going to heads, on the pitch and behind the goal. He's disallowed it! This is where I need the monitor, particularly as the staff alongside me are asking why it was disallowed. "A push, I think" is the best I can offer based on what I've heard in my headphones.

The ref lets us down again, and the absence of the monitor becomes an issue once more, as another ball into the box seems to hit a defender's hand. There's a big shout from the players and the fans, but there's nothing doing from the ref. At times like this, I start to wonder what the extra officials behind the goal actually do. Do they make the call or do they just muddy the waters?

More questions from the seats to my left, "Was it handball?" Commentary suggests it hit a hand, but it's less clear whether it was deliberate. The only certain news I can relay is the score from Belgium, where Bosnia go one up, then the home nation equalise. Anything but a Bosnia win, I guess?

Our game goes on and Cyprus create their first moment of danger from a free kick, a pass to the edge of the box and a shot that flies over. Ashley Williams is marshalling the Welsh defence superbly, he's got makeshift central defenders on either side of him but he's talking constantly, it's a masterclass; particularly as he's up against Mytidis, a big, strong lad who's happy to take part in a physical battle, even if he seems pretty limited. As half-time ticks around, I have a distinct impression this could end up as a draw, meaning a Wales win against Israel on Sunday will still guarantee qualification, if Belgium beat Cyprus here on the same day.

By the time, I've got back to the tunnel, Belgium have gone ahead against Bosnia, if it stays like that, Bosnia can't qualify automatically, and Wales are guaranteed at least a third place finish and a place in the play-offs. It's a start I suppose. As ever, 'don't lose' is the starting premise for any away game. We've got four games to get three points, so there's no huge pressure on for the win.

The second half starts with another flurry of Cypriot activity but, as hard as they work, they just can't make any headway against a rock-solid backline. A shot flying in from outside the area forces Wayne Hennessey, a virtual spectator thus far, to push away for a corner and briefly raises the volume levels from the home support. It's a hot, humid night, I've got beads of sweat on my arm just sitting pitchside, and the energy levels drop off a little. It's pretty quiet around the ground, nothing like the cauldron of hate I'd anticipated. I can hear the players shouting to each other, the instructions from the bench.

Cyprus make changes, the centre-forward's taken off, a decision that seems surprising given his first half performance. It looks good for Wales for sure, Ashley Williams might be able to play that little bit further forward, pushing midfielders in front of him higher up the pitch as well. The game's in something of a lull, but that's fine by me, I'd settle for the draw now.

Except, as the clock ticks down, there are one or two signs that the home team's tiring, passes go badly astray, they don't push men forward as quickly when they're in possession and the back four's content to sit pretty much on the edge of the area.

This is the impressive bit. As I get a sense of a change, so do the Welsh players. With 15 minutes to go and the game under control, they begin to turn the screw. The away fans respond and lift their voices again, it's a stirring sensation. The phrase that comes to my mind straight away is 'rope-a-dope', Ali's description of the tactics for his famous world title fight win against George Foreman. Wales haven't ever been on the ropes, but they've let Cyprus come at them, taken their best shots and now that they're all punched out, Wales go on the attack.

Suddenly, there are crosses coming in again. From one of them, Ramsey arrives late in the box and jabs a shot goalwards, the 'keeper flings himself to his right to push it away. The ball's still with Wales as Cyprus make a hash of clearing it. From where I sit, at the far end of the pitch, I only see the ball sailing into the penalty area and Gareth Bale rising majestically, back slightly arched, smashing the ball with his head; a knockout blow! It flies into the top corner, and now we're all up and shouting. To my right, the entire bench has spilled onto the pitch and Bale has charged into their midst, one big, seething mass of joy. To my left, all around me, similar scenes. Fitness coaches, psychologists, soft tissue specialists, players, fans, kitmen, all leaping up and down, punching the air, hugging each other. The Twitter kids have a simple, snappy phrase for it, #scenes.

Talking of hashtags, in the commentary coming through my headphones, Bill uses the phrase, Together Stronger. Never has a marketing slogan seemed so successful. It doesn't jar with the image of what people are seeing, it fits. As things calm down a little, it's my time to try and shine, and the short journey back to the tunnel begins. There have been high fives and handshakes all evening, now James

Collins offers his hand as I pass him, then Sean, the physio, catches my eye and sees my broad grin, "Told you, didn't I?" he smiles. I nod in acknowledgement of his wisdom.

I arrive at the tunnel feeling emboldened, nothing's going to stop us now. Cyprus are out on their feet, aren't they? Well, maybe not. As I arrive at the interview position and glance at the monitor I see Ashley heading the ball down into the ground. It hits the legs of a Cypriot attacker and loops towards goal with Wayne Hennessey no more than a spectator. The other spectators behind the goal watch open mouthed as it drops a yard wide of the far post. I'd have taken a draw at the start of the night, but an equaliser now would feel like a defeat. Out of nowhere, Wales are having to do more defending in their box in the last couple of minutes than they've had to do all night. As I'm trying to concentrate on events on the monitor, the UEFA delegate's pestering me for names for her list of interview requests. It's Bale and Williams at full-time, then Ramsey, then Ben Davies so I can offer something to S4C as well, then Osian Roberts, another interview that'll be done in Welsh. This causes a real problem. Osh isn't named on the official team sheet, so she has nothing to refer to and she doesn't seem to have encountered an 'Osian' before. In the end she hands me the pen and clipboard and I write his name in the relevant box. This is all somewhat distracting as I try and see what's happening on the pitch, but I guess we're all meant to be the model of calm professionalism down here, seconds from the end of a vital Euro qualifier that could take your team to within one win of a first tournament for 57 years. Calmness personified.

Even as I hand the clipboard back, Wayne catches a ball into the box and as he does so, the ref raises the whistle to his lips. The tall 'keeper can celebrate his 50th cap with yet another clean sheet, his fifth in seven games. Wales can celebrate another amazing away win. I restrict myself to another yelp of relief and pleasure and a double fist punch. It's not been pretty, and often in the balance, but brilliant in its execution nevertheless. For the fans who've made their way over in such great numbers it's the cue to start a party that will carry on long into tomorrow morning. It's 11.30pm after all. The players dance around in front of them, then make their weary way back towards the dressing room.

Ashley appears first, bare-chested apart from the shirt he's swapped slung over his shoulder, Gareth nips off to get a new top. As we get ready to start, a Cypriot TV guy tells Ashley he has to wear a shirt. I've not heard this one before, Ash often appears bare pelt straight after a game. The Cypriot guy's insistent so there's a comedy moment as the barrel-chested Wales captain attempts to pull a shirt, made for a much smaller torso, down over his head and shoulders. Not only that, but, as he remarks, he's now got someone else's sweaty shirt on. The shirt's inside out as well, but I suspect he'll have to be cut free from it later so I've got to plough on.

Both lads offer another bravura performance in playing things down. They've found a thousand different ways to say 'we take it one game at a time' and seem determined not to feed the hype machine, but both accept they'd like to get qualification nailed on Sunday – sooner rather than later.

There's no MOTM bottle tonight, that's for home games only. But for me it was Ashley, no question. It was a brilliant header though!

After they depart, there's a wait for someone else. I've got a message from Jim telling me to get as much as I want, as there's a lot of time to fill post-match, but there's no sign of anyone emerging from the dressing room. For the first time in the campaign, the usual queue hasn't formed. I know people will be getting agitated back at base, studio guests can only 'fill' for so long, we need more. I can't get anywhere near the away dressing room, it's down a long corridor and I'm plugged into an audio box. It's a few minutes before I see IG emerge with a purposeful stride with Chris Coleman behind him.

Chris looks almost as shattered as the players. I think he had this one down as a potential banana skin, hence his agitation last night. I mention that the commentary described him as having a 'smile as wide as the River Taff' when the goal went in, It was a lovely line and as I say it, we see the smile again. He bemoans the state of the pitch, the heat and the decisions that didn't go Wales way, but doesn't have to linger on any of them. He accepts the performance wasn't great, but the application of the players was once again spot on. He knows what Sunday could bring but expresses a note of caution. It's been a tiring trip, and Israel will be another hard game.

After that, we wait. For ages. Nobody else comes out. I'm now getting increasingly agitated messages in my ear from Sarah, who's in touch with Jim. They need someone, anyone, quick! Messages are fed to the dressing room. Ben and Aaron are in the shower so that'll be a while. Jazz Richards appears, he'll do! I shout down the corridor to him, "Come on Jazz, we need you". I've never interviewed him before and he seems reluctant, "I don't usually do TV", he says, as he walks. I can't take no for answer this time though, "Come on, just two questions", I plead. "Just two, you sure?" I nod to confirm, even as I'm manoeuvring him into position. And he's good. He sticks to the party line but speaks really well. I ask three questions. He doesn't walk away, and at the end of the interview I express my gratitude. Another on the list of good talkers in this eloquent group.

I think we're almost off air now, which takes some of the pressure away but Ben Davies appears swiftly after Jazz and I do need him, in English and Welsh. He knows the score after our earlier conversation. I've been thinking of my questions whilst everything else has been going on around me, but I have to concentrate hard before I start the bit for S4C. I want it to be right, I want it to be good. I owe it to my mum, my nain and taid and all the people who taught me Welsh at school. It's actually a great honour to have this opportunity. I don't want to blow it.

I keep it simple, so does Ben, we get through it okay. Once again, I have great cause to be grateful. He could have made a monkey out of me, thrown something back at me in Welsh, he didn't, top lad.

One down, one to go. Osian appears. This is the guy who runs the coach education system that I help out with, and now I'm interviewing him, in Welsh. It's a bit bizarre but he's a confident broadcaster; Welsh speakers tend to get plenty of opportunity to practise as their services are much in demand in the Welsh media. Again, I play a straight bat, but I cut loose a little at the end, "Ac, rŵan, Osian, ar Ddydd Sul, y siawns i wneud hanes?", which I hope translates as "Now, on Sunday, the chance to make history?" Osh is great, answers at some length, and we're done. "You didn't understand any of what I was saying did you?", he laughs. He's got a point!

Only one more to go, but I'm on a roll now. Aaron is the final interviewee on the list and I've set myself one more challenge. Aaron can speak Welsh but he prefers to do his interviews in English. I just wonder whether I can coax an answer out of him. If I do, I'll be given the freedom of S4C.

It would be wrong to ambush him, so I ask him if he's up for it before we start. He put out a Tweet in Welsh recently which provoked a mixed response from his many followers, but earned him praise from the Welsh-speaking community in particular.

My own status as Welsh language hero is denied as Aaron says he only wants to do it in English. Ah well, I tried.

And that's it. Game over. Job done. It's way past midnight now, and still really hot. I retreat to the TV compound, where the guys are already well into the process of packing everything up. Dave Weinstein's procured a pile of light blue baseball caps that were distributed to all the home fans by the Cyprus FA, a nice souvenir of the trip. Then, we jump aboard the minibus and head back to base.

The hotel lobby's pretty busy, the Cardiff group are back already and preparing for a walk out to a bar called Reckless in the Old Town, I'm invited along, which is good of them, but I've got my own crew outside around a table, with a round of drinks on their way so I go and join them for a quick debrief. I'm pretty tired, I'm sure everyone is, but it'll be nice to sit back and reflect on another top trip. As the minutes pass, members of the group drift away to their beds and the lights go off in the lobby. That leaves me and Bill in the darkness, sipping the last two bottles of beer we've managed to beg from the night porter, who's keen to sit with us and reminisce about about his beloved Fulham, the team he followed when he lived in London.

He's got a better memory of football than he has of sandwiches. He had us all in stitches as he tried to take an order of four ham and two chicken, but kept getting it wrong. "Right, so you want four ham and two cheese and tomato?" Laughter. "Okay, got it. Three ham and three chicken, right?" On and on it went, like a bizarre but hilarious dream!

It's 3.30am and I also head back to my room for a few quiet moments on the balcony, enjoying the warm night air. Reflections? Well, three hours ago, at 00.33, Bill took a screenshot of his phone, showing the exact time and date. He did that to mark the moment when, for the very first time, he heard me say that I thought Wales would qualify.

Friday 4th September

Five and a bit hours later, I'm awake again. A very important task must be performed before I can go down for breakfast, I need to sing

Happy Birthday to Megan! Technology will be enlisted to achieve this to maximum effect. I use my iPad to make a FaceTime call to Rachel. Millie answers, then Megan appears and I launch into my rendition. Then, I want to see Megan open her presents, starting with the watch I ordered from this very hotel room only two days ago. Being able to see everybody and everything's just brilliant, and makes me a feel a little bit better about being away.

Once we've said our goodbyes, I go down for breakfast where the rest of the gang are gathered. We're checking out at 11.30, Barry's making his own way with a flight much later on at 9.30 tonight. The FAW party have left already, but I figure they'll still be on the ground so I send IG a couple of requests looking ahead to the next game. There's been a suggestion we might get an interview with Gareth Bale ahead of the key fixture, which has now arrived, so I make the request. Jim has also asked if I can get players to say 'Together Stronger' into the camera for an opening sequence featuring the FAW's marketing phrase.

The Bale request gets a fairly swift knockback, Chris wants to keep everything to the normal, standard, routine, so only the captain and manager are available tomorrow. Then we get a no to the second request as well, apparently for the same reason. So, it'll be Ashley in the hotseat for the interview for the live show again. I hope, at least, to get him and Chris to use the Together Stronger phrase.

We say goodbye to Barry and get going on time, a good job as it turns out. The flight's full, in fact they've oversold. We're offered £400 to stay behind and get the next one. It's tempting, but we resist. Latecomers may find their seats already taken.

Now, there's a first to report. We finally gain access to a business lounge, thanks to a couple of frequent flyer cards and something called the Air Angels app.

Once inside, we descend on yet another buffet. I emerge onto the outdoor terrace with a plate full, "Why have you got yoghurt on your bread?", Alex asks incredulously. "It's not yoghurt", I answer somewhat sniffily, "We're near Greece. It's taramasalata." Then I take a bite. He's right, it's yoghurt, fruits of the forest I think. 'Team Sky' collapse in laughter again.

I sleep a lot of the way home. Back at Heathrow, Bill and I pile into Alex's car and we set off for Cardiff. *En route*, I take a call from

Barry, he has that exasperated note in his voice again. Sure enough, his halting message carries another tale of travel woe. 'Flight delayed up to 21 hours...need the emergency number for Sky travel...got to get back for work tomorrow'. I find the number he needs and text it over. We stay in contact as escape routes are closed off. His flight's completely full, but so are all the others back to the UK, probably because a lot of Wales fans are heading home. When we arrive at our hotel in Cardiff, Barry's still on the ground in Cyprus. I vow to buy him a St Christopher medallion ahead of next month's trip to Bosnia.

At the hotel – not the Radisson, which is fully booked due to the rugby in town tomorrow – I make contact with Megan again. She's had a great day, out pony trekking and now a sleepover with pals. I'm planning an early night, so we have a quick drink in the bar and then call it a day, a very long day. My last act is to watch the highlights of the game on SkyGo, the first time I've seen any of the coverage of the match. The disallowed goal should have stood, and Wales should have had a penalty for handball, better late than never I guess?

8

"We've waited 57 years, a few more weeks won't hurt us"
Wales v Israel

'Simon Church my Lord, Simon Church'

Saturday 5th September

There's a little envelope and a gift in my bag when I get round to unpacking, placed there by my wife prior to departure. These are to mark our anniversary, and I sit and open both as I enjoy my first cup of tea of the day. I have left a card for her as well, so no danger of an angry phone call sometime mid-morning. To back it up, I send a text message as well, all bases covered. Our interviews have been put back an hour to 11.30, so breakfast is leisurely and fairly late. Then we take two cars over to the Cardiff City Stadium. As we leave, the city centre streets are already busy with the rugby international this afternoon. They're expecting a gate of around 50,000 for the final warm-up fixture before the forthcoming World Cup.

It's the usual routine on arrival, the away dressing room's been allocated for our purposes. Bill's come along to hear what's said and to watch the training session afterwards, so we have an extra pair of hands to help us carry everything in. Alex is almost ready when Chris arrives, a little earlier than the scheduled time. As Alex tweaks stuff, I chat. He seems in a good mood so I regale him with the latest tale of Barry's travel troubles. I'd got a text from him at 3am saying he was hoping to take off soon and that he'd be going straight to work from the airport; under-12 trials this morning you see?

Our job done, Alex goes off to film training while I sort out sending the material back to HQ. There's no interview needed from Israel this time and there'll be a shorter build-up to coverage, but I'll come back later with Bill to watch the media conference and training, just in case anything of interest happens.

In-between, I do as I did pre-Belgium and go to the barber's for a haircut. The city centre's thronged with people now as kick-off in the rugby gets closer. It's a very different crowd from the football. Lots of families for one, lots of groups of females for two, rugby matches in Cardiff are a big draw in the midst of a hen party excursion. Much of the merchandise on offer on the streets is directed at this market, big daffodil hats, sparkly cowboy hats with a Welsh dragon on, that sort of thing. There'll be an awful lot of drinking, a bit of singing but will anyone will be too bothered if Wales win, lose or draw? I'll be honest, having grown up in north Wales, I don't really get the rugby thing. We played it once at school. Somebody grabbed my shorts as I was running with the ball. I kept going and stopped only when my shorts were round my knees. That was the end of my rugby career.

Hair now short, Bill offers to drive us both back to the CCS, not such an easy task with roads closed now that the rugby is underway. I know a long cut, and we get there with time to spare before the Israelis' arrival. We sit through a fairly dull media conference in which Tal Ben Haim makes it clear they haven't come here as guests at a party, then wander down the tunnel to watch them train. Up in the stand, two armed police officers are keeping an eye on proceedings. Security's been ramped because it's Israel.

When we leave the stadium, after our permitted 15 minutes, the car park is full of police vans. The security operation around this fixture is much more obvious than it was in Israel. It probably doesn't help that there's a pro-Palestinian protest planned for tomorrow. The FAW are also worried about pitch invasions. If political protestors or Wales fans come on to celebrate there could be a UEFA punishment to follow, potentially even a points deduction, especially as Wales have already been punished for what happened in Andorra last year. The

FAW will have twice as many stewards on duty than usual. It would be so utterly 'Wales' to qualify, then have a load of points deducted for the celebrations that followed!

We take the long route back, as members of the Sky crew have already been caught in horrendous hold-ups trying to make the two mile journey to the hotel. My local knowledge ensures a trouble-free drive back.

Things haven't gone quite so smoothly for the rugby team, two key players, Webb and Halfpenny have both suffered serious injuries and look like missing the World Cup. In the case of the latter at least, that's the equivalent of Gareth Bale getting injured just before Euro 2016. If we get there, of course.

Tea is taken at the hotel, watching Spain v Slovakia, no big night out. Cardiff tends to get pretty messy post-rugby and besides, it's my football Christmas Eve and tomorrow I'm hoping Santa's going to be bringing a gift I've wanted all my life.

Sunday 6th September

MD8, or DWD1, which stands for Date With Destiny 1. I've slept surprisingly well, considering. I've been here before, of course. Wales needing a win to qualify. For that reason, I'm determined to try and stay calm. That said, never mind butterflies, I feel like I've got an Atlas moth fluttering around inside me.

I cast my eyes over the morning paper as I take breakfast. Front and back, it reflects the contrasting emotions for followers of the two national sports. The rugby writers are reeling from the catastrophic 'warm-up' game, the football writers are looking forward to an almighty celebration. There's often a rivalry between the two sports in this part of Wales. Everyone's chasing the young talent, Bale was a good rugby player as well, and the battle for hearts and minds, for commercial deals and for spectators could hinge on the events of the next few hours, certainly the next four weeks. If the football team qualify and the rugby team have a bad World Cup, the round ball's in the ascendancy again after many years in the shadows.

I chat with Bill and Sarah. Both are keen to get a real sense of what lies ahead, it's important that they know the narrative so their coverage can best reflect that. Bill asks me if I think it would be right to mention Gary Speed's name, if things go the right way. I reassure him that would definitely be alright – in fact I've already been weighing up whether I should ask the manager and players to talk about Gary's influence on their success. Sarah says she expects to see me running onto the pitch to celebrate with everyone else at the final whistle. She's joking but it shows she gets it. She's a mad football fan herself, so understands how much this means to the supporters, including me. She speculates how emotional I might get. I must confess this is a concern, there's a job to be done after all. Me blubbing isn't going to make for a good post-match interview with the manager.

Cardiff's going to be a lively city today. There's already a lot of activity on the streets, as it's the 10k this morning. Bill and I tried to get ourselves a late sign up once we realised it coincided with our visit, but it's a no go from the organisers. I have to do my pre-match run still and the route of the 10k, around Bute Park and Sofia Gardens, is largely the one I tend to follow. I head out anyway, I could probably just join in, who'd notice that I had no number? Instead, I manage to go anti-clockwise whilst the masses are going clockwise, it works, although I end up doing the last few hundred metres right down the High Street, dodging between the shoppers. I pass the Owain Glyndŵr pub on my way. It's a place with a special resonance in this story. In 1993, I was standing on a table in there, singing *'We're on the march with Terry's Army and we're going to the USA'*, before the game against Romania. The mood was incredibly positive, we just 'knew' that we were going to do it, the whole pub was up and singing. Then Bodin's penalty hit the bar and things have never been the same since. I changed. In Barry's weekly newspaper column this week, he's described me as 'The Most Pessimistic of Pessimists', before claiming that, after Cyprus, even I was now prepared to admit Wales would qualify. Sounds like silly talk to me, I must have had a Keo or two that night.

I shower and change, then nip out again – this time to buy my wife an anniversary gift and to get a few little things for the girls. I also acquire a rather cool free-standing speaker. Back in my room, I plug my phone into it and start pumping out Super Furry Animals tunes whilst I begin to get ready. I have brought the same suit I wore for the Belgium game, with a Euro 2016 badge attached to the lapel. The tie's different though, the one I wore in Brussels has acquired a prominent stain , something I only noticed as I packed. This is a concern.

Alex is waiting for me in the car at 1pm. Bill's made his own way as he's heading straight off afterwards. He's had to wrestle with that one a bit, desperate to be around town if Wales qualify, but also mindful of the fact that tomorrow is his son's first day at 'big school'. Happily, family beats football. I missed both my children's first days at primary and secondary school because of internationals; not good.

I check Alex's feet as I enter the car. The red and grey stripy socks are on. We can proceed. At the stadium, there's much more activity than usual, even though it's nearly four hours before kick-off. We enter the car park behind a minibus from north Wales, the train operator having failed to provide any way to get supporters from north to south and back again in a day, despite the fact that the game starts at 5pm. The transport infrastructure of this country is a real joke. Israel fans can get to and from London by train, but Wales fans can't get to and from the north, hence the fleets of coaches beginning to arrive. Those who can't get here will be watching on TVs in towns and villages, north, south, east and west. I'd bet loads more people are watching across the UK as well, to see what all the fuss is about perhaps, but also to see if this story's finally going to have a happy ending.

There's a real buzz about the OB compound and on the catering bus as well. Everyone knows they could be involved in something pretty special. Neil the Rigger, the most Mancunian Manc I've ever met, a massive City fan, wishes me all the best. One of the great strengths of the way Sky have covered the game is that everyone's a fan. Whatever the perceptions of Sky's influence on the game in general, the actual coverage has always been fantastic and that's because the people responsible love it and get it.

I see Laurence on the bus, the guy who came over for that first 'green screen' shoot way back. He's been putting together a piece to follow the game if Wales win and've been discussing suitable music in the days since Cyprus. He's gone with Men Of Harlech this time but he's keen on my suggestion, a song by Mike Peters that has the chorus, 'And it just don't get any better than this'. Mike's from Rhyl, a big football fan, he'd be chuffed to hear his song in this context. Next time, maybe?

I sit down with Simon, the presenter, and Duncan, the studio director, they are both keen to ascertain my emotional state, knowing that I've got quite a bit invested in this 'project'. I try to explain that I'm very nervous but it's difficult when every neutral will look at the group and say that Wales are certain to qualify. It's utterly illogical to be nervous, there are three games to go but there's a whole generation or more of Welsh football fans who've become hardwired for failure, often at the final hurdle. I predict a river of middle-aged tears if Wales actually, finally, manage to do it and win today.

Of course, there has to be consideration of the chance that Wales might not win today. I've already put some contingency plans in front of the FAW in the event of a draw. If that happens, Cyprus v Belgium becomes crucial and we're showing that game straight after this one. I've struck a deal. We'll have a satellite truck parked outside the team hotel and a reporter and cameraman on standby, but we won't film anything unless a mini-miracle happens and Belgium fail to win. If Wales do win, we'll be there anyway, for the celebrations. I've already been asked to stay on in Cardiff tonight by Sports News in case it's a big story in the morning. I've agreed but with the provision that I intend to party with the best of them if it comes to pass; they're happy to take the gamble! On the QT, I know a party is planned and the FAW have provisionally scheduled media access tomorrow, if... .

Jim's on the bus, and we talk through the Coleman pre-match interview. Then, we discuss what might happen at full-time. If Wales win, there'll be a 'super-flash' interview with someone on the pitch, but UEFA rules say we're only allowed one and it can only last a minute. That seems hugely restrictive for these potential circumstances, especially as the players are likely to stay out on the pitch for ages. There's much about the hands-on UEFA involvement that's been of benefit, but these directives aren't amongst them.

Barry and I have our first job to do after we've had lunch. He and I will be doing our usual bit for Sky Sports News. He's bounced back from the horror trip home from Cyprus and is on good form. He'd love to be staying over tonight as well, but he's got year five Physics first thing in the morning.

In the tunnel area, Smartie's already taking control. Lydia, the UEFA delegate's on duty for this one again as well, and she's got another UEFA blazer watching over her. Whether it's his presence or not, I don't know, but there are changes to the way we're allowed to work. We aren't going to be allowed to walk in front of the Welsh dugout as we usually do when it's time for post-match interviews in the tunnel. Instead, it's a long hike around the stadium involving a door which has to be opened for us from the other side. It's going to take minutes to make a journey that usually takes a few seconds. This seems very silly.

Almost immediately after the two pieces with Barry, including an extra one for Sky News, I'm on standby for the arrival of the team bus and my interview with the manager. As we wait, various members of the coaching staff come over for a chat. They're every bit as keyed up as I am, not as nervous perhaps, but anxious to see the job, their job, done. There's a lot of English guys on the backroom staff, and one Irishman, but nobody could suggest it doesn't mean as much to them as it does to me. Steve Williams makes an appearance as well. He's not on liaison duties anymore, he's trained up a new guy. Steve's now the treasurer of the FAW, a fantastic achievement, as a 'Caws Mawr'(Big Cheese), he's not able to fulfil the old duties. This is good for him, but won't help my badge collection.

Then the coach arrives and the expectation levels move up a notch. The players walk through the tunnel first, a couple of minutes later Chris appears. I've heard a suggestion that it's the same starting XI as Cyprus, which he confirms before we start. My final question is "what's the message?" He asks the fans for backing and patience, and the players for focus and another massive effort.

There are three games to go. One win will do and Andorra provide the opposition in the final game, so we could all wait for that. But it feels like Wales have to do it today, that anything else will feel like failure, even though it isn't. For those who've been involved throughout the campaign, there's another desire to see it done. Every game's brought pressure. The more the campaign's gone on, and the more the interest has grown, so the more the pressure has increased. I was talking to Amanda about this in Cyprus. Normally, by this stage, we're talking about building for the next campaign and everyone bar the diehards has pretty much lost interest. For the first time in a long time, everyone's still got to be at the top of their game, on and off the pitch, eight games into a qualification tournament. The players have managed it well, and everyone else has to match their level of application.

Those players start assembling in the tunnel as kick-off approaches. Israel line-up closer to me. Not a big side, physically, and they're missing some key players including their leading scorer. It's difficult not to hope this might prove helpful.

John Smart makes sure everyone's where they should be, when they should be and they walk up the tunnel on time, emerging to a huge roar. I take a second to look around and soak it in before I turn left and head for my usual seat. I shake Osian's hand. James Collins looks unusually tense. He's normally the most laid back of players, it's getting to everyone! The Israeli anthem has nothing like the same impact without the ageing rocker singing it and 'Hen Wlad Fy Nhadau' blasts out from over 30,000 voices. Tears? Yeah, of course.

And then, we're off. I settle into position, Andy alongside me as ever, not expecting much by the way of conversation. Today, for the first time, the result is significant, not quite 'make or break', but certainly 'make', as in 'make me ecstatically happy'.

The opening signs are good. Israel are clearly set up to defend, barely playing a striker. Wales race into the space in front of them. It looks like the manager's sent them out to get the goal as soon as possible. A minute in and Ramsey connects sweetly with a volley that's swerving towards goal before a defender gets his body in the way. From the corner, he gets another strike on target. This is good. Israel are rattled, as in Haifa,and start giving the ball away. They already look a poor team. Jazz Richards wrestles the ball off a defender on the right touchline. He gives it to Kanu, whose great pass sends Andy King clear, but the drilled shot lacks power and the 'keeper saves. The ball loops up towards the head of Ramsey, the goal gaping, but he can't direct it down and it sails over the bar. At this moment, it feels like a matter of time. One goal, get the one goal. Israel will collapse. Instead, Israel survive the onslaught and already I'm wondering whether that long, hot night in Cyprus might have an effect. The visitors gradually play themselves back into the game. They don't create anything resembling a chance, but they do start to get a bit more possession. The stadium clock is now counting down as if minutes were seconds. How does that happen?

Noise levels drop a little as Wales struggle to break down this rugged rearguard, marshalled well by Tal Ben Haim. A point would suit Israel in their quest for what will most likely be a third place finish.

The whistle blows all too quickly, and we're heading back down the tunnel. In one sense, I'm calm. I can't see Israel scoring against our own brick wall and I think a penalty or a set piece might win this for Wales. We're 45 minutes closer to a conclusion that will bring its own relief.

The moment arrives right at the start of the second half. A foul conceded on the edge of the area, a push on Kanu only inches away from being inside. As Gareth Bale prepares himself, it feels like a penalty anyway. It's in the middle, in the D. He scored from further out in Haifa, and in Andorra. It'll go to the 'keeper's left, I'm guessing low and hard, it's so close to goal. The stadium's at fever pitch as he steps up and strikes. He's fooled me, it goes up and over the left side of the wall, it dips, but not enough and it lands on top of the net. There's almost an air of disbelief in the stadium. How did Gareth not score that? It's about this time I begin to seriously consider the prospect of a draw, and the need to keep an eye on the Cyprus game later. The seconds fly by. Israel have changed their formation and their line-up, but that doesn't make them any more of an attacking threat. Williams is again outstanding in the heart of the home defence. Taylor and Richards are pushed up high, but they're not seeing much of the ball. Ramsey and Bale start dropping deeper to collect possession, but we need them higher up, where they're a threat. Still, chances are created. Another corner drops perfectly on the head of Andy King, who directs the ball goalwards from a few yards out, but the 'keeper's quick to react and leaps to his left to make a catch.

Then a deep cross from the left. Kanu chases a defender as the ball sails towards the goalline, the defender has his arm stretched out and as the ball passes him, there's a roar of 'Handball!' from players and fans, Kanu in particular. He was closest to it, his reaction suggests he's certain. Once more, there's a massive question mark over the usefulness of the officials behind the goal. The replays show the ball brushed off the arm, but they give nothing.

Because of the long route back to the interview position, I have to get up out of my seat with ten minutes left of the 90. This is awful, anything could happen whilst I'm walking round the concourse back to the tunnel. Indeed, I'm level with an Israel player as he crosses and a diving header is tipped over the bar by Wayne, just about the only save he's had to make all game.

Andy's with me, we disappear out of sight of the pitch and head for a door that needs opening by a steward from the other side. But there's no one there. Andy alerts the gallery to let them know we're stuck. We can see members of the coaching staff moving around inside, but they don't know we're waiting to get let back in. The game goes on in our absence but then I hear a huge roar and the commentary in my earpiece tells me a Bale shot has been saved. Let me in!

Eventually, our doorman appears to grant us entry to a position about ten seconds walk away from where we were sitting. I consult with Jim about the location for the interviews. As it stands, a draw means we're staying in the tunnel. Mark's there, a reassuring sight, pacing up and down furiously. The monitor that UEFA had demanded were switched off before the game and during half-time, is now switched back on so I can see what's happening. The request for interviews is submitted; Bale and Williams. Then the manager. Andy King and Aaron Ramsey. Just as I'm telling Lydia, there's a huge roar and I can see people at the end of the tunnel leaping about. I race out to join them, arms stretched wide, but even as I arrive in the sunlight, I hear the word 'offside' in my earpiece. Now, hands are clamped on heads. As I spin round, a steward hands me the mobile phone that flew out of my pocket as I sprinted passed him. I get back to the monitor in time to see a replay. Simon Church nodded it in, about two yards offside.

With that I hear the collective sigh that greets the final whistle. Then there's applause and the players stay out a little while to acknowledge the gesture. Israel have done to us what we did to Belgium, dig in and claim a precious point.

I actually feel better now than I have done all day, more upbeat. The maths are even more favourable now. One more point will do it, from either of the two games. As the players start to pass me, I make sure I give them a clap, a little 'well done'. They look so disappointed, none more than Ashley Williams. He appears at the interview point looking really upset, so much so that I feel compelled to try and gee him up, "Come on Ash, it's fine. Another point, another clean sheet.. it's alright". He raises a weak smile. We're waiting for Gareth until we're told he doesn't want to do it, so we crack on with the captain. His frustration's obvious but he does a good job of masking it and talking positively. He takes the MOTM bottle and heads off to what will be, I suspect, a quiet dressing room.

The players are out swiftly for their media duties today, in fact Tal Ben Haim's brought out as soon as we've finished with Ashley. I think it's worthwhile getting his perspective. I point out that he said before the game that he didn't want to be present at Wales' party and the gameplan ensured that was the case. He acknowledges their pleasure at the point but describes Wales as a very good team that he'll be glad to see qualify. Andy King appears next, still in his kit. He knows he could have won it, twice, and he's big enough to acknowledge that. It would actually have been great if someone like Andy could have been the hero today. Whatever might be said, this is not a one-man band.

Aaron follows straight on after Andy. He probably hasn't had his best game in the red shirt but he's still more upbeat than the other two lads. In a sense, there's not an awful lot to say. They couldn't have tried any harder today, on another day they'd have got the goal that would have won the game. Aaron's right when he says four points from the last two games would have looked a decent return in advance.

Chris Coleman's our last interviewee. Before we start the chat, he's keen to clarify the significance of tonight's Cyprus v Belgium game. I tell him it's only significant if Belgium don't win. He doesn't seem entirely convinced and, to be fair, it took me, Bill and various others at Sky most of yesterday afternoon to sort it all out. In the interview, he makes it clear he expects things to be delayed until next month, "We've waited 57 years, if we have to wait a few more weeks, so be it." He does, however, express the hope that maybe Cyprus can 'do Wales a favour'.

After the interview, Mark Evans comes over for a quick word. They've had their number crunchers looking at it, and we're right. A draw will do. I confirm with Mark that we'll be on standby to visit the hotel. He says that's fine but the manager won't be there, he's going home, as are a few of the big hitters. Gareth's probably got his private jet idling on the tarmac at Cardiff Airport.

Alex is idling in the car outside the stadium, he's all packed up and ready to go. I've formulated a plan. We go back to our hotel and keep

259

an eye on the Cyprus game. If things are going well, we'll head down to the team hotel later. The Sports News reporter's heading there now, but it's probably not worth him hanging around. The fact that I know the players, particularly the less well-known ones, means I should be there. I pop into the OB truck to let Jim know what's happening. He's staying on site to produce the next game, and then the highlights of all the qualifiers that will follow. It's a long haul for him and the studio team, Simon Thomas, Dean Saunders and Mark Bowen. If, by some minor miracle, Wales qualify tonight, we might be able to get material to Jim that he can use whilst his show's still on air.

It takes us about ten minutes to drive back to the hotel. I've been busy sending emails to everyone to make sure they know the plan, and I've told the reporter and his cameraman they can go home. Alex and I will be around if required. I'm pretty hungry by now, so I suggest we adjourn to Alex's room, order something to eat and watch the match on his TV. By the time we get up to the room, there's 15 minutes on the clock and it's still 0-0. Oh God, here we go again, remember the phrase 'It's the hope that kills you'?

By now, others seem to be switching on to the fact that the longer the game remains goalless, the closer Wales edge to France. Twitter starts to quiver with it. I'm guessing that a lot of Wales fans who were expecting a quiet pint rather than a party are beginning to get revved up again. Half-time arrives and it's still 0-0. Not only that, but Belgium are playing really badly.

I set a new deadline for our departure. If it's still 0-0 by the hour mark, we're off to the St. David's. It's a ten minute drive max. The room service arrives at 55 minutes so we wolf down the sandwiches, then, with the game still at 0-0, it's 'go time'! As we're getting into the car, I get a message from Jim suggesting we scramble, so we're a few steps ahead. Alex has rigged his phone up so I can watch the game on SkyGo *en route*. If Belgium score, we can pretty much turn right around and finish for the night. The only team that looks like scoring, though, is Cyprus, they are the better team. We reach the hotel on 70 minutes, still 0-0. We rush into reception where we run straight into James Chester. "Hi mate, you watching this?!", I jabber excitedly. We both stand and look at the frozen image on Alex's phone for a few seconds before he points out that the rest of the lads are watching in the team room, just to the left of reception. We push through the doors and find a large group watching, all eyes fixed on the TV. Actually, there's most of the starting XI here. IG's in the far corner, looking nervous. We've now entered the inner sanctum, the lads are standing around, some of them cradling a pint. I make a beeline for IG, "Don't worry, we won't shoot anything unless it stays like this." He says ok, but goes off to give the manager a call anyway. He comes back and says Chris doesn't want us to film any players with a drink in their hands. "IG, if Cyprus hang on, it'll be history we'll be filming here, we can't not film it", I point out. Even as we're talking, Alex is getting the camera ready. There's 10 minutes to go now. Hal's sitting on a sofa right in front of the screen. he calls me over, "So, if it's draw, we qualify?"

It's like they're still seeking the final clarification. The excitement levels are rising palpably. There are nervous shouts when Belgium get a free kick just outside the box, Neil Taylor shouts at the 'keeper, "Save it with your knees again!" He doesn't, this time he punches it away and as he does so there's a big cheer in the room. IG goes off again to make another call. There are just five minutes left now, my phone rings and it's Jim, it's hard to hear him amidst the shouting but we start to discuss what we're going to do on the final whistle, I'm thinking he might want to get a player out to the satellite truck to talk about it? Then Belgium score, Hazard, and the balloon's burst. I swear, and the room goes quiet.

Cyprus won't equalise, they haven't got the energy left, nor the attacking potency. Taken to the brink for the second time in a day seems a little cruel. I suddenly feel drained, and just want to get out.

IG reappears, phone in hand, Chris says it's alright to film the players now. No need.

Our evening ends quietly, with a pint in The Crockerton, one of our old haunts. We look ahead, Bosnia in a month's time. One point there and the job's done. As the highlights of Wales v Israel come up on the big screen, we both agree, we've had enough for one day, and it's time to go to bed.

9

"The best defeat of my career"
Bosnia v Wales

'Bryn Law Bryn Law, what's the score?
Bryn Law, what's the score?'

Monday 5th October

Here we go again! All the preparation, all the packing, then big hugs and kisses for my wife and daughters, a pat for the dog and I head off on the highway to..? Well, Cardiff, obviously, but, symbolically, where am I bound? It should be the state of ecstasy, shouldn't it? The facts are these, one more point from the last two games guarantees qualification and the second of those games is at home against Andorra.

This tiny Catalan principality are currently 205th out of 208 FIFA countries, Wales are now at an all-time high of 8th. Andorra have never won or drawn an away qualifier. Did I mention, Wales only need a point? Add to that an almost full-strength Wales squad with Bale fit again after an injury scare, and Bosnia look like being without Džeko and Bešić: the outlook could hardly seem brighter. So, why the hell do I still feel so ruddy nervous!?

Somehow, despite all that, despite the fact that the bookies will give you 10,000/1 odds on Wales not qualifying, despite the fact that someone clever, and bored, has calculated that there's a 0.2%

262

likelihood of Wales not qualifying, there remains a doubt. And whilst there's a doubt, we will worry. In any other country, parties would have been planned, national holidays scheduled, bunting put up. Not in Wales. Indeed, as I drive into Cardiff the only visual manifestations of momentous sporting moments to come are concerned with the Rugby World Cup. Wales have just beaten England in that tournament and, like the round ball team, are now ranked higher than their neighbours. They play Australia on Saturday afternoon, a warm-up to the Bosnia game. Cardiff is hosting some games, so there are RWC road signs and there's a great big 3D rugby ball sculpted to make it look like it's crashing through the wall of the castle. But the football game's bigger, much bigger. Not many nations play rugby, so a world cup features half a dozen good sides. The other teams, apart from the occasional upset, are generally there to make up the numbers. The fact that the FIFA ranking list goes down to 208 tells you which is really the world game.

There's been a longstanding rivalry between football and rugby in Wales so some will support both teams on Saturday, but not all. It's an ongoing battle for the hearts and minds of the nation's youth for a start. Gareth Bale was a really good rugby player, so was Aaron Ramsey. Both could have opted to pursue that at a high level. They chose football. Others may have chosen rugby. In a small country, talented athletes are a rare and precious commodity and both the FAW and the WRU are competing to attract and nurture those identified as talented. If Wales win the World Cup, a generation of youngsters might be inspired to be like Sam Warburton. If Wales qualify for the Euros, then perform well, they will want to be Gareth or Aaron or Hal Robson-Kanu.

The World Cup has already had an impact on my plans for the week. It's France v Ireland in Cardiff on Sunday and the closest hotel room Sky's travel department could find for us was in Bridgend, 17 miles out of town. So, we'll be heading west after we return from Sarajevo, unless there's a celebration party to attend, of course! In that event, a bench in Bute Park will suffice. There's work to be done first, of course, starting today. It wouldn't be Wales if plans weren't a little 'flexible' and I arrive in the Radisson to read an email informing me that this afternoon's open training session has been cancelled, and rescheduled for tomorrow morning. This comes as no great surprise. Lots of the players were in action yesterday, which means they'll only be doing a recovery session today. No point inviting the cameras along if the big hitters aren't there.

My journey hasn't been wasted however. Tonight's the FAW awards night and I've been invited, not as a host but as a guest. This year, I've kept my toys in the pram and accepted. Alex is going, of course, and so is Bill, the first time our commentator's ever been invited in all the years we've been covering Wales! It's a fact that's discussed over a pre-event drink in the hotel. What is it he's done to deserve this so soon in his international career?

Suitably kitted out in evening suits, we walk up to the venue through the city centre, looking a little like members of a male voice choir. Alex has his camera and kitbag. We're expecting to do interviews with the winners, as has been the custom in the past, particularly as Gareth Bale appears to have won just about everything. It's only a surprise he hasn't got the Women's Player of the Year as well!

So, we go to work and to play. We've got an extra assignment as well, Jim wants us to film people saying 'Together Stronger' for something they're planning at the start of the programme on Saturday. He also wants good luck messages for another piece due to go out just before kick-off. We did have a clear day to shoot it all tomorrow and I've had to reschedule aspects already because of training but we've still got plenty to go at.

First though, a glass of bubbly courtesy of the FAW. It's nice to have a chance to catch up with a few people, and there are lots of familiar faces. I've never been to one of these nights as a guest. At this stage in the evening, I've always previously been trying to make sure I've got an up-to-date running order and that I know the PA system works.

When we check the table plan, we've all been placed on one of the media tables, the one furthest away from the stage as it happens. My seat turns out to be right in the corner of the room, it feels like I'm being kept as far away from the podium as possible! Do they fear I might suddenly race up to the stage, grab the mic and announce the name of the Players' Player of the year award? Obviously, I've thought about it. Now, I'm so far away, I wouldn't have breath left to speak by the time I got to the MC's lectern. Needless to say my colleagues take great delight in asking why I'm not presenting this year, just as

I predicted 12 months ago. I laugh and shrug and wish Frances, the hostess, all the very best, from a great distance.

As it turns out, the best bit of the night is at the beginning. Mike Peters has been booked to sing a couple of songs. As a massive fan of his band, The Alarm, this is great news. It's just been reported that Mike's long-term battle against cancer has again taken a worrying turn but, as ever, he turns in a great performance and gets the night off to an upbeat start.

There are a lot of awards to work through, as well as a meal to serve, and everyone going up on stage is interviewed. My aim was always to ensure we'd got everything out of the way to ensure the players could leave by 10.30pm at the latest, there's training in the morning remember. I've had previous managers tapping their watches at me, if they felt things were overrunning. Tonight, Gareth Bale might as well establish residence on stage, he's invited up that often. So much so that our hostess has pretty much exhausted her well of Bale questions by award three and she's forced to resort to. "So, what is it that you like about football then Gareth?"

By 11pm, it's all over bar the clapping, and Alex and I rouse ourselves to go and get the customary interview with the winner of the main award. We're waiting outside the hall as Gareth arrives, arms full of trophies, but he's led straight past us and away, pursued by the FAW's in-house media team. IG appears next. I ask if we're getting Gareth tonight? Apparently not. Nobody is, except the FAW. They'll be distributing the interview for general use later. It's the first time this has happened. There's always been a chance to talk to the winners in previous years. It's a real shame, I think fans would like to hear from Gareth at the start of what could/should be a momentous week. And it means we're coming away empty-handed.

Actually, not quite. I bump into Mike Peters in the lobby, and he's only too happy to do us a Together Stronger and a good luck message. He's a big fan himself and he's hoping he'll have cause to sing a celebration song when he appears at the Millennium Centre in Cardiff Bay on Saturday night, at the same time as the Bosnia game. I suspect there'll be a few in the audience keeping track on events in Zenica, even as they're enjoying the show.

After the evening's over, we adjourn to a nearby bar for the post-show party. Again, it's a chance to chat with people I haven't seen for a while, in some cases since the last of these I attended. As I do some mingling, I get a real sense of the extent to which this potentially historic achievement is being played down. The FAW don't appear to have any special plans. I talk to commercial backers who don't seem to realise just how massive it's going to be.

Or maybe I'm wrong. Will it only be middle-aged men like me getting lost in the euphoria of something we've spent a lifetime longing for, but never really expected to see? I can only go on what I've seen elsewhere. When we played Belgium as they celebrated qualification in the final game of the previous campaign, the stadium was awash with stuff given away by the Belgian FA's backers. Even I got a t-shirt and there were branded hats and flags, thousands of them. Never mind jumping on the bandwagon, it doesn't look like they've even got the wheels on yet in Wales!

Tuesday 6th October

I'm a little tentative this morning, I'm used to sipping water through the Awards evening, awaiting my next stint on stage. Sitting back and being able to enjoy the Brains beer was good last night, not so good today.

Lots to do though, so no time to dwell. There's a training session to cover! We get the 'Together Stronger' and 'Gyda'n Gilydd yn Gryfach', messages from Chris Coleman and Osian Roberts before the players arrive. There's a bit of banter flying around, most of it aimed at IG for kiboshing a plan to do something similar last month because of a misunderstanding about which Sky programme would use the footage. Chris makes a big point of asking him if it's alright for him to do it? There's a lot of laughter, and everyone's in high spirits, the perfect way to start the serious work.

David Cotterill is injured while Ashley Williams and Neil Taylor have an extra rest day, but the rest of the squad alights from the team bus a few minutes later. Joe Allen and Joe Ledley are fit again, so are Jonny Williams, David Edwards and Emyr Huws. As they descend the steps to take to the pitch, Alex stops filming for a moment. "Blimey, strong squad!" he observes, and he's right. This is probably the strongest squad Wales have assembled in the 11 years we've been covering the games. Nobody wants to miss out. David Cotterill is planning to travel to Bosnia with the squad despite not being able to play. They know they are on the brink of something very, very special.

Our 15 minutes up, we're off to the first of our 'Together Stronger' locations. I've arranged to visit a primary school in Cardiff, Ysgol Pwll Coch. It's a Welsh-language school, suggested by Alun, whose son, Twm attends. We're booked in with Twm's class, and they've all brought in Welsh flags, hats and scarves. Twm's a bit nervous as his big moment arrives. He's delivering the good luck message, in Welsh and English. He has a bit of trouble with the word 'Bosnia'. In takes one and two, it's Bonsia, but he nails it in take three. Da iawn - well done Twm!

Next up, we're off to Cardiff High School. The under-14 girls football team, Welsh champions, are waiting for us. Their coach is Gwennan Harries, a former international herself, and she's got it all set up brilliantly. The team emerge in their kit and throw themselves into the filming. It's really good fun, they're confident but not in any sort of arrogant way. There's a real sense of 'team' about them, a bit like the atmosphere around the national men's team. The rise of women's football has been fantastic, and there's a really nice back story in this school. Gwennan suffered a bad injury and, instead of going to play in the States, she took up a teaching qualification. She started this team, the first the school had ever had, and they won the Welsh Cup in their first season. She describes the moment when the whistle blew at the end of the final as the proudest in her career.

There's one more location to come on our mini-tour of Cardiff. We're off to see the Boore brothers, Gwilym and Rhys, at their Gôl football centre. I really wanted them to be involved in this, because they are the people this is really all about, the guys who've travelled all over the world supporting Wales. In good times and, more often, bad, they've been there. Not just Gwilym and Rhys, but a hardcore of a couple of hundred who've never given up on the team, even when everyone else had lost faith. It's not so long since one sports journalist wrote a piece in the *Western Mail* suggesting the national football team should be scrapped, as it was a waste of time.

The bar at the Gôl centre is a cathedral to their devotion. They have a fantastic collection of match posters, gathered on their travels. It's the perfect backdrop for what we're doing. Gwilym and Rhys have their sons with them, both in their early teens, wearing Spirit of '58 bucket hats and the Adidas shirt that Wales wore in the very early '80s. As a lad, I had this kit; shirt, shorts and socks. Now, someone has discovered a box of these tops in the backroom of a sports store in Gabalfa, in Cardiff, in near perfect condition. The two lads have one each, home and away. These shirts are now selling for hundreds of pounds on eBay, but these lads will treasure them long after they grow out of them.

Before we start filming, we chat. Rhys confesses to feeling anxious, he says he's not sleeping properly and has to keep refilling the confectionery and drinks machines just to keep himself occupied. He hasn't grasped the concept of imminent qualification either. He says we'll lose in Bosnia, then lose at home to Andorra, but that won't matter because results against the bottom team in the group don't count. That, it appears, is his best stab at being an optimist. And they call me pessimistic!?

Some won't get this, but that's how it is when you've been following, and suffering, with this team, our team, for so long. Gwilym has another theory. We lose in Bosnia, beat Andorra, but a fan stumbles on to the pitch to celebrate, and Wales suffer a 10 point deduction as a punishment.

The good luck messages they deliver convey all of this frustration, disappointment, pride and hope in a few well-chosen sentences. Gwil actually gets very emotional. We have to start again, and he just about holds it together the second time. It's brilliant stuff. This is what it means when you love football and you love your country. Needless to say, Gwil and Rhys are off to Bosnia, so we say our goodbyes and tentatively, very tentatively, plan to meet up in Cardiff when we all return on Sunday, you know, if... .

It's been a good day. Upbeat, and good to break out beyond the usual confines of training ground and team hotel. There's no doubt about it, people are getting excited about this big sporting Saturday in the life of the Welsh nation. The footballing news from up north is more mixed. Wrexham can only draw at home with Tranmere, but the crowd's nearly 7,000, which is remarkable.

Wednesday 7th October

This was originally going to be the big day before our departure, the player media day and then the chance for a 'sit down' with Aaron Ramsey, for broadcast in the build-up before kick-off on Saturday. Plans, however, have changed. Aaron's keen to do it on Thursday instead, which isn't a problem.

Before we go to the team hotel, there's one more 'Together Stronger' to do, the one that had to be rescheduled due to the training session being rescheduled! Are you keeping up with this? It's the former 400 metre runner and world champion, Jamie Baulch. He was on my list of Cardiff-based celebs to try and get, and he's proved tremendously willing to help. He's agreed to meet us in front of the Millennium Centre, and good to his word, he bounds into view, shakes hands, records a couple of high energy 'Together Strongers' and a good luck message, then bounds off again. It's another gold medal performance!

My pace is somewhat less impressive as I take the chance of a fairly long run before our next job, not helped by taking a couple of wrong turns. How did that happen? I know this route so well! Truth is, I can't get the game out of my head. I'm distracted. I just want it to happen.

So it's appropriate that the first person we see at the hotel is Sean, the physio. "Here he is, the most nervous man in football!", he shouts by way of a greeting. I smile weakly, and wonder what he'd make of Gwilym and Rhys and their altogether higher level of pessimism? We're directed upstairs to our designated room. There's no hurry as the players are taking a later lunch, and what happens next is well worth the wait. David Edwards, Hal Robson-Kanu and Chris Gunter are duly brought in. Each in turn gives a great interview. These are some of the best interviews I've ever heard, in 23 years! All three are really good on the need for the players to maintain a sharp focus on the next game, and not the potential prize that awaits. The context is spot on. It's down to daft old sods like me, Gwilym and Rhys to get wound up, nervous, and overwrought. It's down to them to do just what they've been doing all the way through the campaign. As Chris explains that means concentrating on the game and, within that context, only on the performance, not the result. One leads to the other. They know what it means to win or draw in Bosnia, but also know they can only focus on what they have to do to get there.

Amidst so much energised, articulate talk, one bit stands out for me. Chris Gunter's take on the bond between the players is genuinely fascinating. He says you can't 'make' team spirit, it doesn't come from taking the players go-karting. He says it's to do with trust, wanting to do well for yourself but also for the bloke sitting next to you in the dressing room, because he's your mate – and he's your mate because he wants the same for you.

He's impassioned when he talks about this, it's brilliant. I do thousands of these interviews, and for the first time in a long, long time, I'm hanging on every word. We laughed before we began, he said he was "in the zone"! There's another moment when he almost gets me, he says the players want to do it so much for the fans, "People like you who've supported this team for all those years." My eyes moisten. We're all on the brink.

As he gets up to go, Chris stops and says, "Now we're not recording, if we do it, can you make sure there's plenty of beer on the flight home?" And that is also brilliant.

Thursday 8th October

Our interview with Aaron Ramsey is not until after lunch, so there's time for a morning run in the bright Cardiff sun. I get my route right, and return in good time to get set for an audience with Aaron. Before we head off, Alex has chance to show me the fruits of his labours – the good luck message he's edited together for the players. It features some of the goals he's filmed through the campaign, and all the words of the people we've filmed this week. He's had a go at it with a few different tunes as backing music, but has settled on a track I suggested, Kelly Jones' version of 'Can't Take My Eyes Off You'. It's been a fan favourite for many years, since featuring in a popular BBC promo for that vital qualifier against Romania. The Stereophonics frontman's version is slower than the original, just guitar and vocal, and it was played at Gary Speed's funeral. Alex has done a fine job. It ends with Gwilym's emotional address. There shouldn't be a dry eye in the house when they've finished watching it! He sends it across to the FAW video analyst for distribution to the players.

The fine weather turns out to be a good thing when we arrive at the team hotel a little later. A slightly harassed-looking IG emerges from the lift as we walk into reception. It seems there are no rooms available at the inn. All the usual places are in use, so our only option is to set up outside, on the terrace adjacent to the spa and health club. In fairness it all looks rather splendid, with blue skies and a fine view across the Bay to Penarth. Sounds are more of an issue. There's a car alarm blasting somewhere in the distance, a helicopter overhead, the audio commentary from the little boat that takes sightseers around the Bay; and there's nothing we can do about any of it.

Aaron arrives with IG, we get him settled in and start the interview. One question in, there's an almighty crunching noise close to hand. It's IG, who has attempted to cross the pebbled path back to the spa. All eyes turn to him and he looks back, horror-struck, holding up a hand by way of apology. We respond with gales of laughter, and pick up where we left off.

It's another top interview. Having dealt with the nervous 19-year-old Aaron, it's hard to believe it's the same guy sitting here, talking confidently and eloquently about Wales, Bosnia and what lies beyond.

Job done, we pack up and head towards the door to the leisure club reception. Alex goes ahead and, as he enters, there's a big cheer. Two steps later I see why. It appears there's a birthday party going on, and a dozen elderly ladies are celebrating with a bit of pampering. They're sitting at a long table, in their towelling robes with glasses of bubbly in front of them. We're not exactly the Chippendales, but their reaction to our appearance in their midst suggests we might be the best available alternative. As I resist the temptation to whip off my reporter costume to reveal my thong, we both wish the birthday girl all the best, and flee back to the safety of our own hotel.

There's now some packing to be done as we fly with the team tomorrow, the first time in this campaign or the last that we've been on the same flight. Flying on the team charter used to be the standard arrangement for away internationals but, for whatever reason, it had lapsed. Undeterred, I asked about travelling with them when we were in Cyprus, realising that there were no direct flights from the UK to Sarajevo. A fan always books early, and old habits die hard.

We're lucky, and I'm grateful to the FAW for letting us on. While fans, and others travelling for Sky, have already started their journeys to hub airports across Europe, Alex, Bill and I will be the only members of the media pack to enjoy a direct two and a half hour trip over to the Balkans.

The so-called 'week of football' gets underway tonight with some top games, and Sky are showing all of them. Northern Ireland, the Republic and Scotland are all playing games key to their qualification hopes. The aim is to find somewhere we can watch all of them at once, at the same time as getting something to eat. That challenge proves too great for Cardiff's sports bars. The first venue has two games but no food, the second has all three – including the Republic game on a cinema size screen, but no food (or real ale) – and the third just has the Republic game on. We try venue two for a bit, but it's actually really difficult watching three games at once. Whiplash injuries are a realistic prospect as my head starts twisting from side-to-side as commentators' voices rise, first in the game on the far left, then the far right. Plus two of the games involve teams in green playing teams in white. And we're hungry.

So, venue three, an Irish bar, gets our longer term custom and we settle down to enjoy the game in the company of a sizeable contingent of Irish fans. I guess it's the advance guard, ahead of the RWC game between Ireland and France at the Millennium Stadium on Sunday.

It proves a good choice. The game's thrilling, the more so as we also see Scotland take a 2-1 lead against Poland in the same group. All sorts of scenarios are possible, but a draw isn't a great result for the Republic. Germany miss loads of chances, then a long punt from the 'keeper lands at the feet of Shane Long. He crashes his shot in and the pub goes wild. Nervous moments follow, but the tension eases in the final seconds as Poland equalise and Scotland are out. Elsewhere, Northern Ireland have won to qualify, for the first time. It's an amazing achievement with a squad full of lower league players, and a striker who was a goalie until quite recently!

All in all, it's been a cracking night and just what UEFA must have hoped for from their revamped tournament; meaningful games right to the end of the qualification process. On the other hand, they might be dismayed to see minnows getting through when countries like Holland are struggling. Even Germany aren't yet sure of automatic qualification. But we look forward to another so-called minnow joining the list of qualifiers in the next 48 hours!

Back at the hotel, chances of an early night are reduced as an old mate, a cameraman working on the rugby for ITV, appears in the bar. We catch up for a bit but, just as we're heading up to our rooms, Bill arrives in reception. So there's more catching up to do before I can finally put my head on the pillow.

Friday 9th October

Even though we're flying to Sarajevo with the team, we don't actually see the players until we're sitting on the plane. The usual protocol in these situations is for 'guests' to go to the back rows, then the FAW staff and councillors, then the players, with the coaching staff and manager right up front.

There have been instances of official flights being overbooked and on one occasion, fans who'd paid to travel on the charter, were actually turned away at the airport because the plane was apparently 'too heavy', still casts a shadow over the FAW to this day.

Unfortunately, there have been a number of instances when fans travelling on the official charter flights have been let down badly by the FAW, such as the occasion when fans were turned away at the airport because the additional baggage brought by the association meant the plane was 'too heavy'! For many loyal fans, this type of treatment still casts a shadow over the FAW.

Happily there are spare seats on this flight, and we get off the ground on time. This is important, as we're on a pretty tight schedule when we get to Bosnia. We're due to land at 4.45pm, and have to be at the stadium for the usual pre-match media appearance from the manager and captain at 6.30. In that time we have to get off the plane and collect luggage, get Alex's 'carnet' – his kit list – signed by customs, pick up our hire car and make the one hour drive to Sarajevo. There's not a lot of 'wriggle room'.

The flight bit's fine. We come in over the mountains that surround the city, drop through the low cloud that shrouds their peaks, and get our first view of the place. It's just about as much as we're going to see of Sarajevo, which is a real shame. It was lodged in collective consciousness by the assassination in 1914 of Archduke Franz Ferdinand, an event which started the First World War and forewarned what was to come nearly 80 years later during the Balkan War. For nearly four years Serbian forces besieged the Bosnian capital, dropping shells on to its streets and houses. Fourteen thousand people, nearly half of them civilians, died. As we peer from the small windows of the descending plane we look for signs of the destruction wrought during that time. That we don't really see it shows, I hope, that the resilience that got people through the siege has also helped rebuild their city. I'd like to take a closer look but, sadly, there's no time for sightseeing.

We're into passport control minutes after landing. As we queue, my phone links up with a local network and pings away as various messages appear on the screen. Ominously, there's one from Barry Horne. Needless to say, Barry is travelling separately from everyone. He taught Year 5 physics before heading to Manchester airport for a flight to Vienna. Except that, as the text message tells me, the flight to Vienna has been cancelled. The tale of woe continues. He is now booked on a 23.45 flight to Istanbul, then a connection which gets him into Sarajevo at 07.30 tomorrow, match day! Our reaction to this awful news is predictable. As I read the text out, my travelling companions burst out laughing. Barry's travel nightmares are now a key element of this campaign. We speculate that Chris Coleman, who knows all about them and is also a superstitious man, has perhaps arranged the cancellation to keep up the routine!

It's pretty harsh, Barry will be wiped out by the time he gets to our hotel, which is another hour from Sarajevo, but taking the mickey out of each other is probably what we do best. Still, we have our own travel concerns to contend with. Alex goes to get his documents checked and signed while Bill and I seek the hire car desk, which turns out to be a hut. We watch the players get on their coach and their kit loaded into a separate van. But when they pull away, we're still waiting for Alex, and there's a problem with the hire car. The guy in the booth claims it's not been confirmed. Alex has all the paperwork, but he's still not got through arrivals. The clock is ticking!

Alex, when he does reach us, has a piece of paper confirming that Sky have paid in advance, but the guy in the booth still doesn't seem sure. However he eventually wilts in the face of Alex's increasingly brusque and businesslike demeanour, and processes the booking. He even gives us an upgrade after looking at all our luggage, but when this turns out only to be an Astra we wonder what on earth we were in before!

It's a game show in-waiting; three adults plus luggage and full camera kit in one car, an hour's drive from a media conference at the stadium, which begins in 55 minutes. In haste, I snap a vital connection on the tripod box. If Alex is angry, and he probably is, he hides it well. This is no time to fall out. We squeeze into the car and it groans into life. Power is something else our car distinctly lacks. The engine whines as we start to gather speed while looking for signs to Zenica. The hire car bloke said it was straightforward, left, left and then straight on until you hit the traffic jam. His description is accurate.

Now I know we're in trouble. I convey that message to all the people that need to know; Sarah at the stadium, IG who is already well on his way to the stadium and Sports News, expecting interviews with captain and manager in the next hour. At least they'll have a fallback since the media conference will be filmed anyway.

Away from the airport, our mobile phones are not working very well. Sarah has asked me to call her, but I can't make any outward calls, it's texts only. Emails won't download either. Another text pings up from Jim, the producer. Are we okay for the Asimir Begović interview I've requested at his behest? All this is going on whilst Alex guns the hire car onto the first stretch of open road. It screams its unhappiness at being asked to go so fast whilst taking the strain of luggage and passengers. "I've only got a 1.2 litre engine!", it shouts, "What do you expect of me?"

At least the satnav is working. I keep glancing at the ETA, which says we're going to be at the stadium 15 minutes after things start. IG helps. He says he'll take Chris and Ashley in together, then we can do them straight afterwards. Sarah also has better news, she says the media room's packed and it hasn't started on time. With luck this means plenty of questions, so we can park up, get the gear out and get set up, all in a stadium we've never visited before. Tension levels rise as high as the car's RPM indicator. We hit 5,000 on approach, then screech around the corner and into the TV compound. It's a wonder the wheels don't all fall off, like those clown cars.

We race into the ground through a gate behind a terrace. Inside, it's pitch black. No floodlights on, no lighting of any sort, so we stumble over seats and down steps and feel our way round the perimeter fence to the glow from the tunnel on the far side.

275

Then there are two flights of stairs to ascend before we get to the dressing rooms. Bill's gone ahead and has the reassuring news that the press conference is still going and Peter Barnes will bring Chris and Ashley to us. We're actually going to be okay. It's a massive relief, I hate missing anything. I guess that's why we usually fly out the day before. The team like to travel as late as possible but they get things like police escorts or cars provided by the host association to speed them on their way.

Still we are good to go, sweat wiped from brows, by the time Ash and Chris appear in the long corridor between our interview position and the media room. There's handshakes all-round, and a quick chance to reassure the manager that Barry has taken one for the team again. Then we get our interviews.

The next request is for Begović who's just arrived for the Bosnia media conference. I haven't had time to introduce myself to their head of media, but we'd met in Cardiff when the interview with Džeko was arranged. Their star striker has since picked up an injury playing for Roma, so whilst he is here he seems unlikely to play, leaving Asimir as our prime interview target. Bosnia's media head honcho told me by email that we can do it if he has a couple of minutes to spare. I've told her that we'll be set up ready to go, which we are.

I wait at the side of the room until the last question is answered, then make my approach. I'm also wearing my Sky Sports coat as a visual reminder. When I ask if we're on, she says he's already done his British TV interview. This is puzzling. I ask who with, but she says just that it was 'British TV'. I mention my email, but she says she has no recollection of it. I try to get it on my phone to show that she replied, but the curse of the lack of signal strikes again. She says he's not got time now, he has to go training. Request denied!

It turns out the other crew who've done the interview are from our competitors. My guess is that when they asked the Bosnia media head, she got confused and assumed 'they' are 'us'. It's frustrating. I have to go back to Jim and tell him I haven't managed to get the interview. He's probably now got a hole in his running order. Others higher up the ladder may view it seriously. TV companies pay a lot of money to secure broadcast contracts, and they expect their rights to be protected.

Back in the compound, all the footage is winging its way back to the UK. Neither team is training at the stadium, so we're pretty much done. We now have another journey. All three hotels in Zenica are booked up, so we're staying in Vitez. You might ask how the Bosnian FA are allowed to stage a major international football match in a place with just three hotels, but this is their preferred venue for games. The BBC guys are staying in the same hotel, and Kevin Ratcliffe's in their travelling party. I've had a quick chat with Kev between media conferences and it seems it's a bit of a tricky drive, over a mountain on unfinished roads. Given how much our car struggled on the straight and flat dual carriageway from Sarajevo, this could be a bit of a challenge.

We reload everything, tripod case protruding through into the back seat, then set off. Next stop, logged into the satnav, is the Hotel Central. Or so we hoped. But the first stop is nearly on the way up the mountainside. We hit section after section where the tarmac's been taken up and bounce along on the pitted, potholed surface that remains. The gradient gets steeper, the road windier and the car nearly gives up the ghost. All the time we're labouring up the mountain, Audis are looming large in the rear view mirror, then overtaking on hairpin bends. I grip the seat belt, Bill goes quiet in the back and Alex fills the void by chattering away at the wheel. "I always talk too much when I'm nervous", he says, which isn't exactly reassuring.

By the roadside, there are numerous cemeteries. They are filled with white markers rather than crosses since this is a predominantly Muslim country, and the relative age of the gravestones suggests these are Balkan War victims. Vitez was home to the main UK forces base.

Once we've got to the top, we come down a bit more quickly, but still the Audis fly past. We hit downtown Vitez some 30 minutes after setting off, 30 fear-filled minutes that I'm not anxious to repeat in the heavy rain forecast after the game tomorrow. Even before we check-in, I suggest that we might be better off staying in Sarajevo tomorrow; a much easier drive, even if it is further away. My colleagues instantly concur. A request will be emailed to the travel department on arrival.

But we're not there yet. The satnav directs us towards the postcode listed on the hotel's website. We peer out of the car windows but it's difficult as there are no street lights and it's really dark. We drive up and down the main road a few times without spotting our hotel, so eventually we stop. Alex gets out to ask a man in a garage for directions. He doesn't speak English but he points and gestures. We try to follow his guidance, but still we can't find it. We turn off the main road and see a policeman who points us in another direction.

This time Bill gets out to investigate. It turns out to be a snooker hall. Then we stop at a little supermarket and gather more directions. For what seems like hours, we're driving up and down the main road and turning the car round in another garage, whose owner peers out of his cabin, getting more suspicious every time we appear. He's a scary looking chap as well, a big fuzz of dark hair and few teeth. By the third or fourth time we stop on his forecourt, we're laughing, almost hysterically, and he's probably reaching under the counter.

After the best part of an hour, a phone call to the hotel puts us out of our increasing misery. When we describe where we are, the receptionist sounds downbeat. "It's difficult from there", she says, her voice trailing off. We're saved when she mentions the traffic lights.

We've only seen one set of traffic lights the whole time we've been in Bosnia, and we've driven through three towns and a city today. They were at the top of the road we've been driving up and down for, seemingly, a lifetime. So, it's left at Bosnia's only set of traffic lights, head for Travnik, then look out for the big FIS building and we're next door. We have been using the hotel's name, 'Central', as a clue in our search, but it turns out that was a complete red herring. It's not even in Vitez really, it's on the outskirts, part of a retail and industrial complex just off the Travnik to Sarajevo highway. The capital may be an hour from here, but the rest of our Sky colleagues are probably already tucking into their late dinner.

We have the same plan on checking-in, but the receptionist who guided us here warns us that the restaurant will close in half an hour. We go to our rooms to dump luggage, and agree to rendezvous shortly. I'm last to arrive back, after a quick call home. It's a big restaurant, almost empty save for the eight BBC guys around a table, two locals plus Bill and Alex. We're all heavily outnumbered, however, by the empty tables and chairs.

Despite this, Alex has been warned that the food could take an hour to arrive, as they're 'so busy'. It's hard to take in, but the prediction gets worse after some cold meats are delivered as a starter and we're told it's now going to be an hour and a half! But there are no other customers; nobody else has come in! There are 12 people in the room in total, and two of them are already eating.

Then, our harbinger of culinary doom goes off shift, or at least retires to the bar for a beer and a fag, and her replacement is none other than our saviour from reception. With her on board, things once again take a turn for the better. "I have good news!", she says, as she brings a round of beers, "It might only be half an hour!" In fact, it's less than that. The food, when it arrives, is okay and the price exceedingly cheap. There's no sign of a bar to retire to and it's been a long and pretty traumatic day, so we head off to bed before the clock ticks round to midnight.

Before we go, I have a little presentation to make. I've had t-shirts made for the people who've worked on every game of this campaign; with the Sky logo, FAW crest and the words 'Tîm Cymru' ('Team Wales') printed on them. Bill and Alex accept their gift with more than good grace, and seem genuinely chuffed. We have a little hug in the middle of an almost empty restaurant in the heart of the Balkans. It's what international football's all about!

Saturday 10th October

MD9 dawns. One point. We only need one point. I want it to be tonight. I think everybody else in the travelling party is of the same mind. I'm certain the 750 fans who've travelled with tickets, and all those who haven't, also feel the same way. They, we, are here to see the moment when it happens.

The omens are good. Wales have a full strength squad to pick from, whilst Bosnia have lost several key players including, almost certainly, Džeko. They need to win to maintain a realistic chance of finishing third but Israel will take that slot if they win both their remaining games. Bosnia, pushing forward, should suit Wales' counter attacking style. I wouldn't go so far as to say I'm confident about tonight, we're not at that stage yet, but I think there's a very good chance of getting at least a draw.

Bill and I chat it over at breakfast, eating ham omelettes and what he describes as the worst cup of coffee he's had in his life. I'm drinking tea, which is fine. Our discussions are interrupted by a familiar voice.

We glance over to the entrance and sure enough, there he is, Phileas Fogg!

It's a slight disappointment that he's not wearing the suit, shirt and tie, which he worn to school yesterday morning, but the careworn expression on his face tells as much as a pair of creased trousers ever could. We usher him over to the table and ask the waiter for more ham, eggs and horrible coffee.

Barry's taxi driver's been telling him a little about our hotel on the way over. According to him, it's based in the midst of Europe's biggest shopping centre. I have my doubts about this, but vow to check it out after presenting Barry with his 'Tîm Cymru' t-shirt. He can add it to those 73 caps*. He's off to get some much needed sleep, it's going to be a long night as it is. I go off to explore my surroundings.

We are indeed in the midst of a shopping centre. In fact, if I look three feet right from the door of my room, there's another door at the end of the corridor. When I push it open, I find myself in a bathroom and kitchen showroom. This could present problems with nocturnal ramblings in search of my own bathroom, but I'll be okay this evening as a message from Alex says we're shipping out later and heading to Sarajevo after the match. It's good news, especially as we've now got Barry along for the ride as well. That hire car ain't going to like us!

I can now confirm that this isn't Europe's biggest shopping centre. I wonder if it's even the biggest shopping centre in Vitez. Alex has also been out, in search of a waterproof. He's forgotten a coat, and the bleak forecast and lack of cover at the stadium suggest we're in for a soaking later. Over lunch, he reveals his new purchase, a snip at 40 marks, about £17, from FIS, the massive shop opposite our hotel and a much more realistic contender for the title of Europe's biggest shopping centre.

We eat well. Barry seeks to boost his energy levels by finishing off with a large piece of cake and a cappuccino, evidently a vast improvement on the breakfast. As well as buying a coat, Alex has been busy sorting out the car. He's found a way to get the tripod case into the boot, meaning we probably won't have to strap Barry to the

---

* I know Barry got 59 caps and 2 goals for his country but he picked someone up on it once when they got the figure wrong so it's been a long-running joke ever since. He takes it in good part, safe in the knowledge that he was a very good footballer, while we weren't.

roof-rack. We agree a departure time that factors in the uneven and slow ascent of the mountain, then go off to prepare.

I've had my pre-match run already, in the hotel gym, so have enough time for a last tour of the shopping centre. Five minutes later, I'm back in my room. I've put my Spirit of '58 hat and scarf in my manbag, just in case there's something to celebrate. I've also got my lucky UEFA badge and my lucky Welton Rovers sticker that's been to every game since Andorra. Gareth in the Turnstile office is a Welton fanatic. In fact, I think he's on the club board. He gave it to me ages ago so that I could stick it on the wall of some far flung stadium. I forgot in Andorra, but we got a good result, and it's been with me ever since.

When we meet by the car, Alex is, naturally, wearing his lucky socks but with the rain now lashing down, his coat is looking an even better purchase. Bags and kit boxes are crammed into every nook and cranny and we squeeze in amongst them. As we're about pull off, I notice the warning signs on the door of the hotel, there's a box with a red line through a picture of a scotty dog and another with a red line through a picture of a handgun. That's what you get for your four stars!

The approach to Bosnia's only set of traffic lights is slower than even we anticipated. The traffic's heavy, and it gives Barry a bit of time to panic about losing, first his wallet, then his phone. Both turn-up after some frantic scrambling in his bag. Still, it helps add to the slightly fraught mood in the car as we begin the climb, off the main road and onto the mountain track. Daylight means we can see just how precariously the road grips the side of the mountain, but at least we can see the potholes and ridges a little more easily than last night. The decision to move to Sarajevo still seems a good one.

We've been warned there's a likelihood the roads will have been shut around the stadium and that there's no parking for us there. Neither turns out to be true, and we get a space right outside the main stand. Still the rain comes down, and there's an opportunistic umbrella salesman wandering round in-between the merchandise stalls. I've also been told it's meant to be 'dry' in the bars and cafes, no alcohol, but the banging techno music and the singing and dancing outside at least one suggests this information might also be inaccurate. It's nearly four hours before kick-off, but already someone's waving a flare around underneath a canopy across the road. We're expecting a lively atmosphere; this has surely to be the reason why the Bosnian FA drag everybody over to this relative backwater for their home games.

We get a better chance to check out the stadium in the daylight as well. It's not up to much. It only holds 13,000, there's not an exec box in sight and, more importantly, very little by the way of cover. The away end is completely exposed. Already large puddles are forming in the plastic bucket seats and water's running down the terrace steps. There are imposing-looking security guards posted at all the entrances as well, their appearance slightly undermined by the black ponchos that are protecting them from the elements.

Before I wander too far from the compound, I need to talk to Sarah about what might happen at the end of the game. I know it's like saying 'Macbeth' at the theatre, but we have to discuss what happens in the event of Wales qualifying. It seems I will have what is known as a 'superflash' interview position in the corner of the ground, closest to the away fans. That's where the players will obviously head when… if… .

We will only have a single 'live' camera, and Sarah will put those pictures out to Sky Sports viewers, whilst the host broadcaster covers shots for the domestic audience and the UEFA feed for other countries who are taking the game. It could be quite tricky trying to cover everything and get interviews with players from just one camera, so I need to be prepared to use my initiative and not wait for direction.

Ben's the cameraman again, as he was in Cyprus. He's an experienced operator and that could be crucial if it's all going mad. It's going to be a time for calm heads. That's easy to say, but may be harder to prove if I'm about to fulfil my lifetime's ambition to see Wales qualify.

My first duty for the evening is the usual interview with Barry. There's been no let up in the rain and our broadcast position is uncovered, so we both stand there getting wet and waiting for our cue. It doesn't come, Sports News are in the thick of other stuff, and we're getting wet. Eventually we get the instruction to record it, so we can get back in the dry for a bit. Barry confidently predicts Wales will qualify, he says he thinks they'll win anyway, certainly draw and points out that even then they might go through. The external factor that will see qualification no matter what happens here is if Israel fail to beat Cyprus. That game's taking place in Jerusalem so the home side are favourites to win and ensure third place, ahead of Bosnia, so there's plenty resting on that game for both sides in Zenica.

All done, Barry heads off to shelter on the TV gantry, and I nip over to the tunnel. As luck would have it, one of the few useful facilities offered to us this evening is a post-match interview position that's actually got a window onto the pitch. In theory, I could almost watch the game from here, rather than the plastic chair that's been placed just to the right of the Welsh dugout, out in the open.

But I'm not going to use it as a viewing position. I need to be closer to the pitch and, anyway, I enjoy the company of the lads on the coaching staff, who'll be occupying the chairs between my position and the actual, covered, dugout. Still, it gives me somewhere warm to hang out whilst I await Chris Coleman's arrival for the pre-match interview. In theory, it's still some time off, so I go for walk to see what there might be in the way of food, drink or hospitality. It turns out there's none, not even a proper media room. I last ate at about 2.30pm and it looks like that'll be my lot for the day, since there's no sign of anything for sale around the ground except for strange-looking sealed paper cups with a straw sticking out of them.

Back at my post, I hear the sounds of activity in my little earpiece. The team bus is arriving, a bit earlier than anticipated. Jim's already said what he wants from this interview, so when Chris appears I'm primed and ready to go. The manager makes it clear he wants this sorted tonight; no more messing around, let's book that place to France. The team he's picked comes, once again, with a bit of surprise. James Chester is fit but Chris elects to keep the same back line as the last two games. That means Jazz Richards keeps his place at right-back and Gunter and Davies continue in the centre. In midfield, no surprise to see the two Joes, Ledley and Allen, back in the team. The rest is as anticipated.

After the interview, I'm clear until kick-off. I contemplate heading outside to sample the atmosphere and check out the merchandise stores, but it's still raining heavily. The ground staff are forking the pitch as puddles form, so I err on the side of dryness.

My services are soon required as well. The head of Wales' security team is outside the door to the interview room. He's a big rugby fan and asks if I know the score from back home, where Wales are playing their final World Cup group game against Australia. A win would mean a easier route to the final. He says quite a few of the players are keen to know, as well. To be honest, I'm not really interested and had forgotten it was on, but I'm happy to help. The only thing I picked up on my walk up to the media conference room was a Wi-Fi code. Still, it takes a while before I can confirm that Wales are narrowly losing, but Australia are temporarily down to 13 players after two yellow cards. I imagine there'll be an awful lot of people packing out the pubs back home for this Welsh sporting doubleheader.

Barry is due to speak to the guys in the studio as we come on air 45 minutes before kick-off, so I head over a couple of minutes beforehand to make sure he's okay. The Wales fans are just beginning to file into the away section to his right and the first flags are going up. Two lads clamber up the wire fence to place their Jack Army Welsh flag. It is not so long since Swansea fans would not have felt comfortable highlighting their presence amidst the travelling support, so it is a great sight. There are few enough of us as it is, without people feeling excluded from supporting the national side.

There's another big flag going up, this time with a Wrexham badge on it and the name of the village of Bagillt. Once he's done his bit on the TV, Barry points at it and asks me to take his picture in front of it. It's where he grew up. The fans have spotted him and are chanting his name. His contribution to the cause, a loyal servant who'd have loved playing in the current side, won't be forgotten. In fact Barry would have been an ideal addition as a midfield enforcer protecting the talent. He's a highly intelligent, cultured bloke, but loved a midfield battle!

As I wander back round to the tunnel, the Bosnian fans are beginning to get warmed up as well. They look a lively bunch. Ben's told me some of the ultras carry guns, and those security guys in the ponchos are mainly ex-fighters from the war. I'll behave myself, then.

I'm back in my box, briefly, but then the signal comes to line-up in the tunnel. As I stand at the top of the stairs and the players go past, there are quite a few little handshakes or high fives, including one from Gareth. He catches my eye and offers his hand. It's a simple gesture but I'd be a liar if I said I wasn't chuffed. He may be aware of the background issues but he's a thoroughly decent lad. On top of that, of course, his performances have taken us to the brink of something amazing.

There are a lot more handshakes and winks as the coaching staff pass. There's an unbelievable sense of camaraderie in this group and, at moments like this, I can almost kid myself I'm a part of it. I then make the long walk around the edge of the pitch to my seat and as I pass the away end, I see Rhys, and give him a big wave. By the time I reach my position, he's already banging out the anthem, along with 700 other diehards, most of them already soaked. They've been herded out of Sarajevo on a fleet of coaches, held in a pen by the ground, then herded in heavy rain into an uncovered section surrounded by high fences and security guards. Would any other form of mass entertainment dare to treat its customers like this?

The Bosnian anthem's a disappointment, a bit of a dirge. But there's no doubting the passion of the fans, who are noisy and boisterous. Another group of ultras, all dressed in the same clothes, form a block of dark blue and gold behind the far goal defended by Begović.

As anticipated Džeko is not starting, but Pjanić – their star in his absence – has an early chance when Ben Davies slips on the edge of the box. He pulls the shot wide. That apart, not a lot happens. I'm clock-watching, as ever, but the tension of previous games isn't quite there. Maybe it's reassurance of the Andorra game to come, or because Wales have got a bit of a grip on the game. Bosnia look a poor side and the crowd goes quiet.

As half-time approaches, Hennessey's not been troubled. In the last few seconds, just like in Israel, Wales almost strike. Ramsey picks up on an error and dribbles his way along the by-line and into the penalty area. Begović comes off his line to block him but Aaron slips the ball across the box, inches from the goal-line. Neil Taylor slides in, needing just the slightest of touches to score, and we rise as one man from our plastic seats to see the net ripple. But, like the last-ditch Australian tackler on the try-line at Twickenham that afternoon, a Bosnian defender manages to slide just ahead of Neil, and the ball stays out. The ref gives Bosnia a free kick, then blows the half-time whistle.

Still, 0-0 is fine. Wales still have not conceded a goal since the flukey free kick in the 34th minute of the home game against Cyprus, three days short of a year ago. There are the usual steely stares when the players emerge from the dressing room, 45 minutes away from 'job done', but James Collins lets the mask slip a little as we walk back out together, "Are you coming back to the hotel afterwards?" he asks, "We'll be having a party!" Good lad!

Truth be told, at this stage, I'd be prepared to accept his invitation. Bosnia don't seem a particularly happy bunch. Results have picked up since the new coach took over, but one of the local journalists has whispered to me about his failings. The home crowd does not feel that intimidating either. As Dai Griffiths said to me during the first half, "They're not as bad as Serbia". Dai's right. Serbia felt like full-on hatred, but while the Bosnians are supportive of their own team, there's no obvious aggression towards the opposition.

So, I feel really confident as I walk back out and take the time to look at the away section as I walk in front of it. There are quite a few familiar faces. There's Pete from Wrexham, chairman of the Supporters Trust, who goes everywhere. I catch his eye and he waves. Like me, he's got twin dreams, club back in the Football League, country to qualify for anything. Of the two, only one currently looks a realistic proposition. Wrexham lost again earlier today.

I feel compelled to clap as I walk along the perimeter fence. These people spend so much money following their team and their support has been magnificent throughout, particularly in this campaign. Any fans who can sing '*We'll never qualify*', and yet still keep turning up, deserve every recognition of their efforts.

Back at my seat, I get the first request for information from elsewhere. The lads in the dugout want to know how Israel are getting on so I ask Sarah, who can check with our people back in the UK. The lack of 3G or Wi-Fi means it's really hard to keep in touch otherwise. We're showing the goals from other games as ours goes on. Nothing yet from Jerusalem, and that's good enough for Wales. Still, it shouldn't matter. Wales have established an even stronger grip on the game in this second half. Joe Allen's doing his thing in midfield again. The defence is watertight, despite the rain that continues to come down and that one question keeps getting asked, with James Collins the most frequent enquirer.

As we get close to the hour mark, I hear Sarah say the name Dossa Junior. He plays for Cyprus, as I recall. So the fact that his name's being relayed to her from base must be good news. Sure enough, a second later, I hear Bill in his commentary confirm that Cyprus have taken the lead!

"Cyprus have scored!", I tell the bench. There are little clenched fist movements all the way along our row of plastic seats. Subs jog past to double-check. It's so close now we can touch it. The Cyprus goal's good for Bosnia as well, and the home fans renew their effort to get their team going. It doesn't really work. I can't recall ever seeing a Wales side so completely in control of an away game, particularly one against such tough opposition.

The only thing they aren't really doing is creating chances, but the players probably don't feel the need to get too adventurous. Keep the unbeaten run going, get the point, qualify.

Then, on 70 minutes, a free kick is given away just inside the Welsh half, right in front of us. It's lumped up towards the area, bounces just outside and the ball loops up so the tall sub, Djurić, can flick a header over Wayne Hennessey and in. It's a goal from nowhere and their fans go absolutely wild in response. It's okay though, because Cyprus are still winning. Nevertheless, there's now an almost constant stream of requests for updates from the Welsh bench. Our game is almost irrelevant. I don't know what the players know of events elsewhere, but where I'm sitting and, I'm sure, up in the stands, it's all about Israel. Bosnia are in with a great shout of claiming third place if things stay as they are. Wales are going through.

Then I hear Sarah say "Bitton". That's another name I recognise, this time from the Israel team. Before Bill's even said it on air, I've turned to my nervous companions, "1-1".

Shoulders slump. There's a slightly familiar feeling to all of this. Somewhere at the back of the mind of everyone in the Welsh camp is a fear. Yes, it's only Andorra next, but what if, what if? I won't say a gloom's settled, but everything feels very different to five minutes ago. False info starts to fly around as nerves start to fray. Adam Owen says he's heard it's 2-1 to Israel, I tell him it isn't. They have to trust me to get the accurate news, it could be important.

The players do their bit to lift it. They push forward. Coleman goes all out for an equaliser. Vokes is sent on, then Church. They don't want to lose. The home fans are back in fine voice, but they really need more good news from Israel, they need an away win. Then, 80 minutes flicks up on the big video screen clock behind the goal and, as we move into the last ten minutes, Sarah's uttering another name in my headphones. This one's particularly familiar. Demetriou, she says. That's our pal from the Cyprus game, the chirpy London lad who gave such a great interview. Jason Demetriou has scored for Cyprus. The lad who plays for Walsall has scored the goal that must now send Wales through to France! Surely Israel can't score twice in the last nine minutes? I turn to Team Wales, "2-1 Cyprus!!!" More clenched fists.

Now, we all start to think about full-time, fans who want to celebrate, reporters who have to interview, cameramen who have to film it. I wait another couple of minutes, then warn the sound man, Brian, that I'm ready to make my move. I know this is going to cause consternation in the Welsh camp. They're seeking almost constant reassurance on the score now, but surely the same scenes will be being played out in the away end?

As I get up to go, with five minutes left, Dai, Ian, Jon, Ronan and the rest almost implore me to stay. I have to go. I'm too far away from the superflash position to take the chance, besides, I need to unplug everything here and replug to the cables down in the corner.

I apologise and take my leave. I actually feel vulnerable without the commentary in my ears. I don't have access to the information that everyone wants. The Bosnian FA have run the score across the video screen but maybe people missed it, or aren't convinced. Not even a PA announcement seems to have reassured the travelling fans. As I walk towards them, I see worried faces. Then things get weird. I'm spotted taking up my position right in front of them, immediately they start calling out for a score update. I've got the headphones on, but I can't hear Bill or Sarah yet, Brian's down on his knees, fiddling with a load of cables. "I need plugging in ASAP!", I shout at him although, clearly, he's going as quick as he can. Finally, after what feels like an age, the voices are back in my ears. I gesture towards any fan who asks, 2-1 with my fingers, and even attempt to indicate three added minutes in the Israel game when Bill says the board's gone up there. That's a tricky one though, what if it looks like 2-3?

The game goes on somewhere in the background, Wales miss a chance to equalise, then Bosnia score a second, but it doesn't matter. Only Israel matters.

There are quite a few members of the FAW staff down in my corner as well, the overspill group that wasn't allowed to sit next to the dugout. They're asking for the score. James Collins jogs up, miles away from the bench, he just wants to know the score. When I tell him, he sprints back towards the bench. Then Bill says there's a minute to go here and in Israel. Now I know. A grin starts to spread across my face, I start nodding furiously, almost jogging on the spot. Then a chant starts, '*Bryn Law Bryn Law, what's the score? Bryn Law, what's the score?*' As they await my response, Bill utters the immortal line, "The referee has blown for full-time in Jerusalem!" and my eyes close whilst my arms pump the air; the microphone with its red Euro 2016 mic cover waving about. The fans know what this means. At last! At last! At last, we've done it, we're there! A wave of euphoria rolls up from my feet, up my body, up my arms, I open my eyes and look at the most fantastic scenes of celebration in front of me. It's the moment we've waited for so many years. Loyal fans have passed away without seeing this moment, many on the terraces in front of me will have travelling companions who are no longer with them. I have a friend who should be here and who isn't. I think of him and look up and point to the dark Bosnian night sky, tears of joy falling down from the heavens on us all. Gary's wearing his FAW suit, the little grin and a nod to me, then he turns and goes back to the dugout.

On the pitch, Chris Coleman, has set off stony-faced towards the tunnel. God knows what's happened in my absence, but he appears not to have heard the score at the edge of his technical area, in his, by now, dripping-wet 'lucky suit'. The players are hovering in front of the dugout, presumably asking their colleagues what's happened. Then Chris Coleman meets Mark Evans midway across the pitch. Mark puts him out of his misery and Chris spins around, changes direction and sprints towards the away supporters. The next thing, the players are all heading in the same direction, all at full pelt, before launching themselves into full frontal, Superman-style slides across the soaked surface. Neil Taylor whizzes past, virtually under my feet. The party, my friends, has most definitely started!

Now there's work to be done, so I've got to hold everything together. Back home, all over Wales and wherever expats live beyond, people will be celebrating but they'll also want to hear from their heroes, the men who've made the cherished dream come true. I see one of the lads most deserving of the highest praise for the part he's played in all this, Chris Gunter, and call him over. Just 26 years old and tonight's his 62nd cap. It's an amazing statistic. I've been interviewing him since he played for the under-21s. He's such an eloquent talker but tonight, to begin with, he's almost lost for words, overcome with the enormity of it all. I'm so pleased for him, his loyalty rewarded, all the long trips for meaningless qualifiers forgotten. As he heads back to rejoin the celebrations, a UEFA official appears asking if we want the manager? Of course!

Before we start, there has to be a big embrace. I really like this guy, he's been nothing but friendly and good-humoured, no matter what's been going on. In the aftermath of the Costa Rica game, Gary's tribute night, me, him and Roger, Gary's Dad, were the last three people left in the bar of the hotel. It was as though none of us wanted to leave, because that would be like a final act. He's a good bloke, one who's known the highs and the lows on and off the pitch. I see a man constantly struggling to be better, to learn and improve.

I interview Chris, as the fans go mad on one side and the players celebrate on the other. We are in the midst of all this, me trying to find the right questions, him trying to find the right responses. We struggle through. He speaks glowingly of the people he's been working with, there's no mention of his own role, he shares the praise around.

They are still showing the pictures from our one camera. So Ben is taking shots of the celebrations whilst I'm grabbing, literally in Aaron Ramsey's case, players. The camera catches me in the act of virtually frog-marching him into position. After Aaron's done, I ask Gareth. He's lying down in the midst of a team shot, he indicates two minutes but he's with me in much less and his interview's great. He describes it as "The best defeat of my career". Again the superstar, the world's most expensive player, wants to talk only about his teammates, the staff and the supporters, not about himself. His goals have been crucial but he'd bristle if you suggested to him that Wales relied on those goals. He ranks this right up there with winning the Champions League and scoring in the final, looks forward to the side going to France and doing well. His last answer's delivered as he's already moving backwards, all talked out, back to daft dancing. Then, a special moment as the players lift the manager off his feet and throw him up into the air, time after time. He looks suddenly helpless in their midst but he has managed by consent, not through power, and the affection the players have for him shines through in a moment like this. They really, really like him and that's why they stuck by him when times were hard.

Last up for me, after a false start, is Ashley Williams. He seems almost drained by the whole thing, but then he has after so many of these games when I've interviewed him. As the saying goes, he leaves everything on the pitch. He laments the loss, something all the other players and the manager have done. They were clearly desperate to stay unbeaten. Still, we qualified!

We're all done on the pitch now, the players have started to drift back towards the tunnel, and I've got to get in there to do some interviews against the backboard. What we've just done is for Sky viewers but UEFA need somebody to do interviews for the international audience. I'm also reprising the S4C role from the last away game.

As I turn to head back, Dai Griffiths is walking towards me. He said he'd been too emotional at full-time to join in any celebrations, he said he'd sit in his chair for a bit instead. It looks like that's exactly what he's done. I walk towards him, we meet and there's another big embrace. This guy's devoted his life to Welsh football, constantly travelling all over Europe with different representative teams. He's another rock-solid member of the backroom staff and, of course, he lost his pal just a few short months ago as well. He'll think of Dai Williams as well tonight I'm sure.

There are more scenes like this on the journey back to my interview room, there's a whole lot of hugging going on. At the top of the steps, Bill's waiting, broadest of smiles across his face. One full campaign, one qualification! He must think it's always like this! The UEFA delegates are buzzing around with clipboards as well, ticking off the names of players we've interviewed and adding those we're still after. I request Ben Davies and Joe Allen so that I can interview them in English, and in Welsh for S4C. I also request Osian Roberts just for S4C. Osian? I get a puzzled look from the UEFA guys, and not for the first time I end up writing his name down on the list for them. Before that, the studio wants to hear from Chris again, this time they want to be able to talk to him. IG goes off to find him and they both return fairly quickly. IG asks if it can be kept short as Chris understandably wants to go back to the celebrations, but it's hard for me to make the promise, it's not my call. Still, I send Jim a text along those lines, which he may or may not receive given the problems with the network.

Chris is asked about Gary Speed in this interview. It's not something I was going to do out on the pitch. Too raw, too soon. It wouldn't have felt right. This is a better time to do it. Chris handles the question well, and they let him go. He's got more duties to perform before he'll be back in the dressing room. The media conference awaits, a moment he should savour after some of the tough ones he endured when things weren't going as well. Some who persecuted him then will no doubt be praising him now, it's the nature of the beast. As he leaves the room, I stop him to say 'thanks'. I don't mean thanks for the interview, I mean thanks for doing this, for me and everyone else celebrating tonight. Thanks for finally making it happen.

Ben Davies pops his head round the door at the behest of IG. "I'm missing everything", he implores, so I send him back to the dressing room to share the moment with his team-mates. The viewing public can wait a little longer. I ask him to come back later. He nods. I know he will.

I've been composing the questions for the Welsh interviews in my head. I kept it very simple last month, just on the game really, but there's an onus to do more than that this time. The game was largely irrelevant, as it turned out, but the events have been hugely significant. I have a check-list of words I want to use, and I'm running through it when Joe Allen arrives. I welcome him in, and the first thing he says, "You won't ask any questions about Liverpool will you?" I assure him that if there was ever an interview when I wasn't going to ask him about his club, this is it.

Joe's good in both languages, so is Ben, who's come back as promised even before we've finished. I hope the people back at S4C are watching all this come in, I can't be sure because I've not heard from them. I've sent Dylan a text to let him know what interviews I'm planning, but he hasn't replied. I carry on regardless as Osian arrives. This is going to be the last interview of the evening. Sky are happy with what they've got. I'm doing Osian's interview just in Welsh, so there's no time for a gentle warm-up and we crack on. The problem I have with these interviews in Welsh is needing to listen really hard to the answer, then translating it in my head, then working out whether there's anything I should be reacting to. It's a similar problem to that encountered by young journalists, when they're so intent on their next question they forget to listen to what is being said to them.

I have a question in my head I want to ask. Even as I'm asking it, I'm not sure if I should. I ask Osian if he's had a moment to remember Gary? The two of them were very close. Gary studied for his coaching badges with Osian, who had clearly made an impact on him and so Gary brought him onto the staff when he became national team manager. It was a bold appointment. Osh had never played the game at a high level, but had devoted himself to coaching from quite an early age. Now, here he is as a key member of the staff that's led Wales to qualification for the first time in 57 years.

Osh maybe isn't expecting the question. For a moment tears well-up in his eyes, he takes a breath and then answers. He's close to the edge, emotionally, but holds it together and delivers a strong answer before I move things back to the present, or future even, as I ask him to look forward to the party in Cardiff on Tuesday. He sits in on most of the media sessions I do for coaching courses, and may well be seeing this interview used as an example in sessions to come, since he's dealt with it brilliantly. Tough for him but I'm sure the S4C viewers will appreciate what he's just done. You don't always see what's real in football interviews. In fact, it's very rare. That was real.

With that, I'm done. I pick up my bag, and head back out to the TV compound. The guys are all there and there's another round of big hugs. There's also a round of beers as Barry's been shopping. He's clutching a small plastic bag full of cans, passes them around and we toast each other and qualification in a puddle-strewn car park in a scruffy little town in the Balkans. Who could have ever predicted it would end like this?

The feedback from base is good. They're pleased with our efforts and Alex has excelled himself with some of his super slo-mo shots. We did our bit to make it good for the people watching back home. That's what it's all about, making it good for the viewer, so job done.

We pile into the little car, relieved not to be heading over the mountain, and the road back to Sarajevo is fast and smooth. There's singing in our car. We give it a bit of '*Hal! Robson! Hal Robson-Kanu!*' and have a couple of cracks at '*Can't Take My Eyes Off You*'. We've had some top road trips on this tour of duty, this is the last one, and harmony still reigns.

It's 1am as we check-in and the bar's already shut, but careful negotiations with the night staff produce a few beers and some wine. I present Sarah with her 'Tîm Cymru' t-shirt. She deserves it, she's been brilliant, great company and a great operator. One of the greatest pleasures of this whole experience has been the people I've worked with. Right from Andorra away, we've shared so much and our own team has displayed that Together Stronger characteristic. They're all sitting around me now, probably for the last time. These have been the best of days. The bar closes, we raid minibars for one more round, then people drift off to bed. It's 4.30 am. I had thoughts of heading into the city to find friends but fatigue beats me. Besides, there's still work to be done. This has been one of the greatest days of my life.

Sunday 11th October

Four hours sleep probably isn't quite enough, certainly not for Bill, who doesn't appear at breakfast in the revolving restaurant atop our hotel. I've knocked on his door on my way up. Alex gives his room phone a call. It rings a few times, then some scrabbling and a sleepy Bill murmurs a greeting. "Five minutes to get ready", Alex warns him, "Oh, really?", Bill replies in his best nonchalant Roger Moore style, completely out of keeping with the reality of his situation. He'll be running round the room, throwing things in a bag, cleaning his teeth and pulling on his pants all at once.

Needless to say, Barry's on a different flight home to us. He doesn't like to do the simple, he likes complicated. He's probably appreciative of the chance of a couple of hours more sleep after his marathon effort two days ago.

Bill makes the deadline and we make the short journey back to the airport, almost sad to see the back of our tiny, slow car, a feeling probably not shared by the car. Departures is busy. Camera crews are waiting for the Bosnian players, who are off to their crucial game. They arrive looking like a Boden catalogue shoot, resplendent in gingham checked shirts, blue blazers and fawn chinos. There are also Wales fans and the first members of the travelling FAW party. We join the line behind them. There are a few tired looking people in the check-in queue, so it would seem we are not alone in having had a bit of a celebration! I wouldn't mind betting many of the Wales fans have just gone straight through the night, no sleep. They're going to get a great treat soon, though, as the history makers arrive. It's not a big airport building, so I'm sure we'll all be sitting together, the perfect chance for pictures and a chat with this group of legends.

Through security and, sure enough, there's one small bar and a few seats. There are at least two flights taking fans to hub airports for the connection back to Britain, so it's pretty busy. Then the players appear, a few looking a bit the worse for wear, hoodies pulled up, sipping from small bottles of water, the classic signs. It's clear they've taken the chance to enjoy the impromptu post-match party in the team hotel. Guitars have been played, songs sung and when the hotel staff wanted to shut things down, they were bribed with bits of kit. Dai's inventory is going to be well down on what he flew out with!

Three of the lads make for the bar and order a beer, but they don't pick them up until the coast is clear. Someone, I'm not sure who, leaves the vicinity and they get the beers surreptitiously delivered to their table. In the olden days they'd have had to wheel all the players into the building on luggage trolleys. They'd have drunk this place dry before the flight was called and then done it all again on the plane. Times have very much changed. Not all the lads even drink alcohol, and instead of going out and causing mayhem last night, they gathered round Dai and his guitar and sang along as he ran through his repertoire of classics.

Talking of Dai, he seems to have overdone the tapping of his feet, or something, as he's limping quite badly. In time honoured fashion, this makes him the butt of everyone's jokes. I fire down a coffee and then two bottles of water by way of refreshment. As I'm drinking, Asmir Begović walks past, "Hi Bryn, Okay?", he asks, I'm somewhat taken aback. I think I interviewed him once at Stoke, but many people have told me what a top bloke he is, always happy to help and good with names and faces.

Then I spy some faces I recognise to go and talk to. There's a couple of lads from Wrexham I know, then TC himself appears, Mr 'We'll Never Qualify'. His face never gives much away, he's perfected the slightly scary look, but I know he'll be feeling on top of the world to finally see his damning prediction disproved and destroyed. He deserves to be here now, amongst the players and management.

Whatever he felt, he's always stuck by the team. Today's for him and all the others who did the same.

There's a delay on our flight. As we wait, Barry appears, looking refreshed and ready for whatever today's travelogue has in store for him. He's on a flight heading for Manchester via Munich. We wish him *Bon Voyage* as we finally get called to the gate. Then something fantastic happens. As the players get up to leave, the fans stand to applaud them out of the terminal building. This is what it means. It's a lovely thing to witness and I know the players will appreciate it. The bond that's developed between them and the fans is unique now. It's common for fans to distrust the people they pay to watch. Huge salaries made players rich but haven't made the fans love them more. These Welsh fans, though, know that their team is honest and the players committed, and they love them for that. I stand and watch, then go through myself, but the guy at the desk stops me. "We are missing one", he says, "Do you know who this is?", and he points at a name on a list. As he does so, there's another round of applause, and the man on the list ambles into sight. "Yes, I know him," I say, "He's James Collins!"

I'd been wondering what the flight home might be like if Wales had qualified. I'd been expecting champagne on tap with singing and laughter, all caught on camera by masses of official and unofficial photos, but it's not quite like that, as it turns out. Sky Sports News asked me to seek permission to film a bit on board, but the request has been turned down. The best they let us do is film the players climbing the steps to the plane. There's no champagne either. There's not even one of those cheesy messages from the plane's captain saying "I'd like to welcome you all on board and on behalf of all the cabin crew, congratulations on qualifying!" In fact, as the drinks trolley gets wheeled down the aisle, it becomes apparent that this will be a 'dry' flight. All things considered, it's pretty subdued. Some of the lads sleep. Others play music and there's a bit of singing, but that's about it.

The low-key nature of this triumphal return is maintained at Cardiff Airport. We land, head to baggage reclaim and emerge to ... a normal Sunday afternoon. I thought there might be a bit of a crowd here, I think the players did too. Maybe the First Minister might have arrived to welcome the team back. After all, this is really going to put

Wales on the map, far more than the Rugby World Cup. It's arguably the country's greatest ever sporting achievement. The players have to settle for a few handshakes from the baggage handlers, then they board the bus to go back to base.

I'm reminded of the scene described in Mario Risoli's excellent account of Wales involvement in the 1958 World Cup, *When Pelé Broke Our Hearts*. After a flight back to London, then a train home, Mel Charles steps onto the platform at Swansea station carrying his case, and is recognised by a ticket conductor who says, "You been on your holidays again Mel?" Wales had just played in the quarter-finals of the World Cup!

Alex and I are heading in a different direction. We're heading east to Bridgend and the nearest available hotel room to Cardiff. Ireland are playing France in the city so everywhere's booked up. The streets will be thronged with sports fans as the bus makes its way back to the Bay, but they'll all be bedecked in blue or green. It's unfortunate timing.

There are, as it turns out, crowds three-deep on the road from Barry to Bridgend, but they haven't turned out to cheer me and Gagey for our interviews and slo-mo footage in Bosnia. Apparently there's an old Vulcan bomber flying over, we can't compete with that.

Our day ends at a table right in front of the big screen in the hotel bar, watching the Republic of Ireland miss out on automatic qualification. I adjourn to my room afterwards and get a text from Barry. He got home on time, everything's fine.

The world really does seem a different place today!

10

"We're so proud of what we've achieved"
Wales v Andorra

'Ain't nobody, like Joe Ledley,
Makes me happy, makes me feel this way'

Monday 12th October

Today is my turn to oversleep. I wake up at the very time I'm supposed to be meeting Alex to leave the hotel. He's already set off for the Cardiff City Stadium by the time I make it down to breakfast, which I'm pointedly told, finished at 9.30am. Ten minutes ago.

There's the usual match day routine to go through, but I have negotiated us a little extra access today. Jim wanted four players talking about the campaign, game by game. The FAW were reluctant to make such a demand on the squad, so we've compromised on one extra, Neil Taylor. That's for this afternoon. For this morning, it's Chris then Ashley. Bill arrives at the same time as me and we help Alex carry the equipment in. Alex has been busy making some more inspirational videos for the players. I saw them last night and the FAW people get a preview today. They're really good and the FAW request copies to show at the reception planned for the players, after the game tomorrow.

We're all set and ready to go when Chris walks in, and I lead the rest of the Sky team in a little round of applause as he heads towards his chair. It's genuine. We've all enjoyed his company over the last

298

year, and he apologises to Bill for not getting him the confirmed team on Saturday; he told me about it instead and I passed it on.

I've got quite a long list of questions, provided by Jim. They're to be asked of all three interviewees, then they'll pick the best bits. Time's fairly short, and some of Chris's answers are quite long, so I've got my eye on the clock throughout. I sense IG appearing somewhere behind me, so skip a couple and go right to the last one, "How did you find out about the result from Jerusalem?"

This produces a belting anecdote. At full-time he had no idea of the score from Israel and thought the bench looked a bit glum. He was also annoyed at the side losing for the first time, so set off for the dressing room contemplating another game before qualification was confirmed.

On his way back, he saw Mark Evans coming towards him, "You know Mark, always looks a bit miserable, he's from Merthyr see, and he had that miserable look on his face now. So, I've said 'what's the score then?' and he said 'Israel won', and paused and then said 'Cyprus two!' I've gone, 'now's not the time for that Mark!!' and turned around to go and celebrate with the supporters."

As the laughter fades at the end of the manager's tale of agony and ecstasy, Ashley's now arrived, waiting for his interview. He also wonders aloud as to why there haven't been celebratory scenes on the players' return to Wales. I get the sense they're all feeling a bit underwhelmed at the reaction. He lifts himself for the interview, then heads off outside for the final training session of the qualification campaign. I'm guessing it'll be a relatively easy going affair.

Our appointment with Neil Taylor is a little later in the afternoon, so we head to the hotel to check-in. Tonight will be my fifth different bed in five days and I've got pockets full of room key cards. We've already been warned space is at a premium at the team hotel, so decide to get down early to try and sort something out. After much umming and ahhing, I suggest we use the kit room and go to seek Dai's permission to get everything set up in there. He's looking a lot better than last time I saw him, suffering on the flight back with a badly swollen ankle. He's had a check-up, nothing broken, and he's back strumming the guitar as I enter his kingdom. If you like football and sports gear, this is a magical place. It's filled with training kits, boots, studs, slips, the lot. All piled up neatly on tables down either side of the room. In the centre of the room is a skip full of this morning's training gear with, I suspect, not much sweat on it.

He offers us the back room, usually the bedroom in a suite. The bed has been taken out and it's full of boots and more training gear. It's ideal for what we need, so I summon Alex and he gets to work making it ready for Neil's arrival. In-between setting up lights, he has chance to share the fruits of his filming and editing with some of the passing players and staff. If the players haven't recorded Saturday's game, these little films will make good souvenirs. They will all be emailed a copy.

Then Neil wanders in. He's also not quite feeling the love. He wonders if their return could have been publicised, so that people could come along to the hotel, give the lads a cheer and get pictures and signatures. It's a strange one really. I've heard someone say, "We don't know how to qualify", and I understand what they were getting at. It's such a new thing nobody really knows how to react, whether to play it down or play it up. I have to say that from a marketing point of view, surely you play it up?

We've already seen how the game in Wales is involved in a battle for the hearts and minds of the young stars and supporters of the future. These players are now all heroes to young and old, so get them out there and let the people see them. They're such a fine bunch of individuals they'd be perfect ambassadors for the game and the FAW. Gareth Bale may have his own commercial agenda, but lots of the other players are about to see their profile rocket as a result of qualification. The Hal Robson-Kanu chant hints at what's possible, but even the main sponsors seem to have failed to recognise the potential.

We were in Brussels when Belgium celebrated qualifying for the 2014 World Cup. Thousands of fans had turned up at the airport to welcome the team back when qualification was secured. Wales was the celebration game that followed and there was a massive fireworks display afterwards. Will we see similar events at the stadium tomorrow? I don't think so. I don't think people have worked out just how massive this is going to be, the biggest event a team from the country has ever been involved in.

Neil's the sort of person you'd want your company to be associated with, super smart, highly articulate and principled. He's definitely going to make an excellent TV pundit, if he fancies it, once his career's over.

Back at base, I get a call from Roger Speed, Gary's dad. He's coming over for the match tomorrow, so we arrange to meet beforehand. It'll be good to see him again, he's one of the nicest blokes I've ever met. I first got to meet Rodge when he was supporting Gary at Elland Road, and I was commentating on the games for Radio Leeds. Gary and I were two lads from north Wales, same age, so we got on well. Then, Roger started to come over to the commentary position for a half-time chat with me and my co-commentator, Norman Hunter. Even after Gary had left Leeds, I kept bumping into his dad on Wales trips, both of us travelling as fans.

Once Gary had retired from international football, our paths didn't cross so much although I spent a lot of time with Gary, especially when he came down to Cardiff to work on the Sky coverage of internationals as a studio guest. Like Neil Taylor, he had always been a confident talker, good in front of the camera and unfailingly helpful. Our post-match nights out in the capital were always a great laugh, he was such good company and an excellent 'people person'.

Then he became Wales manager and in his first couple of days in the job, he invited me out for dinner in Cardiff, to raise a glass to thank me for my help, something that gave me a great sense of pride. The next few months were great, he lifted the game out of the doldrums in less than a year and began the process that Chris has continued to this glorious conclusion.

I knew something was up when I got back to my car at about midday on Sunday, 27th November 2011. I'd left my mobile in it whilst I took my daughters around the butterfly house in Leeds. Calls on days off were a regular occurrence, but then Rachel rang me to say they'd tried to get hold of me on the home phone as well. That was extremely unusual. The kids were in the back of the car, waiting for us to head for home, as I made the call. The news editor answered. He didn't beat around the bush, told me they had heard from a good source that Gary was dead, could I check it out?

I think the girls knew straight away something was wrong. I regret to this day that I didn't make the call out of their earshot, I just had no inkling. I think I almost laughed, it sounded so preposterous. He'd sent me a text the day before, taking the mickey out of my white hair, a regular occurrence. I mentioned this to emphasise how daft this suggestion seemed. The only thing I could think was that maybe there'd been a crash or something, but the person on the other end of the line suggested it was suicide. That made me even more convinced that this was nonsense. "I'll check it out", I said, "But it'll be bollocks, some stupid internet hoax."

I drove halfway home, then stopped to buy butter. In the shop's car park, I called and left a voicemail message on Gary's phone. "Daft story doing the rounds mate, give me a call, cheers." Then I rang Mark Evans at the FAW, who answered immediately. "Mark, you heard this daft story about Gary?" "It's true mate", he replied.

I'll never forget that. The most horrific feeling swept over me. I couldn't really speak anymore. The kids knew. When we got home, Megan ran ahead as my wife came to the door to greet us, "Gary Speed's dead!", she said. Both my girls had met him. I staggered back into the house, and then disappeared upstairs for the rest of the most awful day ever. The phone rang frequently. Some calls were from friends, people like Barry and Kev Ratcliffe, everyone in utter shock. Other calls were from work. Would I be available to cover this story tomorrow? In-between, I just cried and cried and cried.

I worked the next day. I never want another day like that ever. By the end of it, I was broken. My wife and children were watching Sky Sports News as I cried again, on live TV.

The next time I saw Roger was the following Sunday. I'd been sent to cover the Everton game, as they'd be remembering their former player before the kick-off. Barry was there as well, working on commentary. We went down to get a team sheet together. As we passed through reception, there was Rodge. The nicest man in the world looked destroyed, in complete shock.

We hugged there, in front of everyone. I felt awful, but for Roger it must have been indescribable. There are still moments when something brings it all back again but for Roger, his wife Carol, Gary's sister Leslie, Ed and Tommy, his boys, and Louise, his wife, it has to be there, somewhere, every minute of every day. They have been incredibly brave. Ed spoke at his dad's funeral, one of the most moving things I've ever witnessed.

I've spent some time with the Speed family since, fantastic people, which makes it all the harder to understand. I hope in some small way, Chris Coleman's success offers some comfort. He's finished the job his mate started. I'm sure Roger will want to thank Chris tomorrow.

When things were just beginning to turn round for Gary after a slow start to the national job, I went to do some filming with Gwilym and Rhys Boore. I wanted the fans' perspective on how things were going. They were really good, spoke of their conviction that he was the man who was going to lead the team to the World Cup in Brazil. That piece was broadcast before his last game in charge, a 4-1 win against Norway.

Dark times followed, so I'm looking forward to a couple of pints with those lads tonight. They come round to the hotel, and an excellent evening ensues. Bill's not met them before, but they're great company and it turns into a proper celebration. We all leave the bar a little later than would be normal on a school day, but hey, we deserve it!

Tuesday 13th October

Despite everything, I feel pretty chipper when I wake up on MD10. Perhaps it has something to do with the fact that I've got nothing to worry about, finally, nothing to fear. Tonight, for the first time in a long time, I can go through the day without that slightly queasy feeling in my stomach, the dread and anticipation of what lies ahead. We're used to meaningless games at the end of campaigns, we've covered loads of them in the last 11 years, but this sort of 'dead rubber' I could get used to!

Actually, there's one thing left to play for. Top spot is still a possibility. If Belgium don't beat Israel, and assuming we win, we've cracked it. It won't help our seeding in France, we're in the lowest pot, but it would counter the suggestion that we've only qualified because of the extended format. To be honest though, who cares? We qualified!

The match day routine doesn't change, a run, a shower, some lunch etc but a lot of the superstitions can now be dumped. We lost in Bosnia, after all, and Alex was wearing the lucky socks, so they're gone now. It's a good job, actually, as they're looking distinctly threadbare; he should auction them for charity. I don't need to wear the Euro 2016 badge now, although I do, for old time's sake. Me and Dai don't need to swap gum. I don't really need the Welton Rovers sticker in my bag anymore, although I need to find somewhere a bit more exotic than Cardiff to stick it. I'm guessing it'll be one more run out for the manager's old suit, then surely off to a display cabinet in the National Museum of Wales, or Oxfam?

We're planning a 'Team Sky' picture at the stadium. I have a t-shirt for Jim as well. He's done all the games, albeit from afar and this will be the only time when we're all together, at least until next year. There are some friendlies coming up, but they aren't covered by the broadcast contract. So it'll probably be someone else covering them. Then on to the Euros themselves, which have to be shown on terrestrial TV, so no Sky involvement there either. I'm planning on going to France anyway, of course. I've looked forward to this all my life, spent so many summers following tournaments without ever really having that engagement. The Boore boys spent a fortune going to the World Cup in Brazil last summer because they thought it might be their last chance, with Wales unlikely to qualify for anything soon, and unattractive World Cups coming up in Russia and then Qatar; the one I suspect nobody will want to play in or travel to.

I haven't planned anything yet. That isn't to say I haven't thought about it. I think it was Belgium at home when I first started to see a clear route to qualification. I just didn't dare share my vision. Only now can I reveal that I've been looking at clapped-out camper vans and caravans on eBay for some months. I've checked venue locations, dates, even train timetables. Going away for two weeks, bumming round France, just watching football, and supporting Wales sounds like quite a lot of fun. I've been in the thick of it for a long time, time for a change of pace perhaps?

First, one more game to enjoy. It's the usual Sky crew for today. Smartie's on the bus already tucking into a plate of chicken. Kit Symons is on board as well, which is great. He's played a massive part in all of this, and it's fitting that he'll be on the touchline, as Sky's guest, when the players are presented to the crowd later. That'll be after the game. The FAW's got something special organised involving glitter, champagne and loud music. I know this, because they are rehearsing as I walk up the side of the pitch to the tunnel. Before the game, it'll be the Super Furry Animals doing their thing again.

Apart from the pre-match chat with the manager, I'm pretty clear until kick-off. Barry and I don't have to do our usual thing, so I'll be ready for their performance at 7pm. That's some way off though. First, the phone rings and it's Roger. He's just coming up to the stadium now so I go out to reception to wait for him. It's three hours before kick-off, but there are already quite a few fans outside the ground. I really hope there's a big crowd out here when the team bus arrives. The lads deserve to walk off it to a wall of noise.

Then Roger appears, smart as ever, with the slightly bowed legs of an ex-footballer. He's always got a big smile, and there's a big hug. He's one of those people who just exudes friendliness and warmth. I'm trying to arrange and interview with him for Sky Sports News but the reporter's inside the stadium, and Roger hasn't got a pass to get down to the tunnel. He's watching the game in one of the hospitality suites and after the game he'll pop-in to see Chris. I tell him I'll see him again later and go back inside to hang around, soak it up.

The usual tension's missing. Everyone's busy doing the usual stuff but it's relaxed busy, and everyone's got that slightly daft 'just qualified' grin on their faces. I love the atmosphere down here. The stadium's definitely got the feeling of 'home', familiar faces amongst the match day staff, fans having places they like to sit, the Canton Stand has become a proper 'end'. Long may all this continue. I don't want to see the side move from here, even though there's talk of the Millennium Stadium being used for a friendly next month.

The players arrive just after 6pm, I wait for Chris at my interview position. As he arrives, I mention the relaxed atmosphere, "I know, don't like it, I need to feel nervous", he says, so I do my best, "If you don't beat these you'll be under pressure again!", I suggest, tongue firmly in cheek.

Although, in truth, it's a crazy game these days, it might actually happen like that. But Wales won't lose. They'll win. How's that for new-found optimism? And, of course, they do. It's not the procession we'd maybe hoped for, but Andorra play a sort of anti-football that proves horribly effective for 50 minutes. It's a good job Wales didn't need to win this one because the tension levels would have been through the roof by the time Aaron Ramsey forced home the first goal. And how does it finish? As it started, with Gareth Bale scoring against Andorra. There's a beautiful symmetry to that.

Then the party really starts. This is what the players have been craving, the chance to sing and celebrate with the fans. The sound of Zombie Nation is heard again and again, as it has been ever since

Belgium away. The players sang it at the end of the Bosnia game, Joe Ledley produced some ace dance moves and subsequently they've become a social media sensation. Tonight, everyone's at it, players and fans. The Barry Horns, the national team band, have done their bit as well, inspiring a wide repertoire of songs that have done wonders for the atmosphere.

Almost by way of a postscript, in the early hours of the following morning, I join the party at the team hotel. The players have all headed off into the city centre by the time I gate-crash. I'm introduced to Mr and Mrs Bale, Frank and Debbie. We chat for ages and, of course, they're lovely people. The same applies to Mr and Mrs Gunter, who I bump into as I wait for a taxi back to my hotel.

Watching Wales has become fun, exuberant and in these young blokes we see the embodiment of a vibrant, talented, upbeat nation. If Romania at home in '93 left deep scars on the Welsh national psyche, and it certainly changed me, then this achievement should have a healing impact. This fine group of people, men and women, drawn from all backgrounds, from Wales and beyond, have shown what can be achieved with a clarity of vision, good humour and hard work. Together Stronger. These have been 13 quite magical months.

"I didn't know Wales had a Q in it!"
UEFA Qualifying Group B

'One Gary Speed,
There's only one Gary Speed,
One Gary Speed,
There's only one Gary Speed'

'Speedo, Speedo, Speedo, Speedo'

	P	W	D	L	F	A	+/	Pts
Q Belgium	10	7	2	1	24	5	19	23
Q Wales	10	6	3	1	11	4	7	21
Bosnia & Herzegovina	10	5	2	3	17	12	5	17
Israel	10	4	1	5	16	14	2	13
Cyprus	10	4	0	6	16	17	− 1	12
Andorra	10	0	0	10	4	36	− 32	0

St David's Press

'A beautifully written and expertly researched book, which gives an insight into Wales' greatest football triumph'
Nicky Wire - Manic Street Preachers

"…a brilliant book…a thoroughly good read…I warmly recommend it"
Adrian Chiles Radio 5 Live

'If you were to write a surreal football comedy script tinged with pathos, personal tragedy, heroism, politics, adventure and endeavour, you couldn't begin to emulate the story of Wales in 1958 … well-crafted … meticulously researched'
Total Football

'a great tale, diligently researched and well told'
GQ Magazine

'excellent … an intriguing story, compellingly told'
Four Four Two

'terrific … a lovely story, well told and, best of all, you don't have to be Welsh to enjoy it'
The Sunday Times

When Pelé Broke Our Hearts is the definitive story of the Welsh team's remarkable 1958 World Cup campaign in Sweden, the first and only time Wales have played in football's premier tournament.

978 1 902719 023 - £9.99 - 180pp - 44 illustrations/photographs